Indicators of Trends in American Education

ABBOTT L. FERRISS

RUSSELL SAGE FOUNDATION

230 Park Avenue, New York, N.Y. 10017

1969

PUBLICATIONS OF RUSSELL SAGE FOUNDATION

Russell Sage Foundation was established in 1907 by Mrs. Russell Sage for the improvement of social and living conditions in the United States. In carrying out its purpose the Foundation conducts research under the direction of members of the staff or in close collaboration with other institutions, and supports programs designed to improve the utilization of social science knowledge. As an integral part of its operations, the Foundation from time to time publishes books or pamphlets resulting from these activities. Publication under the imprint of the Foundation does not necessarily imply agreement by the Foundation, its Trustees, or its staff with the interpretations or conclusions of the authors.

Copyright © RUSSELL SAGE FOUNDATION
1969

Library of Congress Catalog Card Number   76–92860

A number of individuals assisted in the preparation of this volume. I am particularly grateful to Mildred Ann Konan for assisting in bringing together many of the statistical series and in preparing notes on many of them, and to Carol A. Van Arnhem for her careful editorial attention to the bibliographic sources. For their assistance, I also wish to thank Han Kyu Song, Genevieve V. Berthe, Linda Ruth Lewis, Joanne Holler and Clair T. Olson. Mary Ann Ferguson typed the manuscript and tables and attended to other secretarial duties. For her critical review of the manuscript, I am grateful to Eleanor Bernert Sheldon; and for its generosity in making the study possible, the Trustees of the Russell Sage Foundation.

A.L.F.

Foreword

Indicators of Trends in American Education is the second in a series of publications initiated by Russell Sage Foundation as part of its program on "social indicators." In the first volume of the series, *Indicators of Social Change* (1968) edited by Eleanor Bernert Sheldon and Wilbert E. Moore, a general framework for the analysis and measurement of change is presented, encompassing relevant concepts and measures. The primary purpose of this earlier overview was to provide a basis for subsequent studies. This volume by Abbott L. Ferriss of the Foundation staff emerges from that earlier presentation and from the Foundation's continuing efforts to examine and monitor the changing structure of American society.

A dominant characteristic of American society in recent years is its rapid and far-reaching social change. Concomitant with this change (illustrated by the growth and urbanization of population, the rise of minority groups, and the spread of mass education) is an increasing tendency toward planned intervention in many of the processes involved in change. It was in recognition of both the growing influence of planned social change and of the relative inadequacies of available data for monitoring such changes that the Foundation first developed and then expanded its program on social indicators and social trends.

Integral to the program is an assessment of existing relevant data, emanating from a variety of federal and other statistical agencies, and often left to accumulate in those agencies in a relatively uncoordinated fashion. In this volume, Dr. Ferriss has performed a yeoman's task of assembling, collating, analyzing and assessing those data bearing on trends in American education. The volume is designed to present the principal time-series basic to the description and analysis of changes in American education, which is considered both organizationally and as a characteristic of the population.

Dr. Ferriss presents the basic data on school enrollments, retention and attainment indicating changes in the educational characteristics of the population, and comparable time-series on teachers and school finances reflecting changes in the organization of school systems. His analyses of data examine the interrelations among some of the basic indicators as well as among measures which could be considered extraneous to the educational system, such as business cycle variables.

In relating these data to an explicit statement of educational goals for American society Dr. Ferriss, in his final chapter, provides evidence bearing on the relevance of the time-series to national policy formation. He utilizes the data to provide an assessment of progress toward what appeared to be reasonable and necessary educational goals for the nation some ten years ago. Further, his examination provides an assessment of the adequacy of educational statistics for indicating such significant trends in the system. Dr. Ferriss is careful to point out that these data and his analyses of them do not contribute much to our knowledge of *cause and effect* relationships nor to the *sequences of social change*. Rather, his work is a landmark in identifying, assembling and assessing time-series data that are valuable in examining the achievement of educational goals.

In conjunction with other Foundation work aimed at developing and refining theories of social change and causal models of change, this volume both provides a stimulus for further advances and in itself represents a major contribution in an area of inquiry referred to as "social indicators."

ELEANOR BERNERT SHELDON
New York City
August, 1969

Table of Contents

Acknowledgments — iii
List of Tables — ix
List of Figures — xi
Notes to the Series and Data Series — xv

1. Introduction — 1
    The Interpretation of Trends — 5
    Aggregated and Disaggregated Measures — 7
    Criteria for the Selection of an Indicator — 8
    Major Sources of Data — 10
    The Types of Statistical Series — 11
    The Organization of the Volume — 12
    Conventions of the Statistical Tables and Graphs — 14
    Footnotes — 16

2. Enrollment — 17
    Elementary and Secondary School Enrollment — 17
        Public and Non-public Enrollment, by Level — 21
    School Enrollment Rates by Color — 23
    Retention in Secondary School — 23
    Continuation Ratios, 9th to 10th Grade — 25
    Continuation Ratios, 10th to 11th Grade — 29
    Continuation Ratios, 11th to 12th Grade — 31
    The Effects of War and the Business Cycle
        Upon Continuation in School — 36
            The Unemployment Rate — 36
            Per Capita GNP — 37
            Military Expansion — 37
            Continuation Ratios — 38
    Degree Credit Enrollment — 44
    Junior College Enrollment — 44
    Ratio of First-time Enrollment to the 18-Year-Old Population, by Sex — 49
    Ratio, College Enrollment to Population 18–21 Years of Age — 52
    College Enrollment Ratios by Sex — 54
    Enrollment Rates by Age — 54
    Age Specific Enrollment Rates, by Cohort — 58
    Footnotes — 65

3. Teachers — 68
    Public Elementary and Secondary Teachers — 69
    College Faculty — 69
    Public School Teachers by Sex — 72
    Age of Teachers — 74
    Teachers with Substandard Certificates — 78
    Pupil-Teacher Ratio — 80
        Public and Non-public — 82
    Footnotes — 86

4. The Quality of Education — 87
    Scholastic Aptitude, High School Juniors in Minnesota — 88
    Educational Achievement, High School Seniors in Iowa — 91
    Achievement: College Seniors — 95
    Footnotes — 98

5. Graduates — 100
    Measuring "Production" of the Educational System — 101
    Gross Production of the Educational System — 101
        High School Graduates — 101
    Ratio, High School Graduates to 17-Year-Olds — 104
        Graduates of Colleges and Universities — 106
        Baccalaureate Degrees — 106
    Ratio of Baccalaureate Degrees to High School Graduates Four Years Earlier — 107
    Baccalaureate Degrees Related to First-time Enrollment Four Years Earlier, by Sex — 112
        Baccalaureate Degrees per 1,000 23-Year-Olds — 116
        Master's Degrees — 118
        Doctor's Degrees — 118
    From Baccalaureate to Higher Degrees — 121
        Master's — 123
        Doctor's — 125
    Lapse Time, B.A. to Ph.D. — 127
    Trends in Various Specialty Fields:
        Patterns of Growth — 131
        Baccalaureate Degrees — 131
        Master's Degrees — 135
        Doctor's Degrees — 138
    Projections of Degrees — 138
    An Academic Production Index — 145
        The Gross API — 146
        API per Graduate — 148
        Enrollment per API — 152
        Faculty per API — 153
        API per Faculty Member — 153
        Student Aid per API — 156
        Higher Education Expenditures per API — 156
    Suggestions for Improving Data on Graduates — 159
        Quality of the "Product" — 159
        Characteristics of the Graduate — 160
        Geographic Origins and Destinations — 160
        The Classification of Fields — 161
        A Note on Sampling — 162
    Footnotes — 163

6. Trends in Educational Organization and Finance — 166

The Number of Institutions by Type	167
Size of School Systems	169
Length of Term and Days Attended	173
Institutions of Higher Education	174
Size of Institutions of Higher Education	180
Revenue for Public Elementary and Secondary Schools	182
Expenditures for Public Elementary and Secondary Schools	184
Revenues of Institutions of Higher Education	185
Sources of Revenue for Higher Education	190
Expenditures of Institutions of Higher Education	193
Footnotes	200

7. Educational Attainment — 202

Median Years of Schooling	203
Percentage Attaining Given Years of School	205
Less than Five Years Schooling of an Age Group by Sex and Color	207
Twelve or More Years Schooling, by Age and Sex, for the Population 20–24 Years of Age	210
One Year or More of College for White Females in Three Age Groups	214
Cumulative Distributions of Educational Attainment, 20–24-Year-Old Nonwhite Males	216
Footnotes	220

8. Attaining Society's Goals for Education — 221

Goals Concerning Teachers	222
Goals Concerning Segregation	233
Goals for the Education of Women	238
Goals for the High School Curriculum	239
Goals for Higher Education	243
Goals for Financing Higher Education	253
Footnotes	257

Appendix A What Contributes Most to an Increase in Degrees: A Change in Rate or Change in Population? — 259

Appendix B The Development of an Academic Production Index — 264

Appendix C Age Cohorts of the Population — 269

Appendix D Notes to the Series — 276

Appendix E Statistical Series — 375

Bibliography — 418

List of Tables

2.1 Coefficients of Correlation Between Continuation Ratios and Other Factors — 39

2.2 Partial Correlation Coefficients of Continuation Ratios and Three Variables with the Effect of Time Removed — 40

2.3 Cumulative Percentage of Variance in the Continuation Ratios Accounted for by Successive Addition of Three Independent Variables to the Multiple Regression Equation — 42

2.4 The Reduction of the Percentage Enrolled in School of Two Age Groups (14–15 Years, and 16–17 Years) Over a Two-Year Period, and Two-Year Continuation Ratios, 1947 to 1968 — 61

4.1 Mean Scores for Minnesota Junior Year High School Students on the Minnesota Scholastic Aptitude Test — 90

4.2 Median Standard Scores on ITED of Iowa Seniors, 1960–1966 — 92

5.1 Estimated Completion Ratios, Four-Year Baccalaureate Degrees per 100 First-time Opening Fall Enrollment Four Years Earlier, by Sex, 1967–1976 — 115

5.2 Growth of Doctor's Degrees, 1955–56 to 1965–66 — 122

5.3 Median Lapse Time from Baccalaureate to Several Stages in Graduate Education, Doctorate Recipients, 1958–1966 — 128

5.4 Annual Increments of Change Used by the U.S. Office of Education to Project Degrees to 1976–77, Males — 143

5.5 Annual Increments of Change Used by the U.S. Office of Education to Project Degrees to 1976–77, Females — 144

6.1 Enrollment in Public School Systems by Size of System, 1956, 1961, and 1966 — 171

6.2 Public Schools and Enrollment per School by Number of Schools in the System, for 1956–57, 1961–62, and 1966–67 — 172

6.3 Changes in Institutional Types, 1953 to 1954, U.S. Higher Educational Institutions — 179

6.4 Enrollment and Average Enrollment in Institutions of Higher Education, by Type of Institution, 1950–1964, School Year Beginning — 181

6.5 Expenditures for Public Elementary and Secondary Education by Purpose, Selected Years, 1919–20 to 1965–66 — 187

7.1 School Enrollment and Educational Attainment of Nonwhite Males, 1962 to Present — 213

7.2 Comparison of Two Indices of Educational Attainment of White and Nonwhite Males, 20–24 Years of Age, 1947 and 1967 — 219

8.1 Projected Demand for New Elementary and Secondary Teachers, 1959–74 — 224

8.2 Median 1959 Income of Males 25–64 Years Old in the Experienced Civilian Labor Force, by Years of School Completed, Selected Occupations — 226

8.3 1959 Income Comparison, by Sex, for 1960 Census Professional Workers, 14 Years of Age and Over, with 4 Years of College Completed — 228

8.4 Ratio, Average Earnings of Public School Classroom Teachers to Earnings of Other Professional Occupations, 1960 to 1966 — 228

8.5 Ratio, Median Annual Salaries, Ph.D. Scientists in Educational Institutions to Ph.D. Scientists Employed by Other Employers — 231

8.6 Percent of Negro Pupils Enrolled in Desegregated Schools, Southern and Border States, 1954–55 to Present — 235

8.7 Total Number of Southern School Districts Reporting on Desegregation by State, 1964–65 to Fall 1968 — 237

8.8 Estimates of the Enrollment Rates by Age and Subject, Science and Mathematics, Secondary Schools, 1948–49 to 1962–63 — 241

8.9 Percent of Various Age Groups Enrolled in College, and Percent Total Enrollment of the 18–21 Year Age Group, 1960 to 1968 — 245

8.10 Earned Doctor's Degrees, Actual to 1966–67 and Projected to 1976–77 — 247

8.11 Doctorates in Mathematics and Statistics, by Quality of Faculty — 249

8.12 Public School Districts, Fall 1959 to 1967 — 252

8.13 Expenditures by Regular Educational Institutions, 1956–57 to 1966–67 and Projected to 1968–69, Compared with Gross National Product — 254

8.14 Average Tuition and Required Fees per Full-time Resident Degree-credit Student in Higher Educational Institutions by Type and Control, 1958–59 and 1968–69 (Current Dollars) — 256

List of Figures

2.1 Total Elementary and Secondary School Enrollment (Public and Non-Public Day Schools), 1889–1968, Series A1, and the Ratio of School Enrollment to the Population 5–17 Years of Age, 1889–1968, Series A2 — 18

2.2 Total Population, 5–13 Years Old and 14–17 Years Old, 1880–1968, Series I4 and I35 — 20

2.3 Enrollment in Elementary and Secondary Day Schools: Public, 1911–1967, Series A6 and A7, and Non-public, 1934–1967, Series A8 and A9 — 22

2.4 Ratio, School Enrollment per 100 Population of School Age, Total, and by Color, 1850–1968, Series A3, A4, A5 — 24

2.5 Ninth to Tenth Grade Continuation Ratio, 1910–1966, Series A23 — 27

2.6 Rate of Change in the Continuation Ratio, 9th to 10th Grade, 1911–1966 — 28

2.7 Tenth to Eleventh Grade Continuation Ratio, 1910–1966, Series A24 — 30

2.8 Three Year Moving Average of Rate of Change in the Continuation Ratio, 10th to 11th Grade, 1912–1965 — 32

2.9 Eleventh to Twelfth Grade Continuation Ratio, 1910–1966, Series A25 — 33

2.10 Rate of Change in the Continuation Ratio, 11th to 12th Grade, 1911–1966 — 35

2.11 First-time Degree-credit Enrollment in Colleges and Universities, by Sex, 1939–1968, Series D2 and D3 — 45

2.12 Total Degree-credit Enrollment in Colleges and Universities, by Sex, 1939–1968, Series D4 and D5 — 46

2.13 Aggregate First-time Degree-credit Enrollment in Junior Colleges, by Sex, and as a Percent of Total First-time Enrollment, 1939–1968, Series D6–D9 — 47

2.14 Ratio, First-time Opening Fall Degree-credit Enrollment per 100 18-Year-Old Population, by Sex, 1939–1968, Series D11 and D12 — 50

2.15 Total Population, 18–21-Year-Olds, 1880–1968, Series I25, and Ratio, Higher Education Degree-Credit Enrollment per 100 18–21-Year-Old Population, 1810–1968, Series D13 — 53

2.16 Ratio, Degree-credit Enrollment in Higher Education per 100 18–21-Year-Old Population, by Sex, 1939–1968, Series D14 and D15 — 55

2.17 School Enrollment for Selected Age Groups, 1947–1968, Series A32–A35 — 56

2.18 School Enrollment of Every Other Age Cohort, Series A32, A33, A34 — 59

2.19 Trends in Three Measures of School Enrollment of 18–19-Year-Olds — 63

3.1 Classroom Teachers and Other Nonsupervisory Staff in Public Elementary and Secondary Day Schools, 1890–1969, Series B5 and B6 — 70

3.2 Total Faculty in Higher Education, 1880–1967, Series E5, and Percent of Male Faculty Members, 1890–1964, Series E6 — 71

3.3 Classroom Teachers and Other Nonsupervisory Staff in Public Elementary and Secondary Day Schools, by Sex, and the Percent Female, 1870–1966, Series B2, B3, B4 — 73

3.4 Median Age, Elementary and Secondary Teachers, Total and Nonwhite, by Sex, by Decade, 1930–1960, Series B11–B14 — 75

3.5 Median Age, College Teachers, Total and Nonwhite, by Sex, by Decade, 1930–1960, Series E1–E4 — 77

3.6 Teachers with Less than Standard Certificates, Elementary and Secondary Schools, 1954–1967, Series B7 and B8 — 79

3.7 Pupil-Teacher Ratio, Public Schools, Based upon Pupils in Average Daily Attendance, 1870–1966, Series A11, and upon Pupils Enrolled, 1910–1967, Series A12 — 81

3.8 Pupil-Teacher Ratio in Elementary and Secondary Day Schools: Public, 1910–1967, Series A13 and A14, and non-public, 1890 and 1931–1966, Series A15 and A16 — 83

4.1 Minnesota High School Junior Year: Minnesota Scholastic Aptitude Test, Means, 1958–1967 (Source: Table 4.1) — 89

5.1 Graduates of Public and Non-public Secondary Schools, 1870–1968, Series A17 (Semi-logarithmic Scale) — 102

5.2 High School Graduates as a Percent of the Population 17 Years Old, 1870–1968, Series A18 — 105

5.3	Baccalaureate Degrees Granted, 1870–1967, Series D16, and the 23-Year-Old Population, 1900–1968, Series I31 (Semi-logarithmic Scale)	108	
5.4	Ratio, Baccalaureates to 100 High School Graduates Four Years Earlier, 1884–1967, Series D21	110	
5.5	Ratio, Four-Year Degrees to 100 First-time Enrollment Four Years Earlier, by Sex, 1950–1967, Series D25 and D26	113	
5.6	Ratio, Baccalaureate Degrees per 1,000 23-Year-Old Population, 1900–1967, Series D20	117	
5.7	Master's and Second Professional Degrees Granted, 1872–1967, Series D17 (Semi-logarithmic Scale)	119	
5.8	Doctor's Degrees Granted, 1888–1967, Series D18 (Semi-logarithmic Scale)	120	
5.9	Completion Rates for Master's Degrees, 1872–1967, Series D22, and Doctor's Degrees, 1878–1967, Series D23	124	
5.10	Mean B.A. to Ph.D. Time Lapse by Year for Five Doctorate Fields, 1920–1966, Series D42–D47	126	
5.11	Trends in Degrees: Patterns	132	
5.12	Trends in Bachelor's Degrees in Mathematics, Foreign Languages, and Agriculture, 1949–1967	133	
5.13	Trends in Bachelor's Degrees in Social Sciences, Life Sciences, and Physical Sciences, 1949–1967	134	
5.14	Trends in Master's Degrees in Mathematics, Foreign Languages, and Agriculture, 1949–1967	136	
5.15	Trends in Master's Degrees in Social Sciences, Life Sciences, and Physical Sciences, 1949–1967	137	
5.16	Trends in Doctor's Degrees in Mathematics, Foreign Languages, and Agriculture, 1949–1967	139	
5.17	Trends in Doctor's Degrees in Social Sciences, Life Sciences, and Physical Sciences, 1949–1967	140	
5.18	Academic Production Index: Grand Total, Series D27; Total Arts, Humanities and Social Sciences, Series D28; Total Basic and Applied Sciences, Series D29; and All Other Fields, Series D30, 1949–1967	147	
5.19	Academic Production Index per 100 Graduates, 1949–1967, Series D35–D37	149	
5.20	Student Enrollment Related to Academic Production Index, 1949–1967, Series D31	154	
5.21	Higher Education Faculty Related to Academic Production Index, 1950–1967, Series D32	155	
5.22	Student Aid Expenditures Related to Academic Production Index (in Constant 1958 Dollars), 1952–1966, Series D34	157	
5.23	Expenditures in Higher Education Related to Academic Production Index (in Constant 1958 Dollars), 1950–1966, Series D33	158	
6.1	Number of Public Elementary and Secondary Schools, and the Percent One-Teacher Schools, 1930–1966, Series C1, C3, C4	168	
6.2	Average Length of School Term (in Days) and the Average Number of Days Attended per Pupil Enrolled, Public Elementary and Secondary Schools, 1870–1966, Series C5 and C6	170	
6.3	Four-year Colleges and Universities and Public and Private Junior Colleges, 1918–1968, Series F9, F10, F11	175	
6.4	Higher Educational Institutions, by Type of Institution, 1919–1968, Series F1–F8	176	
6.5	Governmental Support for Public Elementary and Secondary Education, as a Percent of the Total Revenue for Education, and Total Revenue, in Billions of Dollars	183	
6.6	Expenditures in Public Elementary and Secondary Schools (in Constant 1958 Dollars) for Instruction, per Teacher and per Pupil, and for Other School Services, per Pupil, 1920–1966 (Source: Table 6.5)	186	
6.7	Expenditures in Public Elementary and Secondary Schools (in Constant 1958 Dollars), per School, for Various Purposes, 1930–1966 (Source: Table 6.5)	188	
6.8	Total Revenue of Higher Educational Institutions, Series F15, and as a Percent of GNP, 1930–1966	189	
6.9	Major Source of Revenue as a Percent of Total Revenue, Institutions of Higher Education, 1930–1966, Series F17–F25	191	
6.10	Percent of Total Revenue, Institutions of Higher Education, from Three Levels of Government, 1930–1966, Series F19–F21	192	
6.11	Total Educational and General Expenditures, Series F26, and Expenditures on Instruction and Departmental Research, Series F29, per Student in Institutions of Higher Education (in Constant 1958 Dollars), 1930–1966	194	
6.12	Expenditures for Organized Research, per Faculty Member in Institutions of Higher Education (in Constant 1958 Dollars), 1930–1966, Series F31	195	
6.13	Total Educational and General Expenditures, Series F27, and Expenditures on Instruction and Departmental Research, Series F30, per Faculty Member in Institutions of Higher Education (in Constant 1958 Dollars), 1930–1966	196	
6.14	Expenditures for Four Purposes, per Institution in Institutions of Higher Education (in Thousands of Constant 1958 Dollars), 1930–1966, Series F32–F35	198	
6.15	Administrative and General Expenditures, Series F28, and Expenditures for Auxiliary Enterprises	199	

and Student Aid, Series F36, per Institution in Institutions of Higher Education (in Thousands of Constant 1958 Dollars), 1930–1966

7.1 Median School Years Completed for Population 25 Years Old and Over, 1910–1968, Series G1 — 204

7.2 Percent of Total Population 25 Years Old and Over Completing None or Less than 5 Years of Schooling, Series G2, 4 Years of High School or More, Series G3, 4 Years of College or More, Series G4, 1910–1968 — 206

7.3 Percent of Nonwhite Population 25 Years Old and Over Completing None or Less than 5 Years of Schooling, Series G5, 4 Years of High School or More, Series G6, 4 Years of College or More, Series G7, 1940–1968 — 208

7.4 Percent of 20–24-Year-Old Population Completing None or Less than 5 Years of School, by Color and Sex, 1940 to 1968, Series G14, G38, G62, G86 — 209

7.5 Percent of the 20–24-Year-Old Population Completing 4 Years of High School or More, by Color and Sex, 1940–1968, Series G18–G20, G42–G44, G66–G68, G90–G92 — 211

7.6 Percent of White Females with One Year of College or More, for Three Age Groups, 1940–1968, Series G43–G44, G51–G52, G59–G60 — 215

7.7 Cumulative Percentage Curves of Educational Attainment of Nonwhite Males, 20–24 Years of Age, 1940, 1947, 1957, and 1967, Series G62–G69 — 217

8.1 Ratio, Median Annual Salaries, Ph.D. Scientists in Educational Institutions, to Ph.D. Scientists, 1957–1966, and All Scientists, 1968, in Federal Government, Business and Industry, and Self-Employed for All Science Fields (Source: Table 8.5) — 232

Notes to the Series and Data Series

	Notes	Data
A1 Elementary and Secondary School Enrollment, Public and Non-public Day Schools (in Thousands), 1889–1968, School Year Ending on Date	276	376
A2 Ratio, Elementary and Secondary School Enrollment, per 100 5–17-Year-Old Population, 1889–1968, School Year Ending on Date	279	376
A3–A5 School Enrollment per 100 Population of School Age, Total and by Color, 1850–1968, School Year Ending on Date	281	376
A6–A7 Enrollment in Full-time Public Day Schools, by Grade-Group, Kindergarten and Grades 1–8 (A6) and Grades 9–12 and Postgraduate (A7), 1911–1967, School Year Ending on Date	284	376
A8–A9 Enrollment in Full-time Non-public Regular Elementary and Secondary Day Schools (in Thousands), 1934–1967, School Year Ending on Date	285	376
A10 Average Days Attended per Pupil Enrolled in Public Schools, 1870–1966, School Year Ending on Date	286	376
A11 Pupil-Teacher Ratio: Average Number of Pupils in Daily Attendance per Classroom Teacher (Including Other Nonsupervisory Staff), 1870–1966, School Year Ending on Date	287	376
A12–A14 Pupil-Teacher Ratio in Public Day Schools, Elementary Schools Only (A13), Secondary Schools Only (A14), and Total Elementary and Secondary Schools (A12), 1910–1967, School Year Ending on Date	288	378
A15–A16 Pupil-Teacher Ratio in Non-public Elementary (A15) and Secondary (A16) Day Schools, 1890–1966, School Year Ending on Date	288	378
A17 Number of Graduates of Public and Non-public Secondary Schools (in Thousands), 1870–1968, School Year Ending on Date	291	378
A18 High School Graduates as a Percent of the Population 17 Years Old, 1870–1968, School Year Ending on Date	292	378
A19–A22 Estimated Retention Ratios, Public and Non-public Schools, 5th to 6th Grades (A19), 6th to 7th Grades (A20), 7th to 8th Grades (A21), 8th to 9th Grades (A22), Base Years 1924–1962, School Year Beginning on Date	293	378
A23–A25 Continuation Ratios in Full-time Public Secondary Day Schools, 9th to 10th Grades (A23), 10th to 11th Grades (A24), and 11th to 12th Grades (A25), Base Years 1910–1966, School Year Beginning on Date	294	380
A26 Continuation Ratios, Grade 12 to College, Public and Non-public, 1945–1967, School Year Beginning on Date	296	380
A27–A37 Percent of Various Age Groups Enrolled in School, 1947–1968, Fall of Year	298	380
B1–B6 Classroom Teachers and Other Nonsupervisory Staff in Public Elementary and Secondary Day Schools, by Sex, School Year Ending on Date, Total, in Thousands (B1), Male, in Thousands (B2), Female, in Thousands (B3), Female as a Percentage of Total Elementary and Secondary (B4), Elementary Total, in Thousands (B5), and Secondary Total, in Thousands (B6)	304	382
B7–B8 Teachers with Less than Standard Certificates in Public Elementary (B7) and Secondary Schools (B8) as a Percentage of Total Teachers in Each System, 1954–1967, School Year Beginning on Date	306	382
B9–B10 Instructional Staff in Full-time Non-public Elementary (B9) and Secondary (B10) Day Schools (in Thousands), 1934–1964, School Year Ending on Date	307	382

	Notes	Data
B11–B14 Median Age of Elementary and Secondary Teachers, by Color and Sex, 1930–1960	308	382
C1 Total Number of Public Elementary Schools (in Thousands), 1930–1966, School Year Ending on Date	309	384
C2–C3 Number of One-Teacher Public Schools in Use (in Thousands), 1910–1966, School Year Ending on Date (C2), and One-Teacher Schools as a Percentage of Elementary Schools, 1930–1966, School Year Ending on Date (C3)	309	384
C4 Total Number of Public Secondary Schools (in Thousands), 1930–1966, School Year Ending on Date	310	384
C5 Average Length of School Term (in Days) in Public Elementary and Secondary Schools, 1870–1966, School Year Ending on Date	311	384
C6 Average Number of Days Attended per Pupil Enrolled in Public Elementary and Secondary Schools, 1870–1966, School Year Ending on Date	311	384
C7 Expenditures for Public Elementary and Secondary Day Schools per Pupil in Average Daily Attendance, in Current Unadjusted Dollars, 1889–1967, School Year Ending on Date	312	384
C8 Expenditure per Pupil Enrolled in Public Schools, 1870–1965, School Year Ending on Date	313	384
D1–D3 First-time Degree-credit Enrollment, All Colleges and Universities (in Thousands), Total (D1), Males (D2), Females (D3), 1939–1967, School Year Beginning on Date	315	384
D4–D5 Total Degree-credit Enrollment, All Colleges and Universities (in Thousands), Males (D4), Females (D5), 1939–1968, School Year Beginning on Date	315	384
D6–D9 First-time Degree-credit Enrollment, Junior College (in Thousands), Males (D6), Females (D7), and as a Percent of Total First-time Degree-credit Enrollment (D8, D9), 1939–1968, School Year Beginning on Date	317	386
D10–D12 Ratio, First-time Opening Fall Degree-credit Enrollment in Institutions of Higher Education, per 100 18-Year-Old Population, Total (D10) and by Sex (D11, D12), 1939 to 1968, School Year Beginning on Date	318	386

	Notes	Data
D13–D15 Ratio, Higher Education Enrollment per 100 18–21-Year-Old Population, Total (D13), 1870–1968, and by Sex (D14, D15), 1939–1968	318	386
D16–D18 Degrees Conferred by Institutions of Higher Education, Bachelor's (D16), Master's (D17) and Doctor's (D18), 1870–1967, School Year Ending on Date	321	386
D19 Doctor's Degrees Conferred (NAS–NRC), 1880–1968, School Year Ending on Date	323	386
D20 Bachelor's Degrees per 100 23-Year-Old Population, 1900 to 1967, School Year Ending on Date	324	388
D21 Ratio of Bachelor's Degrees per 100 High School Graduates Four Years Earlier, 1884–1967, School Year Ending on Date	324	388
D22 Master's Degrees per 100 Bachelor's Degrees, Two Years Earlier, 1872–1967, School Year Ending on Date	325	388
D23 Doctor's Degrees per 1,000 Bachelor's Degrees x-Years Earlier, 1878–1967, School Year Ending on Date	325	388
D24–D26 Ratio, Four-Year Bachelor's Degrees per 100 First-time Enrollment Four Years Earlier, Total (D24), and by Sex (D25, D26), 1950–1967, School Year Ending on Date	326	388
D27 Grand Total, Academic Production Index (in Thousands), 1949–1967, School Year Ending on Date	327	388
D28 API, Total (in Thousands), Arts, Humanities and Social Sciences, 1949–1967, School Year Ending on Date	327	388
D29 API, Total (in Thousands), Basic and Applied Sciences, 1949–1967, School Year Ending on Date	327	388
D30 API, Total (in Thousands), All Other Fields, 1949–1967, School Year Ending on Date	327	388
D31 Higher Education Enrollment per API, 1949–1967	327	388
D32 Higher Education Faculty Members per 100 API, 1950–1967	328	388
D33 Current Fund Expenditures for Higher Education, per API, in Hundreds of Constant 1958 Dollars, 1950–1966, School Year Ending on Date	328	390

	Notes	Data		Notes	Data
D34 Expenditures for Student Aid in Higher Education, per API, in Constant 1958 Dollars, 1952–1966, School Year Ending on Date	328	390	F1–F7 Number of Institutions of Higher Education, by Type, 1950–1968, School Year Beginning on Date: Universities (F1), Liberal Arts Colleges (F2), Teachers Colleges (F3), Technological Schools (F4), Theological Religious (F5), Schools of Art (F6), Other Professional (F7)	336	392–395
D35 API Grand Total, per 100 Graduates, 1949–1967, Academic Year Ending on Date	328	390			
D36 API, Total Engineering, Mathematics, Physical Science, per 100 Graduates, 1949–1967, Academic Year Ending on Date	329	390	F8–F10 Number of Junior Colleges, Total (F8), Public (F9), Private (F10), 1918–1968, School Year Beginning on Date	339	394
D37 API, Total Biological Science, per 100 Graduates, 1949–1967, Academic Year Ending on Date	329	390	F11–F12 Total Number of Four-Year Institutions of Higher Education (F11), and Total, All Institutions of Higher Education (F12), 1870–1968	340	394
D38 API, Health Professions, per 100 Graduates, 1949–1967, Academic Year Ending on Date	329	390	F13 Number of Medical Schools, 1850–1966, School Year Ending on Date	341	394
D39 API, Social Science (Excluding Social Work), per 100 Graduates, 1949–1967, Academic Year Ending on Date	330	390	F14 Number of Dental Schools, 1860–1966, School Year Ending on Date	342	394
D40 API, Education, per 100 Graduates, 1949–1967, Academic Year Ending on Date	330	390	F15 Total Income of Institutions of Higher Education, in Thousands of Current Dollars, 1930–1966, School Year Ending on Date	343	394
D41 Current Fund Expenditures of Higher Education, in Billions of Constant 1958 Dollars, 1930–1966, Academic Year Ending on Date	330	390	F16 Total Expenditures in Institutions of Higher Education, in Thousands of Current Dollars, 1930–1966, School Year Ending on Date	344	394
D42–D47 Mean Lapse Time, B.A. to Ph.D., 1920–1961, by Field and for Total, 1920–1966, as follows: D42, Total Physical Sciences, 1920–1961; D43, Total Biological Sciences, 1920–1961; D44, Total Social Sciences, 1920–1961; D45, Arts and Professions, 1920–1961; D46, Education, 1920–1961; D47, All Fields, 1920–1966	330	390–393	F17 Income from Student Fees as a Percentage of Total Income of Institutions of Higher Education (F15), 1930–1966, School Year Ending on Date	345	396
			F18 Endowment Earnings Income as a Percentage of Total Income of Institutions of Higher Education (F15), 1930–1966, School Year Ending on Date	346	396
			F19–F21 Income from Governmental Sources, Federal (F19), State (F20), and Local (F21), as a Percentage of Total Income of Institutions of Higher Education (F15), 1930–1966, School Year Ending on Date	347	396
D48–D50 Estimated Average Starting Salary (per Month) Offered by Selected Business Concerns to Male Bachelor's Degree Graduates Specializing in Engineering, Accounting and Sales, 1947–1968, School Year Ending on Date	331	392	F22 Income from Private Gifts and Grants as a Percentage of Total Income of Institutions of Higher Education (F15), 1930–1966, School Year Ending on Date	348	396
E1–E4 Median Age of College Teachers, by Color and Sex, by Decade, 1930–1960: Male Total (E1), Male Nonwhite (E2), Female Total (E3), Female Nonwhite (E4)	334	392	F23 Income from Organized Activities Related to Instructional Departments as a Percentage of Total Income of Institutions of Higher Education (F15), 1932–1966, School Year Ending on Date	348	396
E5 Total Faculty, Institutions of Higher Education, 1880–1967, School Year Ending on Date	334	392			
E6 Male Faculty as a Percentage of Total Faculty, Institutions of Higher Education, 1880–1964, School Year Ending on Date	335	392	F24 Residual Income as a Percentage of Total Income of Institutions of Higher Education (F15), 1930–1966, School Year Ending on Date	349	396

		Notes	Data			Notes	Data
F25	Income from Auxiliary Enterprises and Student Aid as a Percentage of Total Income of Institutions of Higher Education (F15), 1930–1966, School Year Ending on Date	350	396	**F36**	Expenditures for Auxiliary Enterprises and Student Aid in Institutions of Higher Education per Institution, in Thousands of Constant 1958 Dollars, 1930–1966, School Year Ending on Date	358	398
F26–F27	Total Educational and General Expenditures in Institutions of Higher Education, per Student (F26), and per Faculty Member (F27), in Constant 1958 Dollars, 1930–1966, School Year Ending on Date	351	396	**F37**	New Public Construction Expenditure Estimates, Non-residential, Educational, in Millions of Dollars, 1920–1965	360	398
				G1	Median School Years Completed for Population 25 Years Old and Over, 1910–1968	361	400
F28	Administrative and General Expenditures in Institutions of Higher Education per Institution, in Thousands of Constant 1958 Dollars, 1930–1966, School Year Ending on Date	352	396	**G2–G13**	Percent of the Population 25 Years Old and Over, and the Population 25 to 29 Years Old Who Have Completed (a) Less than 5 Years of Elementary School (G2, G5, G8, G11), (b) 4 Years of High School or More (G3, G6, G9, G12), (c) 4 Years of College or More (G4, G7, G10, G13), for Total and Nonwhite Population, 1910–1967	364	400
F29–F30	Expenditures for Resident Instruction and Departmental Research in Institutions of Higher Education, per Student (F29), and per Faculty Member (F30), in Constant 1958 Dollars, 1930–1966, School Year Ending on Date	353	398				
F31	Expenditures for Organized Research in Institutions of Higher Education per Faculty Member, in Constant 1958 Dollars, 1930–1966, School Year Ending on Date	354	398				
				G14–G109	Percent of the Population Completing Various Levels of Educational Attainment, by Color and Sex for the following Age Groups (a) 20–24 Years, (b) 25–34 Years, (c) 35–44 Years, 1940–1967	365	402–407
F32	Library Expenditures in Institutions of Higher Education per Institution, in Thousands of Constant 1958 Dollars, 1930–1966, School Year Ending on Date	355	398				
				G110–G125	Labor Force Participation Rates of the Civilian Noninstitutional Population, 14–17 Years of Age and 18–24 Years of Age, by School Enrollment Status, Color and Sex, 1959–1967	367	408
F33	Expenditures for Plant Operation and Maintenance in Institutions of Higher Education per Institution, in Thousands of Constant 1958 Dollars, 1930–1966, School Year Ending on Date	356	398				
				G126–G157	Labor Force Status of the Civilian Noninstitutional Population, 14–17 Years of Age (G126–G141), and 18–24 Years of Age (G142–G157), by Fall School Enrollment, Color and Sex, 1959–1967	370	409–410
F34	Expenditures for Organized Activities Related to Instructional Departments in Institutions of Higher Education per Institution, in Thousands of Constant 1958 Dollars, 1932–1966, School Year Ending on Date	356	398				
				G158	Percent Illiterate Among Persons 10 Years Old and Over, 1870–1959	370	412
F35	Expenditures for Extension and Public Services in Institutions of Higher Education per Institution, in Thousands of Constant 1958 Dollars, 1930–1966, School Year Ending on Date	358	398	**H1–H3**	Median Income of Males, Age 25 Years and Over, Who Have Completed: 8 Years of Elementary School (H1), 4 Years of High School (H2), and 4 or More Years of College (H3), 1939–1966	371	412
				I1–I35	Population, by Sex, for Selected Ages and Age Groups, 1880–1968	373	412–417

Introduction

This volume presents statistical time series on trends in education in the United States. The principal purpose is to bring together time series that indicate changing characteristics of education -- education considered both organizationally and as a characteristic of the population.

In "laying out" statistical time series and in searching for indicators of educational change, many single-time studies of the educational system had to be neglected. Similarly, time series of trends in limited or localized areas are disregarded, except in using them to illustrate a series not otherwise available for the nation as a whole.

The educational system offers a variety of statistical evidence on itself. One may be surprised to find so many time series available on trends in education. Upon closer inspection, however, one may be equally amazed that so "literate" a system as Education, with a capital E, does not provide more evidence on many vital aspects of the system, such as the amount of learning that takes place or the qualifications of the teaching staff. Such omissions become evident when the data are assembled in one place.

By assembling in one place a great part of the statistical evidence one may then identify the missing elements, the data needed for adequate monitorship of the system.

"Monitorship of the system" may have several functions. Statistical measures across time serve to identify changes. Whether a characteristic is increasing or decreasing may be intrinsically interesting to us, such as whether a larger or smaller percentage of the 17-year-olds are enrolled in school, or whether the number graduating from engineering colleges is increasing or decreasing. Such intrinsically interesting indicators may be called criterion indicators and monitored from the viewpoint of the society.

A change in a statistical measure may also indicate a forecast of a future change in another, perhaps more important, statistical measure. Thus, a decrease in school enrollment of one population category may herald a decline in educational attainment of that population cohort five or ten years later, or a decline in Bachelor's degrees may forecast a decrease in Master's degrees a few years later, as did first-level degrees in Agriculture when they began to decline in 1958-59. Just as "leading indicators" have proven quite valuable in business forecasting, herald (or mercurial) indicators, when identified and when the systemic linkage is verified, may prove equally valuable in signaling the need for counter-moves or other adjustments to forestall an unwanted future consequence.

However, the linkage between indicators may not always be obvious. The change in one indicator may be associated with a change in another but the important, causative force may be a third variable whose influence is not understood or suspected. A third purpose, then, in monitoring social indicators is to identify significant changes that cry to be explained. There are two approaches in discovering the interactions and interconnections among elements of the social system which will identify such cause-effect linkages. Ideally, both would be firmly grounded in a theory of how the system functions, a model.

One approach would associate the criterion indicator with other indicators of changes in the system, indicators theoretically relevant to the criterion. Regression analysis of time series rests upon the adequacy of the theory and the precision of the indicators. It leads to statements of what "accounts for" changes in the criterion. As an example, the continuation of students in secondary school from one class to another is analyzed (chapter 2) in relation to changes in unemployment, in per capita expenditures, and to changes in the size of the Armed Forces. Such a regression analysis offers some explanation of the change in the criterion indicator and leads to identifying other measures needed for more complete explanation, in this example, marriage rates by age and sex, fertility rates, etc.

A second approach in identifying cause-effect linkages would develop a basis for predicting the indicator at successive points in time through establishing the interrelations at one point in time. Intensive cross-sectional studies would be made using both the measures comprising the time series and other variables. Thus, an indicator of achievement in a subject might be predicted through multiple regression methods, as was done in <u>Equality of Educational Opportunity</u> (Coleman, et.al., 1966: 292-334). Such cross-sectional analyses lead to the identification of important cause-effect linkages affecting the criterion indicator. By introducing the new measures so identified into the system of social indicators in time series, the basis for prediction is enhanced.[1]

In summary, the purpose of this volume is to present a number of indicators of change in the educational system. This assembly is intended to provide a basis for monitoring education (within the limits of currently available statistics). Such monitorship should detect changes in important indices that reflect the adequacy of education in the United States. It also should lead to identifying linkages between leading, or lagging, indicators, particularly in cases where some systemic relationship between the two is theoretically reasonable. Such linkages may be identified through analysis of changes in indicators across time and through cross-sectional studies which establish a basis for predicting a dependent variable (a criterion indicator) upon the basis of a set of independent variables.

The Interpretation of Trends

If a change occurs in an indicator, what has caused the change? To isolate the relationship between cause and effect gives society the basis for adjusting the system so that the desired rather than the undesired end comes about. Knowing the cause-effect relationships sometimes is easy: the return of veterans to school under the G.I. Bill of Rights after World War II stimulated an increase in degrees. Discovering why degrees thereafter continued to increase, after a brief decline, however, is not quite as easy. Did an increase in the population of college age, or an increase in the graduation rate, or both cause the increase? This problem is explored in chapter 5.

In analyzing the basis for changes in the educational system, measures of the resources going into the system and of the results coming from the system provide a model with a great deal of appeal, logically and practically. Such system analysis, however, requires knowledge of the interactions within the system and measures of the relevant variables. One of the disappointments of this study is that such a comprehensive use of the data was not possible. We have a few, and very few, measures of "input" and even fewer measures of "output," but we know almost nothing about interaction within the system. This is perhaps the most important single consideration for those who might wish to develop educational statistics into the needed tools for planning and evaluation. To begin such a development, knowledge first of interrelations among variables in the most elemental unit is needed, interaction in the classroom and the school.

Even so, limited input-output considerations are presented and more undoubtedly may be developed from the data presented herein. Measures of college graduates in relation to first-time enrollment four years earlier is a simple input-output measure that reflects the change in "inputs" needed to produce a given level of "output."

While trends may be interpreted in terms of the functioning of the system, trends also may be interpreted in relation to some goal. To what extent are various educational goals being achieved? To demonstrate this use, some of the (measurable) educational goals in the 1960 report of the President's Commission on National Goals were evaluated by determining the degree to which they had been achieved. This exercise could not evaluate all of the educational goals set by the Commission, for the evidence on many of them was not to be found.

Using goals as the basis for interpreting trends, however, makes social indicators of the educational system a necessary adjunct to educational planning and evaluation. Perhaps serious planning for the educational system should always be accompanied by the development or use of indicators measuring the degree to which the goal of the plan is achieved. This use of indicators however, may contribute little to our understanding of how the system functions.[2/]

Another basis for interpreting trends uses aggregated indicators, decomposed into their constituent parts, a topic discussed next.

Aggregated and Disaggregated Measures

A measure representing the United States, whether a rate or a simple total of those possessing a given characteristic, is an aggregate measure. While such measures may reflect important changes across time in some phenomenon, they also mask much of the variability of the phenomenon. The term, disaggregate, has been used by economists to refer to a global measure that is decomposed into parts reflecting its variability An educational indicator may be disaggegated according to the categories or types of the population composing it, for example by such traits as sex, color, geographic area, income, and others.

Disaggregation by geographic area is highly appropriate for most of the data presented in this volume. Geographic detail by state or county serve to narrow the focus on the situation or problem. However, such disaggregation was not attempted for this volume. Detail by sex, color and age are presented for a few series, where appropriate, and a few aggregates are broken down into subcategories.

Disaggregation becomes especially important, also, when the aggregated statistic exhibits a change requiring an explanation. Then, decomposition into its parts will help identify the elements associated with the change in the aggregate. Thus, the plateau reached in the indicator of educational attainment (12 or more years schooling) in 1964 by nonwhite males 20-24 years of age is explored (chapter 7) in relation to sub-levels of attainment, of smaller age groups, and in relation to the school enrollment of the age cohorts at an earlier date. Such disaggregation, or one might call it analysis into more elemental classes, is a rather important step in the use of social indicators. When the aggregate trend presents a change of interest, the analyst proceeds to examine the more elementary bases for the change, both in time, in place, as well as according to categories of the population. Analytical steps of this kind are needed in monitoring social indicators.

Criteria for the Selection of an Indicator

No single criterion was used to select educational indicators. Several criteria were used. The state of knowledge at present is not adequate to define which indicators are most useful and which are not. Accordingly, some indicators included may prove useless.[3/]

Criterion indicators were included if the series measured a condition of the educational system thought to be desirable or undesirable from the vantage point of an effective system. As an example, a pupil-teacher ratio provides a global index of the adequacy of teacher manpower with respect to pupils to be taught. Generally, the rationale is that the lower the number of pupils per teacher the more likely is the teacher to provide an environment to stimulate sound learning. Another example is the percent of secondary school teachers with less than standard teacher's certificates, reflecting the adequacy of preparation of the secondary school teaching staff.

A number of series are included because they contribute to the development of a criterion indicator and are a necessary part of a criterion measure. Following the preceding paragraph, an example is the number of pupils and of teachers, by level. Space, however, does not permit the inclusion of all such data. The sources of data, set forth in Notes to the Series, provide the key to retrieving such aggregates as one might want to analyze further.

Some indicators were included because they appeared to forecast the future. While school enrollment by age-sex-color groups is a valuable indicator in itself, it also forecasts the educational attainment of a future age-sex-color group. Consequently, if a series appeared to indicate a situation requiring a future adjustment, it was included. Whether or not a forecast is realized in the future depends upon whether an active effort is made to alter the assumptions. Thus, a prediction of a shortage in the supply of teachers may be followed by efforts to increase the supply, efforts that cause the forecast never to be realized. Other examples of indicators which are useful forecasts of the future are the number of 5-year-olds, the rate of enrollment in college, and the percentage of first-time college enrollment in junior colleges.

A few indicators that show changes in a single state, e.g., Iowa, are presented because national measures are unavailable. If available nationally, such an indicator would provide a useful criterion of the educational system. For example, the achievement test scores of high school seniors in Iowa, by subject, reflect the trend in the quality of learning and hence the quality of the educational system. Such measures for the nation would evaluate the system as no currently available measure does.

While these characteristics have provided general guidance in selecting data for this volume, limitations of space also placed bounds upon the number of series that could be presented. Consequently, not all series fulfilling these characteristics could be included.

Major Sources of Data

The data brought together in this volume come primarily from two sources: the U. S. Bureau of the Census, based upon the Decennial Census, the Current Population Survey, or the Census of Governments; and from the U. S. Office of Education, based upon data collected from state departments of education, directly from the institutions themselves, and upon surveys of students or faculty, etc. The virtue of these two major sources rests upon their continuous use of approximately the same data-collection methods, concepts, definitions, etc., and generally upon the length in time of the series.

While these are the chief sources, other primary sources have been used. For example, included also are test results from the Educational Testing Service, from the Minnesota testing program, data on the desegregation of schools from the Southern Education Reporting Service, results of studies from the National Education Association, and data on aspects of scientific manpower from the National Register of Scientific and Technical Personnel of the National Science Foundation, and other sources.

The Types of Statistical Series

Six kinds of statistics are presented in the volume:

1. A simple aggregate or frequency, such as the total enrollment in elementary school or the total revenue of institutions of higher education.

2. Ratios and other quotients, expressing one aggregate in relation to another, such as the school enrollment per 100 population of school age, or the expenditure of public elementary and secondary schools per student enrolled.

3. Percentages, expressing the number in one class per 100 in the total of all classes in the set, such as the percentage of 20-24-year-old nonwhite females who have attained four or more years of schooling, or the percent male of all college faculty.

4. Rates, like percentages, expressing the number in one class divided by the total of all eligible, such as the enrollment rate of an age group.

5. Means, medians, etc., expressing the central tendency of a distribution, such as the median years of school completed by a given age-sex-color group, or the mean score of Minnesota junior year high school students on an aptitude test.

6. Contrived aggregates, based upon the sum of a number of frequencies, each weighted with a different value, such as the Academic Production Index, a summation of the product of degrees and an appropriate value for each kind of degree.

The efficacy of these measures is discussed in the context of review of the series, in the text and in the Notes to the Series. However, it should be clear that means, medians, percentages, and rates are more precise measures than ratios and contrived aggregates. In the case of ratios, it is not always certain that the members of the denominator term were eligible for the characteristic in the numerator. As an illustration, the ratio of first-time college enrollment per 100 18-year-olds is not as precise a measure as the percent of 18-year-olds who are enrolled in college. In the case of contrived aggregates, such as the A.P.I. measures, the procedure of aggregating, often involving the summing of products, produces an indicator that is more general than the detail composing it. Indeed, this usually is the reason for developing such an aggregate. The contrived measure, however, has uses beyond those of the separate parts; for example, expenditures of higher educational institutions per API provides a more interpretable measure than would the ratio of expenditures to 4-year degrees.

The Organization of the Volume

The trends in education are presented in major categories of data and, within categories, are generally organized by level of education. Enrollment of students in school is presented first and is followed by a brief chapter on teachers and another on the quality of education. Data on graduates comprise an extensive chapter. The chapter on trends in institutional organization and finance discusses the number of institutions of various types, the sources of revenue, and the objectives of expenditures, the latter expressed in per capita terms. Then, there is a review of trends in the educational attainment of the population, considered by age, sex, and color. Finally, the concluding chapter assesses the attainment of goals for education as set forth in Goals for Americans (President's Commission on National Goals: 1960).

The statistical series themselves are organized by level and category insofar as this ordering could be conveniently followed. The major categories and the identifying letter of each, follows:

- A - Elementary and Secondary, Enrollment
- B - Elementary and Secondary, Teachers
- C - Elementary and Secondary, Schools and Other
- D - Higher Education, Enrollment and Graduates
- E - Higher Education, Teachers
- F - Higher Education, Institutions and Finances
- G - The Population, Educational Attainment, and Enrollment and Labor Force Status
- H - Miscellaneous
- I - The School-Age Population, by Age and Sex

In addition to these basic statistical series, a few additional time series are introduced here and there in the text. In most instances, these series are short, containing only a few observations, or applying to a region or a state, etc.

Conventions of the Statistical Tables and Graphs

Some educational statistics are logically oriented to the beginning of the school year, such as enrollment, and others, such as graduates, are more logically calibrated to the end of the school year. For this reason, no attempt was made to cast all statistical series in relation to the beginning (fall) of the year or to the end (spring) of the school year. Consequently, the following symbols are found at the head of the statistical columns:

SYEOD: School Year Ending on Date, meaning that the statistic refers to the school year that ends on the date appearing in the row.

SYB: School Year Beginning, meaning that the statistic refers to the school year beginning on the date appearing in the row. This symbol was shortened, that is, OD (on date) was eliminated, in order to more easily distinguish it from SYEOD.

"Base year" refers to the year of the data used as the denominator of the statistic. Continuation ratios, for example, utilize data from two successive years, and are presented on the base year, that is, the year of the denominator statistic.

Depending upon his purpose, the analyst may wish to re-orient a statistical series for another year to which the data may be more relevant to his purposes.

The sources of data are presented as Notes to the Series, beginning on page 276. Here, also, will be found precautionary notes and information on the data collection methods, etc., where such is appropriate to the series. Some of these notes are keyed to specific statistics of the series by use of a superscript which refers the reader to explanations in the Notes to the Series.

In the illustrations, the following conventions are followed:

Solid or dashed lines: Solid lines are used to connect the points in annual series. Dashed lines are used to connect points in biennial or decennial series. This convention is always followed when the series changes from one period to another, as from decennial observations to annual, or from biennial to annual. In other figures, different symbols for lines are used when several trends on the same graph must be distinguished from one another.

The year: The tables identify the approximate date the data refer to, whether fall of the year, spring of the year, or whether the data are for the school year ending on the date, etc. Graphs represent the data according to these dates. In inspecting data series or comparing one series with another, special attention should be given to the specification of the date in the tables. This applies, especially, to data based upon ratios that may involve more than one year, for in these cases the year of reference depends upon the purpose of the investigator.

Footnotes

1/ Of the 21 economic indicators originally proposed in 1931 by the National Bureau of Economic Research, only 11 are included in the 1966 set of 25 indicators thought most indicative of the American economy (Moore, 1967b: 28).

2/ A discussion of some of the pitfalls of complete reliance upon evaluation of goals as opposed to the other more comprehensive approaches (the system-model) is discussed by Etzioni and Lehman (1967: 7-8).

3/ See footnote 1.

2

Enrollment

In this chapter, two types of enrollment data will be examined: enrollment as reported by the institution, and enrollment status as reported by the population. Both provide useful indices of trends in enrollment. A few aggregates of the number of students enrolled in school will be presented, but the chapter will primarily present trends in enrollment upon the basis of (a) the ratio of enrollment in institutions of some particular educational level to the population chiefly served by that institutional type, and (b) the rate of enrollment of the population of a given age group. Where appropriate, rates of retention or of continuation in school also will be introduced as time series sensitive to changes in enrollment. The utility of cohorts to analyze trends in enrollment and retention in school, also, will be demonstrated.

Elementary and Secondary School Enrollment

The volume of enrollment in the public and private elementary and secondary schools has increased tremendously since 1890. The increase results both from an increase in total population and an increase in the rate of school attendance. Both Series (A1 and A2) are presented in Figure 2.1.

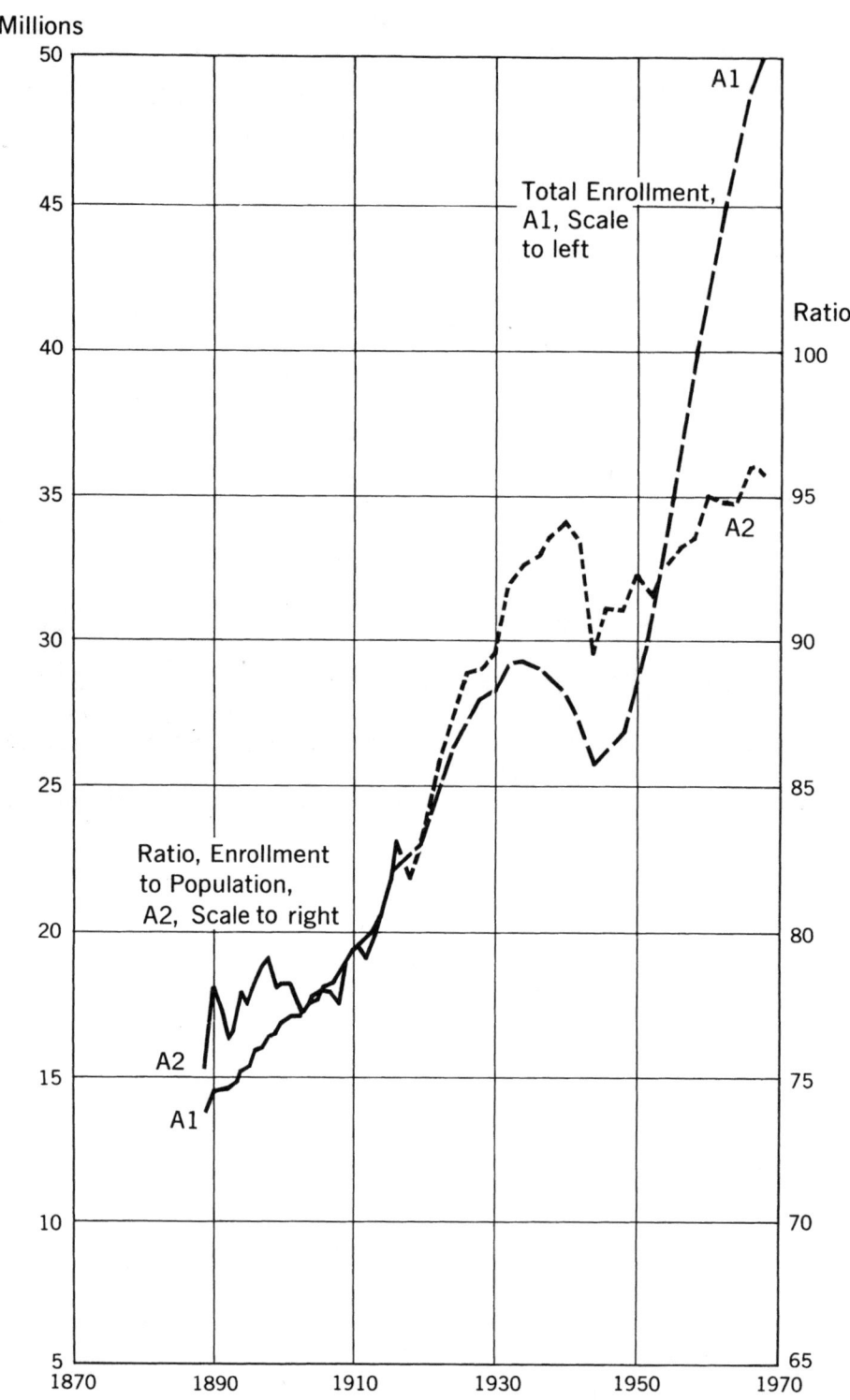

Figure 2.1. Total Elementary and Secondary School Enrollment (Public and Non-public Day Schools), 1889–1968, Series A1, and the Ratio of School Enrollment to the Population 5–17 Years of Age, 1889–1968, Series A2.

The increase since 1890 has been continuous except during the 8 years, 1936-1944 (Series A1), a period affected primarily by a decline in the school age population. Since 1944 the increase in enrollment has averaged about one and one-third million annually. The annual rate of increase since 1960 has been approximately 2.5 percent.

Series A2, the ratio of elementary and secondary enrollment to the population 5 to 17 years of age, gives a long-term series on rate of attendance. The series displays a moderate amount of variation as it dips down during the 1900-1910 period and during the 1940s. The upward climb 1907 to 1926 was quite rapid. The increase since 1944 has been slow but steady and now has reached 96.

The decline in elementary and secondary enrollment during the period 1932 to 1944 resulted from a combination of a decline in population of the elementary and secondary ages (usually taken to be 5 through 17 years), and a decline in the rate of attendance during the period 1940 to 1944. Enrollment is presented as Series A1 (Figure 2.1). The steady increase in elementary and secondary enrollment came to an end in 1932 and thereafter declined to 1944, when it again began to increase. In Figure 2.1 it will be noted that Series A2, enrollment as a percent of the population 5 to 17 years of age, continued to increase until 1940. The decline in enrollment to 1940, then, can only be a consequence of the decline in the population of school age (Series I4 and I35, Figure 2.2).

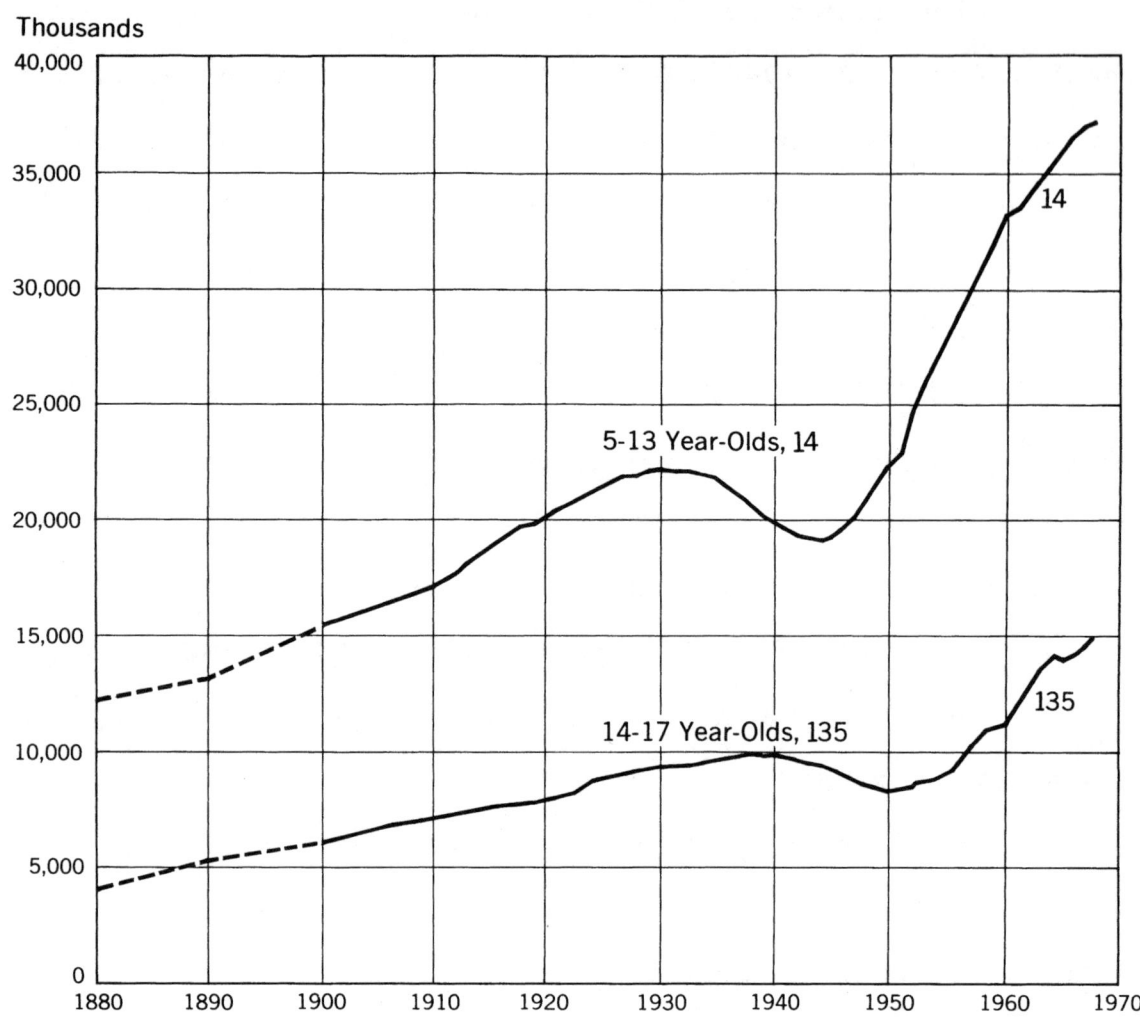

Figure 2.2. Total Population, 5–13 Years Old and 14–17 Years Old, 1880–1968, Series 14 and 135.

In Figure 2.2 the elementary school population, ages 5-13, Series I4, began tapering off at about the same time enrollment began to decline and reached its nadir at exactly the same point that enrollment reached its lowest point. However, during the period 1940 to 1944, undoubtedly as a consequence of dislocations caused by World War II, both population and the rate of attendance were declining. During these war years about as much of the decrease in enrollment must be attributed to a decrease in the rate (57 percent) as to a decrease in population (43 percent).[1]

Following 1944, however, elementary and secondary enrollment continued to increase, and by 1967 it reached nearly 50 million, a ratio of attendance for the age group of approximately 96 percent.

Public and Non-public Enrollment, by Level. The comparison of the relative importance of public and non-public elementary and secondary enrollment is shown in Figure 2.3. While the non-public elementary enrollment has been increasing, particularly since 1950, it has increased very little when compared with the tremendous enrollment increases of the public elementary school (Series A6 and A8). The non-public secondary school plays an even smaller role when compared with the public secondary enrollment (Series A7 and A9). The chief institutional support for non-public schools are religious organizations, the Roman Catholic Church enrolling approximately 90 percent of the non-public pupils.

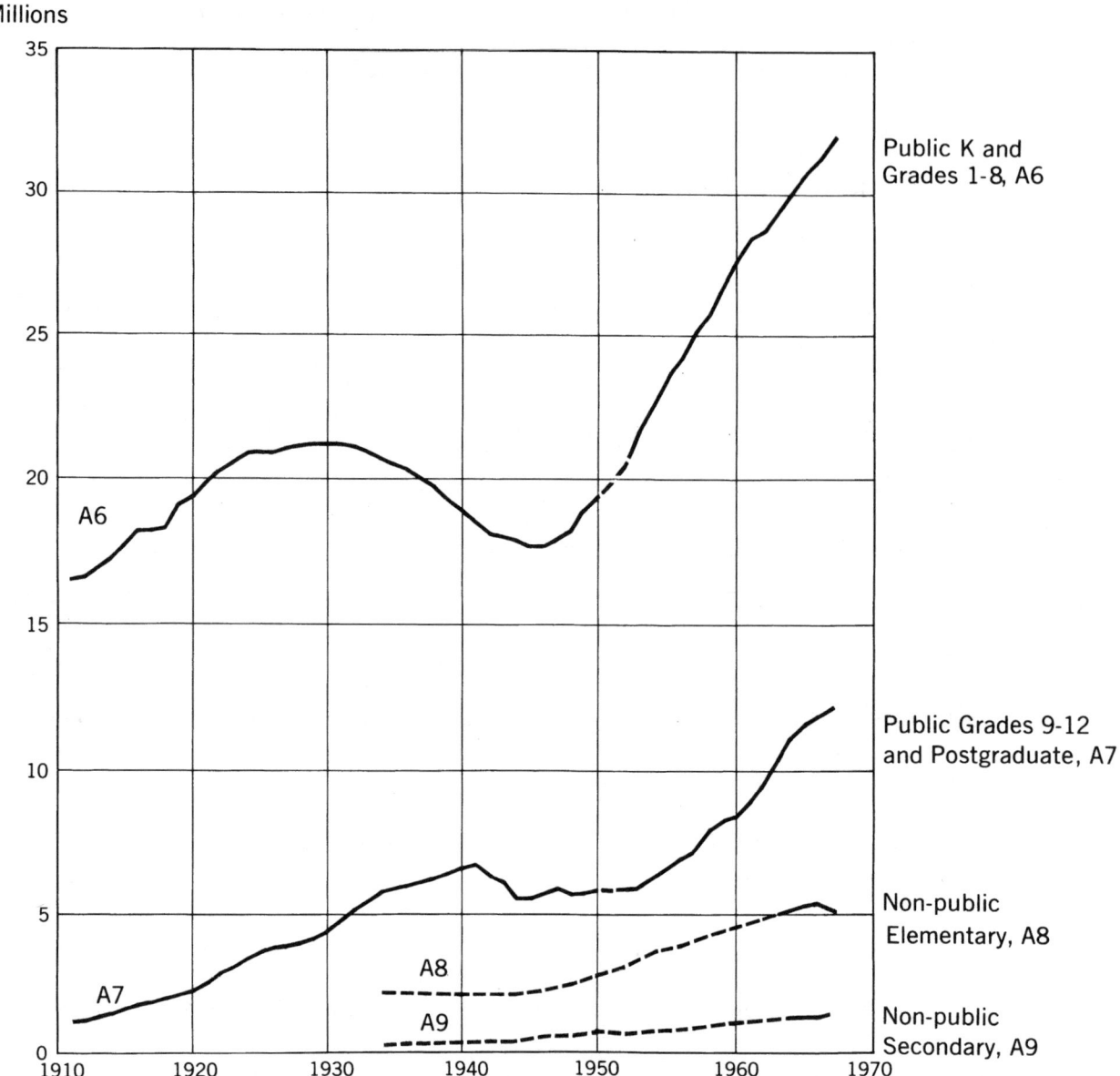

Figure 2.3. Enrollment in Elementary and Secondary Day Schools: Public, 1911–1967, Series A6 and A7, and Non-public, 1934–1967, Series A8 and A9.

School Enrollment Rates by Color

The gains since 1850 in enrollment of the school age population, the total and by color, are presented in Figure 2.4 (Series A3-A5).2/ The nonwhite population, because of its initial position near zero, shows the greatest increase. In the seventy years after 1850, enrollment of the nonwhite population rose to a level about the same as the level of the white population in 1850. During the same seventy years the enrollment rate of the white population increased only about 13 percentage points. Since 1930, improvement in both rates has been parallel. By 1963, the rates were almost the same and had reached a stable point where they were changing very slowly.

Retention in Secondary School

Studies of school dropouts have shown school retention is affected by socioeconomic status of the family, general economic need and a preference for work rather than study (Blough, 1956). Such microsocial studies lead one to infer that school retention would be increased by improving the financial status of the family, or otherwise removing the necessity to work. There is some evidence from macrosocial studies that periods of greater relative family need, as during a depression or an increase in unemployment, are accompanied by increases in school retention, rather than decreases, and that dropouts are somewhat more likely to increase during prosperous periods (Duncan, 1965: 128).

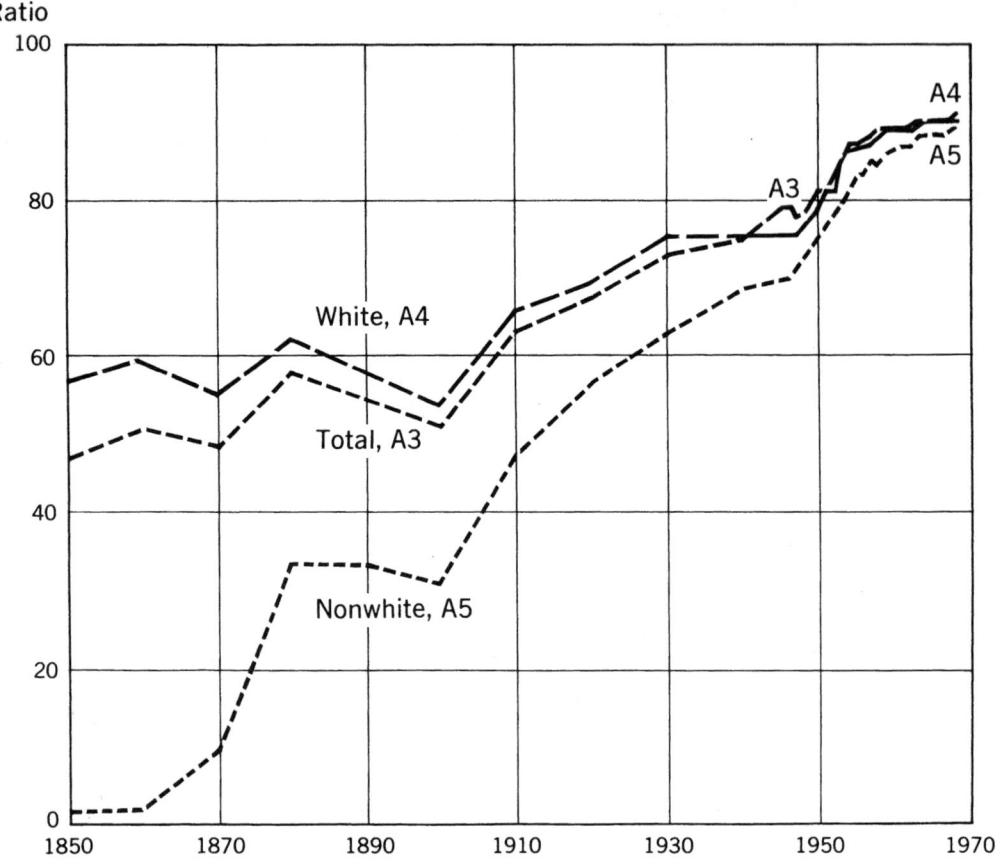

Figure 2.4. Ratio, School Enrollment per 100 Population of School Age, Total, and by Color, 1850–1968, Series A3, A4 and A5.

A logical argument can be made for both hypotheses: (a) When the family financial need becomes greater, as occurs during depressions, the student will be pressed into employment and will drop out of school; (b) when unemployment increases, jobs are less plentiful, and the more marginal worker, such as an enrolled student, will be more likely to remain a student rather than enter the labor market; conversely, when jobs are plentiful, the more marginal worker will be attracted to employment, and hence the enrolled student will drop out of school to take a job.

War is a more obvious force affecting dropouts. Military and industrial mobilization both draft young men into military service and stimulate employment in defense-related industries for both men and women.

The effect of these factors upon school retention now will be explored.

Continuation Ratios, 9th to 10th Grade

In 1910, the probability was .657 that a 9th grader would continue to the 10th grade in 1911 (Series A23). Year after year, this probability has increased at an average increment of approximately .006. By fall 1966, the probability that a 9th grader would continue to the 10th grade in fall 1967 was .978 (Figure 2.5), the highest rate of continuation of a high school grade.

The present 2.2 percent of the 9th grade dropping out of school before entering the 10th remains an educational problem of some dimension, but this rate is a great improvement over 34.3 percent, the percent of the 1910 9th grade who did not enter the 10th grade in 1911. This improvement, however, has not been uniform across the 56-year period.

The continuation ratio has dipped during the following periods: 1915-1918; 1924-1926; 1934-1936; 1940-1943; 1946-1951. These periods reflect wars and changes in the business cycle, events that appear to lure 9th graders from the school system.

In Figure 2.5, the topmost graph traces the observed trend in the probability of continuing in school. The middle graph shows the secular trend, with the increase uniformly spaced over the 56-year span. The lower chart describes the deviation from the uniform increase of .00573 annually, highlighting periods of improved school retention and periods of excessive dropout.

In the light of this trend one may see that the effect of World War I upon the 9th to 10th grade transition was more severe than World War II, suggesting more successful efforts at keeping students in school, and, perhaps, a shifting of the ages of students in these grades to younger ages. The small decrease in the continuation ratio in 1951 -- the time of the Korean Conflict -- shows still smaller effects upon this high school class. Although the 1933-1935 period witnessed a decline in the continuation ratio, net gains continued to be made during the severe depression of the 1930s (1930: 81, 1939: 89).

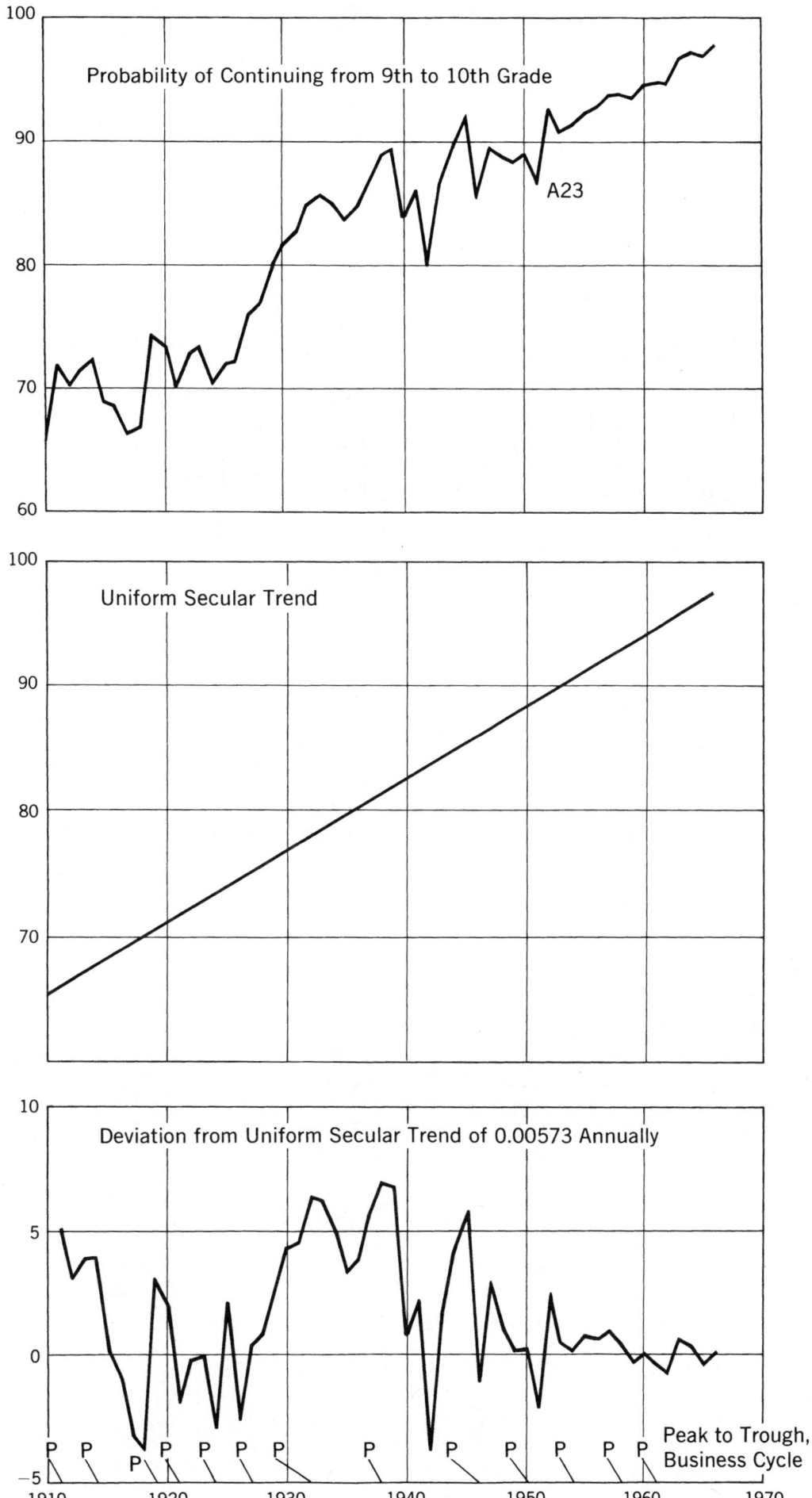

Figure 2.5. Ninth to Tenth Grade Continuation Ratio, 1910–1966, Series A23.

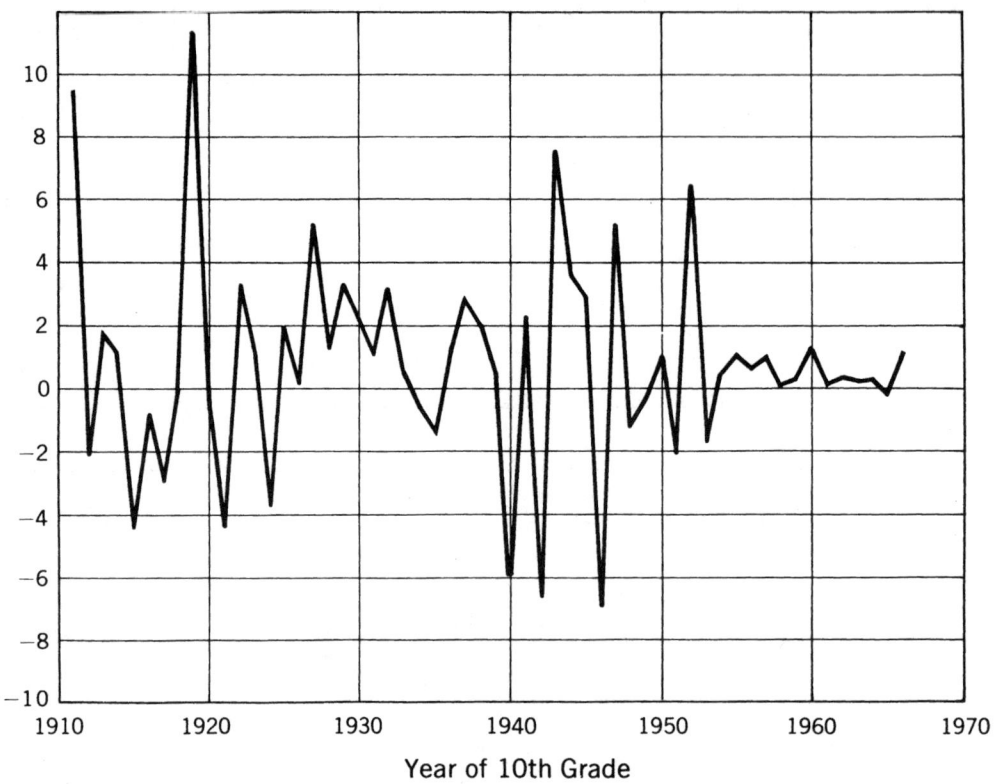

Figure 2.6. Rate of Change in the Continuation Ratio, 9th to 10th Grade, 1911–1966.

Finally, since 1953 the trend has closely followed the uniform secular increase.

The rate of change of the continuation ratio provides another useful basis for examining trends (Figure 2.6). The rate of change was greatest after World War I, but there were fairly consistent increases between 1925 and 1933. During World War II (1943-45) the rate of change increased. During the 13 years prior to 1966, the rate of change has been low, constant, and positive.

Continuation Ratios, 10th to 11th Grade

The probability of a 10th grader continuing to the 11th grade increased from .707 in 1910 to .930 in 1966, an annual constant increment of nearly .004 (Series A24). The year-to-year increase over this period, however, has been far from constant (Figure 2.7).

The transition of 10th graders to the 11th grade -- these are typically ages 15 to 16 -- is beset by more hazards than the 9th to 10th grade transition. The hazard of war -- particularly World Wars I and II, and the Korean Conflict are quite discernible in the trends; the hazards of business recessions extracted heavier tolls in the 1920s than during the 1930s (recessions during the 1920s: 1920-21, 1923-24, 1926-27, 1929-32). The consequences of more recent turns in business activity appear to be less severe than formerly. The lower chart sketches these relations.

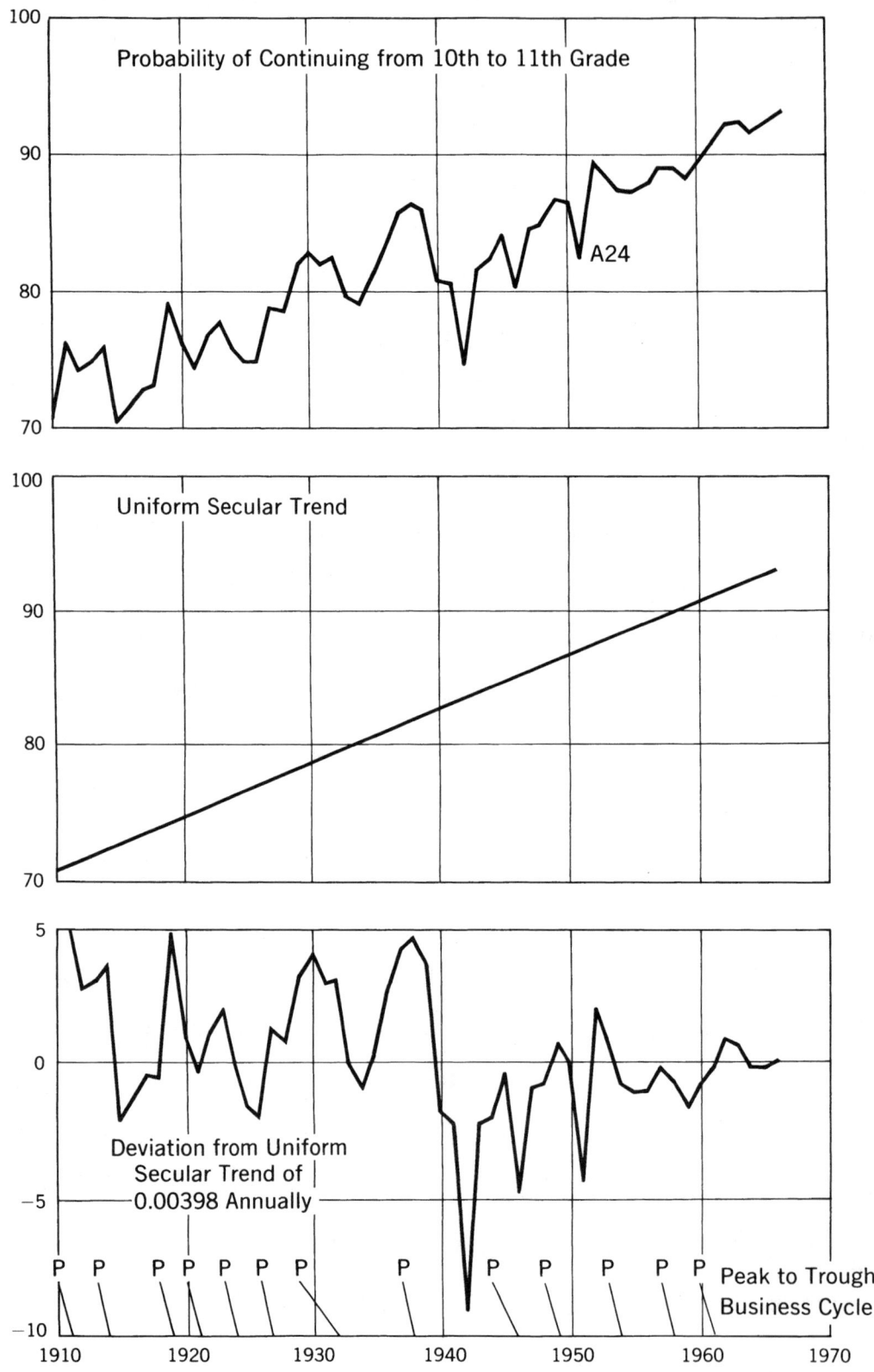

Figure 2.7. Tenth to Eleventh Grade Continuation Ratio, 1910–1966, Series A24.

The rate of change in the continuation ratio of the 10th grade class as it moves into the 11th grade varies more than that of the 9th to 10th transition, as Figure 2.8 illustrates. Were it smoother and more uniform, this graph would resemble the sine curve. Distinct upturns occur after the two major wars and the two major depressions, mid-1920 and early 1930. As we pass the mid-century mark the rate of change continues positive but dwindles to a slower pace. If we may be guided by the past, a major military conflict or a major change in business activity would bring about a sharp decline in the rate of change, but, barring these events, the rate of change may be expected to continue slightly positive.

Continuation Ratios, 11th to 12th Grade

This series begins with the eleventh grade class of 1910. The probability of this class continuing to the 12th grade the next year was .750 (Series A25). By 1966 this probability had increased to .919 (Figure 2.9).

While variations since 1910 appear to follow and to lag behind the peaks and troughs of the business cycle, the correspondence is not as close as the continuation ratio for the 10th-to-11th class. World War I affected the 11th-to-12th grades much less noticeably than it affected the 10th-to-11th, presumably because the latter class had drained off the students for military and civilian requirements, leaving the 11-to-12 transition less affected. World War II, however, affected the

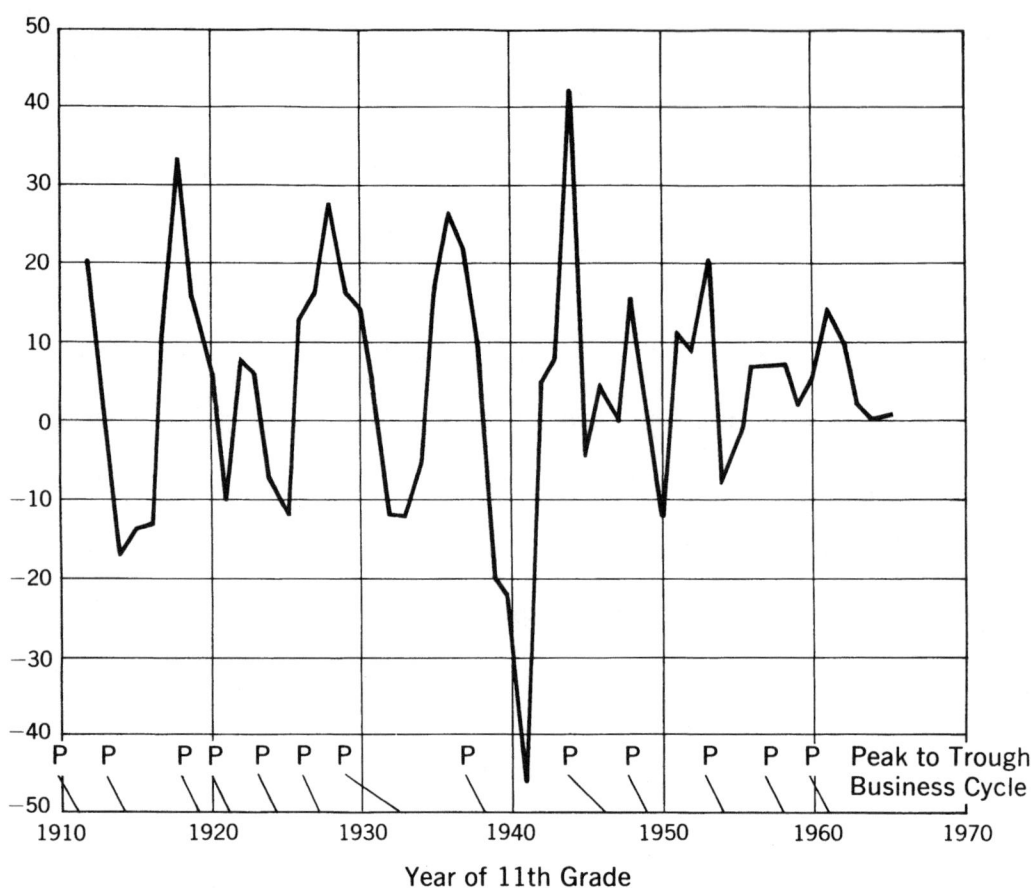

Figure 2.8. Three Year Moving Average of Rate of Change in the Continuation Ratio, 10th to 11th Grade, 1912–1965.

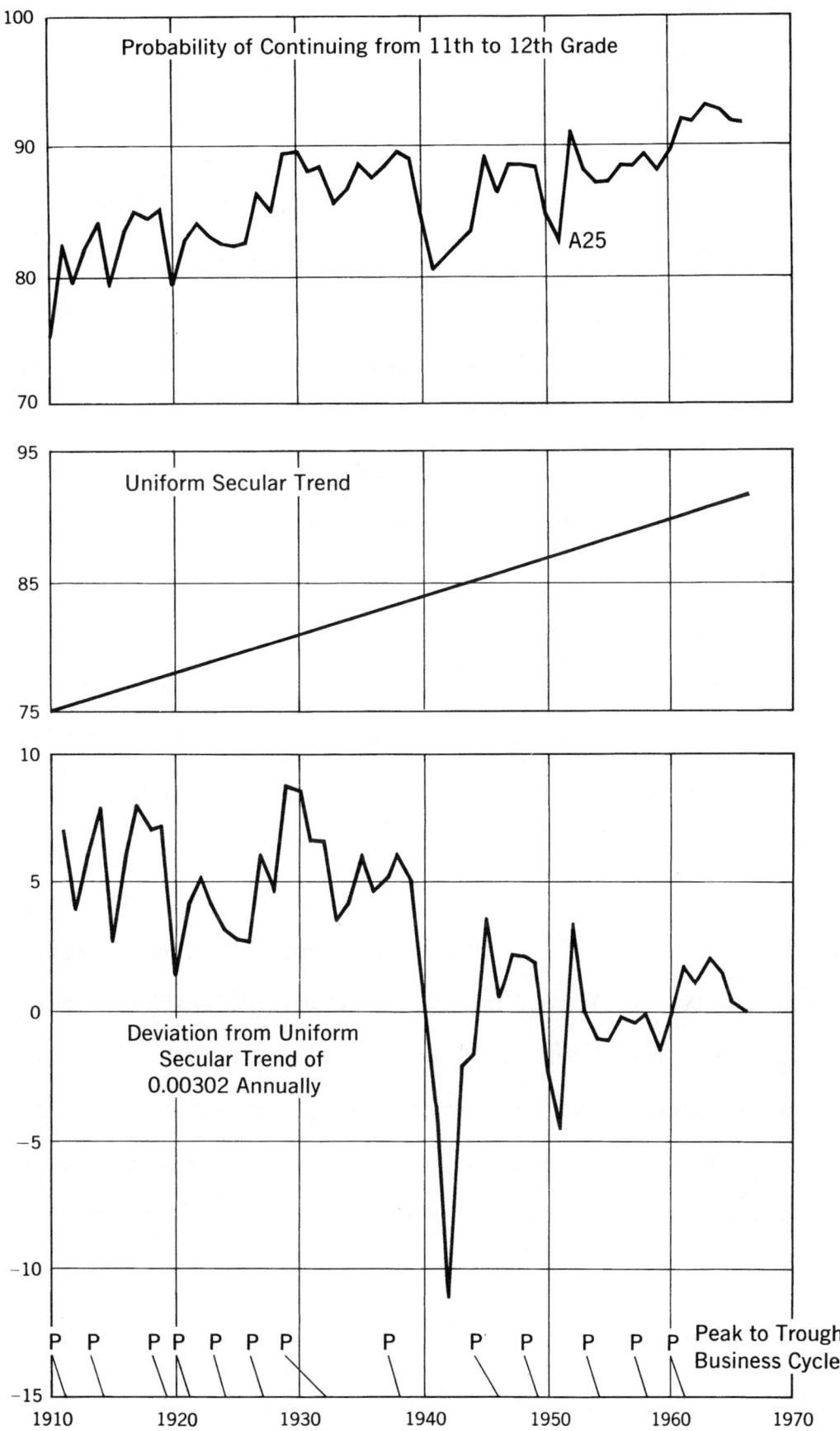

Figure 2.9. Eleventh to Twelfth Grade Continuation Ratio, 1910–1966, Series A25.

11th-to-12th much more directly and the draft for the Korean Conflict in the early 1950s affected the continuation ratio noticeably.

The business recessions of 1924, 1929-1932, 1946, 1949 and 1954 each have affected the continuation ratio of this class. The response of the continuation ratio to these events, however, has not always been immediate: a lag of one or two years seems to be typical.

Most of the long-term improvement in the 11th-to-12th grade continuation ratio occurred before 1940. The deviation of the ratio from a constant annual increase (Figure 2.9), shows the ratio exceeded a constant rate of increase to 1940, but has been below a constant increase about half the time since 1940. In 1939 retention reached .890 and in the next 23 years only gained a net of .028. Actually, some improvement has occurred since 1958, but the present increment is small. Why has retention of 11th graders resisted any but a slight secular improvement since 1940? The present continuation ratio (approximately .920) appears to be near the maximum possible: some will drop out when they pass the legal age of manditory attendance, some girls will quit school to marry, some boys will be lured away to employments and military service, etc.

The rate of change in the 11th-to-12th grade continuation ratio (Figure 2.10) has shifted abruptly as wars and depressions, prosperity and peace, have dominated the country.

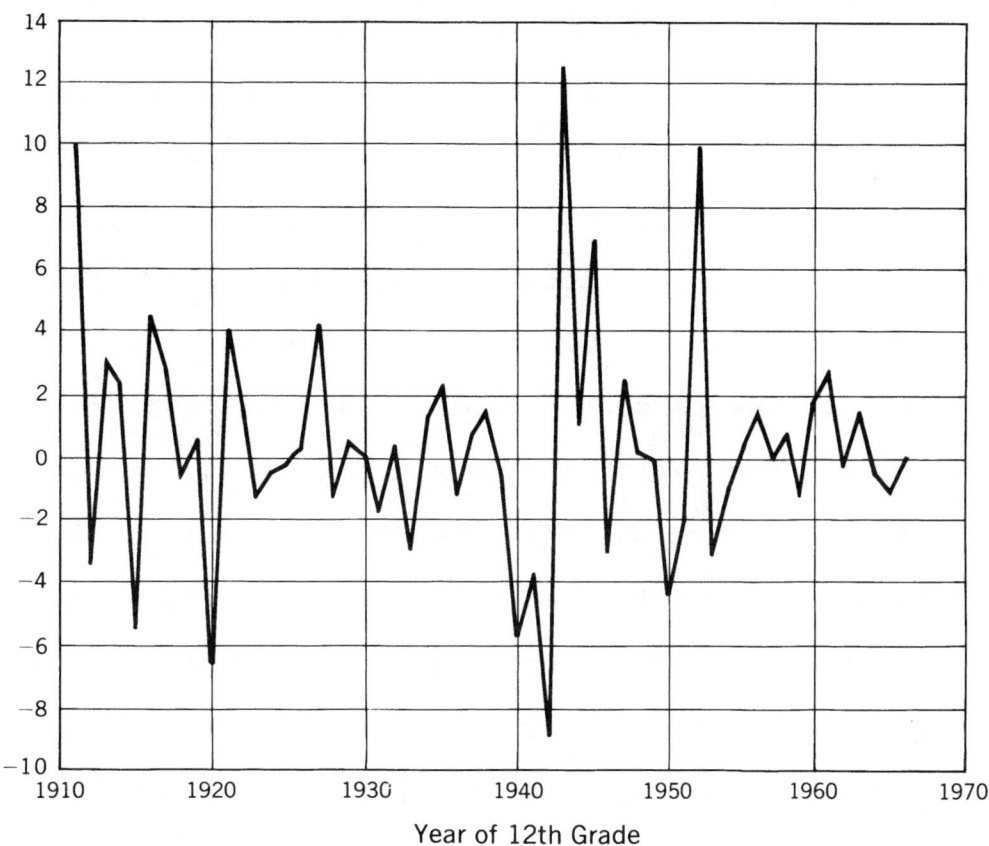

Figure 2.10. Rate of Change in the Continuation Ratio, 11th to 12th Grade, 1911–1966.

The Effects of War and the Business Cycle Upon Continuation in School

The preceding description has suggested the possible effect of the business cycle and war mobilization upon the continuation in school of secondary school students. We will now explore these relationships more empirically through correlation analysis. Trends in the business cycle will be "indexed" by the percent unemployed in the labor force and the per capita Gross National Product, expressed in constant 1958 dollars. A measure of military expansion will be developed and used to gauge the effect of mobilization. After describing each measure, the zero-order coefficients of correlation will be presented, and a multiple regression analysis will be made to identify the amount of variance in the three continuation ratios that can be accounted for by the independent variables.

The Unemployment Rate. Economists have developed estimates of the percent of unemployment in the labor force for all of the years for which the ratios of continuation in school are available.

The unemployment rate from 1910 to 1929 was estimated by Stanley Lebergott (Census, 1966a: Series B1, 190-191) by estimating the civilian labor force, estimating employment, and deducting one from other to estimate the unemployed. Such estimates are not as reliable as those after 1929 from the Bureau of Labor Statistics, based upon employment surveys (Census, 1966a: Series B2, 190-191). Over this period there is a slight long-term decline in unemployment, but the linear trend is insignificant.

In addition to unemployment, trends in the business cycle are reflected in the Gross National Product, expressed in current or in constant dollars, and the Federal Reserve Board index of monthly industrial production (Moore, 1967a:17).

Per Capita GNP. Total GNP in 1958 dollars and per capita GNP in 1958 dollars both reflect trends in business activity. The two measures are highly correlated ($r = .98$) and each is highly associated with the linear trend ($r = .94$ and $.98$, respectively). The per capita GNP is slightly more highly associated with the rate of unemployment ($r = .46$). The per capita measure was selected for analysis as an additional index of trends in the business cycle. The series was developed by the Office of Business Economics, U. S. Department of Commerce (Census, 1966a:Series A12, 168-169).

Military Expansion. Considering that we are attempting to account for the rate of continuation in secondary school, the ideal measure of military expansion would be the number of 17- and 18-year olds in the Armed Forces, annually. While this information is available for recent years, it is not available over the entire range of years under study (1910-1967). Accordingly, a measure of military expansion was contrived by determining the gross change in the size of the enlisted personnel in the Army, Navy, Marines, and the Air Force (Census, 1960a:736; 1965a:103; and 1968a:257). The total enlisted strength was subtracted from the strength the following year to produce a measure of change in gross size. This statistic was attributed to the later of the two years, thereby reflecting the year in which the increase or decrease occurred. This was then expressed as the ratio of the increment to the population of males 17 to 20 years of age. The trend over time in this measure was quite similar to that of the gross increment. Consequently, the gross measure alone was selected for the study. As one might expect, the size of the number of enlisted personnel in the Armed Forces has been very stable over long stretches of time, during the 1920s and 1930s, for example, and also has increased tremendously during periods of emergency, these being

War	Dates of Conflict
World War I	April 6, 1917 - Nov. 11, 1918
World War II	Dec. 7, 1941 - Aug. 14, 1945 Treaty signed: Dec. 31, 1946
Korean War	June 25, 1950 - July 27, 1953

Since the increment increased greatly during these war years and decreased just as dramatically immediately after the conflicts, the time series tends to reflect very little change during most of the years; the mode, in other words, tends to dominate the distribution with a few quite extreme values. Despite these non-normal attributes of the time series, nevertheless, it appears to provide the desired index to the years of rapid military expansion.

Continuation Ratios. The method of computing the continuation ratios has been described, above. Since the continuation ratio is based upon enrollment data from two successive years, the ratio may be attributed to either year, depending upon one's purpose. If one wishes to consider the ratio as the probability that a student continued to the next grade the following year, the ratio would be keyed to the denominator year. If one wishes to consider the ratio in relation to the year the student dropped out of school, the ratio would be keyed to the numerator year. In examining the relation between the continuation ratio and war, the business cycle, and unemployment, the latter procedure was the more appropriate.

Since several of these time series have increased over time, particularly GNP and the continuation ratios, a variable increasing by one unit each year also was introduced into the computation of the coefficients of correlation. In the presentation below, this variable is identified as "time."

The intercorrelation matrix of these factors, is presented in Table 2.1.

Table 2.1. Coefficients of Correlation Between Continuation Ratios and Other Factors

Variable		1	2	3	4	5	6	7
Continuation Ratios:								
9-10	1	1	.95	.74	.08	.82	-.09	.96
10-11	2		1	.84	.05	.79	-.12	.92
11-12	3			1	.20	.49	-.32	.68
Unemployment	4				1	-.46	-.03	-.13
Per Capita GNP	5					1	.06	.92
Military Expansion	6						1	-.02
Time	7							1

The effect of time has been removed in Table 2.2 presenting the partial correlation coefficients of each of the continuation ratios and the three variables, with time held constant.

Table 2.2. Partial Correlation Coefficients of Continuation Ratios and Three Variables with the Effect of Time Removed

Continuation Ratio	Unemployment, Time Constant	GNP per Capita, Time Constant	Military Expansion, Time Constant
9-10	.69	-.54	-.27
10-11	.45	-.36	-.26
11-12	.40	-.45	-.42

To briefly review the above results: The rate of unemployment is practically unrelated to the continuation ratios until the linear trend is removed. However, when time is removed, the association of the ratios and the rate of unemployment increases to a level that is statistically significant. The direction of this relationship is positive: an increase in the continuation ratios is associated with an increase in unemployment. Thus, when unemployment increases, the more marginal worker, the student, is more likely to remain a student than to enter the labor market; conversely, when jobs are more available, the enrolled student is more likely to be attracted to employment, and hence the probability of his continuing in school declines. The same result is reflected in the partial coefficients of correlation between the continuation ratios and per capita Gross National Product, with time constant. The latter relationship is negative, an increase in the continuation ratio being accompanied by a decrease in GNP per capita, and vice versa. These results confirm hypothesis b, page 25.

The index of military expansion is almost unrelated to any of the variables in the study (Table 2.2). It presents a statistically significant relationship only with the 11-to-12th grade continuation ratio. However, as the partial coefficients of correlation show, the association between the continuation ratios and military expansion increases when the effects of time are removed. The relationship, of course, is negative, since military expansion is associated with a decline in the continuation ratio. The coefficients show, also, that the 11-to-12th grade ratio is more highly associated with military expansion than the 10-to-11 or 9-to-10 ratios.

The generally higher association of the continuation ratios with unemployment than with per capita GNP dictated the use of unemployment as a measure of trends in the business cycle, in the analysis next to be reported.

Table 2.3 below presents the cumulative percentage of the variance in the continuation ratios that is accounted for by the successive addition of the three independent variables to the multiple regression equations predicting the continuation ratios.

Table 2.3. Cumulative Percentage of Variance in the Continuation Ratios Accounted for by Successive Addition of Three Independent Variables to the Multiple Regression Equation

Independent Variable	Grade 9 to 10	Grade 10 to 11	Grade 11 to 12
1. Time	92%	85%	46%
2. Percent Unemployed in Labor Force	94%	88%	54%
3. Index of Military Expansion	95%	88%	64%

The linear trend absorbs almost all of the variance in the 9-to-10th grade continuation ratio. The percent unemployed and the index of military expansion are able to add very little additional predictive power. Except for the 3 percent of the variance added by the measure of unemployment, the same is true for the 10th-to-11th grade continuation ratio. However, the situation is different for the 11th-to-12th grade ratio. Time explains 46 percent of the variance in the 11-to-12 continuation ratio; the percent unemployed adds another 8 percent and, after these two are accounted for, the index of military expansion adds another 10 percent of the variance in the 11-to-12th grade continuation ratio, altogether accounting for 64 percent of the variance.

Two factors re-enforce the last result: (1) Compulsory attendance laws have less effect upon the 11-to-12th grade continuation than on the lower grades, since some students will become older than the minimum before graduating; (2) Only the more senior secondary school students reach the eligible age to enter the Armed Forces and only the older students are eligible for regular employment because of child labor laws. As a consequence, when these variables (unemployment and military expansion) are added to the multiple regression equation of the 11th-to-12th grade ratio, they make a greater contribution than they do to predicting continuation in earlier grades. Undoubtedly, a measure of marriage rate for 17-year-olds, if available, would account for even more of variance in the 11th-to-12th grade continuation ratio.

In summary, the rate of continuation in secondary school since 1910 has increased greatly for each of three secondary school grade-steps: 9th-to-10th, 10th-to-11th, and 11th-to-12th. The linear increase across time has undoubtedly resulted from the increased value society generally has attributed to education, by the improved availability of educational opportunities, by the motivational consequences of job opportunities and of educated parents, and by such specifics as compulsory attendance laws and improved consolidated schools with free transportation.

For the 9th-to-10th and 10th-to-11th grade transitions, the business cycle and military expansion have little effect upon continuation. Most students in these grades are below the minimum age to be subject to these effects. However, the greater availability of jobs and the expansion of the Armed Forces decidedly affect the continuation ratio from the 11th-to-12th grades. When employment increases in the labor force, generally, students about to enter their senior year are more likely to drop out of school and seek employment. On the other hand, when unemployment is increasing, students are inclined to remain in school. In addition, an increase in the size of the military service signals an increase in 11th-to-12th grade dropouts.

Degree Credit Enrollment

The first-time degree-credit opening fall enrollment in all colleges and universities, male and female, is presented in Figure 2.11 (Series D2 and D3). Following the post-World War II peak, evident more in the first-time enrollment of males than of females, the enrollment returned to a more normal trend. Since 1951 male and female enrollments have paralleled one another, with the female reaching nearly 700,000 in 1967 and the male, nearly 900,000.

Figure 2.12 shows total degree credit enrollment. Series D4 and D5, for males and females, respectively, follow the same parallel development as did first-time enrollment. By 1967 males had reached 3,867,000 and the females 2,639,000, each enrolled for degree-credit courses.

Junior College Enrollment

The increasing importance of the junior college in higher education is illustrated by Figure 2.13. Enrollments of males and females (Series D6 and D7) have been increasing rapidly since 1951 and dramatically since 1963. The two-year institution and the community college are the major educational responses

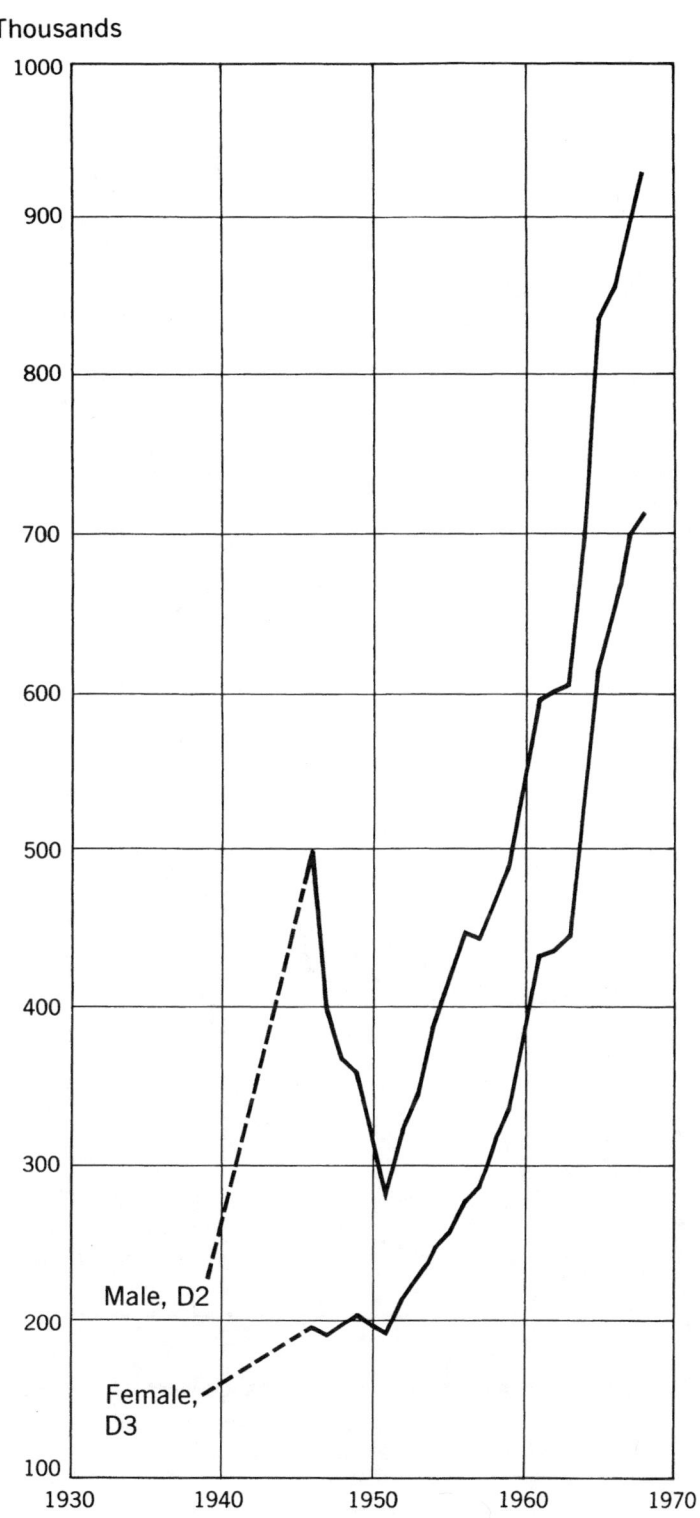

Figure 2.11. First-time Degree-credit Enrollment in Colleges and Universities, by Sex, 1939–1968, Series D2 and D3.

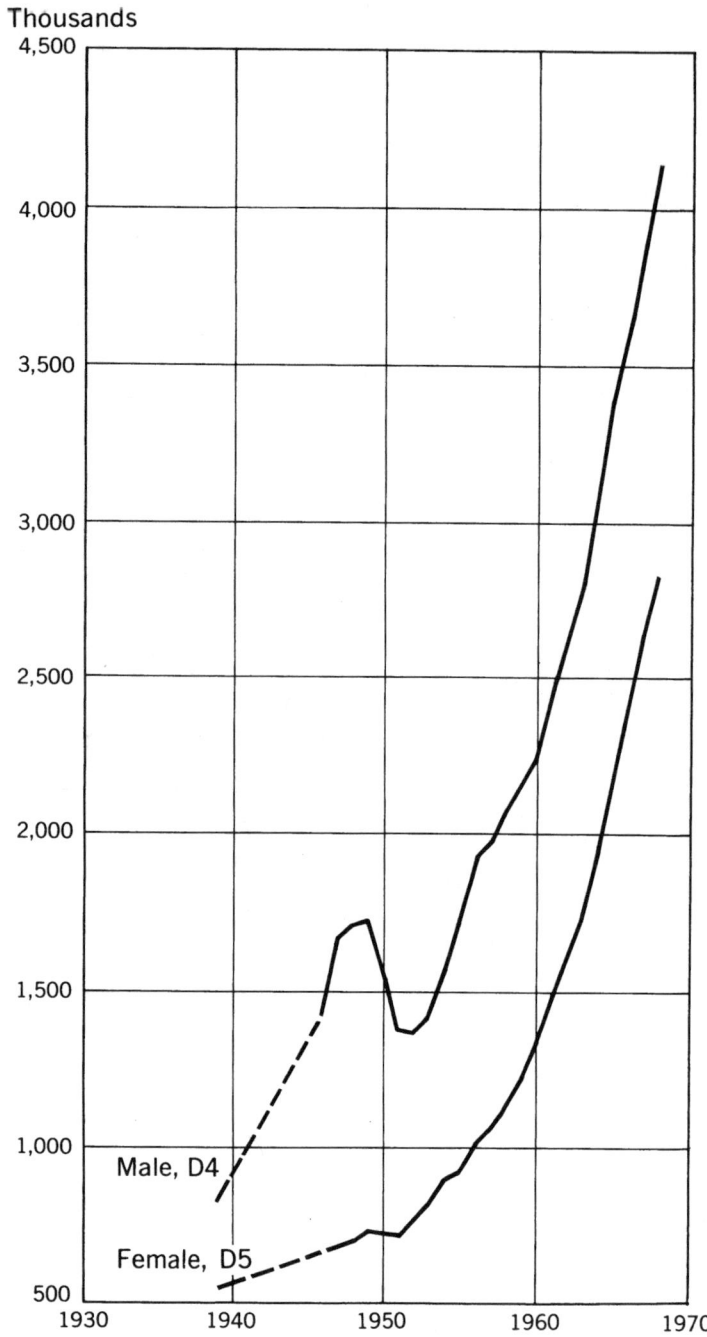

Figure 2.12. Total Degree-credit Enrollment in Colleges and Universities, by Sex, 1939–1968, Series D4 and D5.

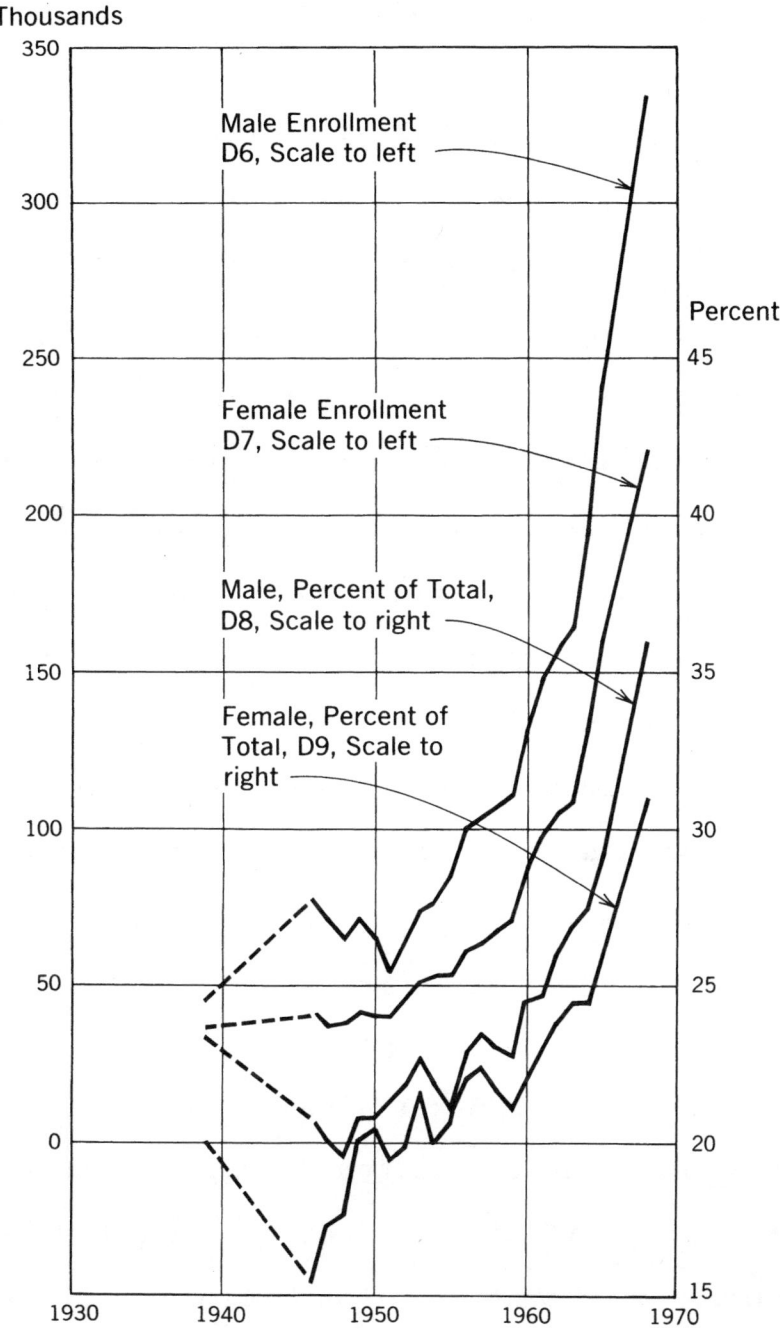

Figure 2.13. Aggregate First-time Degree-credit Enrollment in Junior Colleges, by Sex, and as a Percent of Total First-time Enrollment, 1939–1968, Series D6–D9.

the nation has made to the 1946 spurt in the birth rate, a spurt that affected first-time enrollments about 1964.

The magnitude of the enrollment "load" that is being assumed by the junior college[3/] can best be judged by examining the percentage of first-time enrollment entering these post-secondary institutions, rather than four-year institutions (Figure 2.13). The percent of first-time enrollment in junior college increased slowly from immediately after World War II to about 1960. After this, however, the proportions jumped up quite rapidly. Fall 1969 will probably see 41 **percent** of first-time male enrollees in junior colleges and 38 percent of the female first-time enrollees.

The two-year institution is now assuming and undoubtedly will continue to assume an increasing share of the post-secondary educational task. With approximately 30 percent of first-time enrollments in two-year institutions, "feeder" relations of two-year to four-year institutions should be studied, as Knoell and Medsker (1964a and 1964b) have done.

As <u>at least</u> a junior college education becomes more and more prevalent, information on junior colleges will be needed more and more. A comment upon the nature of the information needed may be appropriate here. Since the two-year institution includes non-degree-credit programs, information on the number of enrollees according to the type of program would provide a basis for judging how adequate training facilities are relative to the need. Similarly, the number of persons graduated with the Arts degree and the number certificated as having completed technical and semi-professional training are needed.[4] Studies following up the educational progress of graduates would provide a basis for decisions on the curriculum and on the quality of instruction.

The ratio of completions of baccalaureate degrees to starters (Series D25 and D26) should be watched for signs of loss of degrees in relation to first-time enrollment (in view of the increasing junior college enrollment). Similarly, a series on the ratio of graduates of two-year institutions to first-time enrollment two years earlier would provide a comparable measure for junior colleges. The educational plan for the two-year institution to feed four-year colleges, a system typified by California, Florida, and other states, might be evaluated through statistical series of these kinds, if compared with the experience of other states having different institutional systems. The process of converting two-year institutions to four-year liberal arts institutions, also, should be observed in assessing change.

Ratio of First-time Enrollment to the 18-Year-Old Population, by Sex

The ratio of first-time opening fall degree-credit enrollment to 18-year-olds in the population, by sex, from 1939 to the present is shown in Figure 2.14 (Series D11 and D12).

The series for females shows a fairly consistent linear trend, increasing steadily at about 1.2 percent per year to

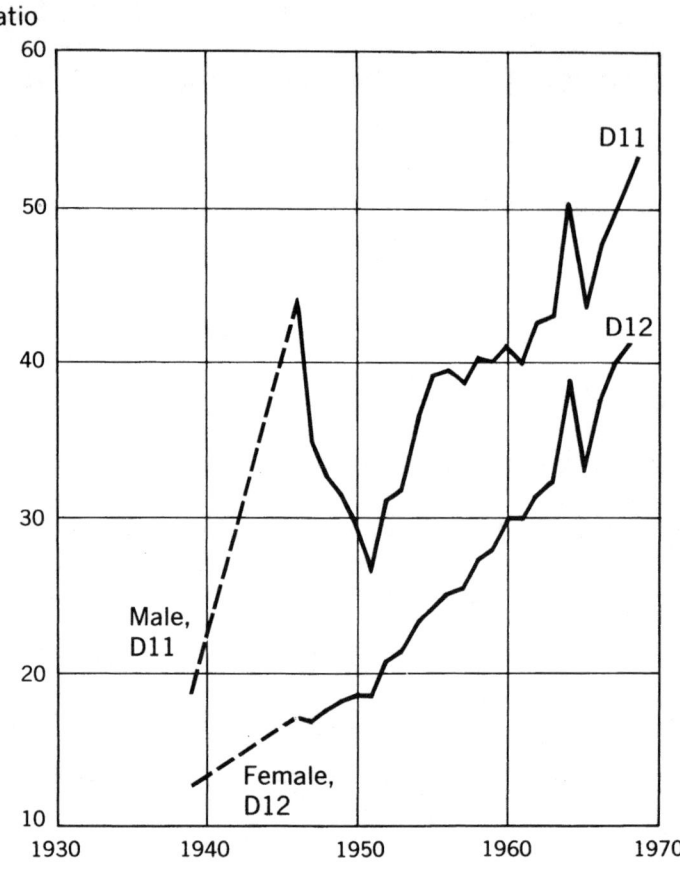

Figure 2.14. Ratio, First-time Opening Fall Degree-credit Enrollment per 100 18-Year-Old Population, by Sex, 1939–1968, Series D11 and D12.

1964, after which the ratio falls off, due to the large increase in the cohort born in 1946.[5]

The pattern of increase for males is about the same as for females, except for the distortion created by World War II and the post-war period. The peak in 1946 and the continued high ratios through 1950 are artifacts of the exceptional influx of World War II veterans to colleges and universities. However, with the return of a normal flow from the high schools into the colleges, the ratio for males climbs fairly uniformly to 1964. Like the female trend, the male trend, also, continues in the same direction after 1965.

The abrupt increase in the ratio both for males and for females for 1964 is a consequence of the 1946 and 1947 increases in fertility and births. The numerator of the ratio for 1964 includes some 17-year-olds who entered college a year earlier than their peers. The ratio, based upon the 18-year-old population, adjusted to a more typical level the following year when a large increment entered the denominator.

Generally, however, the increase over the 25 year period, particularly as illustrated by the female ratio, indicates an improvement in continuation for each successive 18-year-old age group. If present trends continue without further distortion by military operations or by a change in the disposition of youth to attend college, we may expect the male ratio to continue upward to approximately 49 by 1970 or 1971, and, similarly, the female ratio to about 42 by 1971. A significant change in draft policies could alter the trend for males, of course.

Ratio, College Enrollment to Population 18-21 Years of Age

A slow, gradual increase in the ratio of college enrollment to the 18-21 year age group occurred to World War I (Figure 2.15, Series D13). The ratio then increased more rapidly until the Depression of the 1930s, when it dipped slightly, but recovered about 1935, increasing again until the advent of World War II. The decline in the percent enrolled during World War II was greater than the decline during the Depression, and much greater than the retardation in the growth rate during World War I. However, the World War II data do not reflect collegiate-level work on college campuses sponsored by the military services. Recovery after World War II, however, was quite rapid. Higher enrollment ratios were stimulated, and rapid increases continued. There can be no doubt that great strides in enrollment have been made since the mid-1950s. The actual increments in the ratio over the past half century present an increasingly rapid rise: during the 1920s, 3 points increase; during the 1930s, 3 points; 1940s, 10 points; 1950s, 12 points; and during the 1960s, 13 points increase.

The recent data accumulated by the U. S. Office of Education are not entirely compatible with earlier data, making interpretation of the current trend somewhat less certain. However, increases now are about one percentage point per year. At this rate, by fall 1970 this college enrollment rate should reach 50 per 100 population. Some of this increase, however, is a consequence of changing definitions of enrollment.[6]

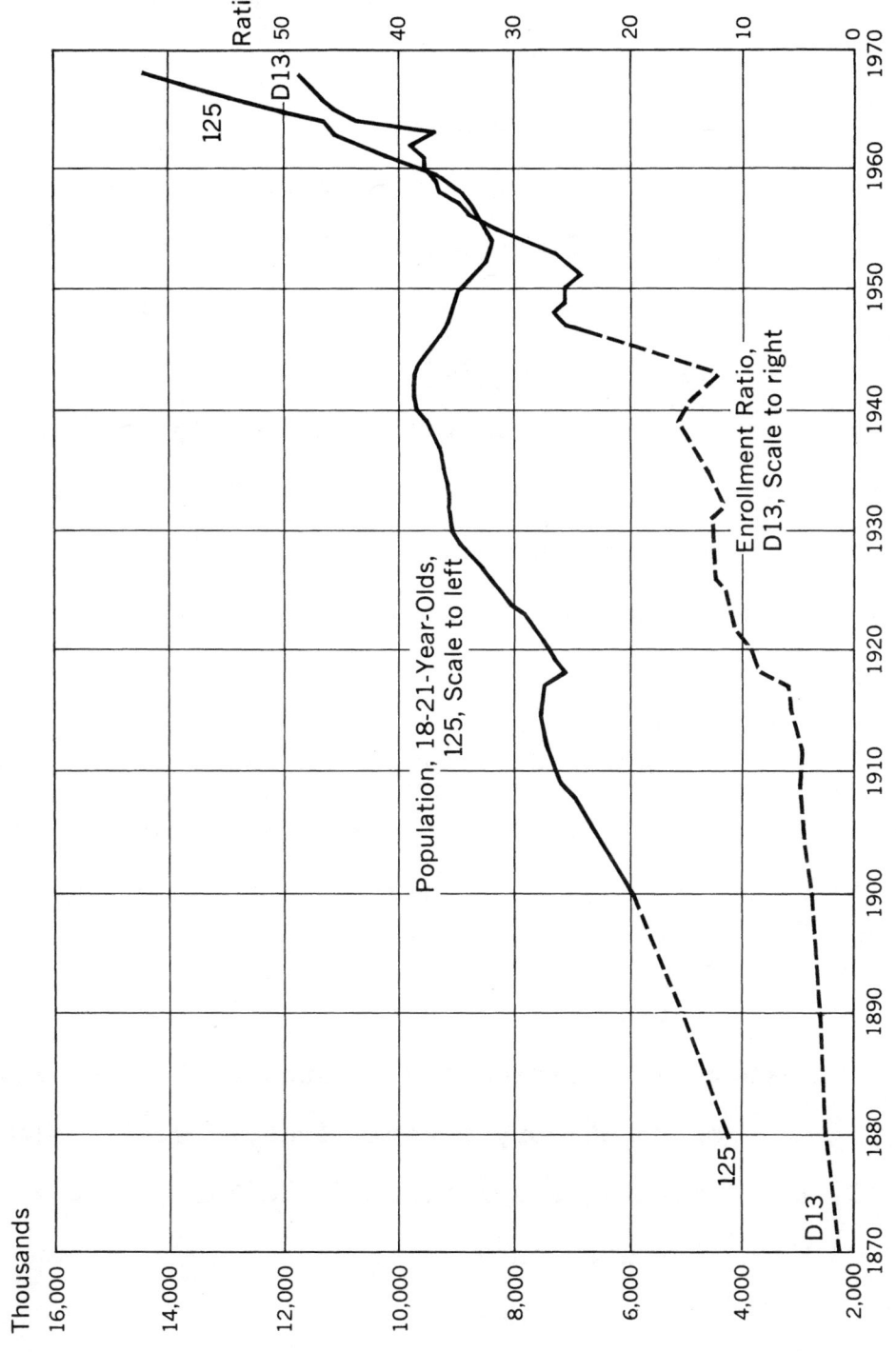

Figure 2.15. Total Population, 18–21-Year-Olds, 1880–1968, Series 125, and Ratio, Higher Education Degree-credit Enrollment per 100 18–21-Year-Old Population, 1870–1968, Series D13.

College Enrollment Ratios by Sex

Series D14 and D15, presented in Figure 2.16, show trends since 1939 in degree-credit enrollment of males and females, each related to the population 18-21 years of age by sex. After the aftermath of World War II, about 1951, both series present fairly uniform trends. The trend in the ratio for females especially appears to be following a uniform increase, 1.17 persons per 100 per year since 1943. Although the ratio for males was buffeted by World War II (1940-1945), influenced by the veteran's educational program,[7/] and then hit by the Korean War, it has settled to a fairly steady growth rate, of 1.62 persons per 100 per year since 1951.

Enrollment Rates by Age

Age specific enrollment rates, 1947 to 1967, provide a sensitive indicator of trends in education, irrespective of level of school.

The population between the ages of 6 and 15 are retained in school remarkably well (Series A28 through A32). Generally, these are the ages of compulsory school attendance.[8/] From 1947 to 1966, the percentages enrolled of the age groups 6, 7-9 and 10-13 have increased only 1 percent or less. When the enrollment rate nears its ceiling, 100 percent, very little additional increase is possible. The 14-15-year-old group has gained nearly 8 percentage points in enrollment during the period, and in 1966 had attained a level, 98.6 percent, very near its ceiling (Figure 2.17, Series A32).[9/] By comparison, the 10-13-year age group reached 99.5 percent enrollment in 1960.

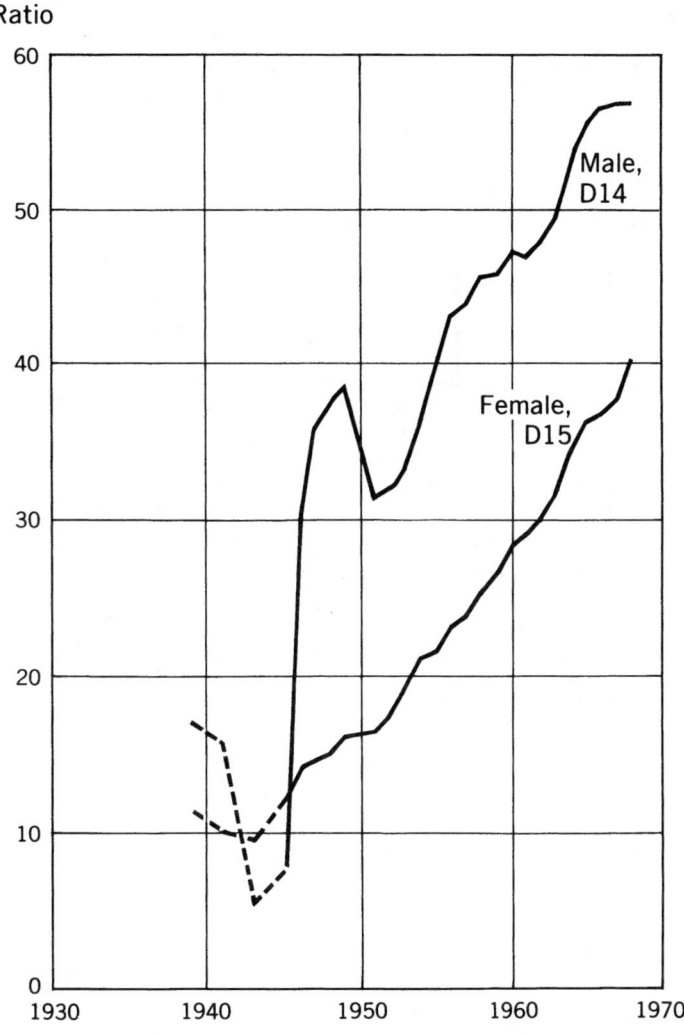

Figure 2.16. Ratio, Degree-credit Enrollment in Higher Education per 100 18–21-Year-Old Population, by Sex, 1939–1968, Series D14 and D15.

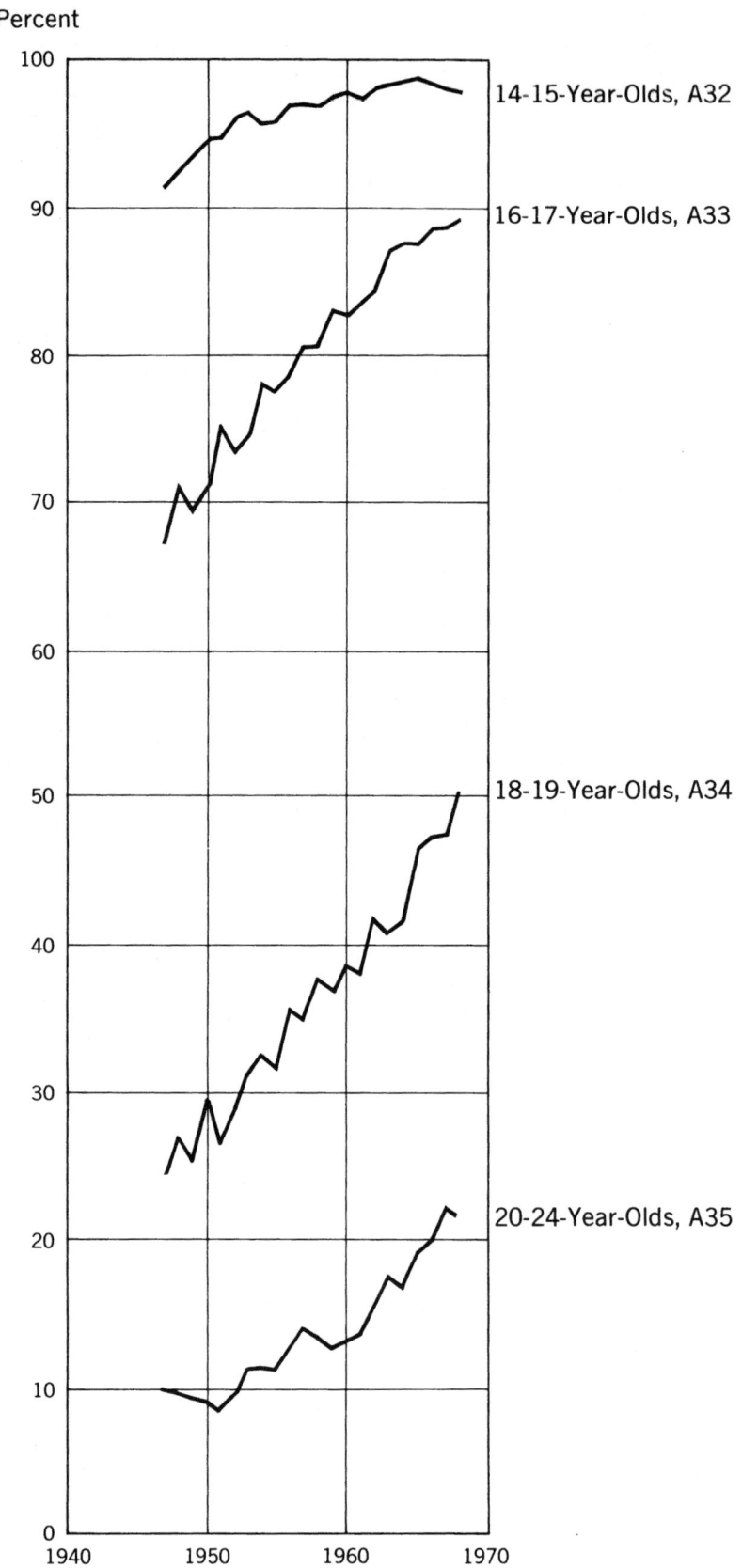

Figure 2.17. School Enrollment for Selected Age Groups, 1947–1968, Series A32–A35.

Among the older age groups, increases in the enrollment rates are more possible and increases have been realized. The 16-17-year age group increased 21 percentage points (Series A33); the 18-19-year age group increased 23 percentage points (Series A34); and the 20-24-year age group increased 10 percentage points (Series A35). Higher age groups have increased slightly over the twenty years, from 3.0 percent to 6.5 percent for the 25-29-year age group and from 1.0 percent to 2.7 percent for the 30-34-year ages, but all levels enrolled, even now, are quite low.

The 16-17-year age group and the 18-19-year age group have been increasing at about the same rate: one percentage point per year on the average. The enrollment rate for 16-17-year age groups now approaches 90 percent, and undoubtedly will achieve this level by 1968 or 1969. The rate of change has been quite uniform, with little variation about the linear trend.

Enrollment of the 18-19-year age group, about three-fourths of it in colleges and universities, also has been steadily increasing during the past 20 years. The rate has fluctuated little about its steady linear increase. Sputnik, the Russian intercontinental ballistic missile, launched in 1957, however much it may have stimulated an interest among educational and political circles in science and technology, did little or nothing to stimulate a spurt in the enrollment rate. In fact, the 20-24-year age group evidenced a decline after 1957, rather than an increase.

The 20-24-year-old enrollment rate has increased very slowly. In fact, during the period 1947 to 1951 enrollment of this age group declined, perhaps a consequence of World War II veterans completing their schooling. Otherwise, there is little or no pattern to the trend in the enrollment rate of the 20-24-year-old group.

Age Specific Enrollment Rates, by Cohort

School enrollment may be analyzed by tracing the enrollment rates of successive cohorts. Series A28 through A37 are grouped according to the standard age grouping used by the Census Bureau.[10/] These are for various age classes: single year, two years, three years, four years and five years. Because of this not all sequences can be followed from year to year as cohorts. However, the 14- and 15-year age group can be followed for four years, to the ages of 18 and 19.

Figure 2.18 (Series A32, A33, and A34) illustrates recent trends in the percent enrolled in school for the three age groups, 14-15, 16-17, and 18-19 years. Every other year only is displayed both for simplicity and to present discrete, independent cohorts.[11/] By tracing the symbols for each age group across time, the changes in enrollment of an age group may be observed. Modest gains have been made in increasing the percentage enrolled among the 14-15-year age group. The age group is enrolled near its maximum, and little additional improvement can be expected. In contrast, the percent of the

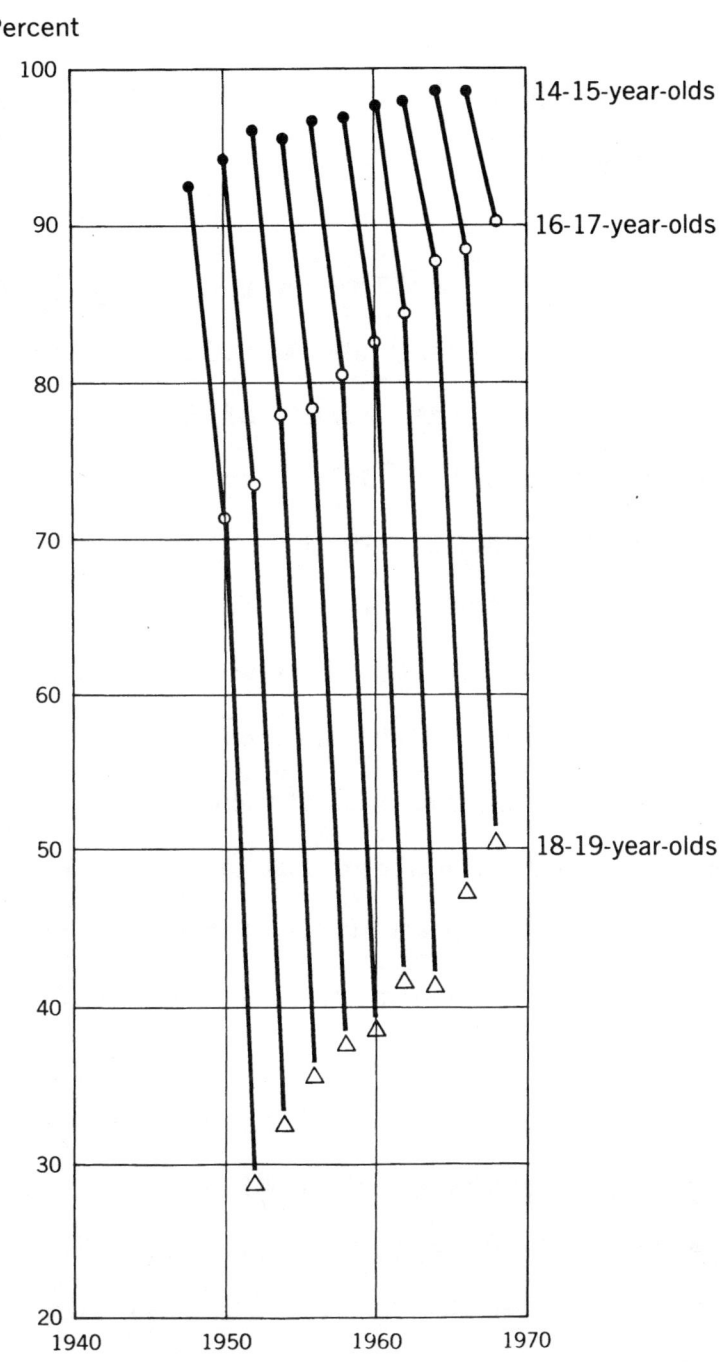

Figure 2.18. School Enrollment of Every Other Age Cohort, Series A32, A33, and A34.

16-17-year-olds has made rapid strides, from 68 percent in 1947 to 90 percent in 1968. Likewise, the increase in the enrollment of the 18-19-year-olds has paralleled that of the 16-17-year-old group.

In Figure 2.18, by following the nearly vertical lines from one symbol to another, the enrollment "progress" of the cohort may be traced. The length of the line from one age to the next is proportional to the loss in the percentage of the cohort enrolled in school over that time period. This "tracing" makes it quite evident that gains in percentage enrolled have come primarily through improving the retention of the 16-17-year-olds. Over the twenty year span of time, little improvement was made in the retention of 14-15-year-olds and almost no improvement was made in retention of 18-19-year-olds that had not been made already by the 16-and 17-year-olds. The latter conclusion may be more evident from Table 2.4 and Figure 2.19.

The first two columns of Table 2.4 have been developed by subtracting the percentage enrolled at the later age from the earlier age for the cohort. The initial enrollment of the cohort of 14-and 15-year-olds was reduced from 1947 to 1949, by 22.1 percentage points. In the next two years enrollment of the same cohort was reduced by 43.2 percentage points. From this 1947 base, the percentage loss in enrollment between 14-15-years and 16-17-years dwindled fairly uniformly, year by year, to 10.1 percentage points loss between 1964 and 1966.

Table 2.4. The Reduction of the Percentage Enrolled in School of Two Age Groups (14-15 Years, and 16-17 Years) Over a Two-Year Period, and Two-Year Continuation Ratios, 1947 to 1968

	Percentage Points Reduction in Enrollment between Ages		Two-Year Continuation Ratios	
	14-15 to 16-17	16-17 to 17-18	14-15 to 16-17 Years	16-17 to 18-19 Years
1947 to 1949	22.1	42.3	.76	.37
1948 to 1950	21.4	41.8	.77	.41
1949 to 1951	18.4	43.2	.80	.38
1950 to 1952	21.3	42.6	.78	.40
1951 to 1953	20.1	43.9	.79	.42
1952 to 1954	18.2	41.0	.81	.44
1953 to 1955	19.1	43.2	.80	.42
1954 to 1956	17.4	42.6	.82	.45
1955 to 1957	15.4	42.5	.84	.45
1956 to 1958	16.3	40.8	.83	.48
1957 to 1959	14.2	43.7	.85	.46
1958 to 1960	14.3	42.2	.85	.48
1959 to 1961	13.9	44.9	.86	.46
1960 to 1962	13.5	40.8	.86	.51
1961 to 1963	10.5	42.7	.89	.49
1962 to 1964	10.3	42.7	.90	.49
1963 to 1965	11.0	40.8	.89	.53
1964 to 1966	10.1	40.5	.90	.54
1965 to 1967	10.1	39.8	.90	.54
1966 to 1968	8.4	38.1	.91	.57

Note: The arrows connect two of the cohorts. See text.

Source: Series A32, A33, A34.

The reduction from 16-17 to 18-19 years, however, was much less impressive. The percentage dropping out has declined and increased irregularly. Only since 1965 does a genuine reduction appear to have occurred in the 16-17 to 18-19 step. This reduction, or loss in percentage enrolled, is shown in the middle chart of Figure 2.19.

The reduction over the 20-year period in the percentage of the cohort enrolled (16-17 to 18-19) was only about 4 percentage points (a reduction of 42 percent in 1948 to a reduction of 38 percent in 1968, Table 2.4). Thus, the gains in enrollment result almost entirely from gains in the 14-15 to 16-17-year-old step, gains which merely were maintained in the next two years to ages 18-19 years.

Figure 2.19 (top panel) also presents the trend in the ratio of continuation in school of the 16-17-year-old group to the 18-19-year-old group. It shows the same trend as the percent enrolled, the lower panel.

The consequences of the above are fairly obvious: (1) The sequential character of experiences is quite important, particularly in school retention. Emphasis upon improving retention over the 14-15 to 16-17 age group will pay dividends in improved retention of the 18-19-year age group. (2) The lack of any marked decrease in the loss in enrollment between 16-17 and 18-19 years deserves attention. This is the age group which discontinues its education, approximately 40 percent of the 18-19 year age group joining the approximately 10 percent of those who

62

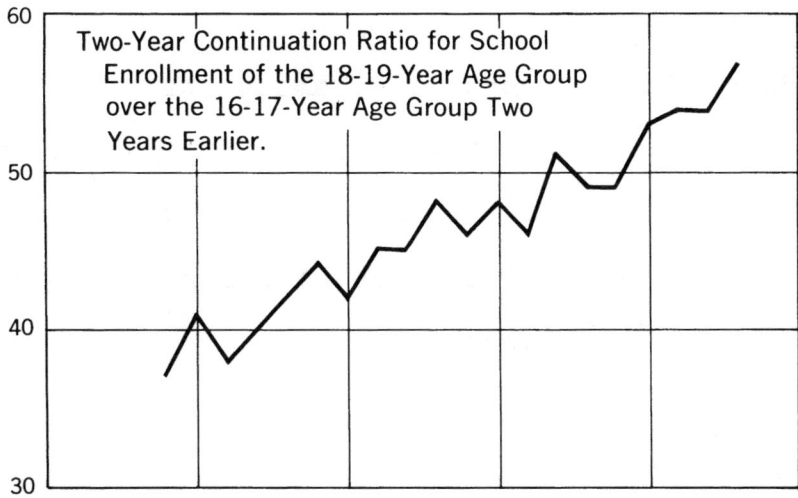
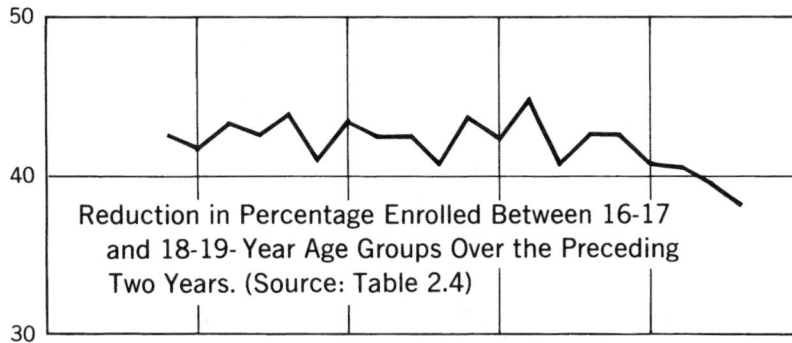
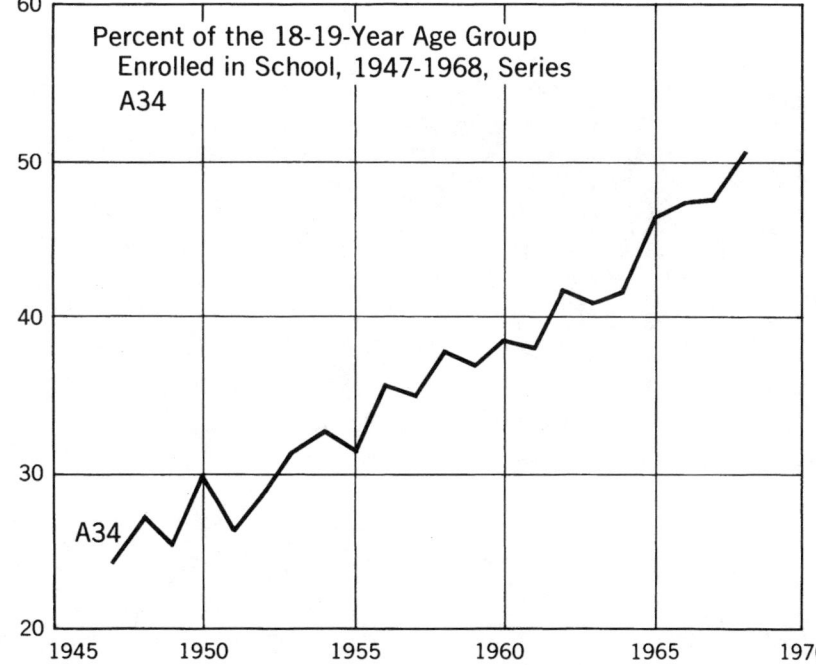

Figure 2.19. Trends in Three Measures of School Enrollment of 18–19-Year-Olds.

already had dropped out of school at about ages 16-17 years. These ages experience a discontinuity in the system: the step from high school to college. Perhaps this educational lacuma should be filled by programs linking high schools to junior colleges and community colleges.

Footnotes

1/ These percentages were arrived at by applying the formula presented in Appendix A to the two periods, 1940-42 and 1942-44. According to this, the decrease in rate of attendance is responsible for a loss of 1,313,000 in enrollment while the decrease in population is responsible for a loss of 996,000 enrollees, over the two time periods.

2/ Series A3 through A5 is the percentage of the population of school age enrolled in school, total and by color. Enrollment may be in schools other than elementary and secondary schools. While most of the series consistently is based upon the population 5 to 19 years of age, there are a few decades prior to 1910 that are based upon other spans of years (see the Notes to the Series). Despite these inconsistencies, the Census series is especially useful because of its length, going back to 1850, and because it affords a comparison in the enrollment of the white and the nonwhite populations (Series A4 and A5).

3/ After 1963, the category of junior college was changed to two-year college. The data for 1965 and 1966 include total first-time enrollment, rather than degree-credit enrollment. These were changes in the survey made by the U. S. Office of Education. The change in the enrollment definition, however, probably affects Series D8 and D9 very little, since non-degree-credit enrollment would be in both numerator and denominator.

4/ The U. S. Office of Education began in fall 1966 to include in its survey of graduates and other awards of higher educational institutions an accounting of graduates of two-year programs by occupational type.

5/ In 1966 and 1967, the U. S. Office of Education did not collect the first-time degree-credit enrollment. By using a rough procedure for estimating these years, it would appear that the ratio recovers and continues the trend at about the same rate of change as before 1964.

6/ See notes to Series D13. The definitions and concepts underlying the data have not been constant. Enrollment to 1946 was the total resident enrollment (to the fall term enrollment was added the new students who entered in the spring). After 1946 the enrollment was defined as the resident degree-credit enrollment in the fall. Later this was augmented by including the extension degree-credit enrollment. The 1966 and later surveys abandoned the degree-credit concept in favor of inclusive fall enrollments. The author estimated 1966 and 1967 from survey data by estimating non-degree-credit enrollment and subtracting it from the total.

7/ The educational program for veterans was provided by Public Law 16 and 346 during the period 1946-1952.

8/ Compulsory school attendance in elementary and secondary schools begins at age 6, 7, or 8, depending upon the state, and continues through age 16, 17, or 18. In 1965, the following states required attendance through age 17: Maine,

Nevada, New Mexico, Pennsylvania, Tennessee, Texas, and Wyoming. The following states required attendance through age 18: Ohio, Oklahoma, Oregon, and Utah (Simon and Grant, 1968: 27).

9/ These statistics from the Current Population Survey have a very small sampling error. For example, the true percentage for the 14-15-year age group may vary, in two samples out of three, only between 98.4 and 98.8. See Notes to the Series.

10/ The age groups change from time to time. For example, 1967 and 1968 data differ from 1966. However, since about 1960 the Census Bureau has tabulated CPS data by single years of age, by sex, although the publication presents primarily age groups.

11/ Cohorts of 14-and 15-year-olds originating each year would not be independent of each other.

3

Teachers

Only a small amount of information on teachers in time series is available. The decennial population censuses have collected some of the characteristics of teachers (age, sex, color, income), and this information has been reviewed by Folger and Nam (1967: 77-109). The U. S. Office of Education has assembled information on the number of teachers by institutional level (sex, certificated or non-certificated, and other characteristics for college faculties).[1] The National Education Association has assembled information on the supply and demand of teachers at both the elementary and secondary and the college levels, with specification of the discipline of newly-hired teachers (National Education Association, 1965b and 1967b). In its National Register of Scientific and Technical Personnel, the National Science Foundation (1968a), has assembled information biennially on characteristics of scientists, the chief occupation among them being teaching in higher education. The above refer to periodic, repeated collection of information. In no instance can it be said that adequate indicators are available on the status of this important occupational group.

Occasionally, each of the above-mentioned agencies has made special studies and surveys identifying with greater specificity the characteristics of the teacher cadre. Perhaps the latter approach, that of sample surveys of teacher populations, repeated at fairly regular intervals, would produce adequate indicators of the status of the occupation, and provide the data needed for manpower planning and policy formation.

Public Elementary and Secondary Teachers

The trend since 1890 in the number of public school elementary and secondary teachers is presented in Figure 3.1 (Series B5 and B6). The growth in the elementary school teacher cadre was retarded during the 1930s and continued to decline until World War II was concluded. Secondary teachers, on the other hand, only declined during the World War II period. The rate of increase for both groups has been more rapid since the mid-1950s, as school enrollments began to rise more rapidly.

Trends in the size of the full-time non-public elementary and secondary schools are presented as Series B8 and B9, but are not illustrated.

College Faculty

The trend in the size of college faculty has followed somewhat the trend in college degrees (Series D16), although with less variation. Figure 3.2, Series E5, shows the slow rise in college faculty from 1880 to 1920, the more rapid rise to the mid-1940s. Following 1946, however, increased enrollments and

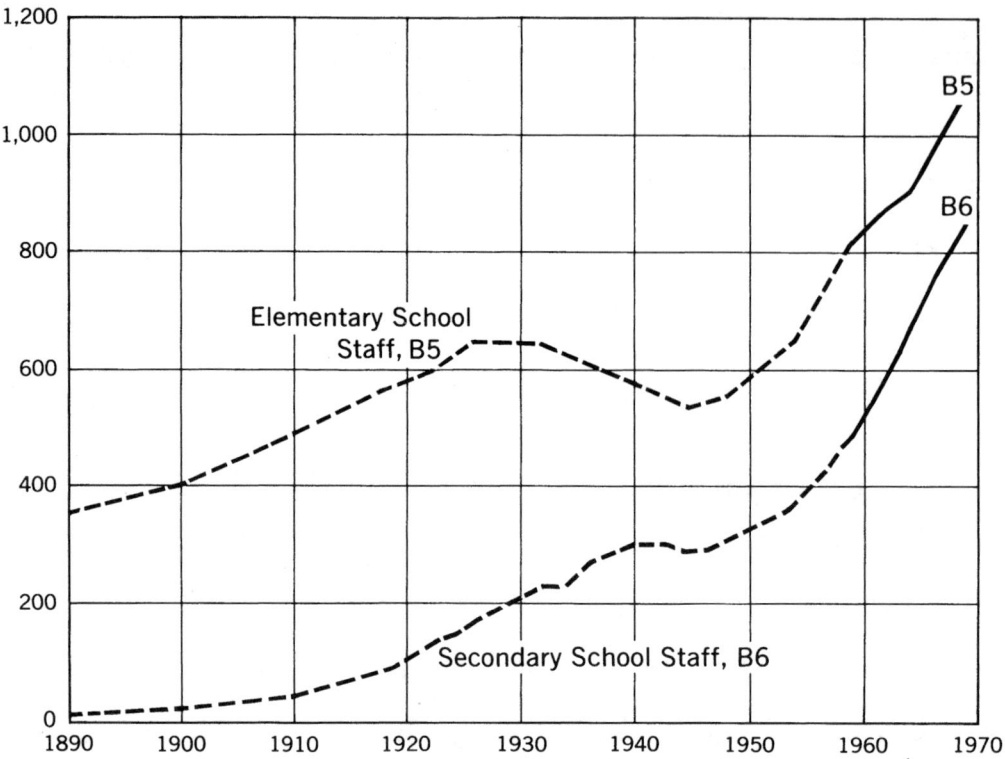

Figure 3.1. Classroom Teachers and Other Nonsupervisory Staff in Public Elementary and Secondary Day Schools, 1890–1969, Series B5 and B6.

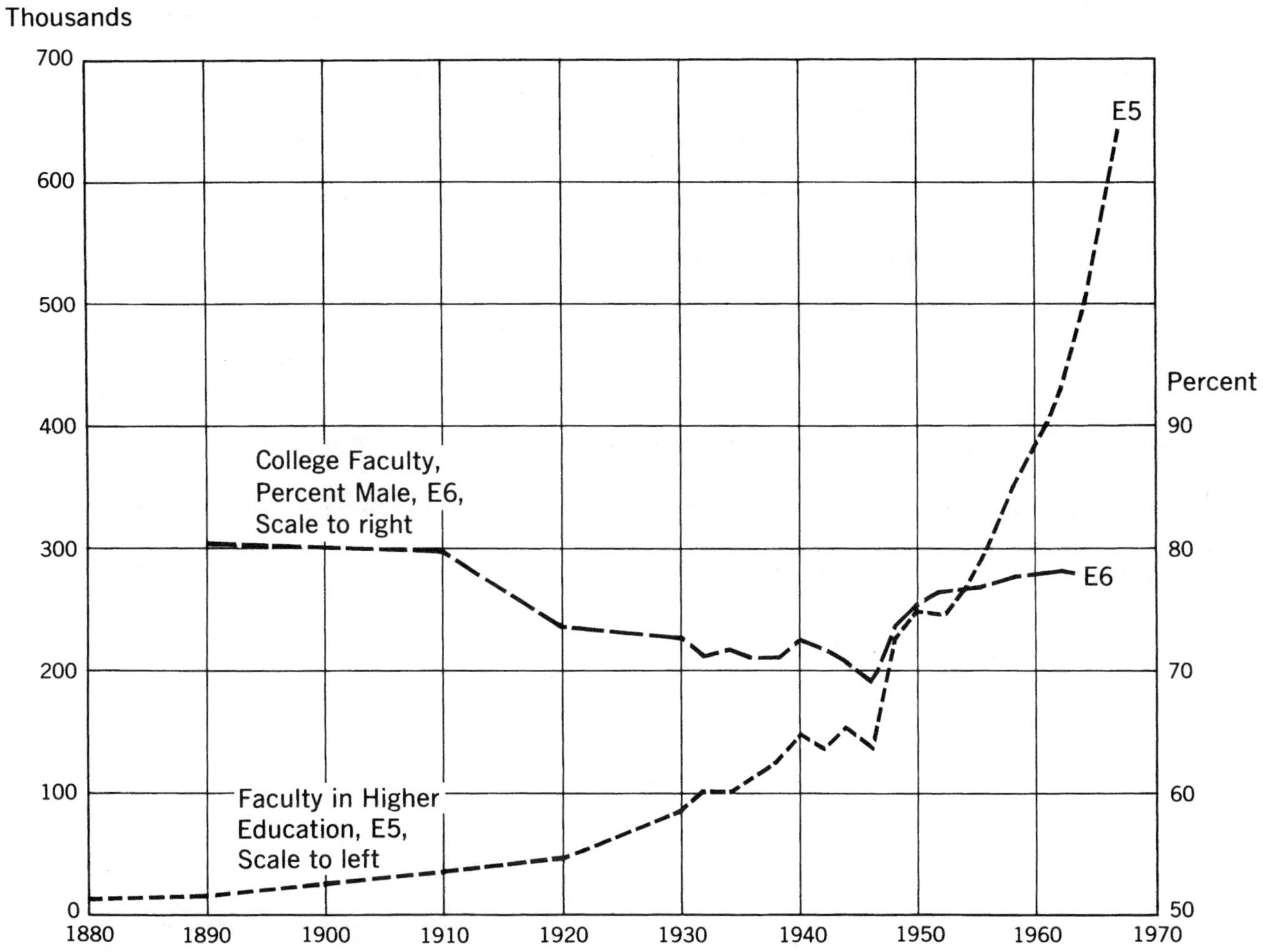

Figure 3.2. Total Faculty in Higher Education, 1880–1967, Series E5, and Percent of Male Faculty Members, 1890–1964, Series E6.

increased research activity in universities caused a much more rapid increase in the staffs of higher educational institutions. The size of the research personnel in colleges and universities increased from 23,000 scientists and engineers employed in research and development in colleges and universities in 1950 to 65,600 by 1966 (National Science Foundation, 1968b: 20).

Presented, also, in Figure 3.2, the percent of males in college faculties, Series E6, shows a decline from 1910 when female instructors began entering higher education in greater numbers, to 1946, when the percent male faculty was slightly less than 70 percent. From that point, the percentage of males has increased to approximately 78, where it has remained to the present.

Public School Teachers by Sex

The number of male teachers in public schools remained fairly constant to 1950, despite an increase in the total number of teachers (Figure 3.3, Series B2). After 1950, however, men began to enter public school teaching in larger numbers. The number of female teachers, on the other hand, has been more responsive to the changing enrollment (Series B3).

To 1880 the balance between male and female teachers was relatively constant, being close to 60 percent. After that point, however, increasing numbers of females entered the teaching profession, increasing to about 70 percent in 1900 and reaching about 85 percent in 1920. Men entering teaching,

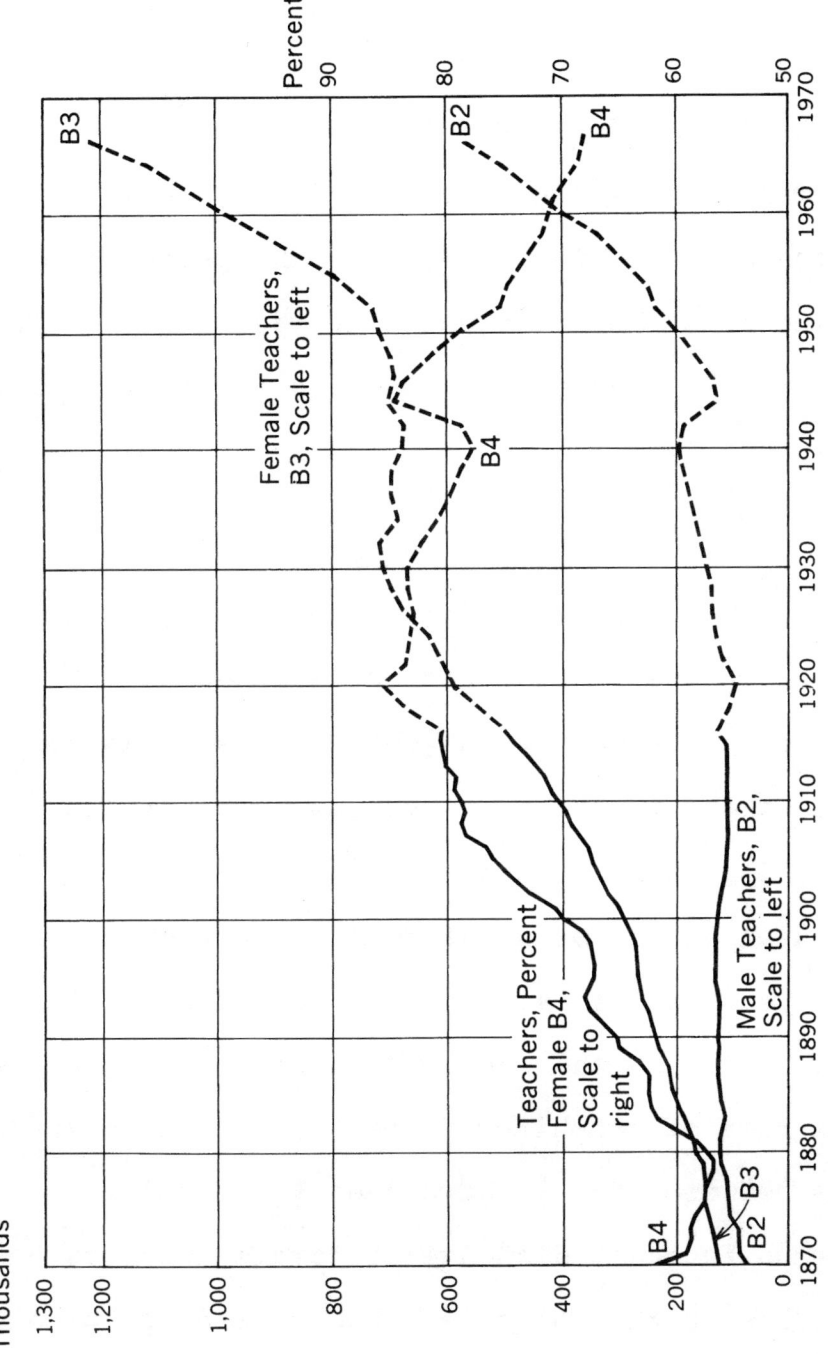

Figure 3.3. Classroom Teachers and Other Nonsupervisory Staff in Public Elementary and Secondary Day Schools, by Sex, and the Percent Female, 1870–1966, Series B2, B3, and B4.

particularly during the 1930s, caused the percent of female teachers to decline (Series B4). As a result of the occupational shifts during World War II, the percentage of teachers who were women increased almost to its 1920 level, but, following the War, declined. By 1966 the percentage had declined almost to the point where it was in 1890. The number of male and female teachers now appears to be following a parallel course.

Age of Teachers

Figure 3.4 (Series B11-B14) presents the median age of teachers, as reported in the decennial censuses, the total teacher cadre in elementary and secondary schools, and the nonwhite teachers in the same systems. The trends have not been uniform for these groups.

The median age of male teachers has varied from about 38 to about 34 years since 1930. The 1960 median age was close to 36 years. In 1930 the age of the total male group was higher than that of nonwhite teachers, but since 1940, the differences between the two have been very small.

The trend in the median age of female teachers has been almost opposite to that of male. The median age of all female teachers has increased, decade to decade, since 1930. In 1960 it was just under 45 years. Nonwhite female teachers' ages, over the thirty year period, have always been lower than the median of total female teachers and the median has not aged

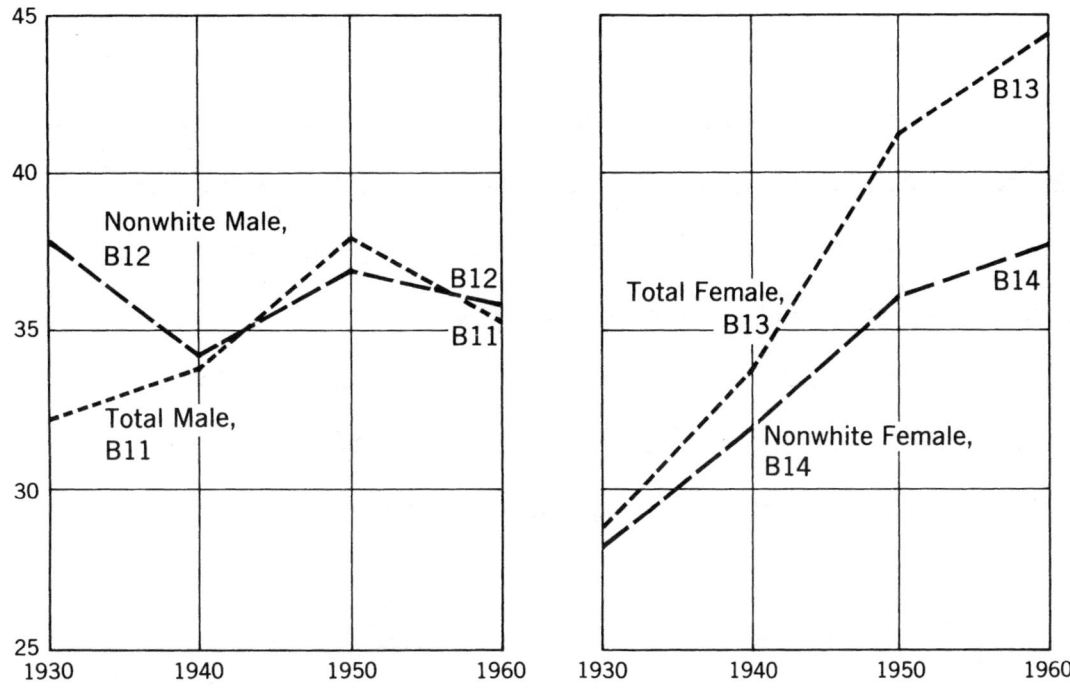

Figure 3.4. Median Age, Elementary and Secondary Teachers, Total and Nonwhite, by Sex, by Decade, 1930–1960, Series B11–B14.

as rapidly as the total. In 1960 the median for nonwhite females was slightly less than 38 years, in contrast to 44.5 years for the total.

The trend in median ages of the college teachers, by sex, for total and nonwhite has followed the same changes as have their counterparts in elementary and secondary schools (Figure 3.5, Series E1-E4).

Male ages have been much more uniform over the thirty year period than have female ages. The median age of nonwhite males has increasingly resembled the median for the total.

The median age for female nonwhite college teachers has more and more come to resemble the median age of the total, and it has "aged" more rapidly since 1940.

The difference in ages between male and female teachers is accentuated by the career patterns of female teachers. They teach for several years following college graduation, marry and drop out of teaching when their children are young. As their children grow older, females return to teaching. In 1960, the age distribution rose between ages of 40 and 50. As Folger and Nam (1967: 84) illustrate, this was not the employment pattern of the teachers in 1930 nor 1940, but it does characterize female teachers in 1950 and 1960.

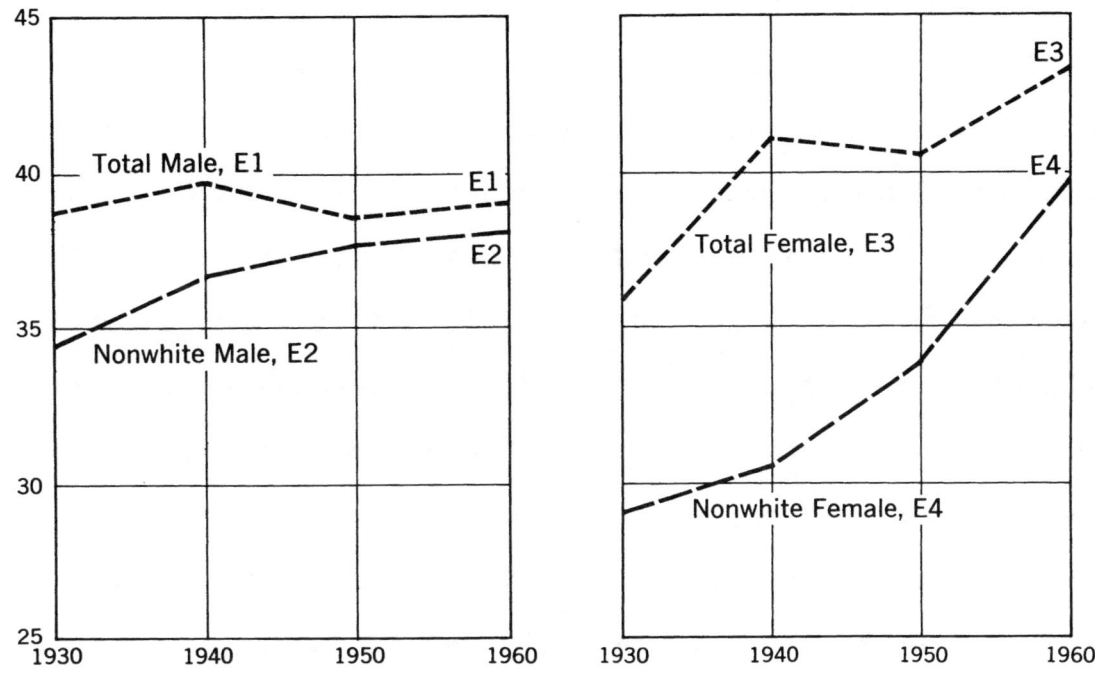

Figure 3.5. Median Age, College Teachers, Total and Nonwhite, by Sex, by Decade, 1930–1960, Series E1–E4.

Teachers with Substandard Certificates

Through state departments of education, elementary and secondary teachers obtain certificates that enable them to teach. Requirements for certificates vary by state, subject, and school level. These requirements are the only standard by which the teacher cadre may be summarily evaluated. The standards apply only for the certification of new teachers, although there are requirements for the renewal of certification, usually in the form of additional college courses.

In order to "man" his classrooms the school principal sometimes must hire teachers who do not possess requisite education and experience to be fully certificated. Such teachers are issued substandard certificates. The percentage of substandard teachers, thus, provides an index to the adequacy of preparation, according to the standards, to teach. We assume that the completely certificated teacher does a better job.

The percentage of elementary and secondary school teachers with less than standard certificates presents a relatively bright picture (Figure 3.6). About 9 percent of elementary school teachers had substandard certificates in 1954. This percent has declined rapidly to its 1966 level of approximately 5.6 percent.

The percent for secondary school teachers, on the other hand, has consistently been below that for elementary school teachers. The former, too, has declined slightly during this period and now is 4.3 percent.

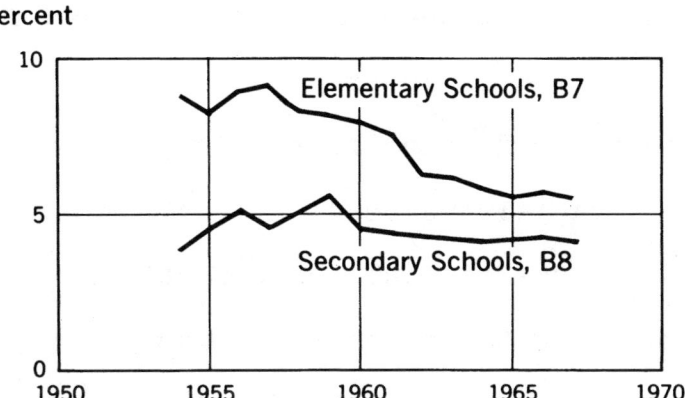

Figure 3.6. Teachers with Less than Standard Certificates, Elementary and Secondary Schools, 1954–1967, Series B7 and B8.

As larger numbers of teachers are graduated from colleges and universities, these indicators may decline slightly. The geographic dispersion of schools, particularly elementary schools, however, may always result in some minimum number of teachers who do not possess full certificates. University extension programs, on the other hand, provide opportunities for teachers to augment their qualifications.

Pupil-Teacher Ratio

To the extent that the student gains more individual attention from the teacher in school systems with fewer pupils per teacher, the quality of instruction may be better and hence the quality of the education the pupil acquires. The pupil-teacher ratio, however, masks a great deal of variation between schools.

In Figure 3.7, Series A11, the pupil-teacher ratio, based upon the average daily attendance, beginning with 1870, shows an increase from around 20 in the 1870s when there were many one room schools, to more than 26 in 1934. Since then, the ratio has gradually declined to its present 22 pupils. Variations in the trend are minor, with a slight decline prior to 1920 and during World War II, and the peak during the Depression of the 1930s. By this index, there has been a slight improvement since 1934, but change appears to be almost imperceptible.

Series A12, Figure 3.7, relates total pupils to total teachers and generally presents the same trend as Series A11, beginning with 1910. This series is included because it may be

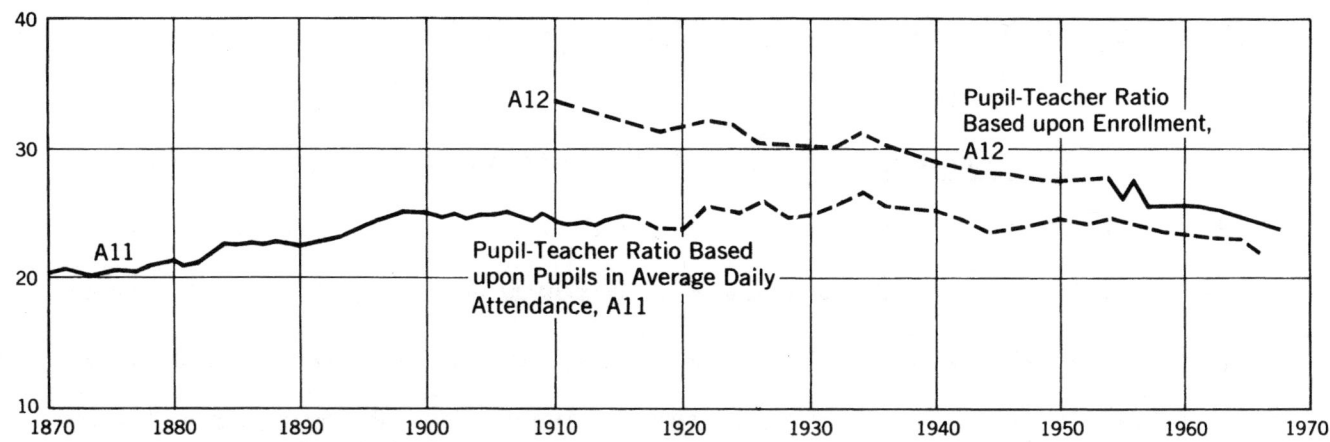

Figure 3.7. Pupil-Teacher Ratio, Public Schools, Based upon Pupils in Average Daily Attendance, 1870–1966, Series A11, and upon Pupils Enrolled, 1910–1967, Series A12.

computed for non-public schools and gives us a comparison of public with non-public.

Public and Non-public. The difference in the pupil-teacher ratio of public and non-public schools is quite clearly shown in Figure 3.8 (Series A13 through A16). In both systems the secondary school has a lower pupil-teacher ratio than the elementary school. At each level, however, non-public schools have more pupils per teacher than public schools.

The differences between the public and non-public ratios in elementary schools seem to have widened as the children of the post-war baby boom began to enter elementary school. The non-public elementary school enrollment increased 47 percent from 1954 to 1964 (Series A8), while the public elementary school enrollment increased only 30 percent during the same period (Series A6). As enrollment in non-public elementary schools increased, teachers were not added proportionately. The non-public secondary schools evidently do not adjust as rapidly to shifts in enrollment as do the public schools. Since 1954, however, as time has passed, the adjustment has improved.

The non-public secondary school pupil-teacher ratio began to increase in 1954 and reached a peak in 1960. While simultaneous occurrence of events may be coincidental, the 1954 decision of the U. S. Supreme Court concerning school desegregation may have stimulated increased enrollment in non-public schools. Certainly the larger birth cohorts of 1946 and 1947 began to enter junior high school about 1958 or 1959 and were

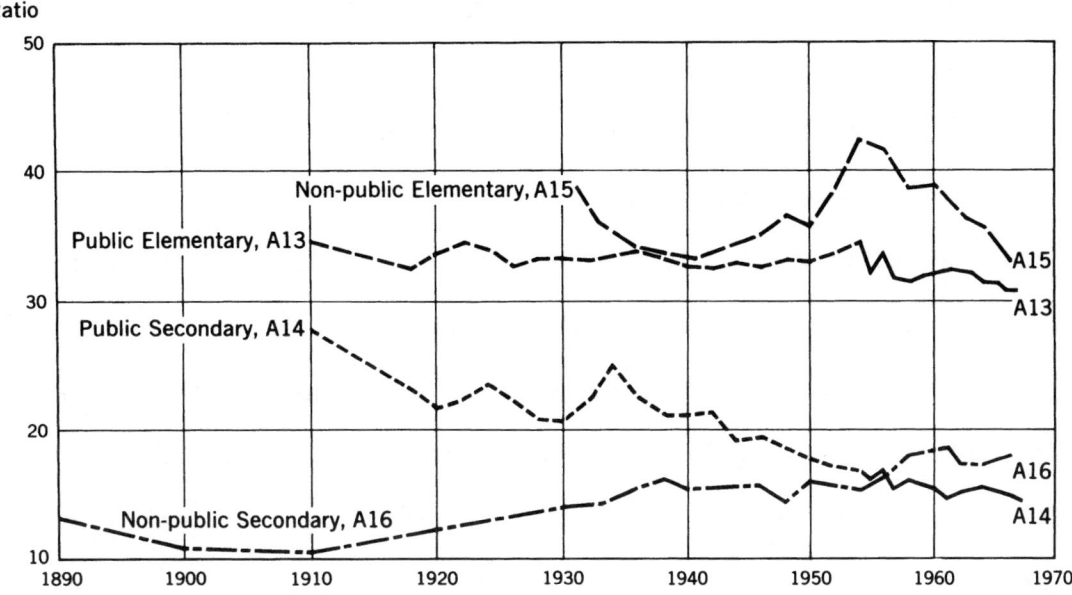

Figure 3.8. Pupil-Teacher Ratio in Elementary and Secondary Day Schools: Public, 1910–1967, Series A13–A14; Non-public Elementary, 1931–1966, Series A15; Non-public Secondary, 1890–1966, Series A16.

in the 9th grade by 1960, the year of the peak of the secondary school series. These speculations assume, also, that the non-public schools adjust less rapidly than do the public schools to increases in enrollment.

In view of the slow change in the public school pupil-teacher ratios, the series will probably vary but little in the future. Other institutional innovations, such as computerized programmed instruction, may alter the effective pupil-teacher relationship, even though the pupil-teacher ratio, as here expressed, remains constant.

Class size in secondary schools has been studied in relation to size of school district and subject (Maul, 1964). Class size is smaller in the smaller school districts, as follows:

Size of School District	Median Class Size	Percent of Classes with Enrollment of 25 or Less
100,000 or more	30.8	25.2
50,000 to 99,999	29.6	29.7
25,000 to 49,999	28.7	34.3
12,000 to 24,999	27.7	40.2

Size of class also varies by subject. Classes in Physical Education and Music led with median sizes of 38.8 and 34.1 pupils, respectively. Classes for the handicapped and in Federally supported vocational education were small (14.2 and 20.1 pupils, respectively).

In using class size as an indicator in secondary school, it would seem sufficient to reflect only the classes in critical educational subjects, such as languages, English, mathematics, science, social science, etc., rather than combine all subjects as if class size were equally important for all. A periodic sample survey of this type would provide useful indices of educational change.

The second column of the above table, the percent of classes with enrollment of 25 pupils or less, also, illustrates another meaningful indicator. The distribution of pupils by size of class with separate distributions for each major subject in the secondary schools, then, would furnish more meaningful indices than now are available in time series.

Trends in one-teacher schools, Series C2 and C3, are presented in chapter 6.

Footnotes

<u>1/</u> See Barr and Foster (1968) and Dunham and Wright (1966) for the latest publication in each series.

4
The Quality of Education

To detect the quality of education is not an easy task and no statistical time series has been developed that tells whether the quality of our educational system as a whole is becoming better or worse.

Each part of the educational system, being devoted to its own purposes and concerned with its own age levels, requires its own basis for evaluation. However, each level essentially is concerned with the same problem: the problem of determining change or growth in the student during the time the student participates in the learning activities of the institution. This "increment added" by the educational system, all other factors being held constant, during the period of exposure by the student, becomes the ultimate criterion.

Such measures have not been developed for the nation as a whole over time at any level of education.[1] Only rarely does one find that a state or a local school system has attempted such measurement, even over a short period of time. In a few instances, however, such measures have shown the potentialities of such assessment. This chapter reviews three of these and discusses a few potentialities of such approaches.

Scholastic Aptitude, High School Juniors in Minnesota

Scholastic aptitude tests attempt to measure and predict the students' future scholastic standing or performance. The results of tests administered to junior year students over a period of ten years to public and non-public schools in Minnesota provide an example of this approach to evaluating the future academic potential of students in a state school system.2/

The average score of a particular high school is fairly stable, year to year. Individual schools maintain a very similar rank order position from one year to the next. Only when a school district is split or consolidated does the relative position of the components change appreciably. However, differences continue to be observed between high schools, the high school means ranging from around 20 to around 60, out of a total possible test score of 78. Because of this stability of average score of an individual school, some of the change in average score for the state might result from increasing size of better schools.

The results of the test, administered to Minnesota junior year high school students, are presented in Table 4.1 and Figure 4.1. Increases in the average scores from 1958 to 1964 are considerable -- from 29 to 34.

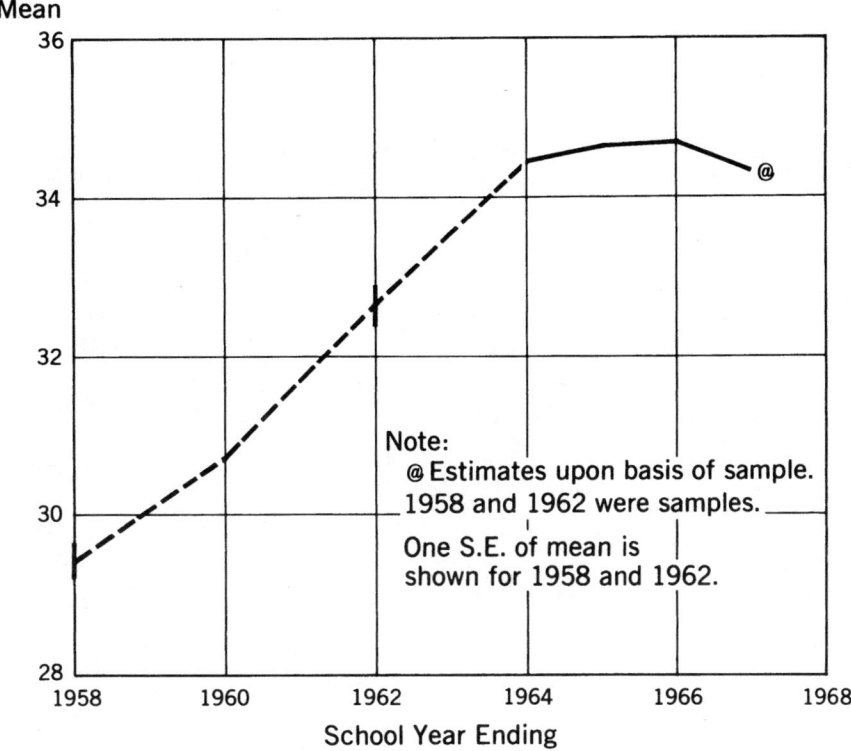

Figure 4.1. Minnesota High School Junior Year: Minnesota Scholastic Aptitude Test, Means, 1958–1967 (Source: Table 4.1).

Table 4.1. Mean Scores for Minnesota Junior Year High School Students on the Minnesota Scholastic Aptitude Test

Year	Mean Score
1966-67***	34.3
1965-66	34.65
1964-65	34.58
1963-64	34.41
1962-63	NA
1961-62*	32.60 ($\pm$.32)
1960-61	NA
1959-60	30.71
1958-59	NA
1957-58**	29.39 ($\pm$.22)

* A 10 percent sample (45,488); one standard error of mean shown.

** A 20 percent sample (41,013); one standard error of mean shown.

*** New form used this year; mean is estimated.

NA Not available.

Source: Private communication from Prof. Edward O. Swanson, University of Minnesota.

Educational Achievement, High School Seniors in Iowa

Iowa Tests of Educational Development have been administered annually, 1961 through 1967, to almost all Iowa seniors in the fall of the year before graduation.[3]

Table 4.2 presents median scores of Iowa seniors on nine achievement tests. The right hand column of the table shows the percentage increase in the median, 1961 to 1967. The numerical change in the median or its percentage change indicates the trend in achievement of Iowa seniors. Comparisons between disciplinary tests should not be made since such comparisons have no meaning.

The disciplinary area showing greatest increase was the Natural Sciences followed closely by the test on "use of sources of information." The interpretation of literaty materials and the social studies followed next in order of improvement. The remaining tests increased approximately 7 to 8 percent. None of the medians show a marked improvement.

The medians show that improvement in test scores ended with the performance of the class of 1965. The last two classes, 1966 and 1967, have shown very little improvement over 1965. For two of the tests, "Correctness of Expression of English" and "Quantative Thinking" little improvement in median test score has been made over the median of the class of 1964.

The examples of time series of test scores from Iowa and Minnesota, above, illustrate the kind of results that may be

Table 4.2. Median Standard Scores on ITED* of Iowa Seniors, 1960-1966

	Test	Class of 1961	Class of 1962	Class of 1963	Class of 1964	Class of 1965	Class of 1966	Class of 1967	% Increase
Basic Social Concepts	1	18.3	18.8	19.0	19.7	20.0	20.0	19.8	8.2
Natural Sciences	2	18.8	18.7	19.2	20.0	20.2	20.3	20.3	8.0
Correctness of Expression English	3	17.6	17.9	18.3	18.9	18.9	19.0	19.1	8.5
Quantitative Thinking	4	17.6	17.5	18.0	18.6	18.8	18.8	18.8	6.8
Reading Interpretation in Social Studies	5	18.0	18.4	18.8	19.6	20.0	20.0	20.0	11.1
Reading Interpretation in Natural Sci.	6	17.4	18.0	18.5	20.0	20.4	20.5	20.5	17.8
Interp. Literary Materials	7	17.4	18.1	18.4	19.1	19.5	19.6	19.6	12.6
Vocabulary	8	18.1	18.3	18.6	19.3	19.6	19.6	19.7	8.8
Comp.		18.8	19.1	19.4	20.3	20.7	20.6	20.7	10.1
Use of Sources of Information	9	18.9	19.7	20.2	21.4	21.7	22.0	22.0	16.4

* - Iowa Tests of Educational Development

Source: See footnote 3.

obtained through one method of evaluating quality of education. At the local and state levels tests have been administered and the results used to advise and assist the student and to project and plan curriculum changes. Some testing programs are thought to have affected the schools by causing changes in the curriculum to more adequately meet the "challenge" of the test (e.g., The New York Regents testing program) as an evaluation of the educational programs (Goslin, 1968: 851-855). This undesirable consequence of testing programs undoubtedly could be minimized or eliminated.4/

Two large scale testing programs, Project Talent (Flanagan, et. al., 1962) and The Equality of Educational Opportunity (Coleman, et. al., 1966) have inquired in-depth into factors associated with aptitude and achievement. The effects of minority group status, region of the nation, expenditures per pupil, teacher characteristics, composition of the school, community and family characteristics, etc., have been analyzed to identify the most significant influences upon the pupil outcomes.

For example, in Equality of Educational Opportunity, per pupil expenditures were found to account for a very small amount of the variance in scores on achievement tests, after family background of the pupils and the social composition of the student body had been considered. It concluded:

"School-to-school variations in achievement, from
whatever source (community differences, variations

in the average home background of the student body, or variations in school factors), are much smaller than individual variations within the school, at all grade levels, for all racial and ethnic groups." (Coleman, et. al., 1966: 296)

In Iowa and in Minnesota over the span of approximately ten years of testing, the social composition of the student bodies of the schools and the family backgrounds of the students were relatively constant. Test results show improvements up to a point but little improvement thereafter. While the possibility remains that the home environments of the successive classes changed slightly, becoming more of a motivational force at the end of the period under observation than at the beginning, this possibility seems less likely than the assumption of a constant environmental background. Can the improvement, then, be attributed to changes in the school system? Why did pupil scores appear to improve to a certain point and then remain stationary thereafter?

The matter can only be resolved by longitudinal analysis of a number of schools wherein sufficient information is assembled on the environmental and family backgrounds, on the composition of the student bodies, expenditures, and on achievement, to determine whether these factors remain stationary or change. Indeed, the Equality study suggests this approach:

"Had a number of years been available for this survey, a quite different way of assessing effects of school characteristics would have been possible; that is, examination of the educational growth over a period of time of children in schools with different characteristics. This is an alternative and in some ways preferable method of assessing the effects of school characteristics." (Coleman, et. al., 1966: 292)

In summary, changes over time in achievement test results and in scholastic aptitude in Iowa and Minnesota illustrate changes in a criterion that might form the basis for longitudinal studies, successively examining the social, economic and school-organizational factors contributory to pupil performance. The increment in growth of pupils when examined across successive cohorts of pupils would provide a definitive indicator of change in the educational system.

Achievement: College Seniors

The performance of senior classes of colleges and universities, also, may be compared to provide an indicator of learning at successive points in time. Data illustrating this method have been collected by Educational Testing Service (Lannholm, 1962). The senior classes of 79 institutions were tested in Social Sciences, Humanities, and Natural Science in 1955 and 1959. The mean scores of all the seniors increased slightly but did not differ significantly. However, the variation among class averages on each test from one college to another was considerable. About one-third of the school means decreased in the Social Sciences, and slightly less than one-third decreased in the Humanities and in the Natural Sciences. Other institutions registered marked gains. The administrators of some of the gaining institutions reported changes in the institution which they considered responsible for the improvement in scores.

An approximation of the means in 65 colleges, based upon testing complete classes of 25 or more seniors at each time is as follows (Lannholm, 1962: Table 1):

Test	1955	1959
Social Science	425.8	434.3
Humanities	438.3	463.0
Natural Science	445.3	453.3

About 17 percent of senior classes did not do as well in 1959 as their predecessors had done in 1955. About 25 percent to 35 percent of the classes, depending upon the subject, performed about the same (within a change of 10 points, plus or minus), and about half of the senior classes performed considerably better on the test in 1959 than in 1955. The Natural Sciences faired slightly better than the Social Sciences. These results are shown below:

Difference Intervals, in Scaled Score Units	Social Science	Humanities	Natural Science
	Number of Institutions		
60 to 99	1	1	1
10 to 59	30	36	37
-10 to 9	23	16	16
-60 to -11	11	12	11
Total	65	65	65

The reasons for the changes suggested by the college administrative personnel included changes in admission policies, in the curriculum (adding, modifying, or discontinuing courses), administrative policies, honors programs, improvements in faculty, library, etc.

The more deliberate and systematic evaluation of higher education, may soon become a reality. The American Council on Education has established a sample of educational institutions and has developed plans for the measurement of student "inputs," college environments, characteristics of faculty and various other "influences" on the student (Astin, Panos, and Creager, 1966). Student outcomes that may be obtained before the student leaves college also will be collected. This research program may create a kind of continuing evaluation of higher education.

In longitudinal studies of colleges, attainment of successive senior classes might be augmented by a freshman-to-senior class comparison of the same individuals, to further gauge how much of senior class test performance should be attributed to the curriculum and how much to a change in the quality of entering freshmen. A testing program of this kind among a number of liberal arts colleges would provide comparisons to evaluate experimental programs. To the extent that the institutions could be sampled to represent higher educational institutions, a continuing indicator of quality of education would be available.

Footnotes

1/ A comprehensive list of state testing programs is presented in Educational Testing Service (1968).

2/ Data from the Minnesota testing program was obtained through the courtesy of Professor Edward O. Swanson, the University of Minnesota. The Minnesota Scholastic Aptitude Test was developed from an early form of the Ohio State Psychological Examination. It is heavily weighted with measures of verbal abilities. The same form has been used from 1957-58 through 1965-66 among all Minnesota schools, public and private, or representative samples of them. A revised form was introduced in 1966-67, but a sample of students took both the old and the new form, enabling an estimate of the 1966-67 mean score on the old form.

3/ Since schools voluntarily participate in the testing program, there may be some upward bias in the selection process, but no evidence is available on this point. For the last three years shown in Table 4.2, 90 to 95 percent of Iowa schools participated. The data, then, appear to have no major bias that may be attributed to selection of participating schools. Data were supplied by Leonard S. Feldt, Director, Iowa High School Testing Program, University of Iowa, Iowa City, Iowa, by letter dated January 5, 1968.

4/ Caroline Hightower (1968) has described the CAPE project, the plans for a national assessment of education developed over several years through support of the Carnegie Foundation and the U. S. Office of Education. The sample selection of student attributes to be tested is one procedure for overcoming the bias mentioned in the text. CAPE plans include tests of 10 subject areas. The national sample would be selected from sample census tracts, with a sampling of residences and schoolhouses in each. The first three-year cycle of testing would be required to establish the base line for the assessment. Only the second three-year period of testing would yield a determination of change in learning.

5

Graduates

This chapter reviews trends in graduates of secondary school and higher educational institutions. Both aggregate numbers completing their education and rates of completion are examined.

The production of the educational system is commonly measured by student days, or student "years" of attendance, and by the number of certificates, diplomas, or degrees granted by institutions.

The product of the educational system is the person certified as having learned a specific body of knowledge. Graduates of secondary school typically are undifferentiated as to subject matter but graduates of higher curricula are counted by field of specialization. Some students may receive two degrees simultaneously, for example, a law student may receive both bachelor of arts and bachelor of law degrees at the same graduation exercise. A university has been known to award two Ph.D. degrees simultaneously to the same person. For practical purposes, the number of such duplications is probably small; we may, then, think of the degree as the person who has achieved competence in a given field of specialization.

Higher education designates the degree, its level and its specialty, e.g., Bachelor of Science (Chemistry). Commonly, this is the first phase in certification of competence which helps to insure the proficient performance of professional and technical roles.

Measuring "Production" of the Educational System

High school graduates and college and university degree recipients are commonly the primary measures of academic production available. However, there are at least 13 gates or metering points where counts might be made of those completing the courses of study. These gates are:

    6th grade primary schools
    8th grade primary schools
    9th grade junior high schools
    12th grade 4-year high schools, senior high schools and
        combined junior-senior high schools
    2-year junior or community college (college grade work)
    2-year technical institutes
    3-year technical institutes
    4-year baccalaureate
    5-year bachelor's or first professional
    6-year first professional degree
    Master's degree
    Doctor's degree
    ? completion of postdoctoral study or research

Gross Production of the Educational System

High School Graduates. Since 1870, when graduates were first reported by state, the flow of high school graduates into society has increased numerically and at a fairly constant rate (Figure 5.1, Series A17). Prior to 1942, the decade to decade increase averaged 87 percent with the 1890s and the 1920s being decades of greatest proportional increase -- more than 100 percent. It would appear strange that such vigorous growth should suddenly come to a halt in 1942, were it

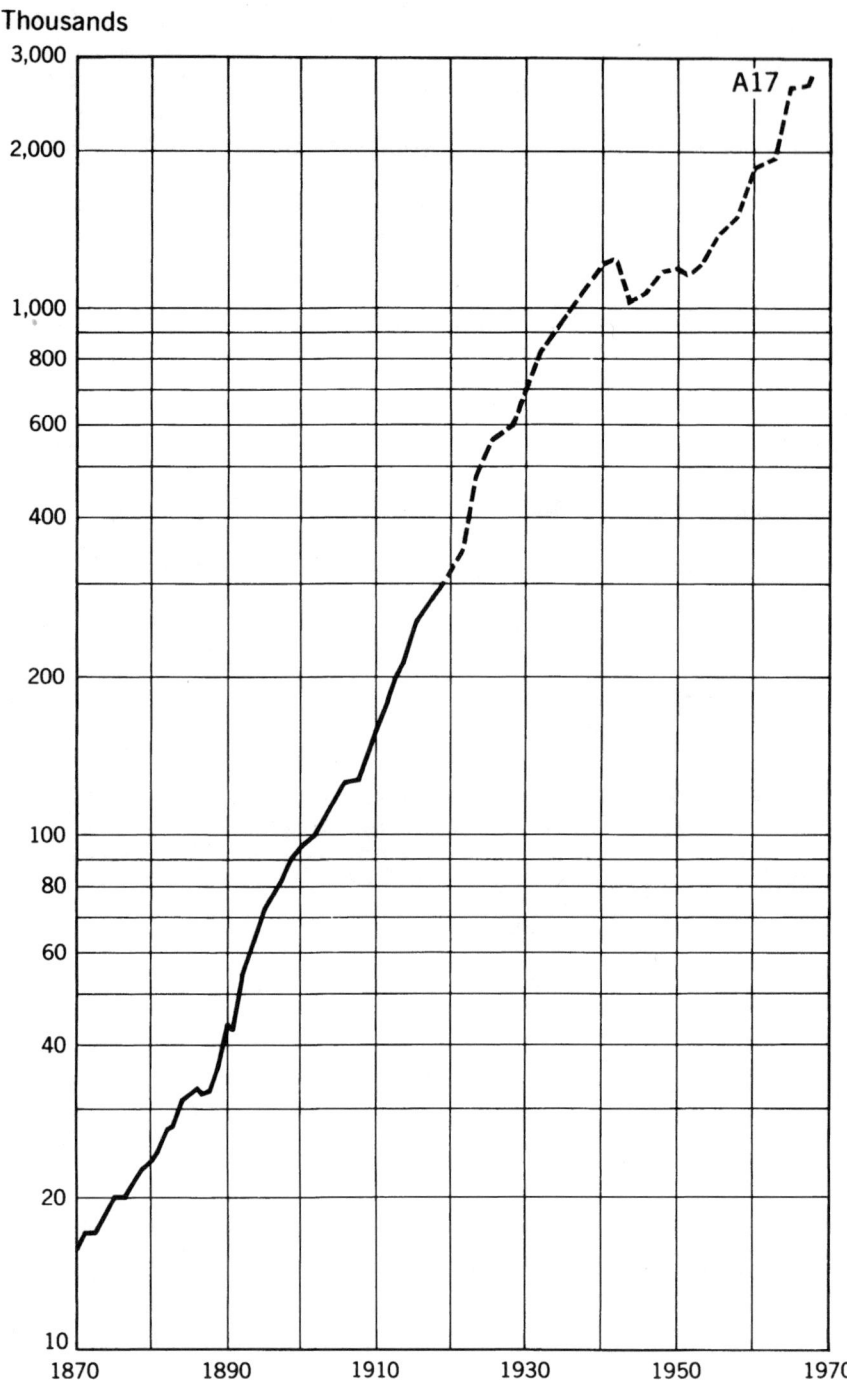

Figure 5.1. Graduates of Public and Non-public Secondary Schools, 1870–1968, Series A17 (Semi-logarithmic Scale).

not for two historical events that together conspired to retard the flow. The first was the decline in the number of births after a peak in 1928. A low point was reached during the years 1932 and 1933, and the number of 1928 births was not again reached until 1938. The depression in the size of high school graduating classes of around 1946 to 1955 is a direct consequence of the decrease in the number of births during the 1928-1938 period.

The second drain on the graduating classes of 1943, 1944, and 1945, of course, occurred during World War II, when military and defense activities siphoned off high school enrollees (Series A18).

Following the decline in graduates during the decade of the 1940s, high school graduates increased during the 1950s. As the numerical aggregates have become larger, the rates of increase have declined. Up to 1940 the decade-to-decade increase averaged 87 percent. The 1940-50 increase was 55 percent. Upon the increases in births alone, we may expect a 43 percent increase in high school graduates during the decade of the 1960s, and a 5 percent increase during the 1970s. With only small increases in the rates of retention, these proportionate increases could turn out to be slightly higher in the next decade.

Ratio, High School Graduates to 17-Year-Olds

In April 1960, 48 percent of the 4th year high school students were 17 years of age (Census, 1963a: 1-349 and 1-377). Being the typical age of graduation from secondary school, the 17 year age group provides a base for Series A18, the high school graduates per 100 17-year-olds, from 1870 to the present. This measure roughly evaluates how adequately the nation has provided schooling to each successive annual 17-year-old age group.

The upward swing of the curve, particularly since 1910, reflects increasingly more universal high school education (Figure 5.2). The graph, however, reveals two retrogressive periods: during World War II, and around 1964. The notch in the mid-1940s undoubtedly reflects the War, and shows that the decline in graduates during this period, discussed in the previous section, was a function of a decline in the rate as well as a decline in numbers in the age group.

The dip in the rate of 17-year-olds graduating in 1964 is a consequence of an abrupt increase in the number 17 years of age coupled with the fact, mentioned above, that only about half the graduates are 17 years old when they graduate. Specifically, those 17 years of age in 1963 and 1964 were born in 1946 and 1947, respectively. The number of babies born in those years were increases of 19 percent and 12 percent, respectively, over the preceding year. There were about one million more 17-year-olds in 1964 than in 1963 (Series I8).

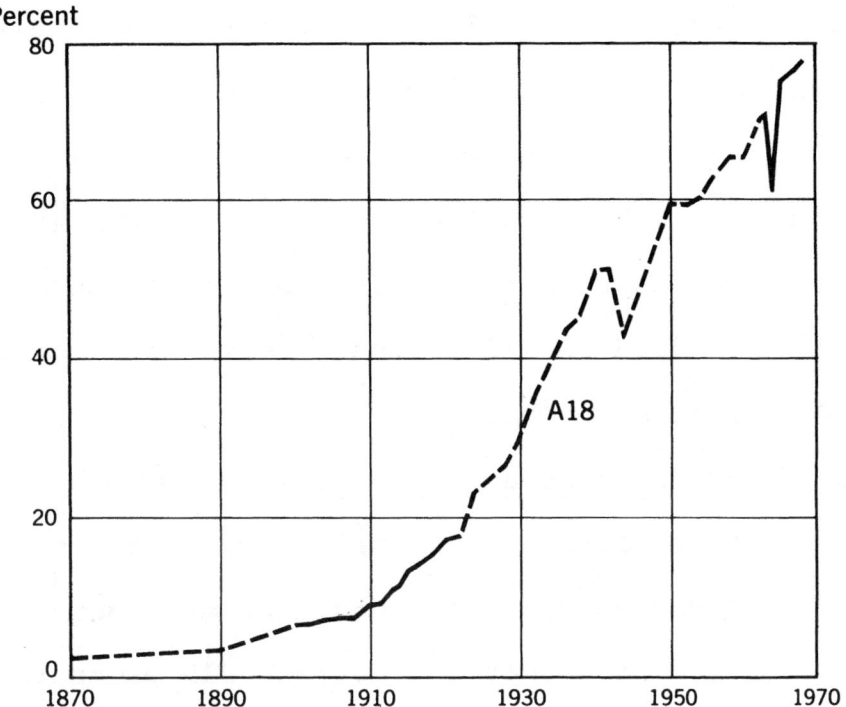

Figure 5.2. High School Graduates as a Percent of the Population 17 Years Old, 1870–1968, Series A18.

The 1964 dip, then, is an artifact of the series resulting from an abnormal increase in 17-year-olds in relation to the age distribution of a normal graduating class.

Viewed in its long-term trend, the ratio at present appears to be increasing more slowly. Having reached almost 78 per 100 17-year-olds in 1968, the rate is now increasing at about 10 percent per year.

Graduates of Colleges and Universities. Trends in degrees at the baccalaureate, Master's, and Doctor's levels are presented in Series D16, D17, and D18, each being assembled by the U. S. Office of Education. Series D19 presents the Doctor's degrees assembled by the National Academy of Sciences.

The other principal outputs of higher education, of which we have only fragmentary information, are the number of Arts (two-year) degrees granted and the number who complete post-high school programs of occupational or technical training. Series on the latter, however, are now being developed by the U. S. Office of Education.

One interested in data on degrees granted is likely to be concerned with a particular field. The presentation of degrees by specialty field involves a great deal of detail. Because of this, we present only a few fields and have selected those with growth patterns of special interest.[1]

Baccalaureate Degrees. The gradual increase in college baccalaureate degrees from 1870 to 1920 reflected the slowly developing higher educational system. However, after 1920 the

106

story was different. From the 1920s to World War II, baccalaureates increased much faster -- about 150 percent increase in the 1920s and about 50 percent increase in the 1930s. The decline in baccalaureates during the 1940s was a consequence of the War. The post-war period saw a dramatic increase in degrees, as veterans returned to complete their education. The decline in degrees granted during the 1950s led to the more normal trend that continued the upswing of the 1920s and 1930s. This upward trend continues today.

The U. S. Office of Education anticipates 736,000 Bachelor's and first professional degrees in 1969-70, an 84 percent increase over 1959-60, and it expects that 1976-77 -- the most advanced year of its projections -- will exceed the degrees ten years earlier by more than two-thirds, reaching 961,000 degrees (Simon and Fullam, 1968: 31).

Figure 5.3 presents the trend in the 23-year-old age group, the typical age of college graduation. The year to year aggregate in this age has increased considerably since 1880 and has especially increased since 1957. These changes, however, are mild when compared with the overall increase and the variations in the number of degrees granted. Ever higher graduation rates of 23-year-olds are apparent.

Ratio of Baccalaureate Degrees to High School Graduates Four Years Earlier

Over the long span of time, both high school graduates and baccalaureate degrees have increased. The ratio of

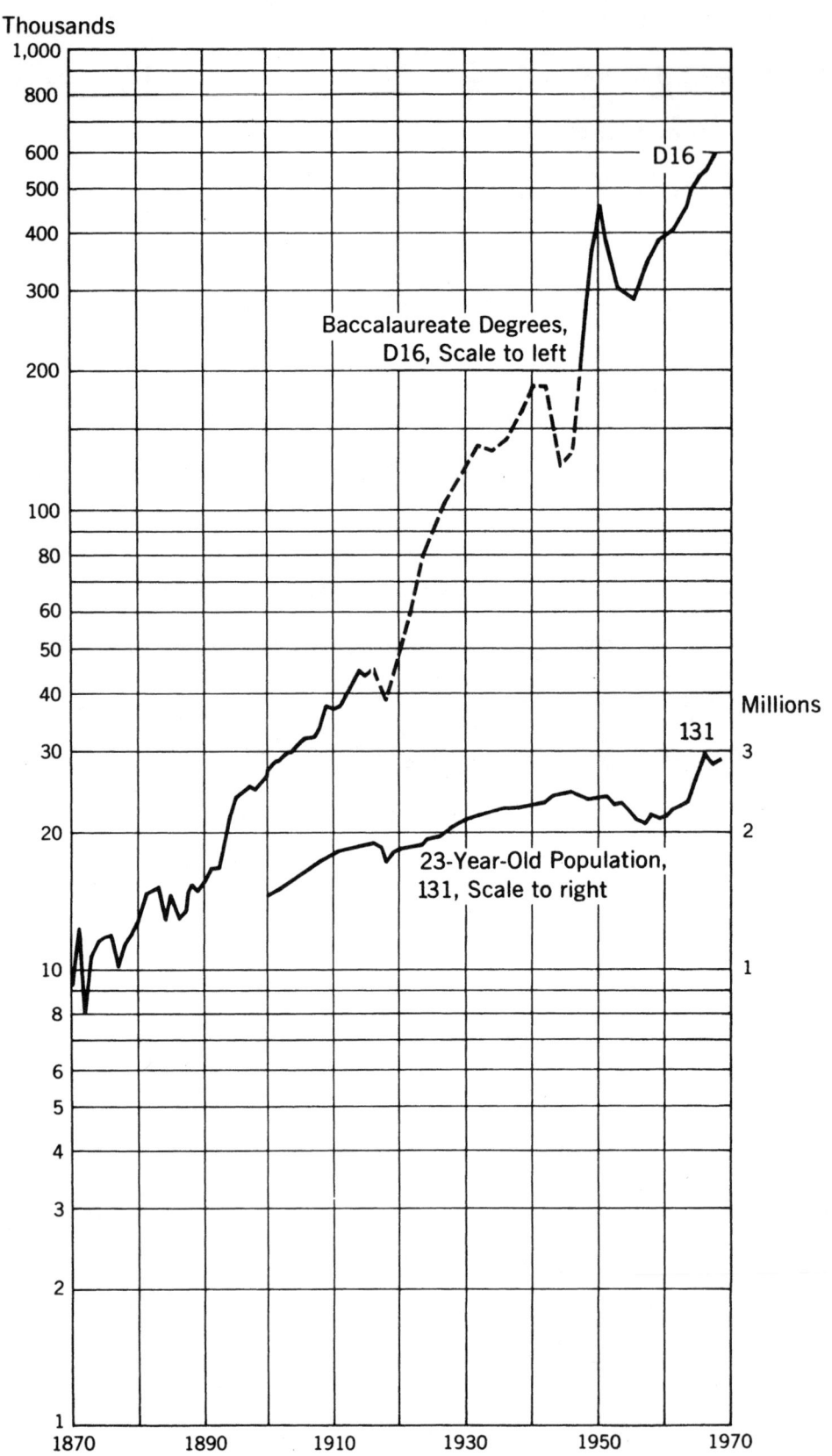

Figure 5.3. Baccalaureate Degrees Granted, 1870–1967, Series D16, and the 23-Year-Old Population, 1900–1968, Series 131 (Semi-logarithmic Scale).

baccalaureates to high school graduates four years earlier provides a gross index of the extent young people continue in formal education (Figure 5.4, Series D21). As with a number of other educational indices, however, this measure to some extent is imprecise: high school graduates do not always proceed immediately to college and, even those who do, do not always graduate within four years. The effect of this defect is illustrated by the 1950 peak. It results from a large number of baccalaureate degrees being granted to veterans whose progress in college was prevented or interrupted by World War II. Despite this fault, the long-term trend dramatically illustrates the changes in American secondary and college education.

Prior to 1895 a baccalaureate degree was granted to about 50 out of every 100 high school graduates four years earlier. During the period 1900-1945 this index decreased to approximately 20 around 1915 and, after gaining during the 1920s, thereafter continued to decline, reaching a low of approximately 10 during the early 1940s. A third "transformation" of the educational system is reflected in the increases in the ratio, currently underway.[2/]

The changes in this ratio (Series D21) actually reflect more fundamental shifts in the purpose, function, and clientele of the two educational systems. Secondary education that ended with the high school graduating class of 1890, approximately, was an elite system, having a curriculum, faculty, and standards of scholarship designed to prepare students,

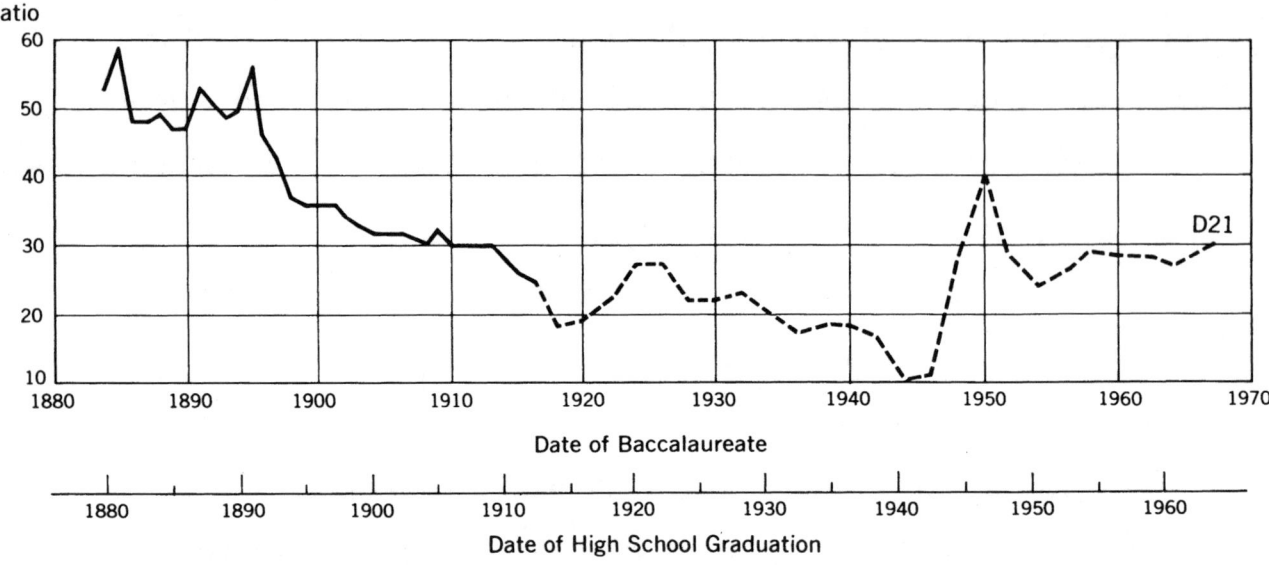

Figure 5.4. Ratio, Baccalaureates to 100 High School Graduates Four Years Earlier, 1884–1967, Series D21.

chiefly young men, for college. As the chart demonstrates, more than half of them graduated from college four years later. This secondary school system was transformed into an educational system designed primarily, not as preparation for college, but as terminal vocational education, a system not for the elite few, but for the masses. As such, continuation of education beyond high school declined. The same "mass" education philosophy was not to be infused into the higher education until after 1940.[3/]

In its long decline from the high school graduating class of 1891 to the class of 1942, the ratio has not decreased uniformly. It declined during both World Wars I and II and dipped slightly during the 1930s. The ratio of the high school graduating class of 1948 represents the real beginning of the third transformation in American education. Not only is high school graduation becoming nearly universal, but the trend is toward higher and higher rates of enrollment in college (see Series A18, D15).

As higher education continues to expand, the current ratio of 30 will climb higher.

The changes that occurred in American industry and commerce after the Civil War created a demand for trained personnel that, by 1890, had reached the system of secondary education. The need for vocationally trained employees resulted in establishing public secondary schools for the mass of youth (Judd, 1933: 325). After World War I changes in industry and commerce set the same forces in motion, creating a demand for college-trained people. Baccalaureate degrees began to increase, but the Great Depression of the 1930s intervened, dampening the trend. This industrial demand really did not begin to permeate higher education until the technological and industrial impact of World War II created the imperative for more highly trained and scientifically oriented technicians and professional workers for industry and commerce. Thus, the "democratization" of secondary education was followed, some half-century later, by the "democratization" of higher education (Trow, 1961). Both junior colleges and four-year institutions share the responsibility of continuing to popularize higher education.

Baccalaureate Degrees Related to First-time Enrollment Four Years Earlier, by Sex

Another index to the production of baccalaureate degrees is afforded by relating four-year degrees to the number of freshmen who entered four years earlier. Figure 5.5 presents two series (D25 and D26) for males and females, respectively. The series for females is more uniform than the series for males. The male graduation classes of the mid-1950s show higher completion ratios, partly because their ranks were swollen by (Korean War) veterans, many of whom were not first time enrollees four years earlier. The series for females is affected less by reentering veterans and presents greater consistency than the male ratio.

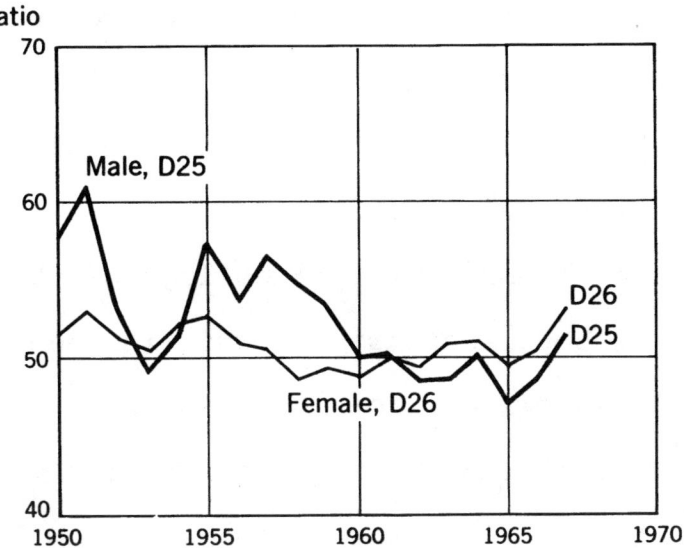

Figure 5.5. Ratio, Four-Year Degrees to 100 First-time Enrollment Four Years Earlier, by Sex, 1950–1967, Series D25 and D26.

Both Series D25 and D26 have declined from the higher levels they attained during the mid-1950s. Other than changes in the enrollment of veterans, what could explain this decrease? There are two possibilities:

1. The ratio of enrollment in college of the population of college age has been increasing. This is seen in Series D13, opening fall enrollment per 100 population 18 to 21 years of age, (Figure 2.15). This ratio has increased (from 31.5 in 1951 to 57.6 in 1966 for males, and from 12 in 1945 to 37.7 in 1966 for females). This may mean that entering college students have a wider range of aptitudes and, correspondingly, a higher proportion of less capable students enter college, lose interest, or fail to complete the four-year course.

2. An increasing share of college students enroll in junior colleges (Series D8 and D9, Figure 2.13). Some junior college students will discontinue their education upon graduating from junior college. The effect of this would be to depress the ratio (Series D25 and D26) of baccalaureates to entering freshmen four years earlier. Better articulation between junior colleges and four year colleges, however, would alter the completion ratios (Knoell and Medsker, 1964a and 1964b).

The immediate future of this index may be estimated from projections of the U. S. Office of Education.[4]

The projection of Series D25 and D26 is presented in Table 5.1. After increasing to 1968, the ratio for both men

Table 5.1. Estimated Completion Ratios, Four-year Baccalaureate Degrees per 100 First-time Opening Fall Enrollment Four Years Earlier, by Sex, 1967-1976

	Men	Women
1966-67	48.5	51.7
1967-68	49.0	52.0
1968-69	45.4	49.0
1969-70	44.7	48.7
1970-71	44.8	48.7
1971-72	45.2	48.7
1972-73	45.3	48.7
1973-74	45.5	48.5
1974-75	45.7	48.3
1975-76	45.9	48.3

Source: Computed from Simon and Fullam, 1966: 7 and 27.

and women declines. The ratio for women declines to about 48 and remains at that level. The ratio for men declines to 45 before it will begin to increase slightly.

In summary, proportionately more high school graduates are eventually graduating from college than was the situation in the 1930s and early 1940s (Figure 5.4). However, as Figure 5.5 shows, the completion ratio based upon the number of starters (the input) is lower now than during the mid-1950s, and may be expected to continue to decline (Table 5.1). This is probably a consequence of a more inclusive population now entering college and of an increasing number of college entrants who complete their college careers when they graduate from junior college.

Baccalaureate Degrees per 1,000 23-year-Olds. Prior to 1920, the production of baccalaureate degrees in relation to the 23-year-old population was fairly steady, about 20 per 1000. In the 1920s, however, the rate began to increase fairly rapidly and continued to increase an average of approximately 6.5 percent per year to the beginning of World War II. The typical response of the educational system to the War -- a decline in the rate, followed after the War by a great increase -- was experienced during the period 1940 to 1954. In the post-war period, the rate did not return to its pre-war trend, but instead increased more rapidly.[5]

The 1965-1966 retrenchment of the ratio occurs at a time when the war in Viet Nam might be a contributing factor. The evidence, however, does not support this notion. During the

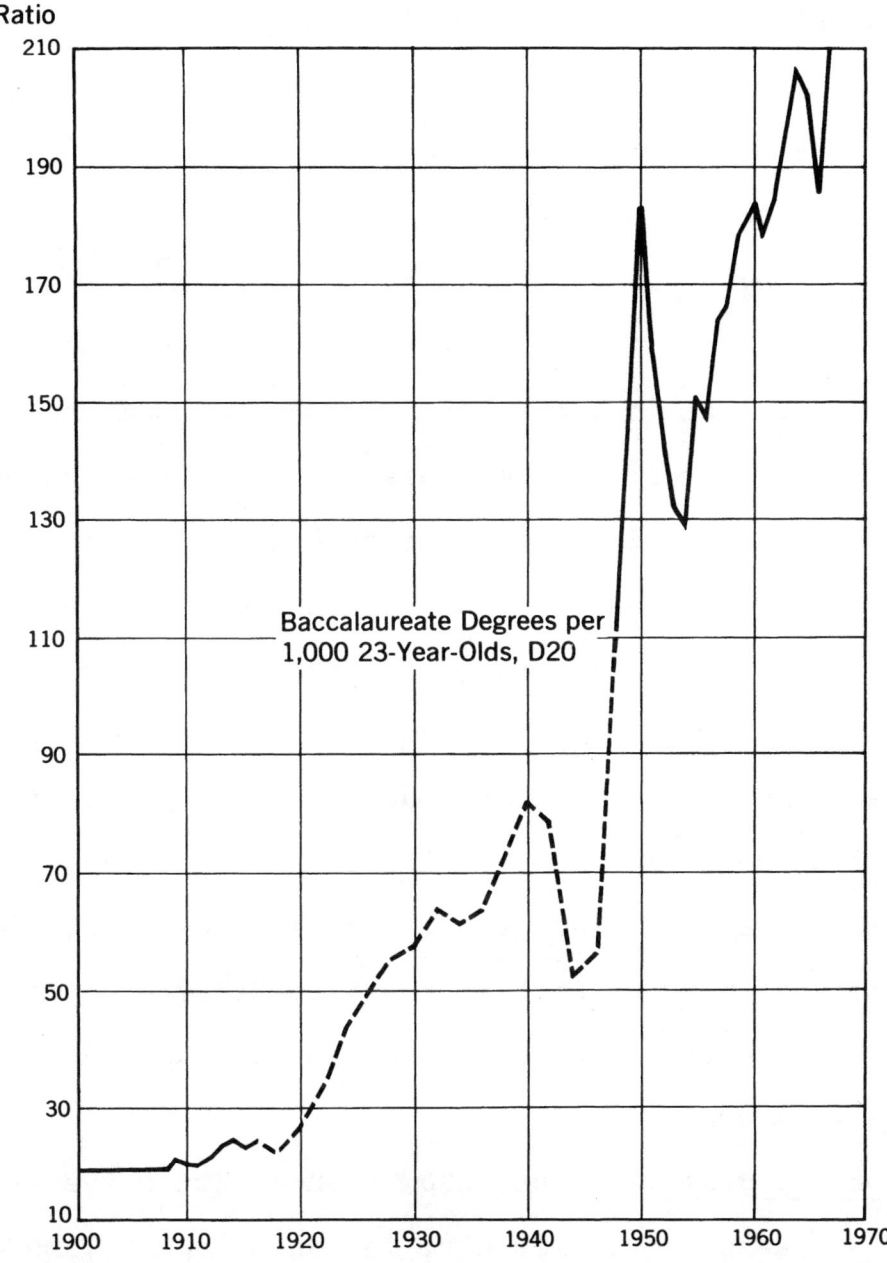

Figure 5.6. Ratio, Baccalaureate Degrees per 1,000 23-Year-Old Population, 1900–1967, Series D20.

period 1962-67, the 23-year-old males in the Armed Forces averaged 16 percent while the four-year degrees per 1000 23-year-old males averaged 20.8 percent, neither figure deviating more than 1.3 percent from the mean.

Master's Degrees. Although the trend in Master's degrees has not been as smooth as the trend in baccalaureate degrees, the general increase has followed the same pattern (Figure 5.7, Series D17). There has been one major exception: the 1950-1955 decline in baccalaureate degrees was not experienced by Master's degrees. The post-war years gave an impetus to Master's degree production that continued with little interruption through the 1960s. While the 1950s saw a 28 percent increase in Master's degrees, the 1960s experienced a 133 percent increase, to 173,600, projected (Simon and Fullam, 1968: 31). The decade that ends with 1977 is expected to see an 86 percent increase to 247,700 degrees. Thus, Master's degrees are continuing to increase faster than baccalaureate degrees.

Doctor's Degrees. Since 1890, earned doctorates granted by United States universities have increased about 7 percent per annum (Figure 5.8, Series D18). There have been periods when this growth rate has not been met, for example, immediately prior to 1920, and during 1941-1945 (World War II). During the periods of "rebound" from these retrogressions in growth, however, the growth rate has exceeded 7 percent and compensated for the losses. In the recent past (1958-1966)

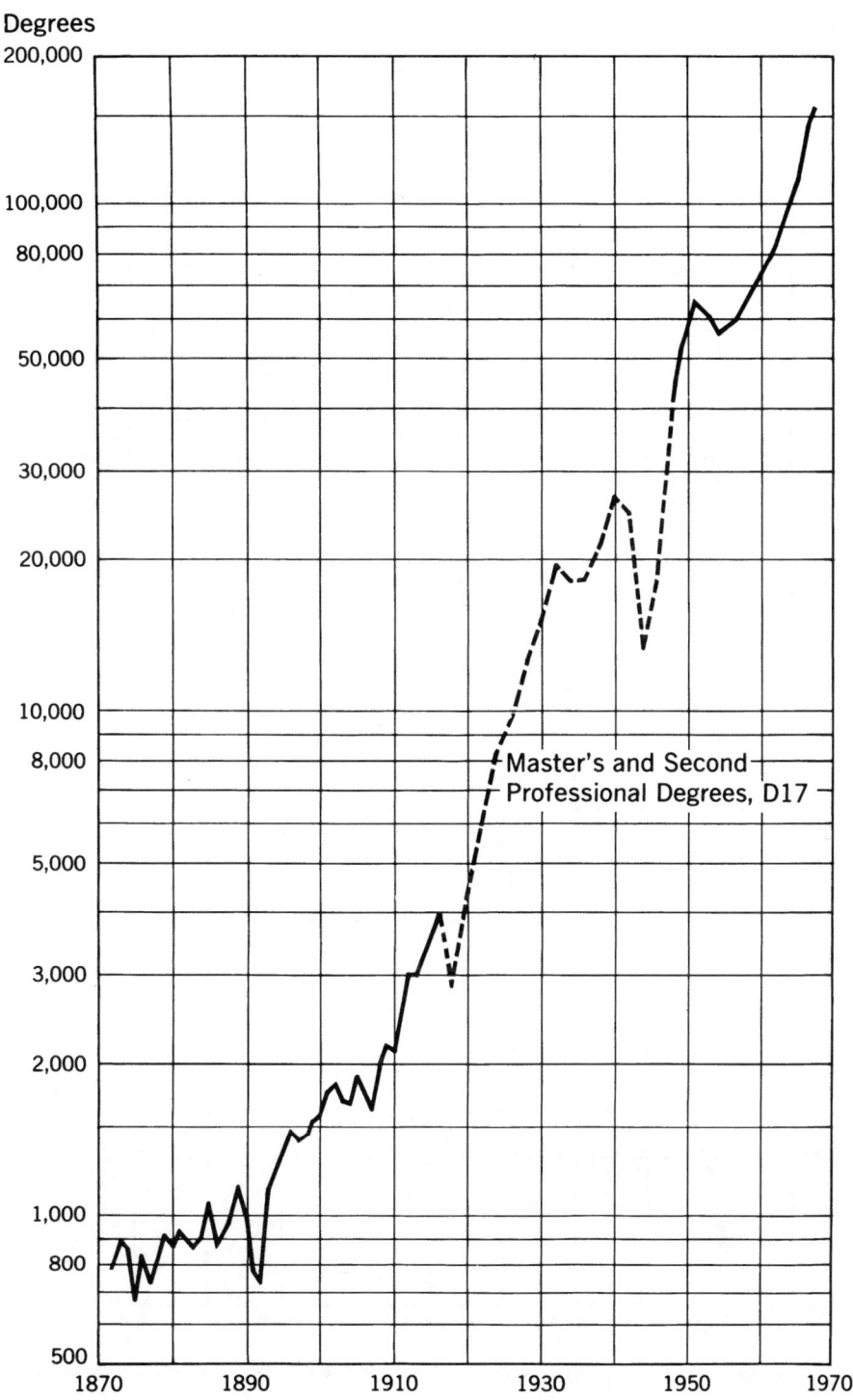

Figure 5.7. Master's and Second Professional Degrees Granted, 1872–1967, Series D17 (Semi-logarithmic Scale).

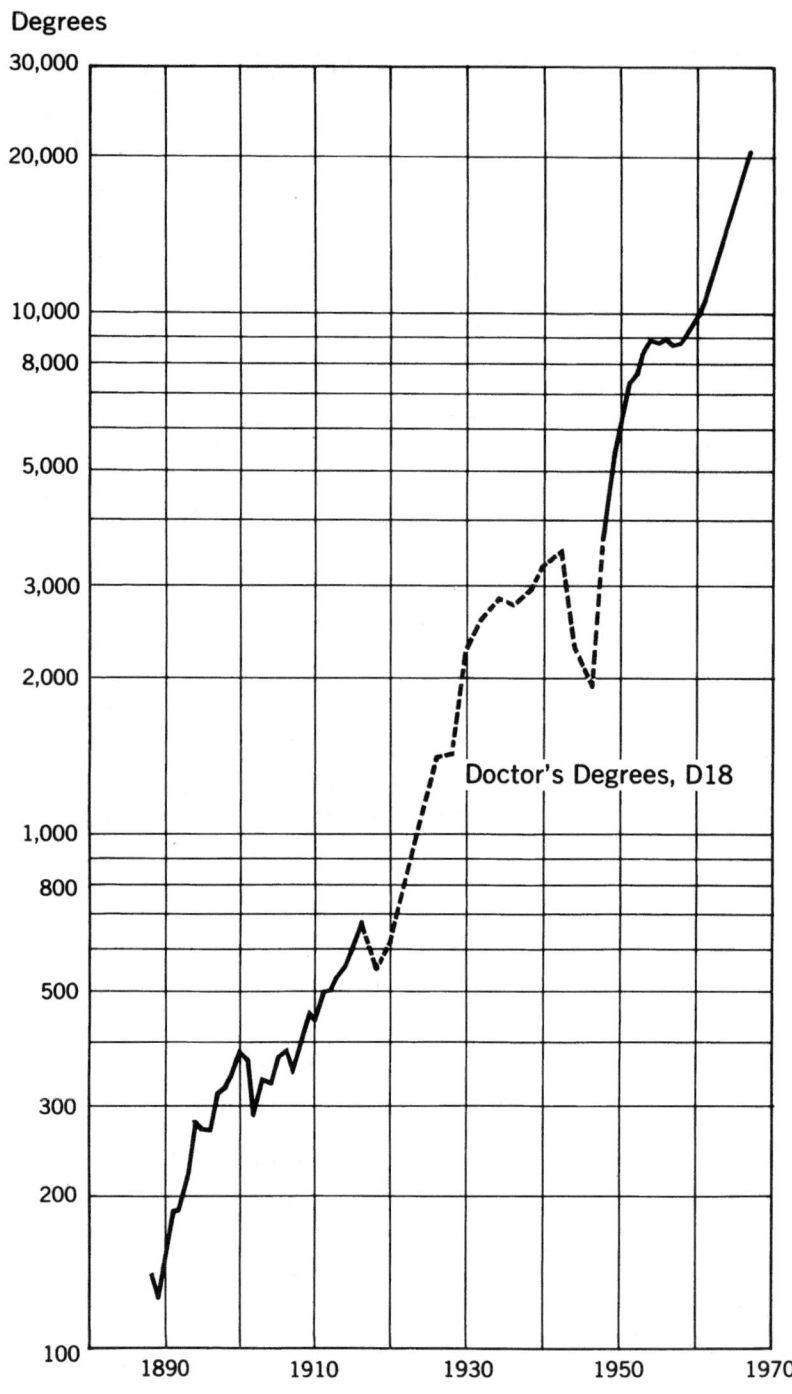

Figure 5.8. Doctor's Degrees Granted, 1888–1967, Series D18 (Semi-logarithmic Scale).

growth has exceeded 9 percent per year. In the decade of the 1960s, doctorates awarded are expected to increase about 150 percent, from 9,800 to 24,800 degrees, a growth rate of 9.7 percent per year. In the decade ending 1976-77, an increase of 106 percent is expected, with 38,700 degrees being granted in 1976-77, a growth rate of 7.6 percent per year for the decade (Simon and Fullam, 1968: 31).

While all fields have increased numerically in Doctor's degrees, they have not shared in equal proportions in the overall growth (Table 5.2). Total Doctor's degrees have more than doubled. Numerically, the Physical Sciences, Engineering, and Education have increased the most, 1955-56 to 1965-66, while the Professions and the Biological Sciences have increased in smaller numbers. The Biological Sciences, the Professions and the Social Sciences did not gain as much, proportionately, as did other fields. Doctor's degrees in the Physical Sciences were 21 percent of the total in 1955-56, 21 percent of the total in 1965-66, and gained 21 percent of the total increase. The Biological Sciences, on the other hand, were 18 percent of the total in 1955-56, 15 percent in 1965-66, and gained 12 percent of the increase over the period.

From Baccalaureate to Higher Degrees

The prospects for higher degrees rests with those who have received the baccalaureate, for this basic degree is almost universally required for entrance to graduate study.

Table 5.2. Growth of Doctor's Degrees, 1955-56 to 1965-66

	Doctorate Recipients		Percent Increase	Absolute Increase	Percent of Increase
	1955-56 1/	1965-66 2/			
Engineering	610	2,304	278	1,694	18
Professional Fields	456	824	81	368	4
Physical Sciences & Mathematics	1,902	3,846	102	1,944	21
Arts & Humanities	1,135	2,255	99	1,120	12
Education	1,438	3,063	113	1,625	17
Biological Sciences	1,567	2,685	71	1,118	12
Social Sciences	1,795	3,262	82	1,467	16
Total	8,903	18,239	105	9,336	100

1/ Rice and Poole, 1957: 18-20.

2/ Chandler and Rice, 1968: 8.

Baccalaureate degrees, then, provide the base for a rate of completion of Master's and Doctor's degrees (Figure 5.9, Series D22 and D23).

Master's. The rate of production of the Master's degree has gone through three stages. From the 1870s to about 1907 Master's degrees per 100 baccalaureates two years earlier varied between 5 and 11 (Figure 5.9). The rate then began to increase and, except for a dip during World War I, climbed to a higher scale. During the next twenty years it oscillated around 15 per 100 baccalaureates. The post World War II Master's production climbed to about 35, a level affected both by the low Bachelor's degree production during the wartime years and the heavy influx of military service veterans after World War II. Consequently, by 1952 the rate had returned to its pre-war level of 15. This did not continue, however. The 1950s ushered in a new stage in graduate education, producing a higher completion rate in what appears to be a new phase.

Graduate education to the Master's level has passed through two important developmental stages and now appears directed toward an increasingly higher production rate. If past experience may be allowed to suggest a pattern, this rate may stabilize and continue at that level for some time to come. From about 25 Master's per 100 Bachelor's degrees in 1965-66, the ratio may increase to 27 by 1975-76 (Simon and Fullam, 1968). Certainly, there is no support in these data for the notion,

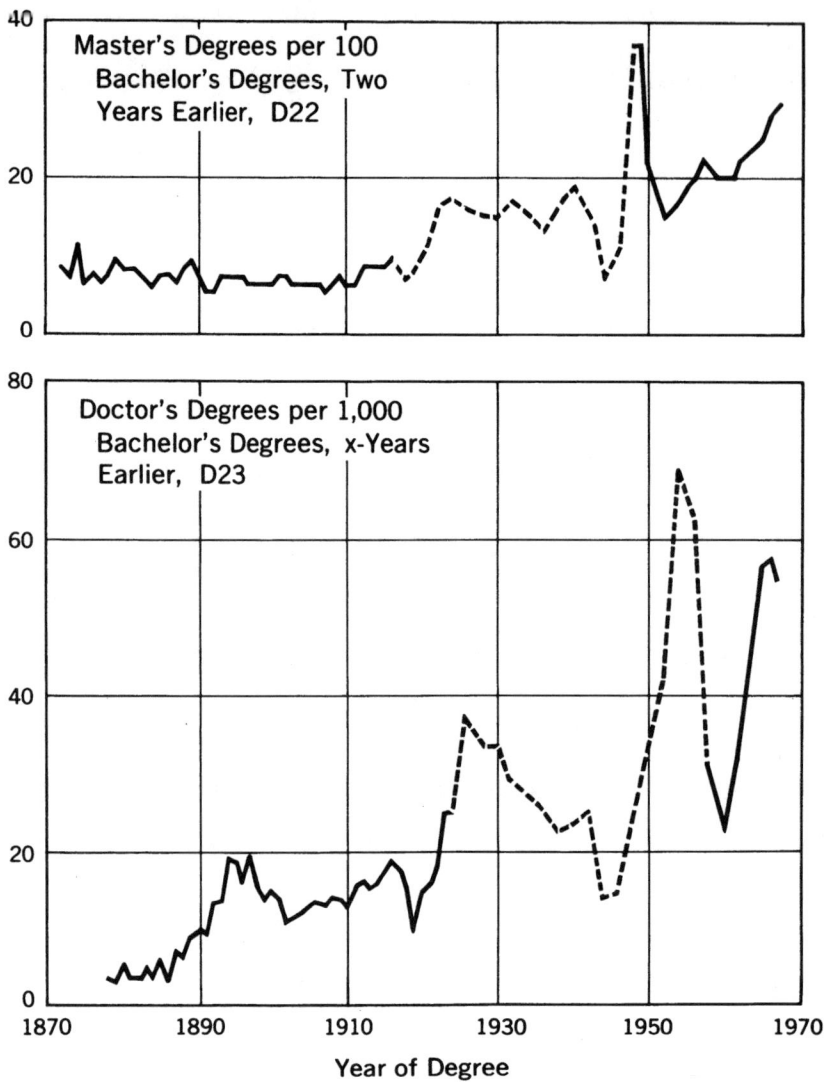

Figure 5.9. Completion Rates for Master's Degrees, 1872–1967, Series D22, and Doctor's Degrees, 1878–1967, Series D23.

sometimes heard, that the Master's degree is declining because of doctorate programs that allow the student to by-pass the Master's degree.

Doctor's. The mean lapse time, baccalaureate to doctorate, has increased from 8 years in 1920 to 10 years at present (Harmon and Soldz, 1963; National Academy of Sciences, 1967). We do not know the average lapse time before 1920, but, judging from the slow rate of change, one would assume that it was not greatly different prior to 1920. In Figure 5.10 a varying lapse time of 8 to 11 years has been used (see Series D47), depending upon the mean lapse time for the year.

The most rapid rate of increase of doctorate completion was the 20 years prior to 1897. The rate declined with the Spanish-American War. Then another upward climb began and continued until World War I. This War, also, instigated a decline. In 1920 an increase began that continued to 1926.[6] However, it is clear that the Depression and World War II brought on an almost continuous decline in the rate of completion.

World War II created a decline in doctorate degrees that ended with 1946. Except for two years, degrees have continuously increased since. The surge upward from 1946 to 1954, the decline to 1958, and the recovery to the present day may be attributed to the shifting baccalaureate base, rather than to great changes in doctorate production. The rate of completion now appears to be approaching a new, higher level, and there seems to be no immediate halt in the upswing of this rate of

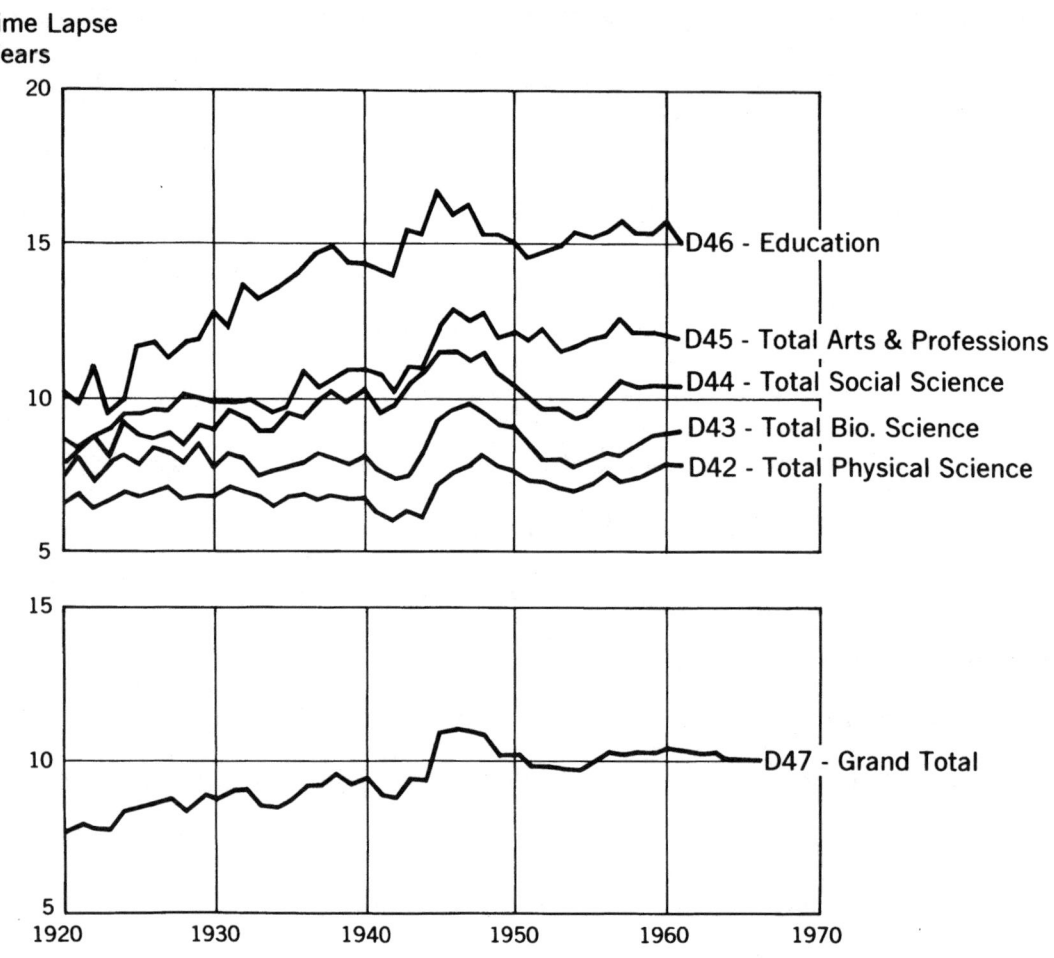

Figure 5.10. Mean B.A. to Ph.D. Time Lapse by Year for Five Doctorate Fields, 1920–1961, Series D42–D46, and Grand Total, 1920–1966, Series D47.

doctorate production. Indeed, the U. S. Office of Education (Simon and Fullam, 1966), always conservative in its projections, predicts a 110 percent increase, 1965-66 to 1975-76, in doctorates.[7/] This will produce a completion rate for the 1975-76 doctorate class of 64.7 per 1000 baccalaureates, compared with approximately 55 in 1967.

Lapse Time, B.A. to Ph.D.

Varying lengths of time after receiving the baccalaureate are required to attain the doctorate. It would seem that the shorter training time would be more desirable both for the student and the educational system, if the quality of the experience is not sacrificed.

The most recent statistics on the career of those attaining the doctorate are presented in Table 5.3. Fields differ little among themselves in time to attain the Master's, a median of about two years after the baccalaureate being typical of all fields. The next step to the doctorate degree, however, varies greatly from one field to the other. The Physical Sciences and Engineering require the least time while Education and Other Professional Fields require the most. The latter may mix work with part-time attendance at a university, and thus extend the time required. The rigorous demands of some of the specialties in the Humanities and the nature of the subject matter, perhaps, require extensive, time-consuming work of the student, in contrast to fields where procedure and method figure more prominently in the objectives of the training.

Table 5.3. Median Lapse Time from Baccalaureate to Several Stages in Graduate Education, Doctorate Recipients, 1958-1966

Median Years from

	Baccalaureate to Graduate School Entry (Total Time)	Graduate School to Master's (Total Time)	Master's to Doctor's (Total Time)	Baccalaureate to Doctorate	
				Total Time	Registered Time
			Years		
Total, All Fields	0.3	2.0	5.2	8.2	5.4
Physical Science & Engineering	0.2	2.0	4.1	6.3	5.1
Biological Science	0.3	2.1	4.3	7.3	5.3
Social Science	0.2	2.1	5.1	9.0	5.3
Arts & Humanities	0.3	1.9	6.2	9.5	5.7
Professional Fields	0.4	2.0	5.9	10.8	6.0
Education	1.0	2.2	8.4	13.8	6.8

Source: National Academy of Sciences, 1967: 69-70.

That the doctorate degree can be earned more quickly without loss of quality has been a topic much discussed (Wilson, 1965). One aim of fellowship support programs has been to reduce the B.A. to Ph.D. lapse time. The ineffectiveness of such efforts may be judged from the attached time series (D45) of mean lapse time 1920 to present (Figure 5.10). Generally, from 1920 to the present, lapse time has increased about 2 years, from 8 to 10 years. This increase has taken place despite large increments in Federal fellowship support that were designed partly to accelerate doctorate production. On the other hand, the onset of a war reduces doctorate completion times, but increases them in the post-war period (see the 1940s in Figure 5.10).

Field of study has consistently been related to time required to complete the degree, as Figure 5.10 shows. Graduate educational programs of the different fields of study impose unique requirements in addition to the overall standards of the university as a whole. Eleven to 12 years mean completion time is experienced in such subjects as English Literature, Religion, Arts and Professions, as compared with the relatively brief lapse time in Chemistry and Physical Sciences (7 to 8 years). The subject matter and educational method require differing time spans.

The relationship between work and study also affects the educational process. For example, doctorates in Education typically enter full-time teaching after receiving the baccalaureate. Oriented to the nine-month school year, they may teach during the regular school year and in the summer attend graduate school. This pattern extends their required completion time.

In addition to field of study, institutional transfer to work on the Master's and the Doctor's degrees affects time spent completing the degree. The National Academy of Sciences study has demonstrated, however, that type of undergraduate institution, itself, has no discernable effect upon the length of time required to complete education, considering only those who actually complete the doctorate degree (Harmon and Soldz, 1963: 40-43).

Indecision in choice of careers after receiving baccalaureate delays one's entrance into graduate school (for those who eventually decide upon additional years of study) and, thus, extends the time. The same "hiatus" may follow receipt of the Master's degree, a period during which the individual may further test his decision to continue in a field of study. Finally, one of the most time-consuming hurdles, the doctorate recipient must develop plans, perform research, and write a doctoral dissertation. This requirement introduces an extensive time lapse which some may never overcome. These may become ABD's -- All But Dissertation -- rather than Ph.D.'s.[8/]

Persons completing the doctorate today take more time than former doctorates took, on the average. Depressions and wars seem to exert an influence upon the time required to obtain the doctorate after the baccalaureate. Field of study and the nature of the doctorate training program appear to affect the time needed to obtain the degree. Those interested in reducing time lapse should examine the curricula in fields requiring shorter average time. The compound of work and study making up the socialization program of a field may impose time-consuming conditions that no rearrangement of curriculum requirements can alter.

Trends in Various Specialty Fields: Patterns of Growth

While the general trend since the mid-1950s appears to be "onward and upward," trends are not equally expansive in every field of study. Growth differs among the three levels of degrees and among specialties. To examine these, we turn, now, to some of the typical trends.

Baccalaureate Degrees. There are three major patterns in the trends in baccalaureate degrees:

I. The degrees achieved a peak in 1949-50, declined to a nadir about 1954-55, and then began an unceasing increase (Figure 5.11). This pattern characterizes baccalaureate degrees in the social sciences, in mathematics, in foreign languages, and the total degrees in the life sciences Figures 5.12 and 5.13). It is the basic pattern in most specialty areas in American education, the basic pattern for total Bachelor's degrees, and "unceasing increase" appears to be the projection of most fields for at least the next ten years in the future.

Figure 5.11. Trends in Degrees: Patterns.

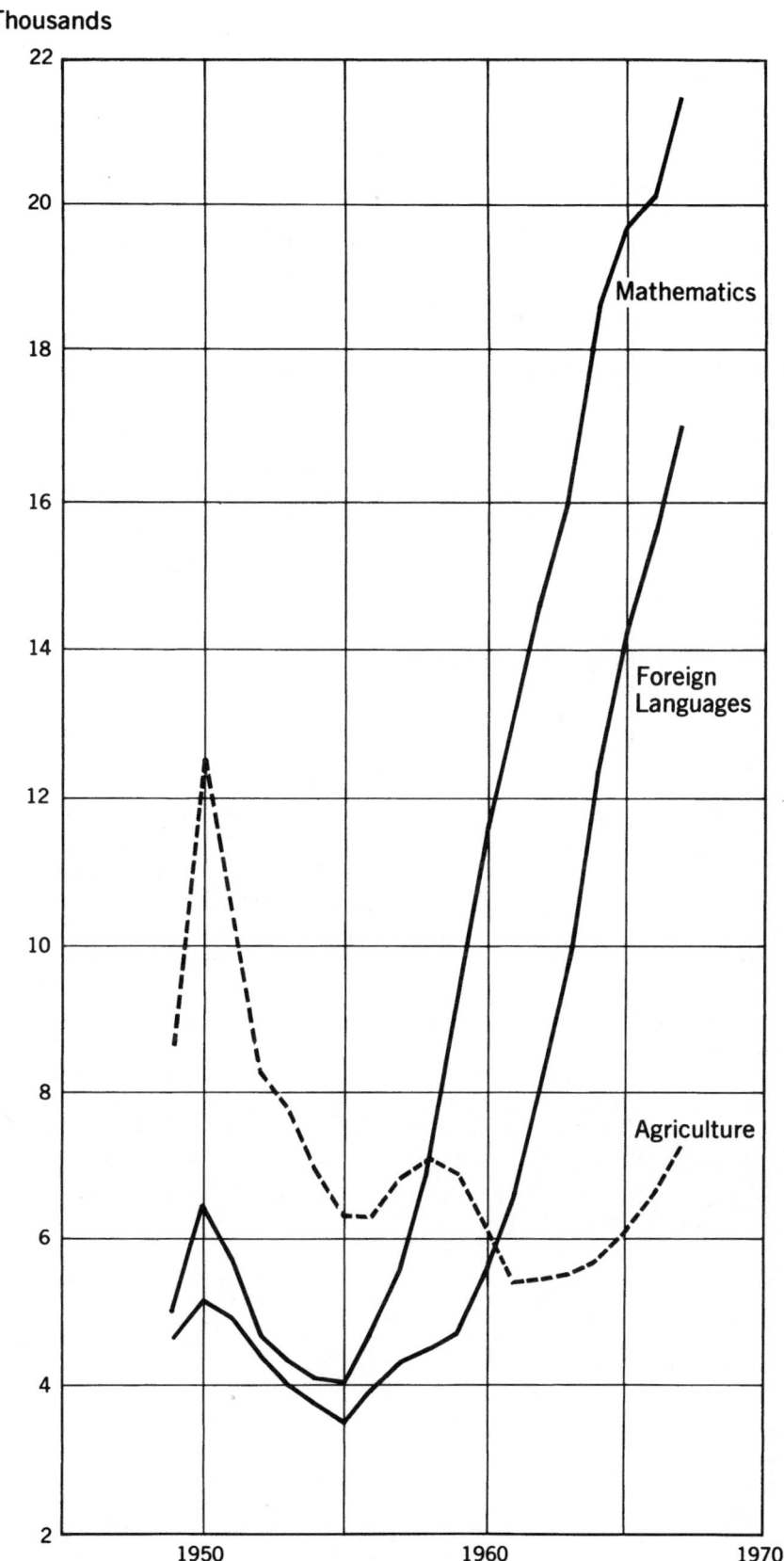

Figure 5.12. Trends in Bachelor's Degrees in Mathematics, Foreign Languages, and Agriculture, 1949–1967.

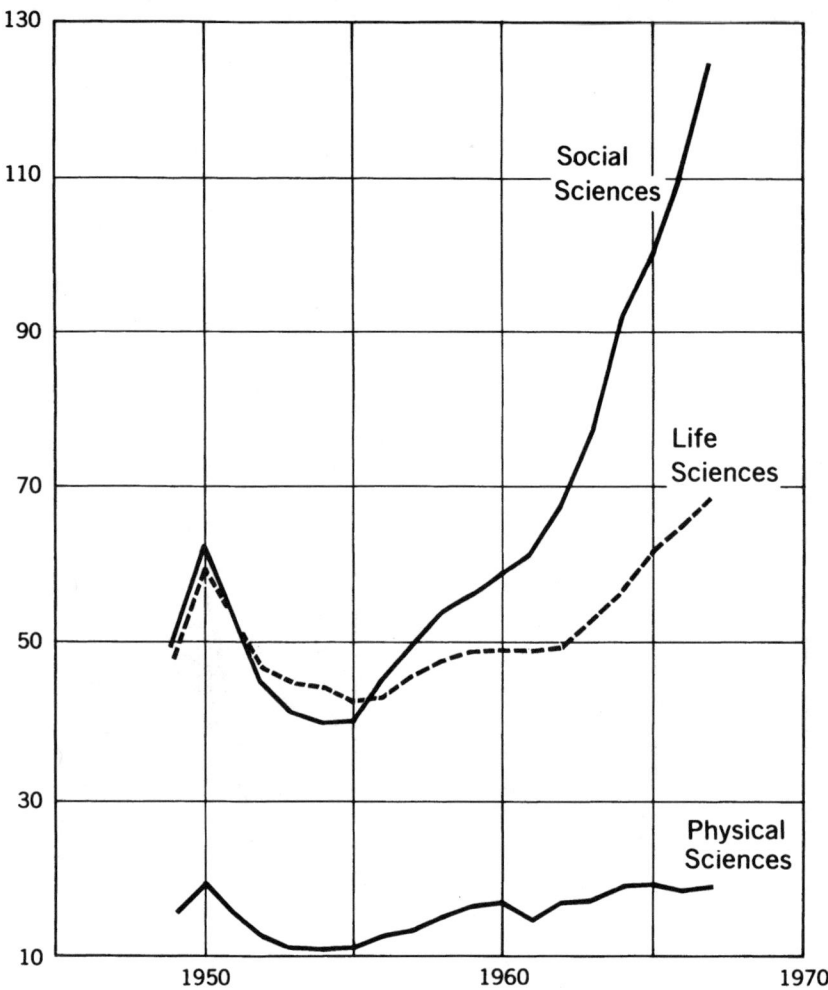

Figure 5.13. Trends in Bachelor's Degrees in Social Sciences, Life Sciences, and Physical Sciences, 1949–1967.

II. The degrees achieved a peak in 1949-50, declined to about 1954-55, then increased to 1964-65, after which there has been a decrease. This characterizes Physical Sciences baccalaureates (Figure 5.13). The decrease, however, may not continue, for degrees are projected to increase. The trend is quite likely to resemble Pattern I.

III. Degrees following this pattern achieved a peak in 1949-50, declined to 1954-55, and then increased and declined successively to lower and lower levels of production. Agriculture and Forestry exemplify this pattern (Figure 5.12). The projections for these fields suggest a continuing decline during the next decade.

Master's Degrees. The only pattern of the above characteristic of Master's degrees is Pattern I, and it must be modified by a very elongated tail. Master's degrees reached a peak one or two years later than Bachelor's degrees: 1950-51 and in some cases 1951-52. The decline that set in after this peak was much smaller than was the case for Bachelor's degrees, but generally the nadir of Master's degrees occurred in the same year as the nadir of Bachelor's degrees. The ascent thereafter of Master's degrees has been equally as swift as Bachelor's degrees and in some cases, proportionally greater (Figures 5.14 and 5.15).

A modification of the above pattern also characterizes some Master's degree fields:

IV. The increase from the nadir of this pattern is a jagged series of increases, each followed by short declines.

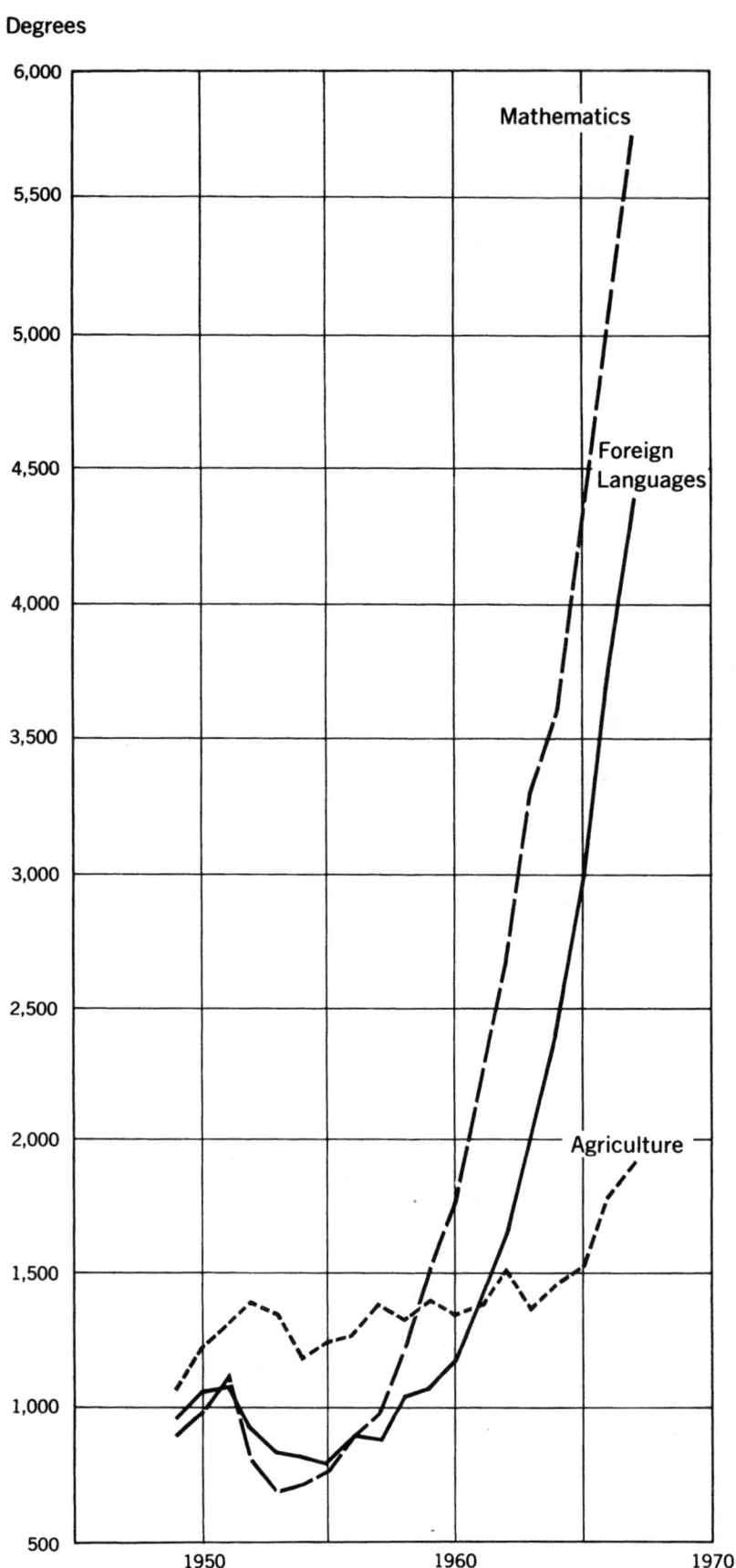

Figure 5.14. Trends in Master's Degrees in Mathematics, Foreign Languages, and Agriculture, 1949–1967.

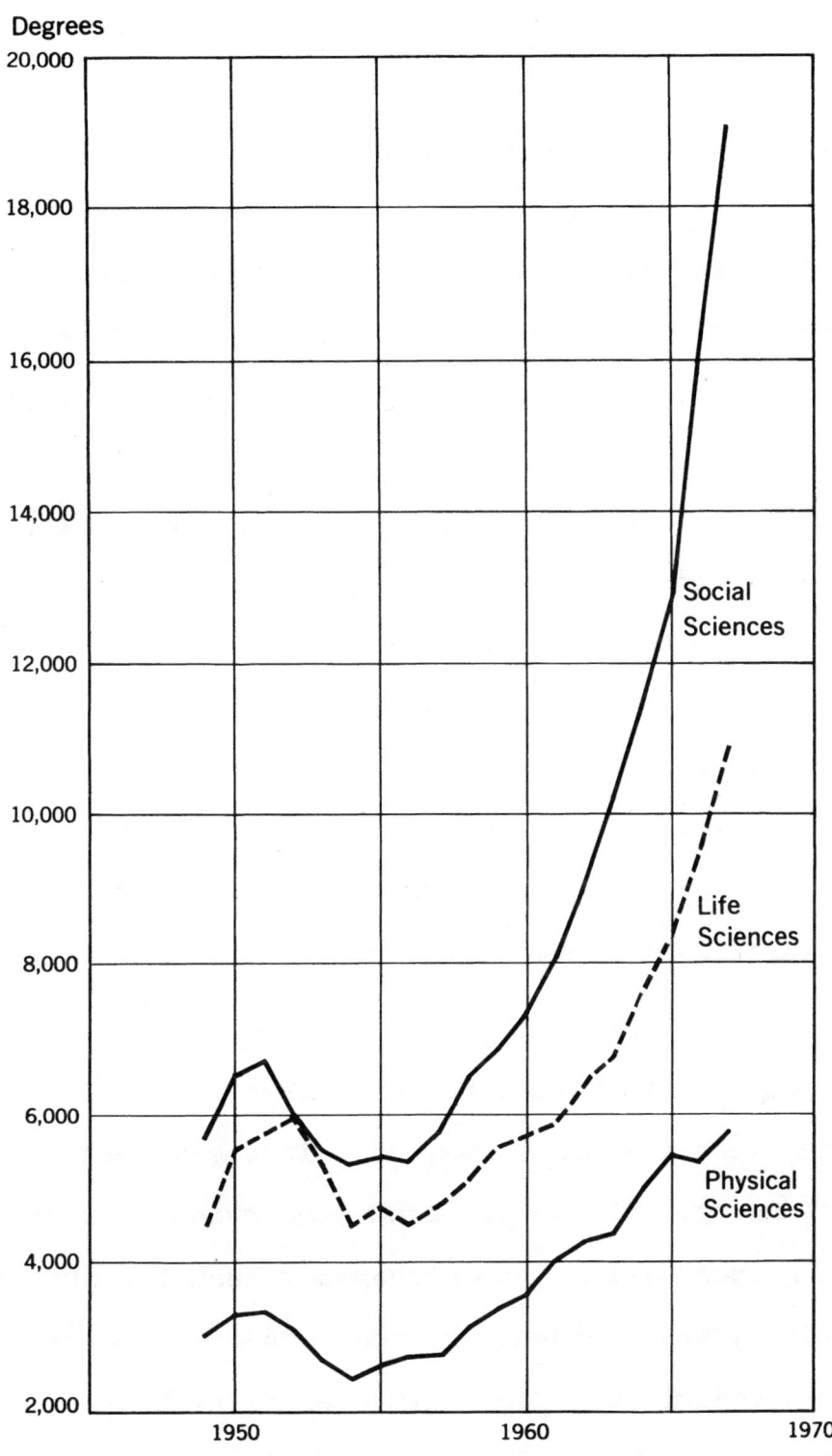

Figure 5.15. Trends in Master's Degrees in Social Sciences, Life Sciences, and Physical Sciences, 1949–1967.

This pattern characterizes Master's degrees in Agriculture (Figure 5.14) and Forestry, Philosophy and Religion, and Social Work. Projections of these fields, however, cannot anticipate such irregular developments, and the projections for these fields, like others, show continued increases.

Doctor's Degrees. Almost uniformly, Doctor's degrees follow a completely different pattern from those described above. This pattern is:

V. This pattern resembles the profile of a seat, coming upward to a plateau, then continuing upward to form the back of a chair[9] (Figures 5.16 and 5.17). This curve shows a temporary interruption in the production of Doctor's degrees during the period 1950-51 to 1957-59, followed by an increase that continues unabated. The primary deviation of Doctor's degrees from the V pattern is Agriculture and Forestry. This area approximately follows Pattern IV.

Projections of Degrees

A projection of degrees to be granted in the future -- say, the next ten years -- provides valuable information for manpower planning. The anticipated production of degrees, by field when compared with the anticipated need for such specialists provides useful guidance to the need for efforts to influence future projection. Many instrumentalities may affect the size of degree classes in particular fields: providing stipends and scholarships to students in the field, supporting faculty research, adding graduate research assistantships and

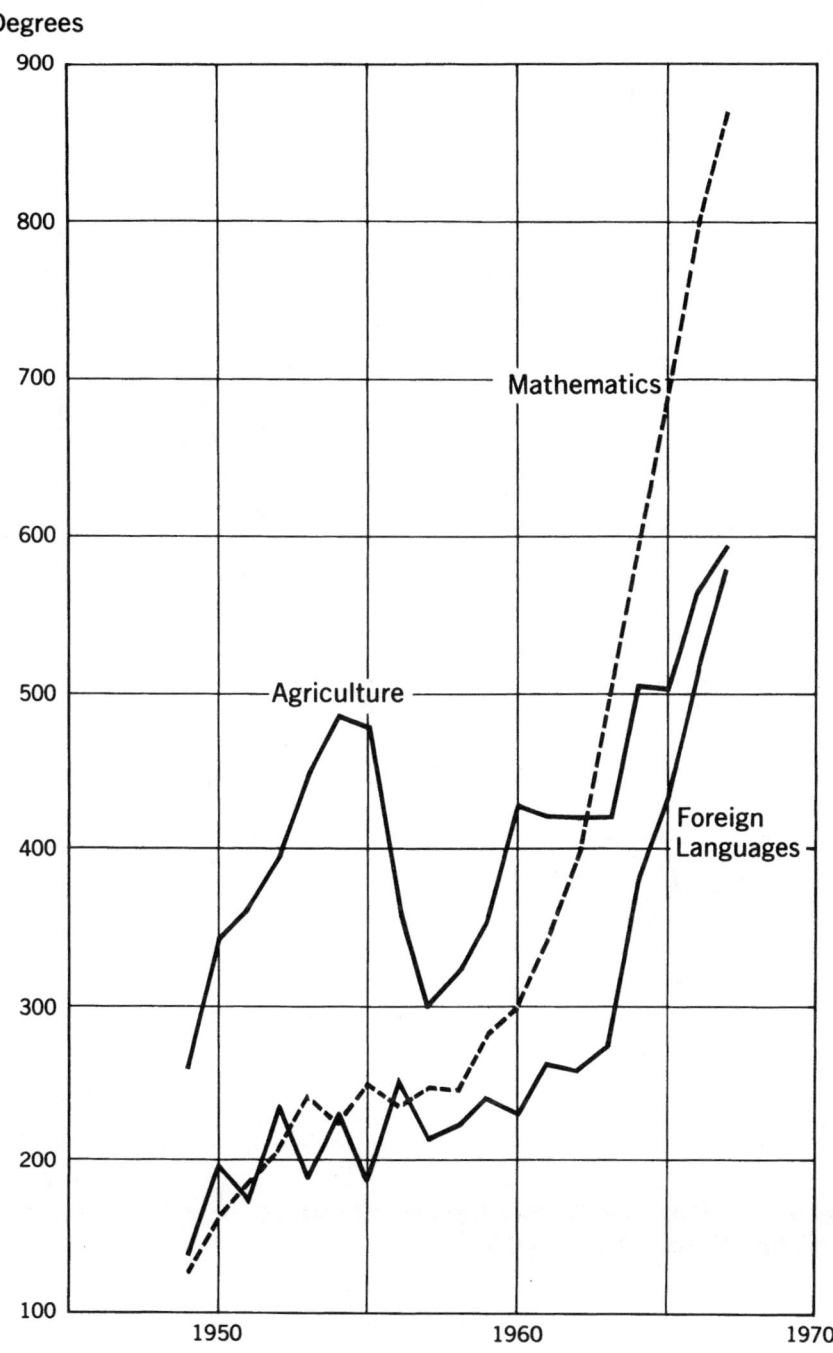

Figure 5.16. Trends in Doctor's Degrees in Mathematics, Foreign Languages, and Agriculture, 1949–1967.

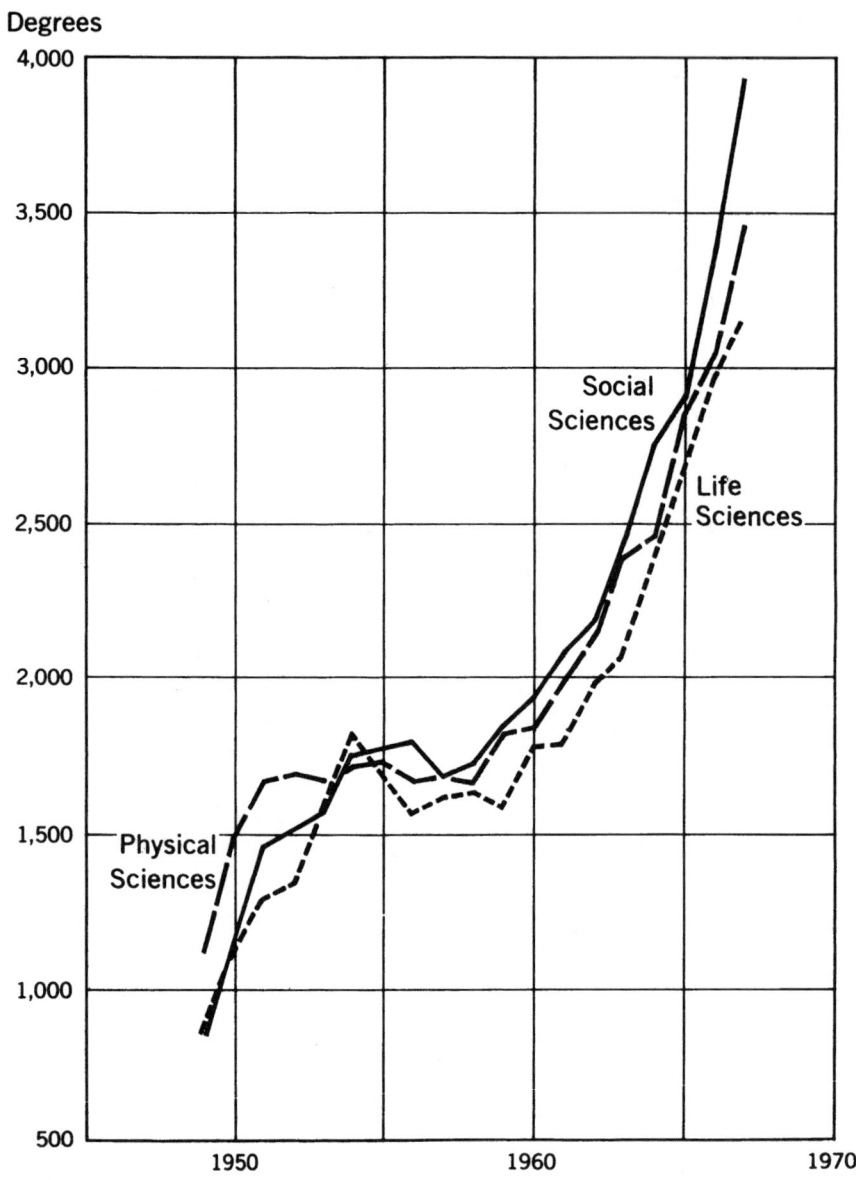

Figure 5.17. Trends in Doctor's Degrees in Social Sciences, Life Sciences, and Physical Sciences, 1949–1967.

teaching assistantships to college faculties, supporting the addition of new departments or colleges in order to increase the number that potentially may be produced, etc. These efforts are made by industries, foundations, and the state and federal government to augment the supply of specialists for the future. To engage in planning of this kind, reliable estimates of the future production of degrees is needed, as well as estimates of the probable demand for specialists.

Estimates of future degree production rest merely upon a continuation of past trends. There are two primary factors that influence these trends: (1) the magnitude of the population group (the age group) that typically receives the degree, and (2) the rate of degree attainment of that age group. While age groups are relatively stable in size from year to year, we sometimes experience changes of large magnitudes. In 1946 and 1947 the birth rate increased to produce 553,000 more births in 1946 than in 1945 and 406,000 more births in 1947 than in 1946. The dynamics of such changes in size of successive age groups, then, obviously will affect degree production. However, experience over the 17 year period ending in 1965 revealed that a change in the rate of degree attainment was a much more important influence upon an increase in degree production than was a change in the magnitude of the age group (see Appendix A). Increases in the rate of attainment of degrees had a greater impact upon the production of Doctor's degrees, somewhat less upon Master's, and least for baccalaureates, for both males and females, but increases in the rates of attainment outweighed by far the effect of increases in the size of the age group typically receiving the degree (Appendix A).

The projected changes in the distribution of degrees at the three levels for males and females, respectively, are presented in Table 5.4 and 5.5. The first row of each table shows the annual increment in the rate of attainment. The increment for baccalaureates is greater than the increment for Master's, and the increment for Doctor's is smallest of the three. The remainder of the table presents the annual increment in the percentage of total degrees by field. The percentage increment of Agriculture, Forestry, and Education are expected to decline among both males and females at each degree level. The percentages of males attaining degrees at each level in the Health Professions are expected to decline. The percentage of male graduate degrees in the Biological Sciences is expected to fall. Among Doctor's degrees received by males, decreases are expected in the proportions for all fields, except and to the advantage of Mathematics and Statistics, Engineering, Fine Arts, and Philosophy and Religion. The rates for all other doctorate fields are expected to decline among males. At the Bachelor's and Master's levels for both male and female, increases are expected among the Humanities and the Social Sciences: English and Journalism, Foreign Languages, Psychology, and the Social Sciences. Conversely, decreases are expected in Philosophy and Religion and the Fine Arts.

Table 5.4 Annual Increments of Change Used by the U. S. Office of Education to Project Degrees to 1976-77, Males

	Annual Change in Percent of Degrees		
	Baccalaureate	Master's	Doctor's
Total Degrees	0.33 [a]	0.24 [b]	0.049 [c]
Mathematics & Statistics	0.38	0.35	0.18
Engineering	-0.25	0.46	0.72
Physical Sciences	0.10	0.018	-0.18
Biological Sciences	0.091	-0.027	-0.12
Agriculture & Forestry	-0.16	-0.16	-0.045
Health Professions	-0.22	-0.064	-0.073
Science, Gen. Program	0.024	0.082	0
Fine Arts	-0.036	-0.15	0.036
Philosophy and Religion	-0.018	-0.0091	0.036
English and Journalism	0.073	0.055	-0.036
Foreign Languages	0.073	0.045	-0.027
Psychology	0.13	0.045	-0.064
Social Sciences	0.40	0.21	-0.12
Education	-0.064	-0.92	-0.20
Library Science	0	0.021	0
Social Work	0.018	0.019	0.0091
Other	-0.40	0.064	-0.018

See Text.

[a] This is the annual change in the percent of the male population 18 years of age four years earlier, expected to receive the baccalaureate degree.

[b] The same as (a), for Master's degrees, based upon 18-year-olds 6 years earlier.

[c] The same as (a), for Doctor's degrees, based upon 18-year-olds 9 years earlier.

Table 5.5 Annual Increments of Change Used by the U. S. Office of Education to Project Degrees to 1976-77, Females

	Annual Change in Percent of Degrees		
	Baccalaureate	Master's	Doctor's
Total Degrees	0.46[a]	0.0845[b]	0.0069[c]
Mathematics & Statistics	0.22	0.18	0.12
Engineering	0	0	0.082
Physical Sciences	-0.018	0.055	0
Biological Sciences	0.12	0.17	0.0091
Agriculture & Forestry	0	0	-0.045
Health Professions	-0.2	0.073	0.018
Science, General Program	0.0055	0.032	0
Fine Arts	-0.082	0.036	0.018
Philosophy and Religion	-0.027	-0.0091	0.045
English & Journalism	0.37	0.43	0.15
Foreign Languages	0.28	0.26	-0.036
Psychology	0.045	0.082	0.35
Social Sciences	0.28	0.21	-0.036
Education	-0.3	-1.56	-0.37
Library Science	-0.0091	0.15	0
Social Work	0.018	0.041	0.055
Other	-0.59	-0.055	-0.073

See notes to Table 5.4, and text.

While these changes in the percentage distribution of degrees, by sex, are expected, it should not be implied that a decrease in the absolute number attaining the degree in these (negative) fields is ahead of us. Because of the increase in the size of the cohorts receiving degrees, increases in absolute numbers of degrees are expected in 1976-77 over 1966-67, for all the 17 degree categories and for each of the three levels, except Bachelor's and Master's degrees in Agriculture and Forestry and Doctor's degrees in the Health Professions, the latter referring to Ph.D. degrees, not M.D. degrees.

An Academic Production Index

Tracing the production of the higher educational system would be facilitated by a statistic that summarizes in a single measure the total production of degrees of all levels. To illustrate the utility of such an approach, an experimental index was developed (see Appendix B). While the method used is not the only approach to compiling a summary measure of academic production, it does produce a statistical series reflecting the total output of degrees from higher education. The statistic may be related to enrollment, expenditures, student aid, faculty, and other aspects of higher education, and it provides a basis for comparing the trends in aggregate production of various specialty fields and areas.

The gross Academic Production Index offers an index to shifting academic production. The measure is roughly proportional to the years of education that end in a given year by the award of a degree. Generally, an increase in API will lead to an increase in the average educational attainment of the population. It may be used to construct other indices, such as expenditures per API, or the Academic Production Index per dollar spent. Thus, it may be related to expenditures for student aid, to enrollment, to faculty, to the number graduating, or to various population categories, such as the labor force. In addition to this gross measure, API may be computed for various fields, by sex, for states or geographic regions, and even for each institution by sex and field.

The Gross API. Figure 5.18 presents the Gross API for all fields. The curve follows the previously-described pattern of degrees. Following the peak year of production of degrees, 1949-50, production declined for four successive years at an average annual rate of -.065. 1954-55 was the turning point, and during the ten years thereafter, the API has increased at an average rate of 0.57 per year.

The school years ending 1968 and 1969 will see abrupt increases in the rate of change of the Academic Production Index, the reasons for this increase in rate having been reviewed, above. Thereafter, however, for the next decade the rate of increase in API will be low and fairly constant, at about 4 percent per annum. At this steady increase the gross API which was 813,000 for 1964-65, will have doubled to 1,600,000 by 1976-77. These future estimates are based upon U. S. Office of Education projections (Simon and Fullam, 1968).

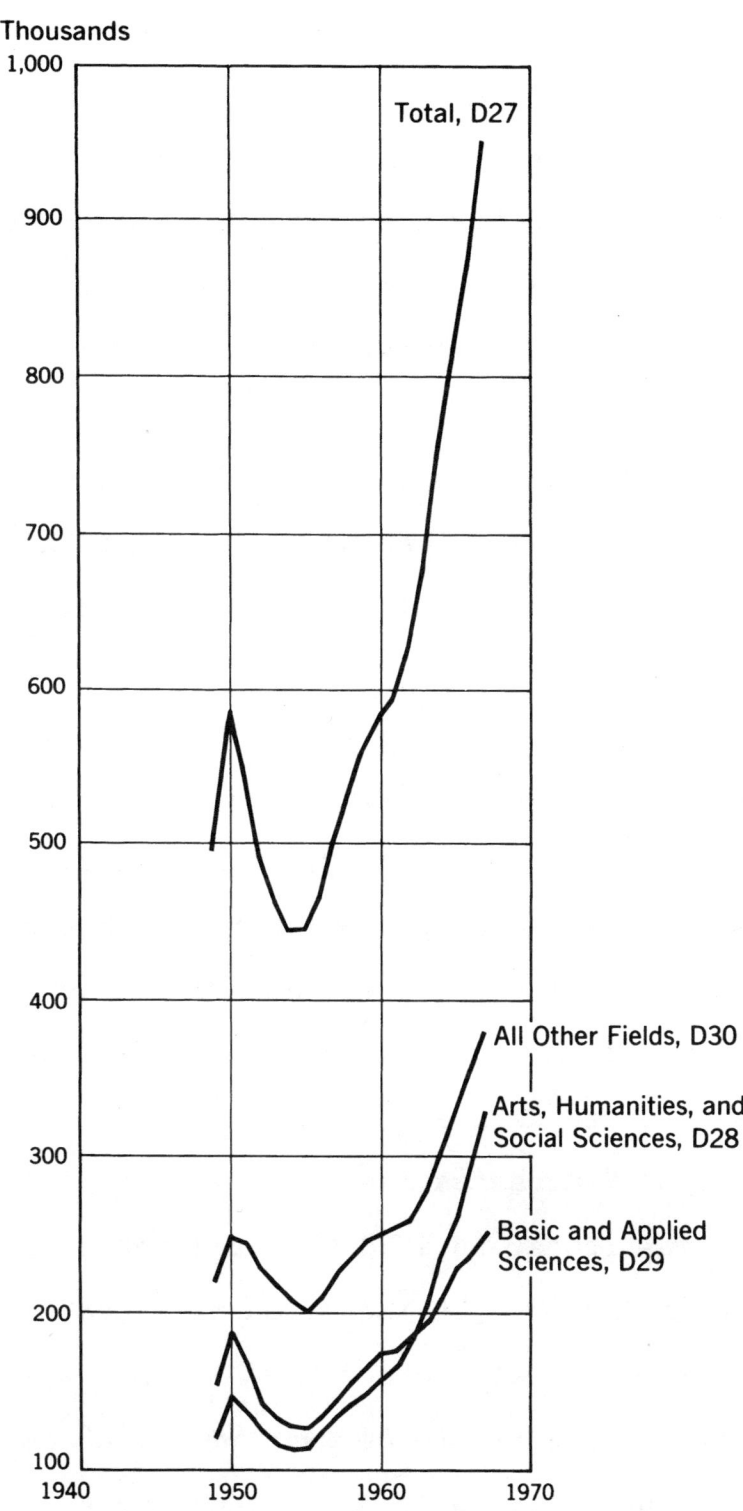

Figure 5.18. Academic Production Index: Grand Total, Series D27; Total Arts, Humanities and Social Sciences, Series D28; Total Basic and Applied Sciences, Series D29; and All Other Fields, Series D30, 1949–1967.

In addition to total API for all fields, Figure 5.18 presents the aggregate API for the Basic and Applied Sciences, the aggregate of Arts, Humanities, and the Social Sciences, and the aggregate of All Other Fields. These curves follow approximately the same pattern as Total API, with the slight modification in the steepness of the elongated arm that begins in 1954.

A few ratios based upon API will be presented, measures suggesting approaches to assessing trends in higher education. This discussion merely will attempt to illustrate a few possibilities.

API per Graduate. An API per graduate value of one would mean that all graduates received the 4-year Bachelor's degree. Any value of API per graduate greater than one, consequently, reflects the presence of degrees with weights greater than one, such as Master's degrees. As API per 100 graduates changes, it reflects variations in the relative number receiving advanced degrees.

Figure 5.19 presents the Total API per 100 graduates, a curve that was lowest in 1950 when a large class of baccalaueates were graduated. It increased to a peak in 1955, a point when the level of most degrees was low but when the "mix" of graduate and baccalaureate degrees was such as to produce a maximum per capita value in API per graduate. Following this peak, API per 100 graduates declined to approximately 120-122, where it has steadily remained. To the extent that graduate

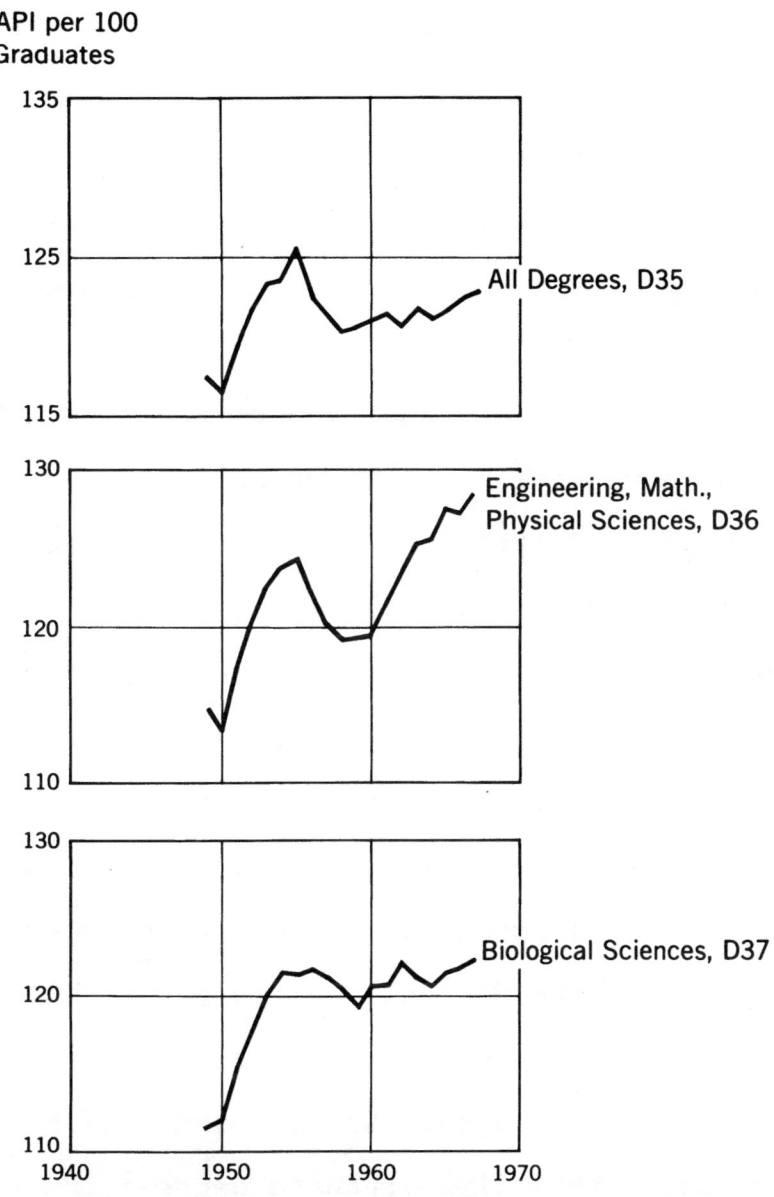

Figure 5.19. Academic Production Index per 100 Graduates, 1949–1967, Series D35–D37.

students increase proportionately within the total student body of higher education, and to the extent that 5-year and 6-year professional degrees increase relative to 4-year baccalaureate degrees, this API index will increase. A gradual increase in Total API per 100 graduate students would seem to be the picture in the future.

The Health Professions produce a higher API per 100 graduates than any other combination of fields. This is because of the large production of medical doctors among degrees in the Health Professions. The value of the index for the Health Professions has been steadily declining, and appears to be going in the direction of 140 API per 100 graduates. This is due to the increasing numbers of first-level degrees being granted relative to higher degrees.

The Physical Sciences, including Engineering and Mathematics, produces the next highest index per 100 graduates. The curve has followed the same trend as the Total API per 100 graduates, reaching a peak in 1955 and declining to about 1960. However, after that time graduate degrees increased relative to Bachelor's degrees and the index began to rise and the rise continues. The future will undoubtedly see a continued increase in this index.

Biological Sciences have followed a different course. They reached a high point in 1954 of slightly more than 121 and have remained at about that level since. The prospects are that this index will increase slightly during the next few years and then remain fairly constant for the remainder of the coming decade.

The Social Sciences, exclusive of Social Work, reached a peak, like the others, in 1955. After declining to 1957, the index for the Social Sciences has remained fairly constant. U. S. Office of Education projections of degrees indicate that the Social Science API will hold its own and increase one or two points by 1977.

The field of Education has followed the same trend as the Social Sciences, except in 1962 when the index dipped to 120, only to rebound the following year and continue its former level. Projections foresee the Education API declining 3 or 4 points to 1977.

As the proportion of graduate degrees to total degrees in a field continues to increase, the API for that field will increase. In fields with a strong demand for highly trained professionals, such as physicists or chemists, the API per graduate is likely to increase. In those fields wherein the primary demand for the specialty comes from educational institutions, the API per graduate is not likely to increase greatly, for the increases in graduate degrees is likely to remain proportional to the increases in undergraduate degrees.

For any single field, there may be a characteristic value for the API per graduate around which it does not deviate greatly, as, for example, Social Work or Library Science, whose balance among levels of degrees is likely to remain fairly constant. For any particular field there may be a minimum value of API per graduate below which the index should not fall in the interest of maintaining an adequately qualified workforce. A criterion for establishing this value is the number of vacant positions that require the specialty. Vacant positions provide an index that reflects an inadequate supply. Thus, the minimum value of API per graduate for a field would be the value that keeps vacant positions near zero.

Another criterion might be the level of educational attainment of those who occupy positions in the field. To illustrate this, a time series of API per graduate in a field will bear some relation to the proportion employed in the field who hold Master's degrees and who hold Doctor's degrees. As the API per graduate declines, the proportion employed who hold higher degrees might be expected to decline, also. Such a clue to the quality of employees in a field is complicated by intersectoral transfers, as between industry and the academy. There is a dirth of systematic and periodically collected information on the quality of personnel employed in a specialty.

<u>Enrollment per API</u>. Increases in enrollment, of course, generate increases in degrees after the period of time required to complete the requirements for the degree. Similarly, decreases in enrollment herald a decline in degrees. The current student enrollment divided by the current API provides an index to a change in API several years in advance. Illustrations of this effect are best observed by comparing the trend in gross API in Figure 5.18 with the graph of enrollment per

API in Figure 5.20. Enrollment per API dropped between 1949 and 1950, and it was followed by a decrease, 1951-1954, in gross API. The first appreciable rise in enrollment per API was between 1952 and 1953; gross API did not begin to rise until 1956. Thus, the ratio of enrollment per API provides a "herald" indicator, two to three years in advance, of a change in API.

Faculty per API. Faculty per 100 API increased during the first half of the 1950s, as shown in Figure 5.21, when API was declining and enrollments were decreasing slightly. By 1956, however, the size of college and staffs and degree production had found an adjustment and the ratio has deviated little from it since. It would appear that 67 or 68 faculty members are required to staff universities and colleges for the production of 100 API. At this rate, college and university staffs will be 1,076,000 in 1977. This compares with an Office of Education projection of 1,006,000 prepared by more rigorous methods (Simon and Fullam, 1968).

API per Faculty Member. The inverse of the above, the API per faculty member, shown below for every other year, has been steadily declining from the peak 1949-50 production year. As colleges and universities have assumed more non-teaching functions, the number of faculty has approximately doubled (to 1963-64) while the net increase in API has been 28 percent. As a result, the API per faculty member has remained fairly constant for the 10 years preceding 1964, at approximately 1.5.

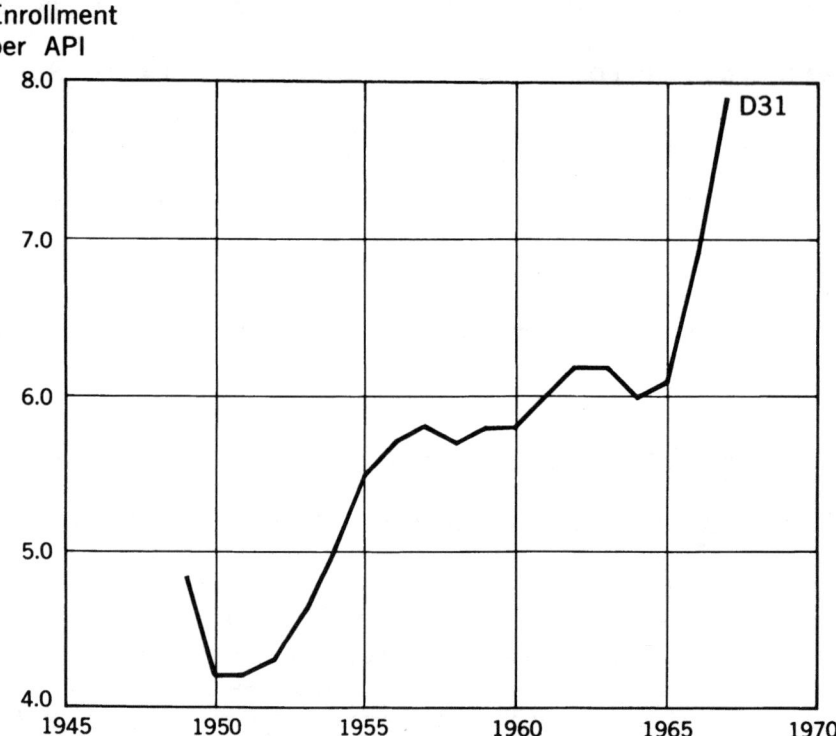

Figure 5.20. Student Enrollment Related to Academic Production Index, 1949–1967, Series D31.

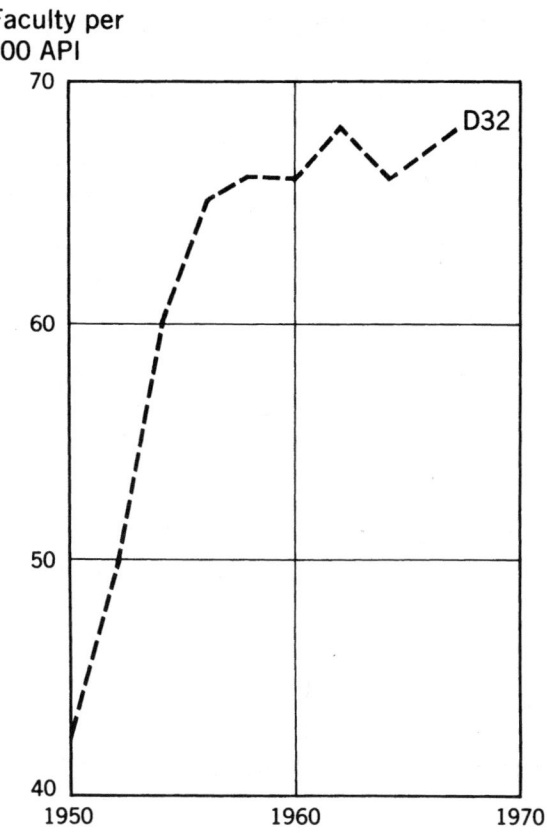

Figure 5.2l. Higher Education Faculty Related to Academic Production Index, 1950–1967, Series D32.

As the proportion of baccalaureates increases, the API per faculty member also may slightly increases.

	API per Faculty Member
1949-50	2.34
1951-52	2.00
1953-54	1.65
1955-56	1.54
1957-58	1.52
1959-60	1.52
1961-62	1.47
1963-64	1.51

Student Aid per API. Student aid per API, expressed in constant (1958) dollars, has been continuously increasing since 1952, as seen in Figure 5.22. The rate of increase, however, may slow down. This index may decline during 1968 and 1969, when larger proportions of baccalaureates will be granted, but thereafter, as larger proportions of students register as graduate students, it undoubtedly will increase.

Higher Education Expenditures per API. Figure 5.23 presents current expenditure by institutions of higher education per API. Expenditures are expressed in thousands of constant (1958) dollars. While the API Index, itself, declined approximately one-fifth, 1950 to 1956, the higher education expenditures per API increased approximately two-thirds. However, over the entire period, 1950 to 1966, API increased 50 percent while expenditures per API increased 164 percent. Absolute expenditures went up 23 percent, 1950-55, and increased

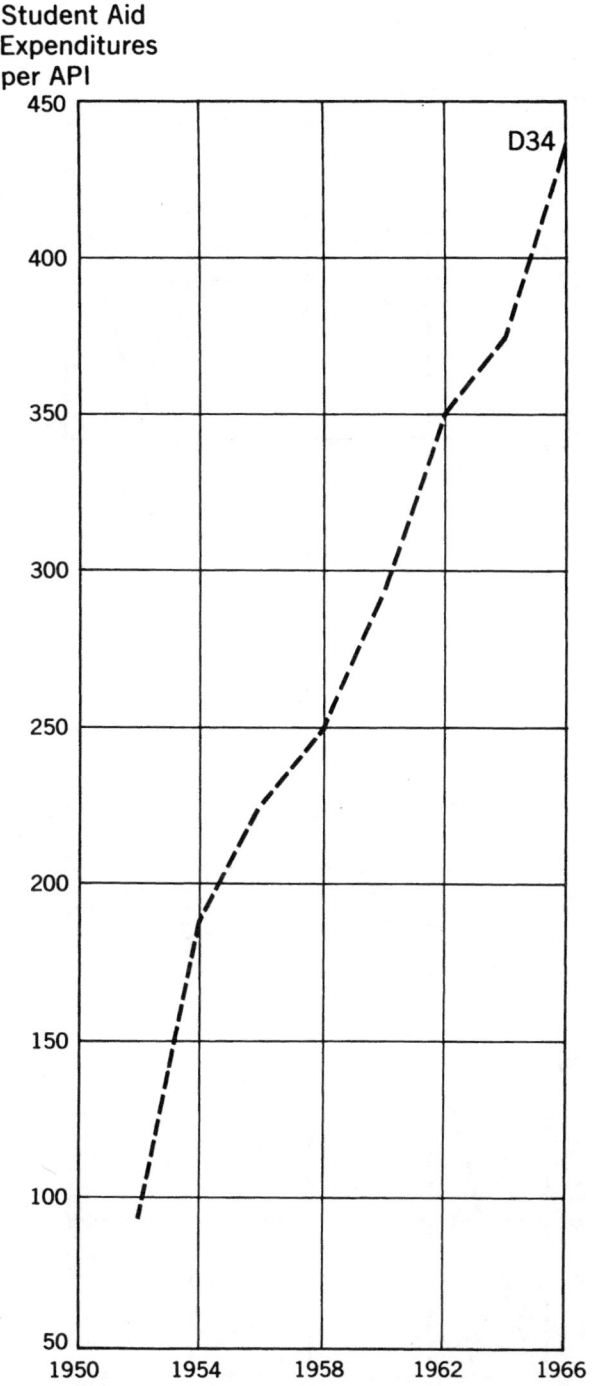

Figure 5.22. Student Aid Expenditures Related to Academic Production Index (in Constant 1958 Dollars), 1952–1966, Series D34.

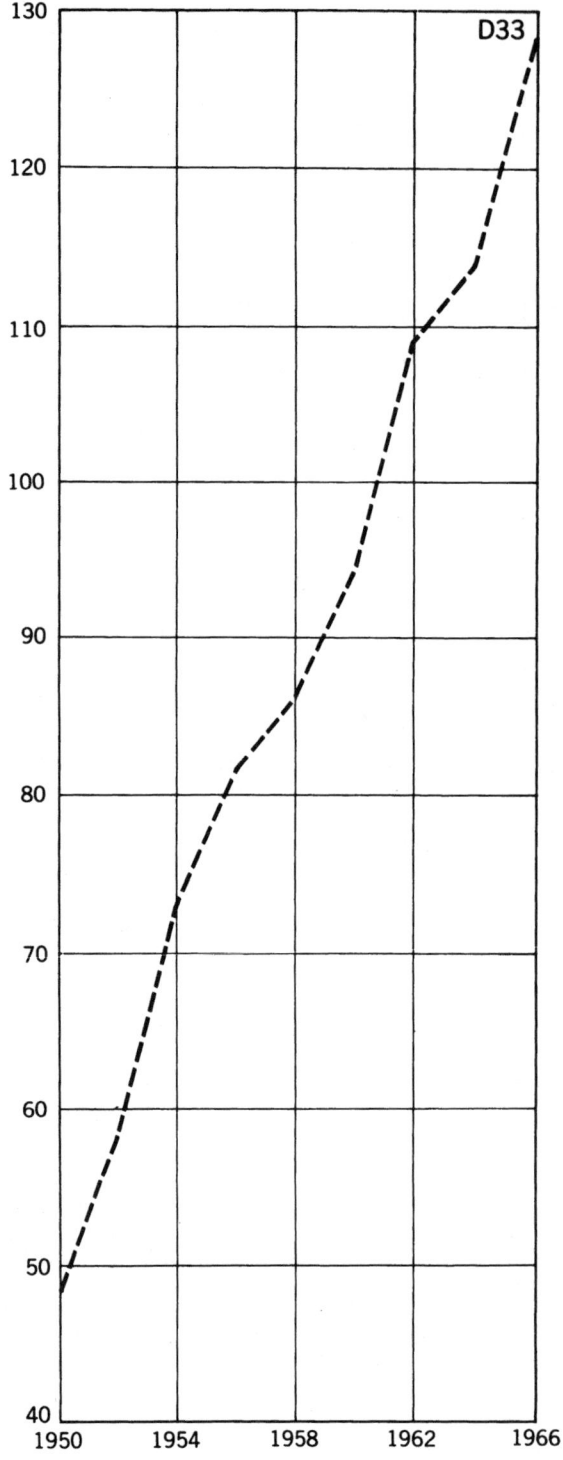

Figure 5.23. Expenditures in Higher Education Related to Academic Production Index (in Constant 1958 Dollars), 1950–1966, Series D33.

53 percent, 1955-65. While expenditures, gross as well as per API, are associated with increases in degree production, an increase in current fund expenditures would not necessarily increase academic production. A direct investment in scholarships and fellowships may have a more obvious influence upon academic production. Demographic factors and retention rates, also, exert an influence upon production.

Suggestions for Improving Data on Graduates

In examining available data on graduates, a few areas for improving the data systems were identified. In some instances the utility of the data would be vastly increased by altering the reporting procedure or augmenting the information assembled. In some instances the use of sampling would make it possible to add to the data assembled, sometimes at lower cost. These suggestions will now be reviewed.

1. *Quality of the "Product."* No information is assembled that classifies the degree according to some quality standard: the quality of performance of the individual, the quality of the program from which graduated, or the quality of the institution. Such an evaluation, over time, would give us trends indicative of strong and weak points in the system and would be a basis for program development at both the institutional, (school) system, and national levels.

To illustrate possibilities:

(a) A distribution of graduates by grade point average, with institutional distributions adjusted to a common standard through a periodic evaluation procedure.[10]

(b) A distribution of graduates by the character of the program from which graduated might be based upon a system of classifying programs, separately developed for each field. Programs also could be "certified," as is now done for undergraduate chemistry programs, as meeting some standard. High school graduates might be classified according to the program of instruction (vocational, college preparatory, etc.).

(c) Graduates might be assigned to "quality" classes upon the basis of a general evaluation of the institution (see Cartter: 1966, for such an evaluation of graduate programs).

2. <u>Characteristics of the Graduate</u>. In addition to some qualitative assessment of the graduate, suggested above, a variety of other characteristics could be identified that would enable more specific tracings of trends of the educational system. The National Academy of Sciences-National Research Council annually assembles information on the population of doctorate recipients (National Academy of Sciences, 1967). The data accumulated has been used in a variety of definitive studies of doctorate recipients, including follow-up studies of the person's eventual work, income, place of residence, etc. Similar data accumulations could be used to improve knowledge of Master's degree holders and baccalaureates.

3. <u>Geographic Origins and Destinations</u>. The present reporting system does not designate whether the recipient is a native or foreign citizen, whether the graduate may be considered an increment of competence for the United States or for

some foreign country, except for doctorate degrees, as was mentioned above. The characteristics of enrollees suggest that some fields have more foreign students in them than others. Among graduate students, such fields as chemical engineering, agriculture, genetics, pathology, and economics have unusually large proportions of foreign students enrolled. Annual information on graduates from foreign countries with an indication of the country of their post-graduation location would provide a basis for knowledge of the geographic "impact" of the educational system.[11]

In a similar manner, data should be assembled on the educational experiences of United States citizens attending in foreign countries.

4. <u>The Classification of Fields</u>. In a society where the division of labor becomes more and more specialized, knowledge, also, has been organized into increasingly differentiated categories. The number of degrees granted by field has been assembled annually since 1947-48 by the U. S. Office of Education. The categories for reporting degrees has increased from 67 (1947-48) to 160 (1955-56) and to 212 (1964-65). This threefold increase in degree categories reflects not merely the feasibility of more detailed reporting by virtue of a greater number of degrees being granted but also the successive elaboration of the curriculum. The expanding curriculum is the product of the ever-increasing differentiation of specialists in the occupational structure.

The continuing elaboration of categories, however, renders difficult the problem of tracing trends of a field over time. Continuing study of the fields of specialization of higher educational institutions is needed in order to systematically augment the classification scheme, as needed to more accurately report the content of the degree and also enable the collapsing of categories to the earlier set for the delineation of trends.

A Note on Sampling. For some purposes information on individual institutions is required. For example, the Fall Enrollment Survey conducted by the U. S. Office of Education provides information of wide interest among educators on the enrollment in individual institutions as well as information on total enrollment. Not all informational needs, consequently, may be served by sample surveys. However, other interests may be more suitably served at lower cost through sample surveys. The Office of Education has used sample surveys to collect much of its data, but these typically have not been repetitive surveys of the type that produce statistical time series. The use of sampling for this purpose is highly advisable. In particular, much of the data suggested above on graduates could be assembled in this manner. An institutional sample of each major institutional type, including each level of education, would form the basis for developing educational indicators of the system that, at present, is possible only on an occasional basis.[12]

Footnotes

1/ The U. S. Office of Education presents the general trends in earned degrees conferred from 1947-48 to 1962-63 (Wright, 1965). Trends for the past 10 years and future projections are presented by field by Simon and Fullam (1968).

2/ These shifts are documented by Trow (1961). The dates of his phases differ slightly from those here presented: Trow's Phase II, for example, is roughly between 1910 and 1940. However, there is no precise delineation of these stages, nor is one possible.

3/ One important sector of "mass" higher education, the Junior College, made modest increases in enrollment during the 1930s and increased along with other elements of higher education after 1946. These increases in enrollment in the 1940s and 1950s, however, were small compared with the strides approximating annual increases of 200,000 enrollees, made by junior colleges during the 1960s. An accounting of certificates awarded and Arts degrees granted by junior colleges has not been uniformly made to provide a series on junior college production (National Science Foundation, 1967a:48). Enrollment data, however, indicate that the junior college of the 1960s began to assume a significant share of the "mass" education mentioned in the text.

4/ In its procedure of projecting first-time opening fall enrollment and degrees, the U. S. Office of Education uses the 18-year-old population, by sex. However, the first-time enrollment is calculated separately for various types of institutions, and the degrees are separately generated with a 4-year time lag. In short, each projection is a function of the numbers annually achieving 18 years of age, each sex separately considered. However, degrees are not projected as a function of enrollment (Simon and Fullam, 1966: 89-102).

5/ The contrast in these two trends is best made by comparing their angle of inclination:

$$1919 - 1940 \quad 51°$$
$$1954 - 1967 \quad 74°$$

This comparison is not influenced by the differences in magnitude of the denominator of the successive rates of change. For example, the rate of change averaged 6.5 percent per year and 4.8 percent per year, respectively, during the two periods.

6/ During the period 1924 to 1956 the data must be presented biennially; consequently, the series lacks the continuity of other years.

7/ The U. S. Office of Education projections (Simon and Fullam, 1968: 95-102) are developed through a two-stage procedure, (1) of projecting total degrees, by sex, by regressing a rate of attainment of the 18 year olds, with a lag in years, on time, and (2) by allocating the total degrees by field through regressing the percentage for each field on time.

8/ A 1963 study found that 22 percent of the non-doctorate teachers in four-year institutions were ABD's (Dunham, Wright, and Chandler, 1966: 70-71).

<u>9</u>/ It is a mathematical function resembling $f(x) = x^3$ with the zero-point and the axis set at about 1953-54.

<u>10</u>/ Davis (1964: 256-268) developed an Academic Performance Index for college graduates upon the basis of their approximate average letter grade and an evaluation of school quality. His procedure, however, reduces nine categories of GPA to three categories with consequent loss of precision of classification.

<u>11</u>/ Information on enrollment of foreigners in the United States is assembled by the Institute of International Education (1966).

<u>12</u>/ The American Council on Education has initiated periodic studies of higher education. See: Astin, Panos and Creager (1966); Creager (1968).

6

Trends in Educational Organization and Finance

This chapter reviews trends in the number of formal organizations, schools and institutions of higher education, which serve the purposes of education. It also reviews the trends in their financial support.

The decline in the small, one-teacher school, the increase in the size of school systems and in the average size of public schools, are probably trends that parallel the urbanization of the population and the growth in size of organizational units of every description. Great increases in the length of the regular school term of public elementary and secondary schools have occurred in the past 100 years. Changes in the number of higher educational institutions of various types have not been spectacular, even though the junior college and the community college have increasingly shown a capacity to meet the educational needs of a growing student population.

This chapter also reviews the revenues and expenditures of public elementary and secondary schools and of institutions of higher education. Revenues are broken down by source and are shown as a percentage of the Gross National Product. Expenditures are expressed by purpose and in terms of students, faculty, or schools, whichever base appears appropriate for interpreting the object of the expenditure. Expenditures are expressed in constant 1958 dollars to provide a basis for evaluating their relative as well as their absolute increase.

The Number of Institutions by Type

Some types of educational institutions have been increasing in number while others have been decreasing. The lower educational level -- elementary schools -- have become fewer and fewer (Series C1) while each unit has increased in size. On the other hand, higher educational institutions -- colleges -- have increased in number and also have become larger (Series F1-F14). The first of these trends is illustrated in Figure 6.1, showing the sharp decrease in the number of public elementary schools and the simultaneous decline in the percentage of public elementary schools with only one teacher. One-teacher and small schools have been consolidated into larger units. The population still is sufficiently dispersed to maintain nearly 10,000 one-teacher schools, but this is only about 9 percent of all public elementary schools. To the extent that our population remains dispersed, we undoubtedly will continue to have some one-teacher schools.

The reorganization of public elementary schools has been a remarkable feat. While the number of schools was reduced by two-thirds -- from 238,000 in 1930 to 73,000 in 1966 -- the population served by them increased nearly 60 percent to over 36 million children (Series I4). The change occurred, of course, as the population moved to urban centers, the small elementary

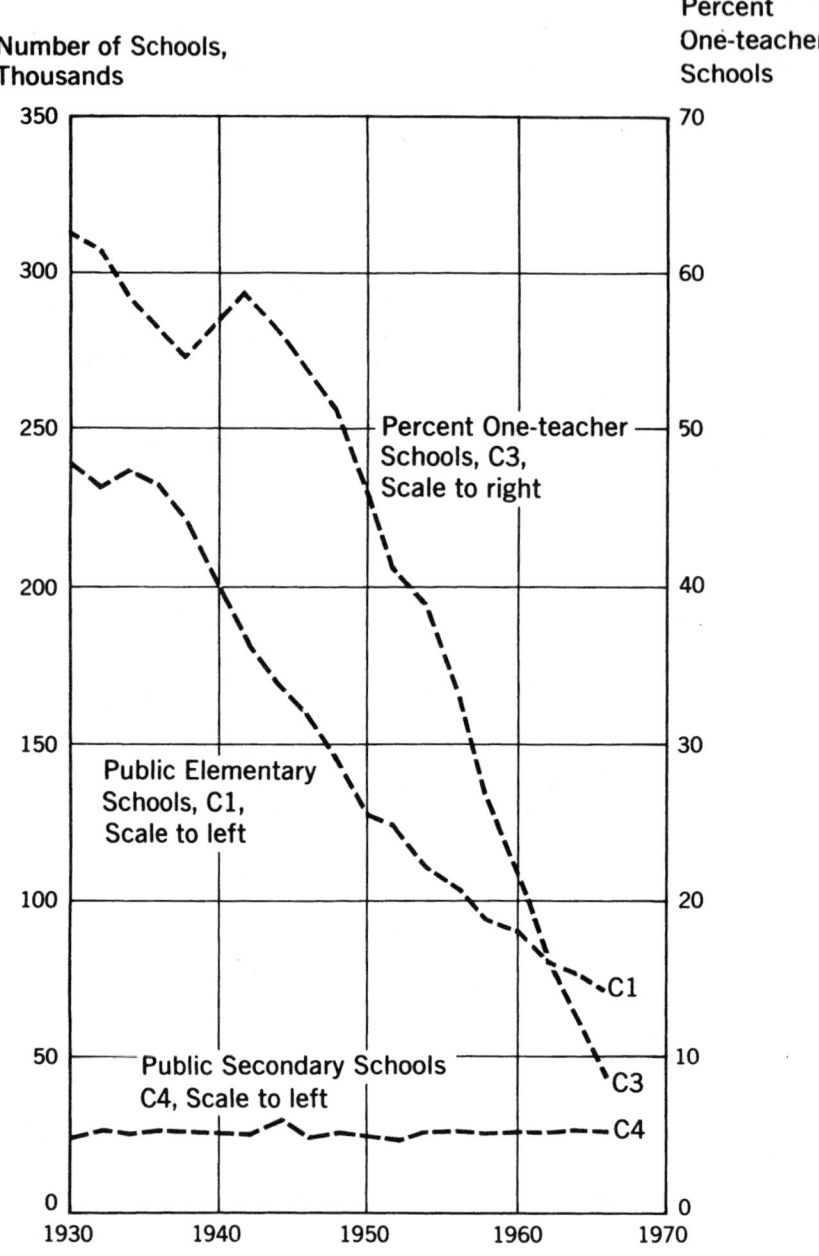

Figure 6.1. Number of Public Elementary and Secondary Schools, and the Percent One-teacher Schools, 1930–1966, Series C1, C3, C4.

schools closing their doors and larger, consolidated ones being built in villages and urban places.

Public secondary schools (C4) have followed the same course of consolidation and reorganization, but their number has remained more stable as the unit size has increased.

As consolidation increased the average size of schools and reduced the number of elementary schools, the length of the school term and the average number of days attended per pupil enrolled have increased (Figure 6.2, Series C5 and C6). This increase in time devoted to studies, per year, represents a real gain to the system.

Size of School Systems

The number of school systems, public administrative units containing one or more schools, has increased in size over the ten year period, 1956 to 1966.[1/] Systems with enrollments of 3,000 or more pupils encompassed 63 percent of public school enrollment in 1956. By 1966 this had increased to 75 percent (Table 6.1). As systems with larger enrollment have increased in size, the smaller systems have become fewer. Enrollment, however, has dwindled only in the two smallest systems (with one or two schools). These changes partly reflect the increasing urbanization of the population and partly, administrative reorganization of school systems in rural and urban areas.

The trend in the number of schools within school systems are presented in Table 6.2. The number of separate schools

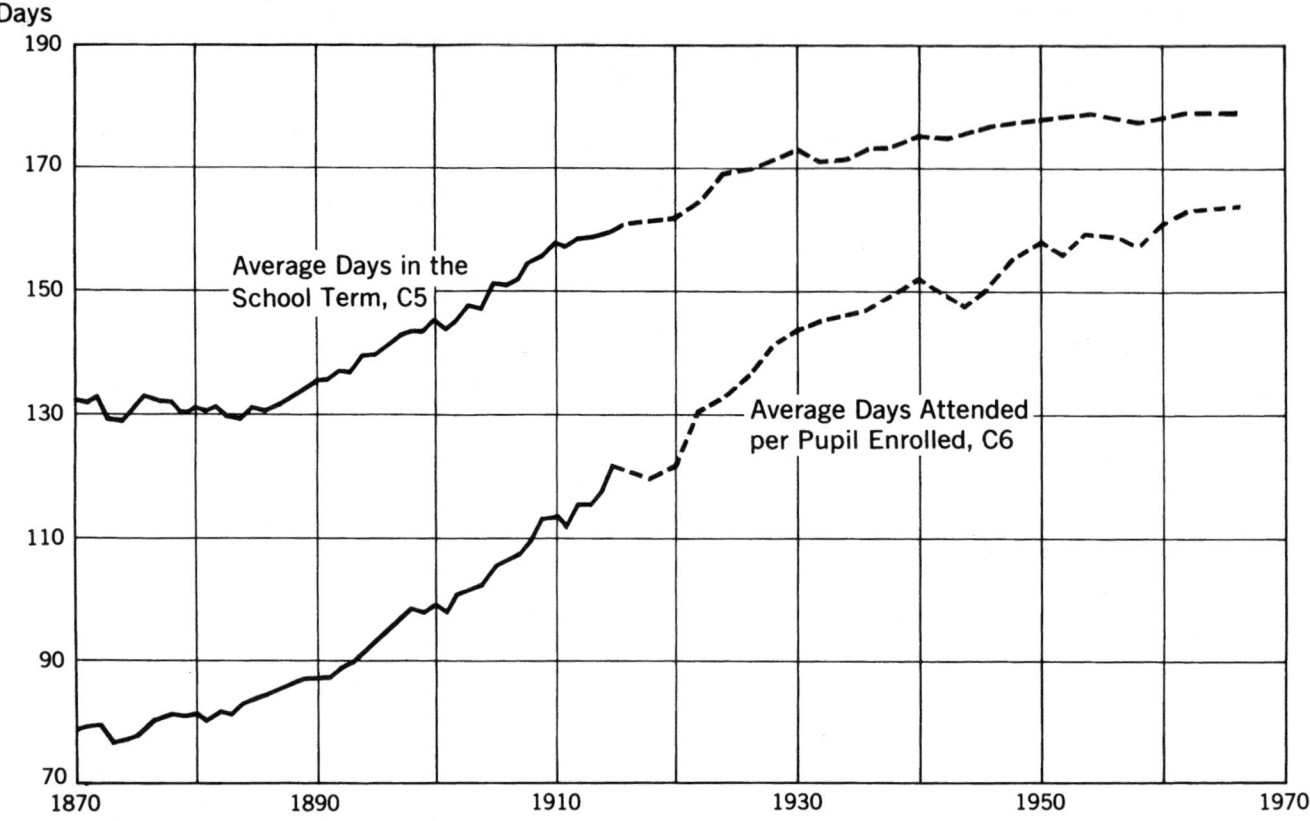

Figure 6.2. Average Length of School Term (in Days) and the Average Number of Days Attended per Pupil Enrolled, Public Elementary and Secondary Schools, 1870–1966, Series C5 and C6.

Table 6.1. Enrollment in Public School Systems by Size of System, 1956, 1961, and 1966.

	1956-57	1961-62	1966-67
Total Enrolled:	31,702,000	37,806,000	43,842,000
Enrollment of School System		Percent of Enrollment	
Total	100.0	100.0	100.0
25,000 or more	24.3	26.3	28.7
12,000 to 24,999	9.0	11.4	13.1
6,000 to 11,999	14.2	14.7	16.6
3,000 to 5,999	15.5	16.6	16.4
1,800 to 2,999	17.1	10.3	9.7
1,200 to 1,799		6.2	5.5
600 to 1,199	8.6	7.1	5.6
300 to 599	5.4	4.0	2.7
150 to 299	2.8	1.8	1.0
50 to 149	1.8	1.0	0.5
15 to 49	1.0	0.5	0.2
1 to 14	0.3	0.1	0.1
None, Non-operating	--	--	--

Note: The data are from the Census of Governments. Approximately 1.5 percent of the enrollment reported was above the secondary level.

Source: Census, 1963f: 7; Simon and Grant, 1968: 46.

Table 6.2. Public Schools and Enrollment per School by Number of Schools in the System, for 1956-57, 1961-62, and 1966-67.

Number of Schools in the System	1956-57 Schools	1956-57 Enrollment per School	1961-62 Schools	1961-62 Enrollment per School	1966-67 Schools	1966-67 Enrollment per School
Total	144,566	219	100,339	377	91,930	477
20 or more	30,663	N/A	29,409	528	28,186	657
10 to 19	14,283	N/A	15,449	437	17,483	492
3 to 9	28,760	N/A	28,707	370	30,027	412
2	9,192	N/A	6,948	283	5,316	356
1	31,668	N/A	19,826	148	10,918	224

Note: The Census of Governments for 1956 did not tabulate enrollment by number of schools in the system.

Source: Census, 1963f: 8; Census, 1968e: 24.

decreased by one-third from fall 1956 to fall 1966. Systems with one or two schools have decreased in number while systems with 3 to 9 schools and 10 to 19 schools have increased. The number of schools in very large systems, 20 or more, have declined slightly (Table 6.2).

With these changes in the organization of school systems, the total enrollment increased 38 percent. The "retrenchment" in institutions has been accompanied by increasing the average enrollment per school. The average school in 1966 was more than twice larger than the average institution in 1956. Both large and small school systems increased in average enrollment size over the period 1961 to 1966. Judging from the decrease in the number of schools in the system and the overall increase in enrollment (Table 6.2), one would assume, also, that the average size of school was smaller in 1956 than in 1961.

The trend toward larger public school systems and toward schools that, on the average, enroll more pupils, is undoubtedly consistent with changes taking place in corporations, factories, and other organizational complexes.

Length of Term and Days Attended

The average length of the school term (Series C5) remained relatively constant during the period 1870 to 1890, but from 1890 to approximately 1925, the length of school term was extended a great deal. From 1925 to 1955, the term continued to be extended, but after that the length of term appears to have remained fairly constant (Figure 6.2).

The average number of days attended per pupil (Series C6) has shown more uniform progress. Increases in the average were made fairly uniformly from 1885 or 1890 to World War I. The average days attended per pupil began to increase again after 1920 and continued to increase until 1940. There was a decline during World War II. The improvement since 1945 has been slower than the pre-World War II pace, but the average days attended still shows signs of increasing (Figure 6.2).

Institutions of Higher Education

Figure 6.3 presents the trends in the number of four-year colleges and universities and in junior colleges.[2/] Four-year colleges and universities (Series F11) have been increasing fairly steadily since about 1954, at an average rate of 19 new institutions annually. Meanwhile, junior colleges also have been increasing in number (Series F9 and F10).

From 1920 to World War II private junior colleges increased parallel to public junior colleges. After the War, however, private junior colleges remained relatively constant in number, while public junior colleges began to increase more rapidly, particularly after 1958. Since 1961, private junior colleges have shown a slight spurt in growth, but public junior colleges now comprise about two-thirds of the total.

Figure 6.4 (Series F1-F8) presents the number of institutions by type. The categories of independently organized professional schools are not inclusive classes, since many universities also have professional schools of various types which are

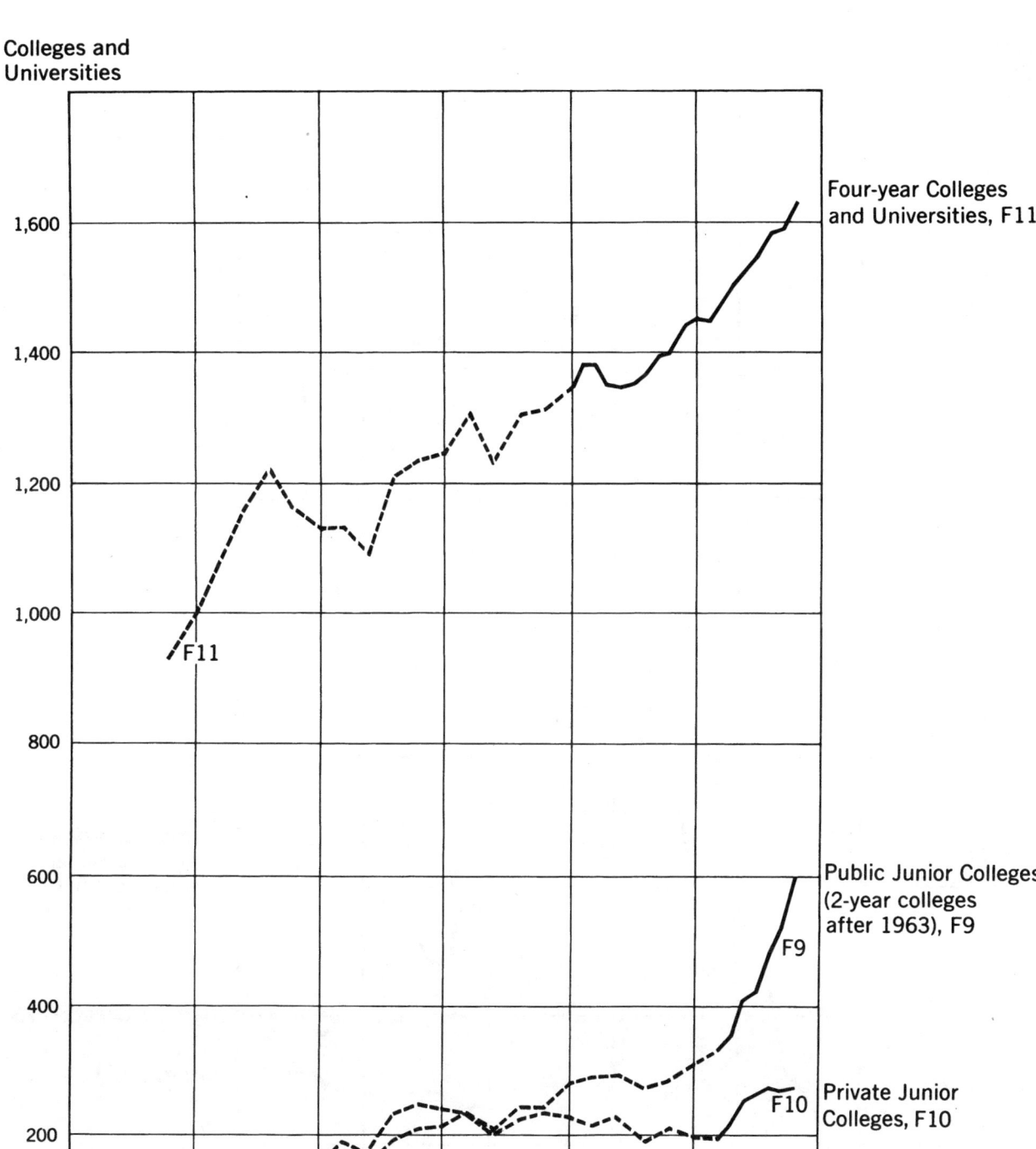

Figure 6.3. Four-year Colleges and Universities and Public and Private Junior Colleges, 1918–1968, Series F9, F10, F11.

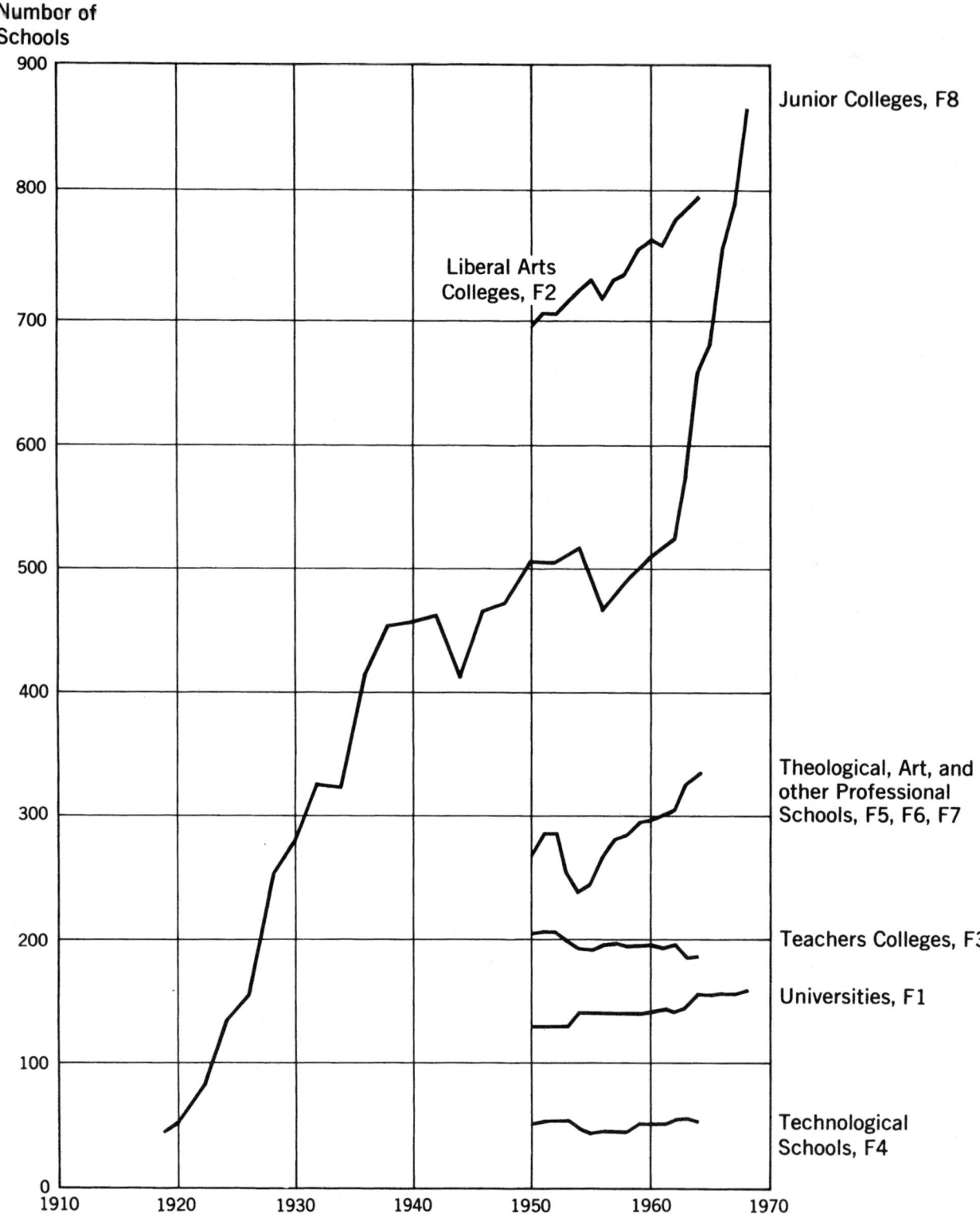

Figure 6.4. Higher Educational Institutions, by Type of Institution, 1919–1968, Series F1–F8.

not counted in Series F3 through F7. Despite this objection to the data, a few trends in institutional types, as defined, may be identified.

Total higher educational institutions have increased 28 percent from 1950 to 1967, there now (1967) being 2,382 included in the listing maintained by the U. S. Office of Education. Two year institutions have increased faster than any other type, from 506 in 1950 to 789 in 1967, a gain of 56 percent. They have increased, particularly, since 1961. Universities increased 20 percent, 1950 to 1967. The liberal arts college, the largest category of institutions, numbered nearly 800 in 1964.[3]

Among the independently organized professional schools, the following changes had occurred by 1964:

Theological and religious schools had increased 70 percent, the greatest percentage increase of any institutional type. Teachers colleges had declined nearly ten percent. Technological schools and schools of art appeared to remain constant. These changes represent the net change. Many institutions have changed from one type to another.

A higher educational institution may change its program and become another type of institution. Universities become liberal arts colleges and liberal arts colleges become universities. Institutions also merge, and some go out of existence. New institutions come into being. To document such changes is difficult.

To illustrate these changes, Table 6.3 presents shifts in institutional type from 1953 to 1954.[4/] Shown are 52 institutions which changed from one status to another, 37 institutions which merged or went out of existence, and 23 institutions, newly hatched, which entered the academic world. Combined, all of these changes resulted in a meager net loss of 0.7 percent, only 14 institutions, from 1,871 in 1953 to 1,857 in 1954.

"Other" separately organized professional schools merged or went out of existence at a higher rate (12 per 100) than any other type, 1953 to 1954. However, nearly 10 percent of the technological schools moved into the university category. Six percent of the universities and 25 percent of the teachers colleges became liberal arts colleges. Although its rate of change was not great -- 2 percent -- 13 liberal arts colleges moved up to university status. Junior colleges and liberal arts colleges led in numbers of newly-created institutions, 1953 to 1954.

The growth or change in the institutional composition of higher education affects the capability of the system to supply education for the nation's youth and to perform research to expand the store of knowledge. From the standpoint of economics both quality and cost of education vary with the institution. To find the composite of institutions that would give maximum educational and research benefits for the investment made requires measurement that goes beyond our present capability. Such an

Table 6.3. Changes in Institutional Types 1953 to 1954, U. S. Higher Educational Institutions

From 1953				To 1954					
				Separately Organized Professional Schools					
	Total	U.	LAC	Teachers	Tech.	Theo.	Other	Jr. Coll.	Deleted and Merged
Total		141	723	193	48	114	125	513	
Universities	131		8				1		
Liberal Arts Coll.	713	13		1	1				8
Sep. Org. Professional schools									
Teachers Coll.	200	1	5					1	1
Tech. Schools	53	5					1		1
Theo. Schools	115	2							2
Other	138	1						1	16
Junior Colleges	521		10			1			9
Nonexistent (1953)			7		1	2	3	10	

Source: Jaracz, 1955: 10-11.

approach, however, may eventually guide policy formation to improve the higher educational establishment.[5]

Size of Institutions of Higher Education

The size of the educational institution affects a number of educational outcomes. Enrollment of the institution is related to the level of the highest degree granted, to the level of educational and general income of the institution, and to the amount of federal funds for academic science received by the institution (Consolazio, 1967: 42, 46, 171, 175). The number and variety of educational programs is greater among larger institutions. So, also, is the administrative overhead, bureaucratic routine, and other dysfunctional aspects of large educational organizations (Barzun, 1968: 12-33). In short, enrollment size is a meaningful indicator of several aspects of higher education. It is important, then, to analyze its trend over time.

Table 6.4 presents the number of institutions by type and the average enrollment of each at four points in time, 1950, 1955, 1960, and 1964.[6]

Institutions of all types are increasing in size. Universities, the largest in average enrollment, increased from 8,527 students to 13,055. Similarly, liberal arts colleges approximately doubled in size, and so, also, did various independently organized professional schools. Junior colleges more than doubled in enrollment. Theological schools remained practically stable in size.

Table 6.4. Enrollment and Average Enrollment in Institutions of Higher Education, by Type of Institution, 1950-1964, School Year Beginning

	1950	1955	1960	1964
Total Enrollment	2,297,000	2,679,000	3,610,000	4,988,000
Average	1,216	1,472	2,016	2,285
Universities	1,117,000	1,241,000	1,551,000	2,111,000
Average	8,527	8,801	10,922	13,619
Liberal Arts Colleges	566,000	708,000	1,028,000	1,396,000
Average	817	967	1,346	1,752
Independently Organized Professional Schools	395,000	419,000	578,000	768,000
Average	589	873	1,062	1,338
Teachers Colleges	191,000	245,000	359,000	498,000
Average	932	1,276	1,813	2,663
Technological Schools	104,000	83,000	107,000	123,000
Average	2,039	1,886	2,140	2,278
Theological Schools	27,000	34,000	42,000	48,000
Average	223	274	239	233
Schools of Art and Other Professional	73,000	57,000	70,000	99,000
Average	490	475	583	780
Junior Colleges	218,000	309,000	454,000	713,000[a]
Average	411	662	871	1,085

[a] Category for this survey year was changed to "2-year institutions."

Source: Computed from data in Story, 1950b; Huddleston, 1961; and Education, 1964.

These indices of institutional size may be slightly misleading in cases where extension enrollment is counted as well as resident enrollment. This is the case for some public supported universities and teachers colleges.[7]

Revenue for Public Elementary and Secondary Schools

Of the two sources of support for elementary and secondary schools -- governmental and private -- almost all of the support comes from public sources: 91 percent of it in 1930 and 92 percent in 1965.[8] The several levels of government, towns and cities, counties, states and the Federal government, support the schools. By far the chief sources of educational revenue -- more than half at present -- are local: cities, towns, and counties. The share from local sources, however, has been declining, as Figure 6.5 shows. Local sources supplied more than 80 percent of school revenue in 1930; provided below 70 percent in 1940; and had fallen below 60 percent by 1950. Since then local sources have provided between 50 and 60 percent of the revenue for schools.

As local revenues have declined, proportionately, the support of elementary and secondary education has shifted to the state government -- not the Federal government. The states now provide just below 40 percent of the revenue. In 1964 the Federal government gave under 5 percent. An estimate for 1966 places its present share at slightly more than 7 percent.

While these changes have been taking place, the total revenue in current dollars, has increased, particularly since the mid-1940s.

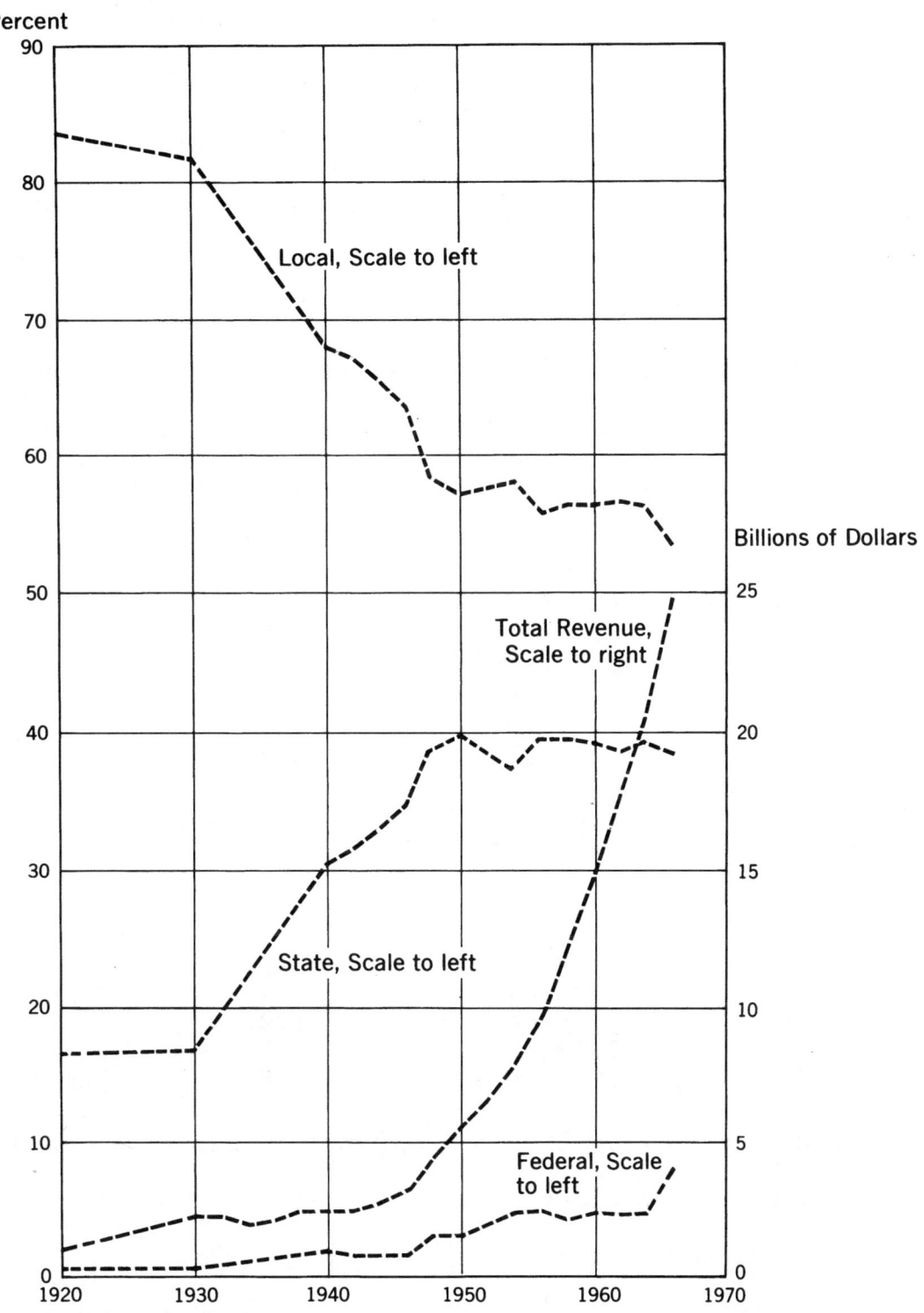

Figure 6.5. Governmental Support for Public Elementary and Secondary Education as a Percent of the Total Revenue for Education, and Total Revenue, in Billions of Dollars, 1920–1966.

Expenditures for Public Elementary and Secondary Schools

Prior to World War II, the schools' share of the Gross National Product was about 1 percent and increasing slightly. After the War, however, the percentage began to increase more rapidly. From 2.2 percent in 1949-50, the percentage increased gradually during the 1950s to 3.2 percent for the 1959-60 period. By 1963-64 the percentage had reached 3.5 percent of GNP. Estimates of public school expenditures since that date bring the percentage up slightly: the estimate for 1967-68 being 3.8 percent. Total expenditures of public elementary and secondary schools, as a percentage of the Gross National Product, is shown below for recent years.9/

1929-30	2.4
1939-40	2.5
1949-50	2.2
1953-54	2.5
1955-56	2.7
1957-58	3.1
1959-60	3.2
1961-62	3.4
1963-64	3.5
1964-65	3.6
1965-66	3.8
1966-67	3.7
1967-68	3.8

It is instructive to examine where increases in expenditures are going, considering them in relation to the number of teachers, students, or schools, as appropriate.

Instruction is the largest single item of expenditure, approximating more than 14 billion dollars in 1965-66. Considered either as dollars per teacher or as dollars per student, expenditures for instruction -- in constant 1958 dollars -- has increased greatly since 1920 (Figure 6.6 and Table 6.5). Increases in both indices during the 1930 to 1950 period were moderate, but after 1950 the amount spent for instruction began to increase faster. Increases in expenditures for instruction per pupil have increased faster than have increases per teacher.

Expenditures per school in constant 1958 dollars are shown in Figure 6.7 and Table 6.5. While these costs were fairly close together in 1950, they have increased at quite different rates and now are widely separated. Administration remains the lowest element of expenditure, but, as new school buildings have been built, fixed charges have increased, and the cost of plant operation and maintenance per school has gone up greatly, to more than $21,000 per school. It should be remembered that, in the face of school consolidations and the movement of the population to metropolitan areas, the number of schools has declined since 1950 approximately one-third. Pupils per school, on the other hand, have increased from approximately 164 in 1949-50 to 429 in 1965-66 (Simon and Grant, 1968).

Revenues of Institutions of Higher Education

Figure 6.8 (Series F15) presents the trend in total revenue of institutions of higher education. The income changed little from 1930 until after World War II. After 1946, however, revenues began to bound upward and even now appear to be set upon a continuously increasing course. Even when expressed as a

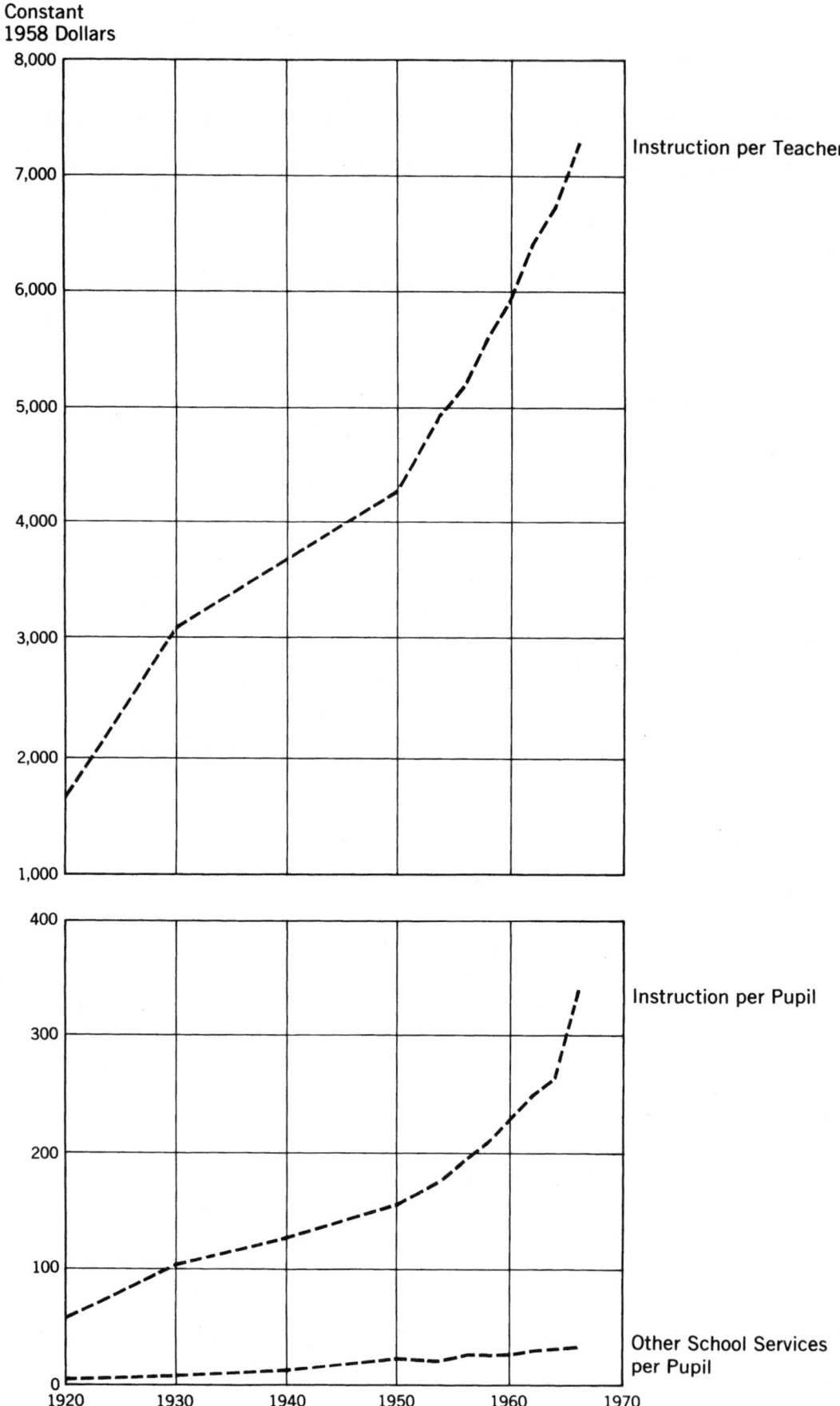

Figure 6.6. Expenditures in Public Elementary and Secondary Schools (in Constant 1958 Dollars) for Instruction, per Teacher and per Pupil, and for Other School Services, per Pupil, 1920–1966, (Source: Table 6.5).

Table 6.5 Expenditures for Public Elementary and Secondary Education by Purpose, Selected Years, 1919-20 to 1965-66

(constant 1958 dollars)*

	Administration $ per school	Plant operation & maintenance $ per school	Fixed charges $ per school	Instruction $ per teacher	Instruction $ per pupil	Other school service $ per pupil
1919-20				1,615	50.9	2.94
1929-30	601	2,252	3,844	3,089	102.7	7.95
1939-40				3,683	126.7	11.66
1949-50	1,808	5,275	2,148	4,273	155.5	22.57
1953-54	2,560	7,473	3,674	4,911	177.5	22.37
1955-56	3,094	8,897	4,409	5,181	191.1	26.83
1957-58	3,712	10,904	5,986	5,543	208.5	26.89
1959-60	4,385	12,514	7,547	5,877	225.9	27.94
1961-62	5,744	15,596	9,544	6,331	248.9	30.48
1963-64	6,628	16,063	11,957	6,692	265.1	31.46
1965-66	8,362	21,283	15,170	7,199	337.2	32.89
% increase over 1930	1,291	845	295	133	228	314

*Based upon the OBE implicit price deflator, using the average of the years represented in the academic year, Series B63 of <u>Long Term Economic Growth</u> (Census 1966a: 200-201).

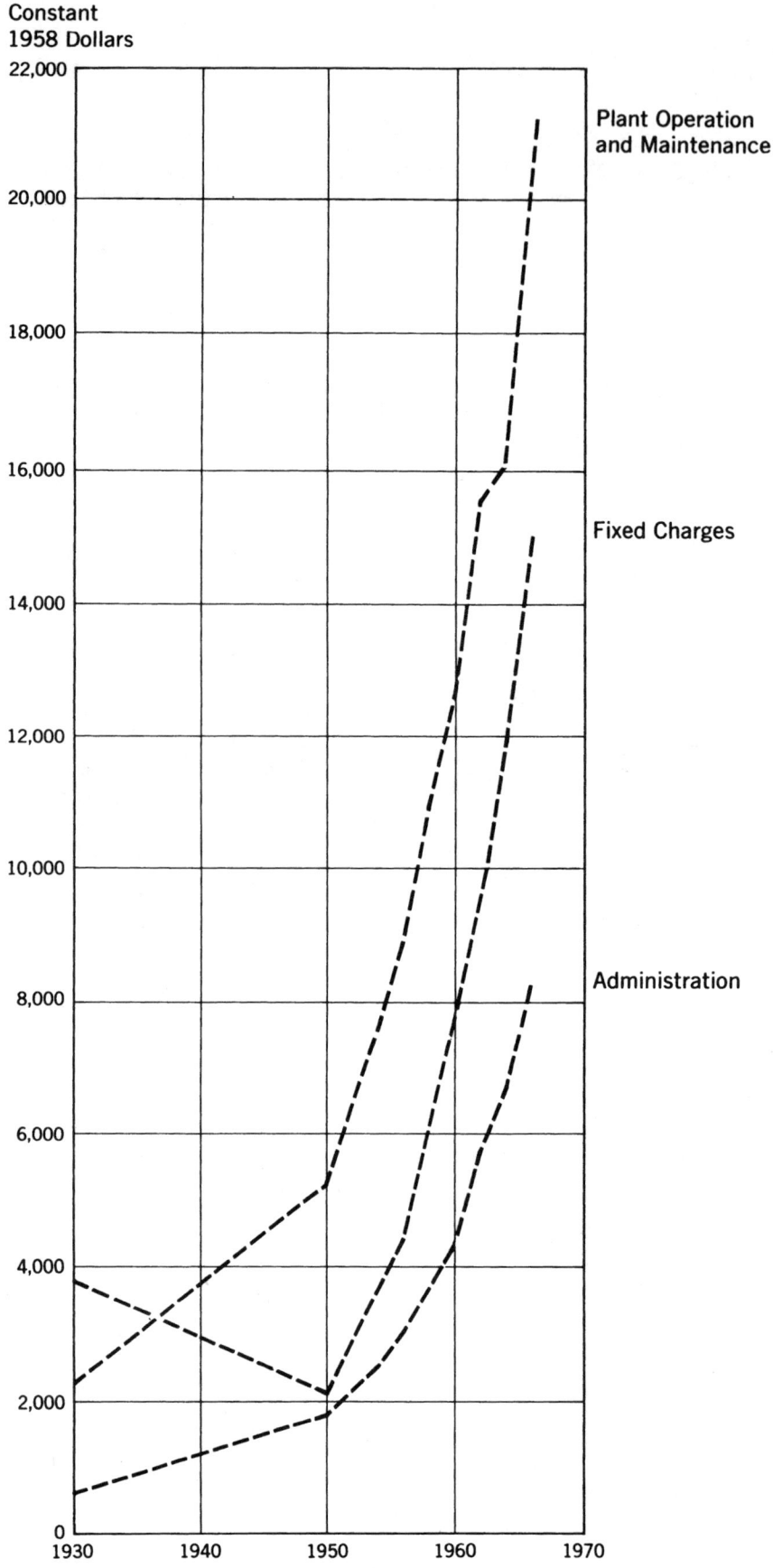

Figure 6.7. Expenditures in Public Elementary and Secondary Schools (in Constant 1958 Dollars), per School, for Various Purposes, 1930–1966 (Source: Table 6.5).

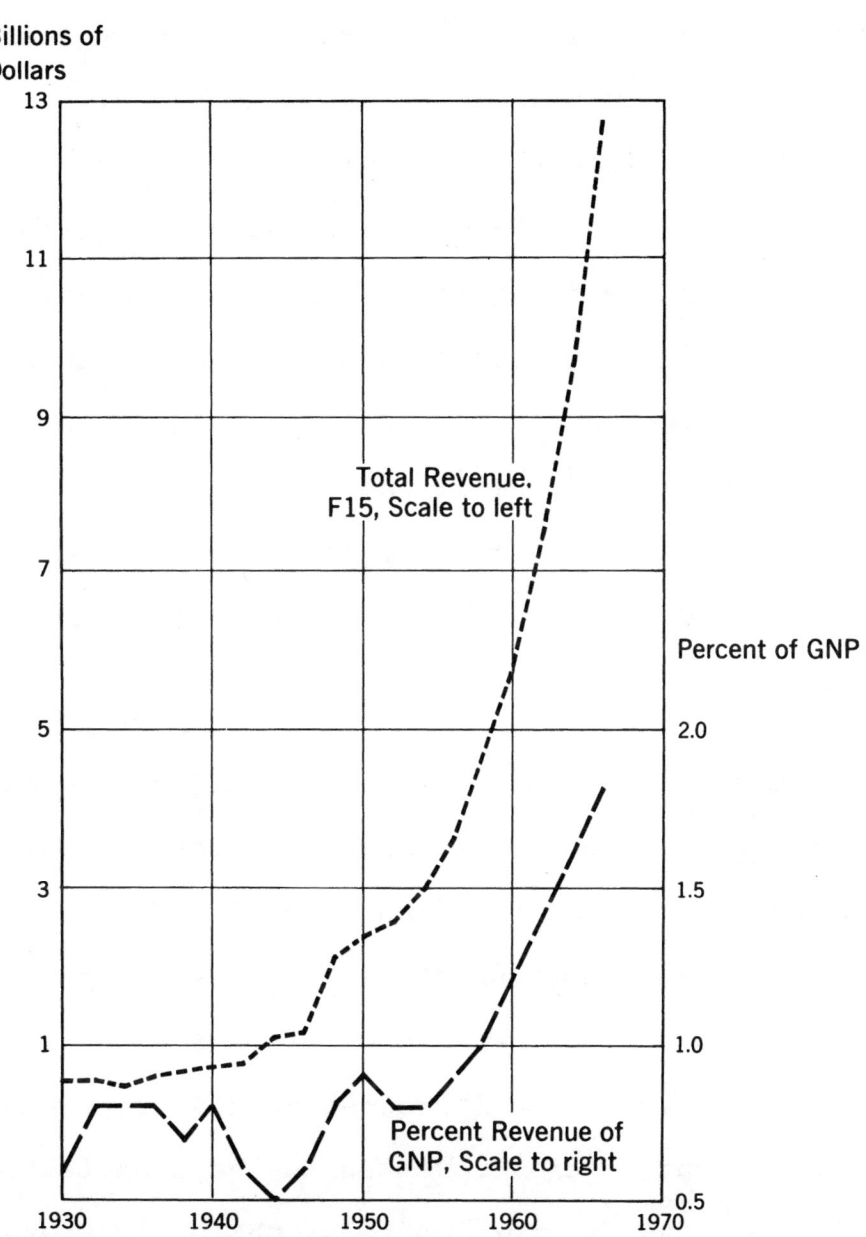

Figure 6.8. Total Revenue of Higher Educational Institutions, Series F15, and as a Percent of GNP, 1930–1966.

percent of the Gross National Product (Figure 6.8), the revenue appears to be increasing rapidly. The proportion of the GNP was rising steadily from the mid-1930s until 1950. During the 1950s, however, when GNP was increasing an average of 6 percent per year, revenues to higher education faltered, and did not keep pace again until 1958, when revenues to higher education regained their strength. As will be seen, this was the time that the Federal government increased its proportionate contribution to the support of higher education, when student fees increased, and when private gifts and donations increased.

Sources of Revenue for Higher Education

Figure 6.9 (Series F17-F25) identifies the major sources of revenue for institutions of higher education, public and private. The relative importance of the several sources has shifted somewhat since 1930. Government has increased its proportionate share. The sharp increase in government's contribution during the 1940s resulted from increases in revenue from the Federal government, but Federal revenues to the institutions declined during the 1950s, proportionately, while the share coming from state governments increased (Figure 6.10).

In the 1930s student fees made up the second most important source of revenue (Figure 6.9, Series F17), but during the 1940s this source fell below that of auxiliary enterprises and student aid funds (Series F25). By 1966 the two were about equal in importance.

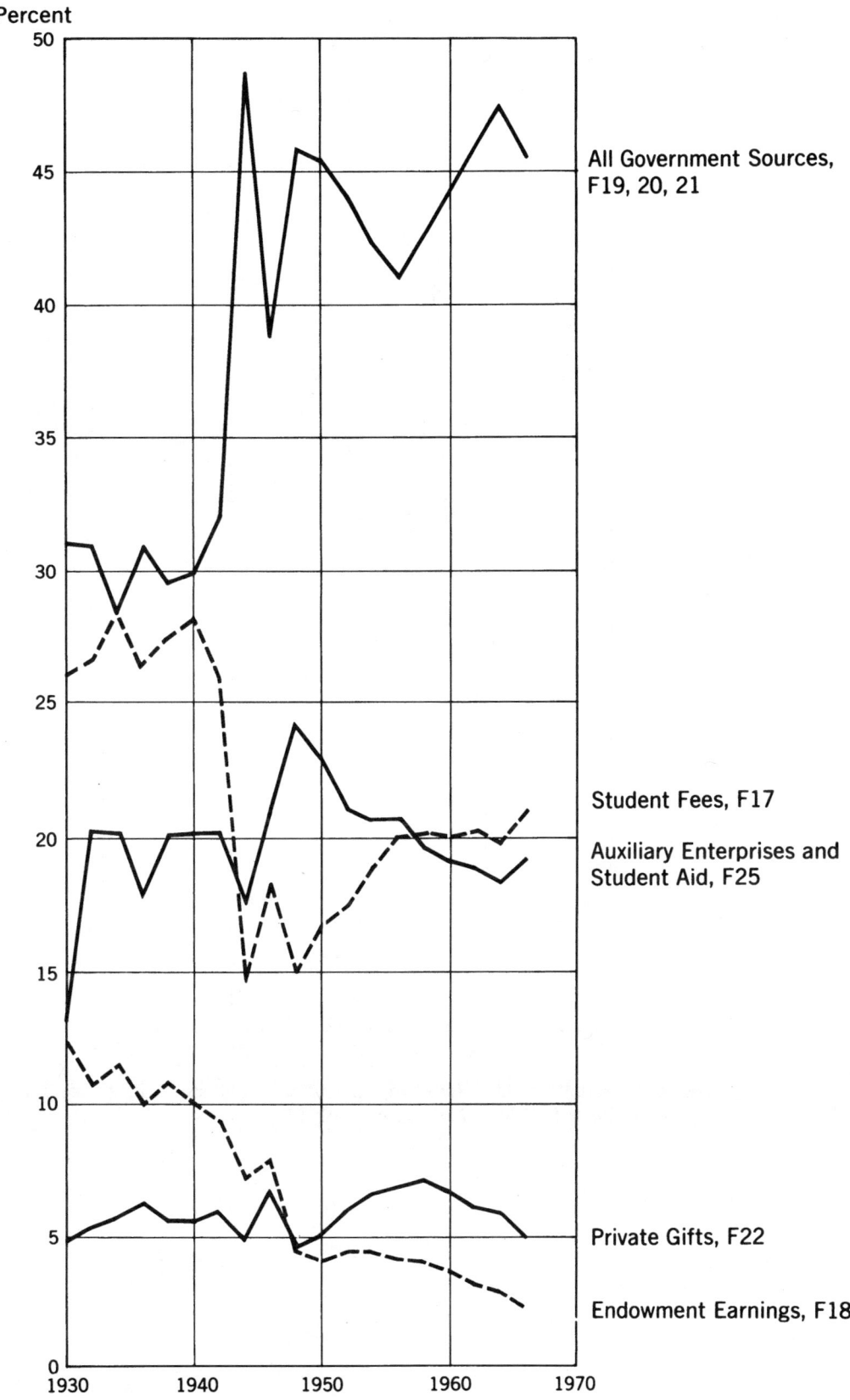

Figure 6.9. Major Source of Revenue as a Percent of Total Revenue, Institutions of Higher Education, 1930–1966, Series F17–F25.

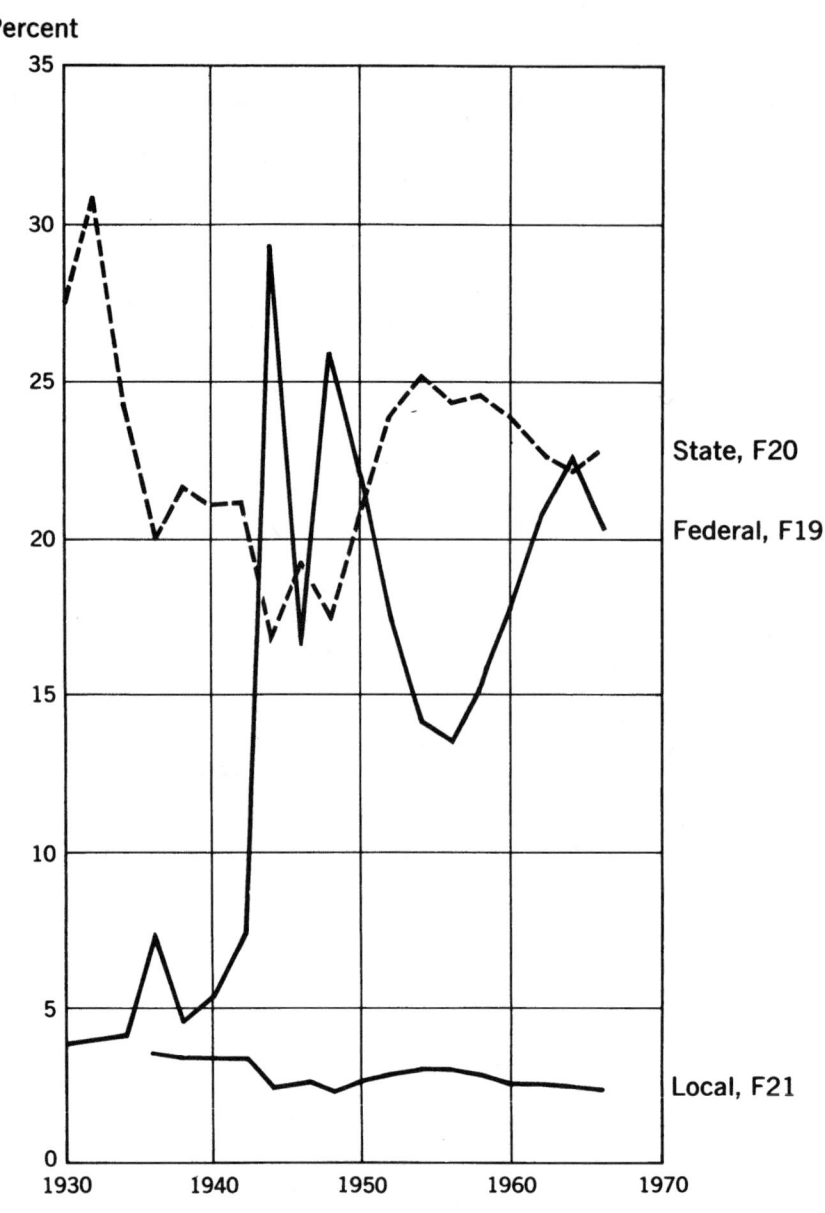

Figure 6.10. Percent of Total Revenue, Institutions of Higher Education, from Three Levels of Government, 1930–1966, Series F19–F21.

Private gifts (Series F22) have remained a relatively constant part of higher education revenues, while earnings from endowments (Series F18) have declined as a percent of the total.

Figure 6.10 illustrates the relative shares of revenue provided by the three levels of government (Series F19-F21). Local governments (Series F21) since 1930 have contributed a fairly constant proportion of the total, while the Federal percentage (Series F19) has increased since 1940 and the state has declined somewhat over the 24-year period. Federal and state (Series F20) each now contribute 20.3 percent and 22.8 percent, respectively, of total higher education revenues.

Expenditures of Institutions of Higher Education

Figures 6.11 through 6.15 present expenditures of institutions of higher education for various purposes, each expressed in terms of students, faculty members, and institutions, as appropriate, and in constant 1958 dollars. These trends show no marked variations. They are either relatively constant or are increasing fairly regularly.

The important expenditures for educational and general purposes, per capita student or per capita faculty member, have been increasing since the early 1940s (Figure 6.11, Series F26, and Figure 6.13, Series F27). The continuous increase in enrollments since the mid-1950s has been accompanied by small increases in expenditures, per student, for instruction and departmental research (in constant dollars), but the increases have not been dramatic (Figure 6.11, Series F29).

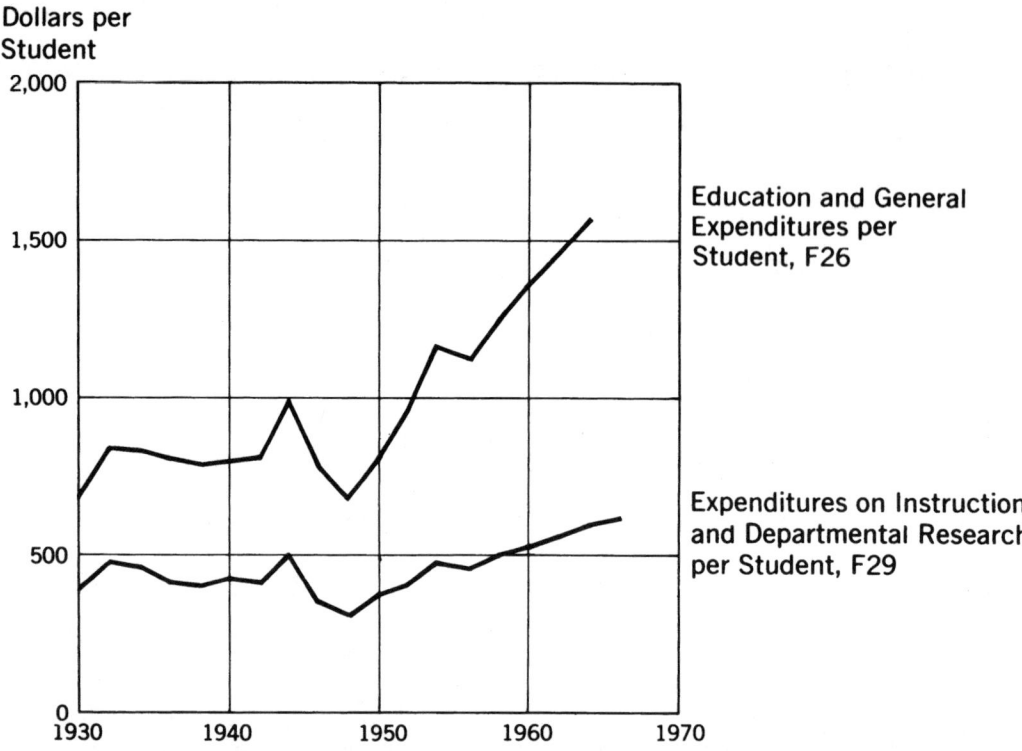

Figure 6.11. Total Educational and General Expenditures, Series F26, Expenditures on Instruction and Departmental Research, Series F29, per Student, in Institutions of Higher Education (in Constant 1958 Dollars), 1930–1966.

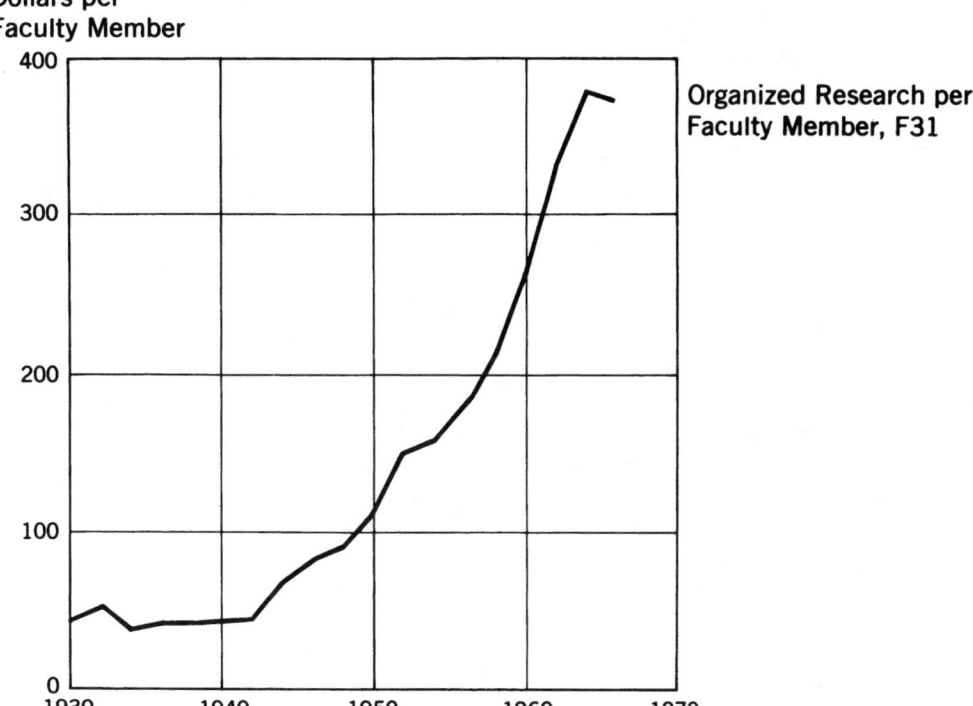

Figure 6.12. Expenditures for Organized Research, per Faculty Member in Institutions of Higher Education (in Constant 1958 Dollars), 1930–1966, Series F31.

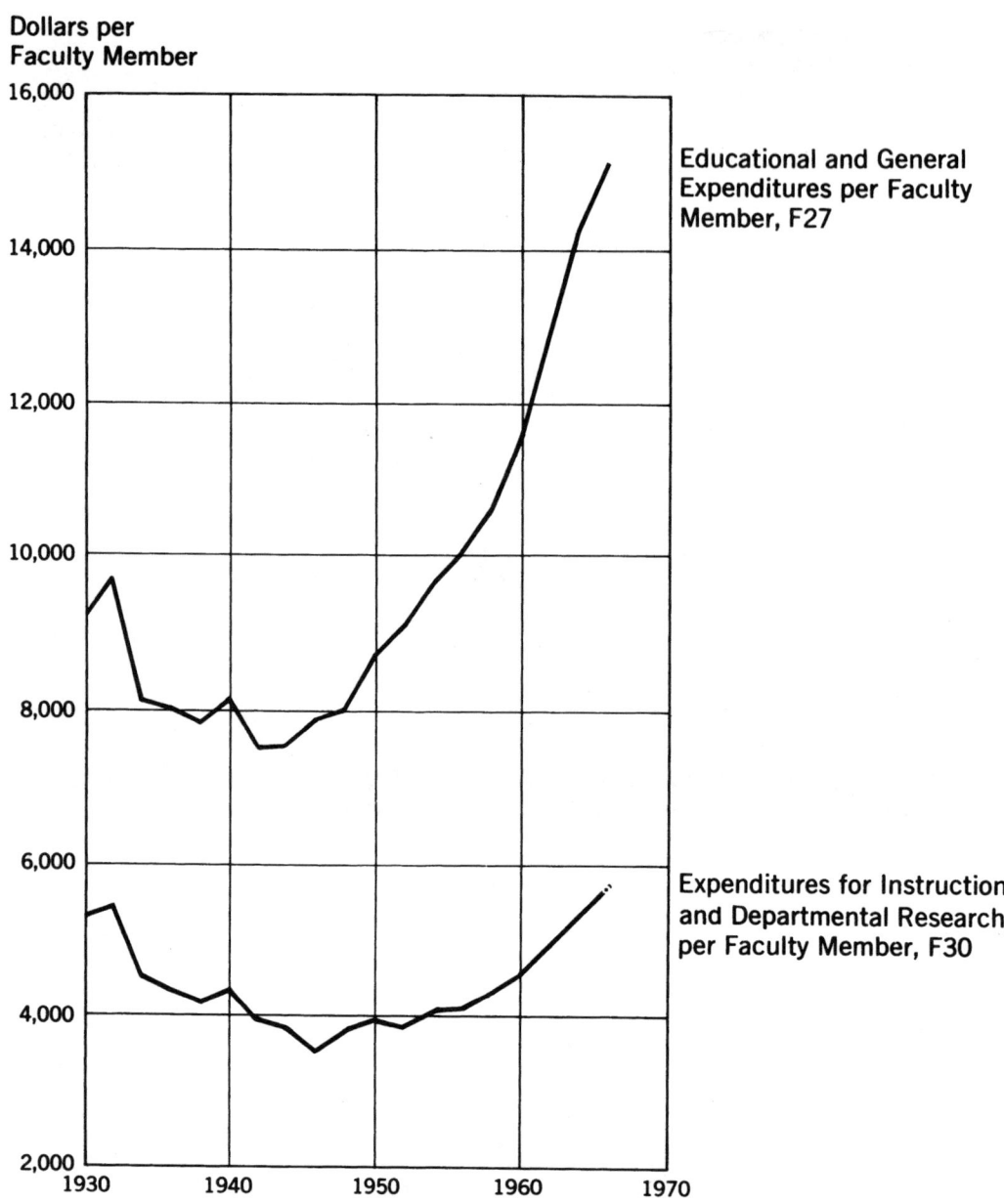

Figure 6.13. Total Educational and General Expenditures, Series F27, and Expenditures on Instruction and Departmental Research, Series F30, per Faculty Member in Institutions of Higher Education (in Constant 1958 Dollars), 1930–1966.

Expenditures expressed on a per school basis, those for plant operation and maintenance, for organized activities relating to instructional departments, for extension and public service, and library expenditures have each increased since the end of World War II (Figure 6.14, Series F32-F35). Plant operation and maintenance has moved ahead more rapidly than the other indices.

Administrative expenditures and those for auxiliary enterprises and student aid, expressed on a per school basis, also began increasing after World War II and have paced one another consistently since the early 1950s (Figure 6.15, Series F28 and F36).

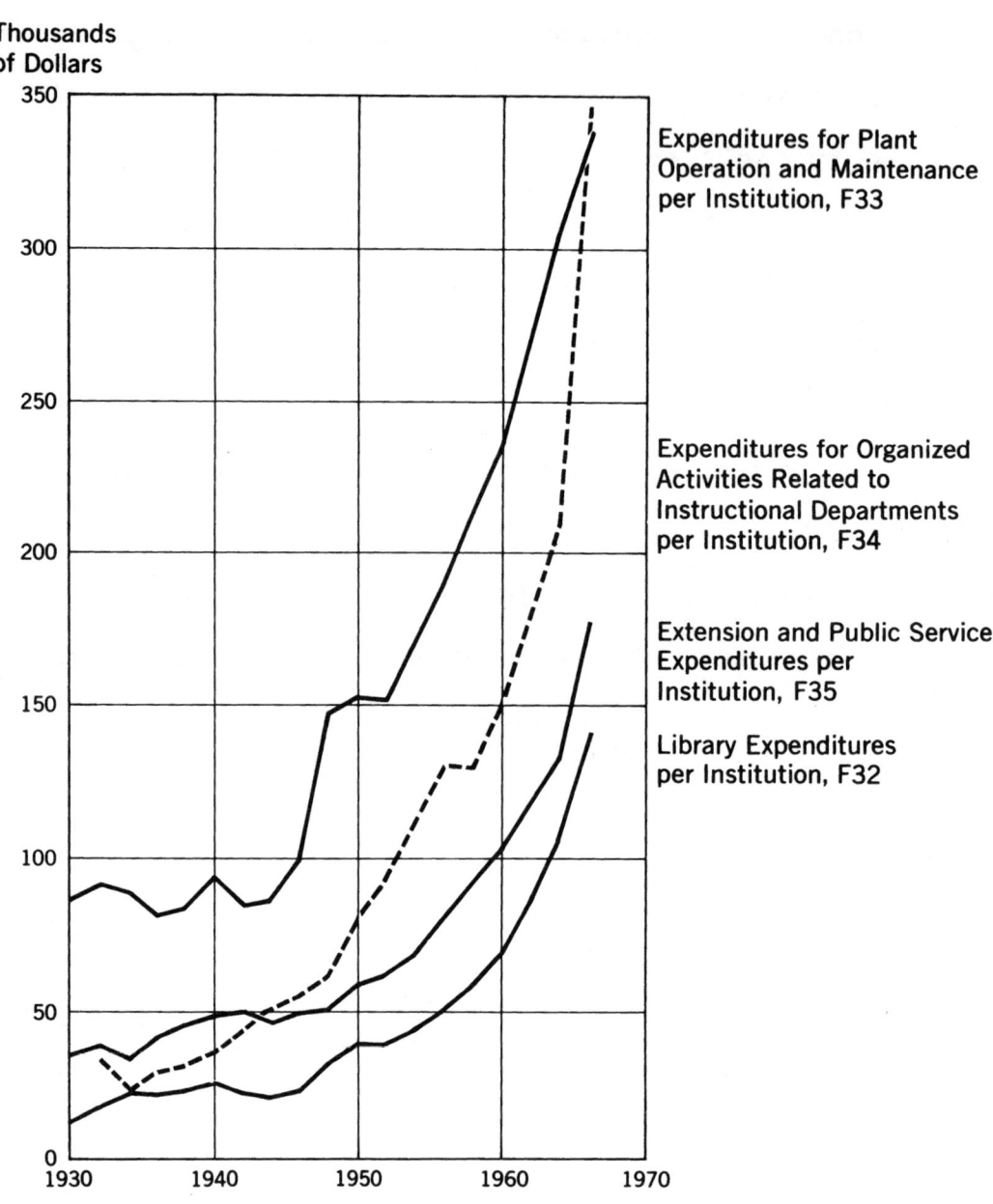

Figure 6.14. Expenditures for Four Purposes, per Institution in Institutions of Higher Education (in Thousands of Constant 1958 Dollars), 1930–1966, Series F32–F35.

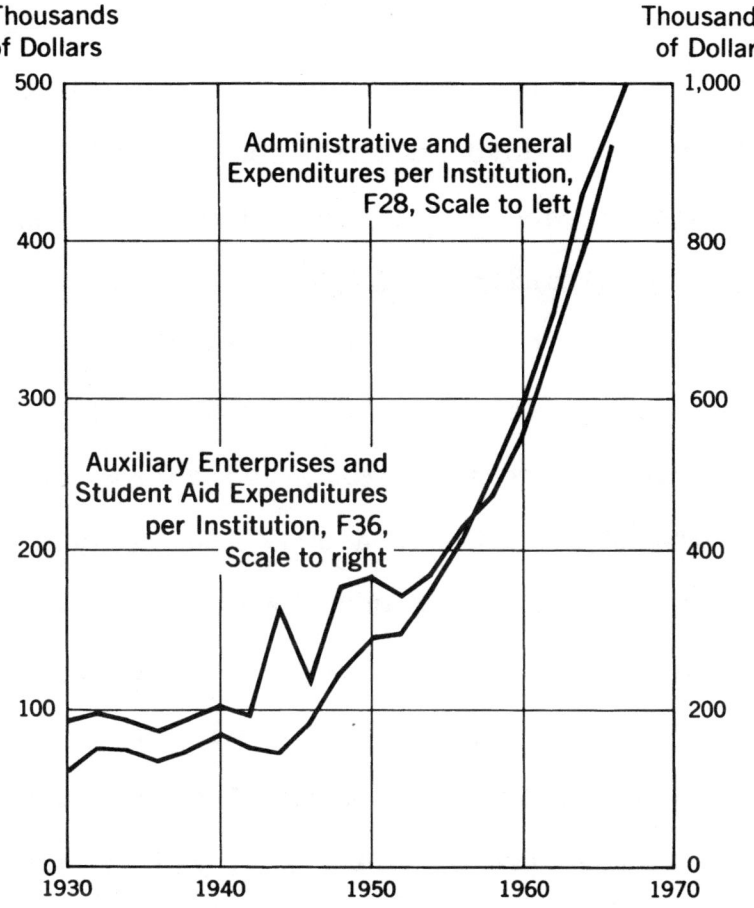

Figure 6.15. Administrative and General Expenditures, Series F28, Expenditures for Auxiliary Enterprises and Student Aid, Series F36, per Institution in Institutions of Higher Education (in Thousands of Constant 1958 Dollars), 1930–1966.

Footnotes

<u>1/</u> The Census of Governments uses the term "public school system" which includes governmental entities of two levels of independence: (a) those administratively and fiscally independent of other governmental units, and (b) those lacking the autonomy to be so classified (Census, 1963f: 5-6).

<u>2/</u> Many student characteristics differ by type of institution. Highest degree planned, major field, and career orientation, religious background, parents' income, high school grade point average, and a number of other characteristics differ among types of institutions (Panos, Astin, and Creager, 1967; Astin, Panos, and Creager, 1967b). The classification of types of institution used by the American Council on Education is not the same as that of the Office of Education, but several categories are comparable.

<u>3/</u> The Survey of Opening Fall Enrollment of the U. S. Office of Education has been the source of the number of institutions by type and the enrollment in those institutions. However, 1964 was the last year that the Office used these classifications. See notes, Series F1-F8.

<u>4/</u> The year 1954 was chosen because the data on changes in type were carefully assembled.

<u>5/</u> Just as the field of economics has gained insights through studies of the firm, bankruptcies, and the like, loss of educational institutions and mergers, if tied to the demographic setting, the character of the educational program, and the state

of public and private finance of education, would reveal many of the critically important forces that have shaped the educational system. Similar forces in the future may bear upon the development and vigor, or lack of it, of higher education.

6/ Data for 1965 would provide a more uniform series, but they could not be obtained since the survey (Education, 1967c) of that year did not classify institutions by type and hence enrollment by type was not tabulated.

7/ An attempt to identify the geographic subdivisions of institutions has been made in Education (1967b).

8/ In recent years among non-public elementary and secondary schools, approximately nine out of ten pupils were enrolled in Catholic schools (Education, 1967a: 17). Consequently, the information on public schools assembled from state departments of education by the U. S. Office of Education represents all but approximately 8 or 9 percent of expenditures for elementary and secondary education (U. S. Department of Health, Education and Welfare, 1966:561).

9/ GNP data are from Council of Economic Advisers (1969b: 227). Adjacent years are averaged to give a GNP estimate for the Academic Year. Public elementary and secondary school expenditures, total, is from Simon and Grant (1968: 59). Expenditures include capital outlay and interest. Estimates for recent years are from Simon and Grant (1968).

7

Educational Attainment

The educational attainment of the population, measured by years of schooling, has been analyzed recently in several studies (Folger and Nam, 1967; Duncan, 1968; Cohen, 1967). The approach has been the utilization of the median year of schooling or the percentage completing a given number of years schooling to examine educational differentials in terms of age, sex, color, region or state of residence, religion, place of residence, migratory status, income, occupation, and various other characteristics. Duncan (1968) has gone further and has used decennial census data to examine the educational attainment of successive population cohorts. Insofar as a year of formal school attendance reflects a real increment of education, the variable provides a meaningful indicator.[1]

In study after study the number of years of schooling has been found to be related to a number of other socially significant variables. There can be no doubt that measures of educational attainment other than years of schooling are needed, as Cohen (1967) has pointed out, but much can be learned from this measure.

The approach of this chapter is to examine the general trends in educational attainment over time and to illustrate the different measures of attainment which may be developed from the years of school completed.

Limitations of the data have been discussed at length by others (Folger and Nam, 1967: 134-135, 243-249), (Duncan, 1968: 603-608, 614-618). Except for the review appearing in the series notes (Series G1 -G13 and G110-G125), no additional comment on the limitations of the data will be made.

Not all available series are included here. For the population 25 years of age and over, the median year of school completed (Series G1) is given, the total completing each of the three major levels of school (Series G2-G4). Similar information is given for the nonwhite population (Series G5-G7). The same series are repeated for those entering the "adult" population, persons 25 to 29 years of age. The next series present the percentage achieving one of eight levels of schooling, for white and nonwhite populations, in each case by sex, and for three age groups: 20-24 years, 25-34 years, and 35-44 years (Series G14-G109).

Median Years of Schooling

The most general indicator of the educational level of the population is the median years of school completed by the population 25 years of age and over (Figure 7.1, Series G1). This index is estimated to have stood between 8 and 9 years of schooling from 1910 to the decade of the 1940s (Folger and Nam, 1967: 132). The 9.3 median years of schooling achieved by the

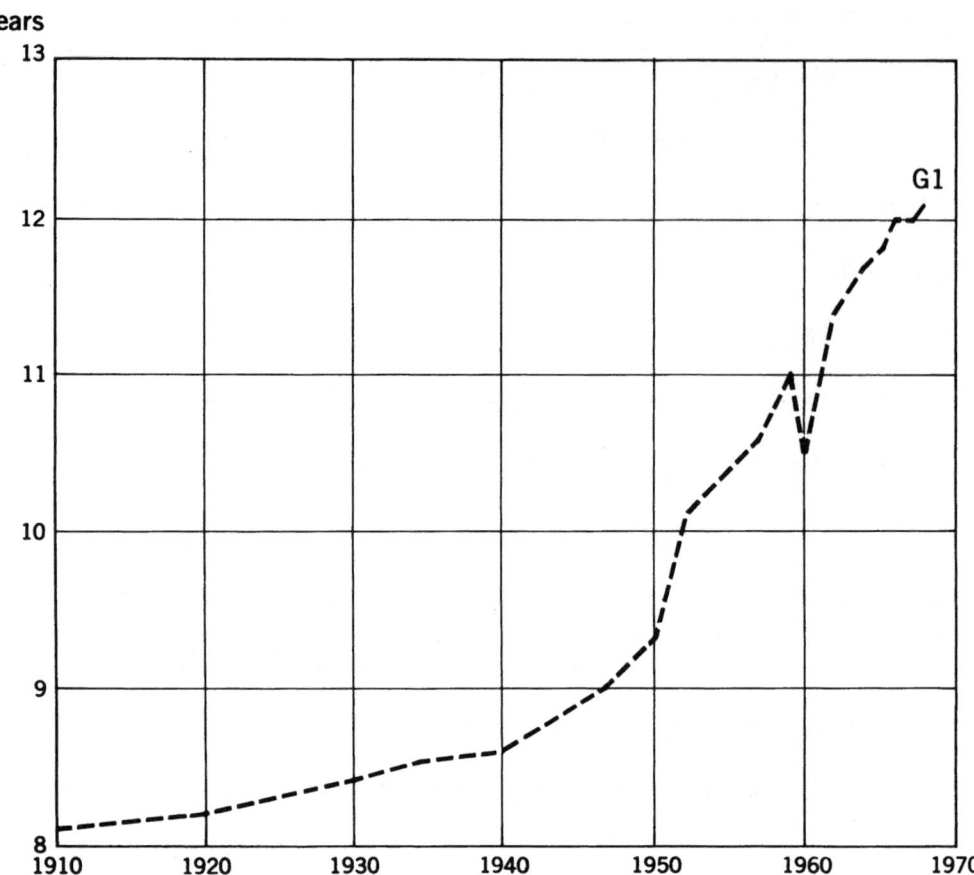

Figure 7.1. Median School Years Completed for Population 25 Years Old and Over, 1910–1968, Series G1.

population in 1950 was quickly surpassed during the following decade.[2] By 1968 the median for the adult population was a high school education (12 years).

Percentage Attaining Given Years of School

A high school diploma now represents the educational attainment of half the adult population (Figure 7.2, Series G3). Since larger proportions of the population have been graduating from high school (Series A18), the numbers of those with 12 years of schooling or more among the adult population may be expected to continue to increase.

The "cream" of educational attainment, the population completing four years of college or more, is shown in Figure 7.2, Series G4. From 1910 to 1950 this proportion increased very gradually and since 1950 has gained more rapidly. By 1968 approximately ten percent of the adult population had at least graduated from college.

From the other end of the distribution is another revealing measure: the percent of persons 25 years of age or older who have had less than five years of schooling (Figure 7.2, Series G2). This index was more than 20 percent before the mid-1920s. From then until immediately after 1950 it declined to below 10 percent. Since about 1952, the measure has declined more slowly, and now stands slightly above 6 percent. Since each on-coming generation is increasingly educated beyond this level, this indicator (Series G2) will gradually decline as the older, less educated population dies.

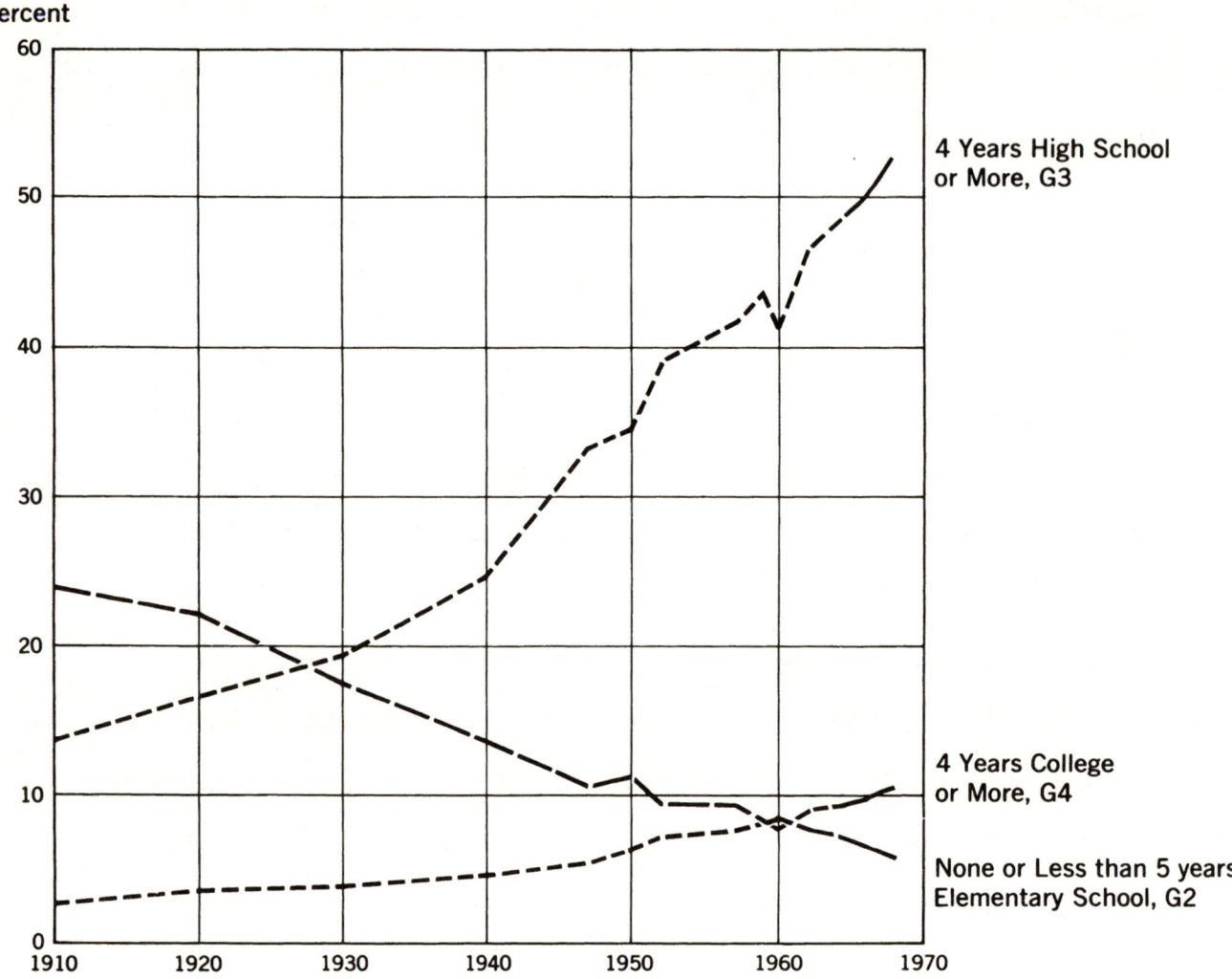

Figure 7.2. Percent of Total Population 25 Years Old and Over Completing None or Less than 5 Years of Schooling, Series G2, 4 Years of High School or More, Series G3, 4 Years of College or More, Series G4, 1910–1968.

The nonwhite population has consistently exhibited the lowest levels of schooling in the adult population. Figure 7.3 (Series G5, G6, and G7) presents three indicators of trends in educational attainment of the nonwhite population.

The percent completing four years of high school or more has increased from less than 8 percent in 1940 to nearly 30 percent in 1968. The percent completing college has increased more slowly and has gained only 3.7 percentage points since 1940.

The percentage with less than five years of schooling has declined most rapidly, from more than 40 percent in 1940 to 18 percent in 1968. This index will continue to decline as the older, less educated nonwhite population dies and the better educated younger population enters the "adult" population category.

Less than Five Years Schooling of an Age Group by Sex and Color

Figure 7.4 (Series G14, G38, G62, and G86) demonstrates the point last made: that the cohorts entering the "adult" population are less and less the poorly-educated segment. White males and females, 20 to 24 years old, who have less than five years of schooling declined 2 to 3 percentage points, 1940 to the present, and in 1967 less than 1 percent of them had less than five years of schooling.

Nonwhite males and females of the same ages, however, have shown the most progress in this indicator. Nonwhite males have

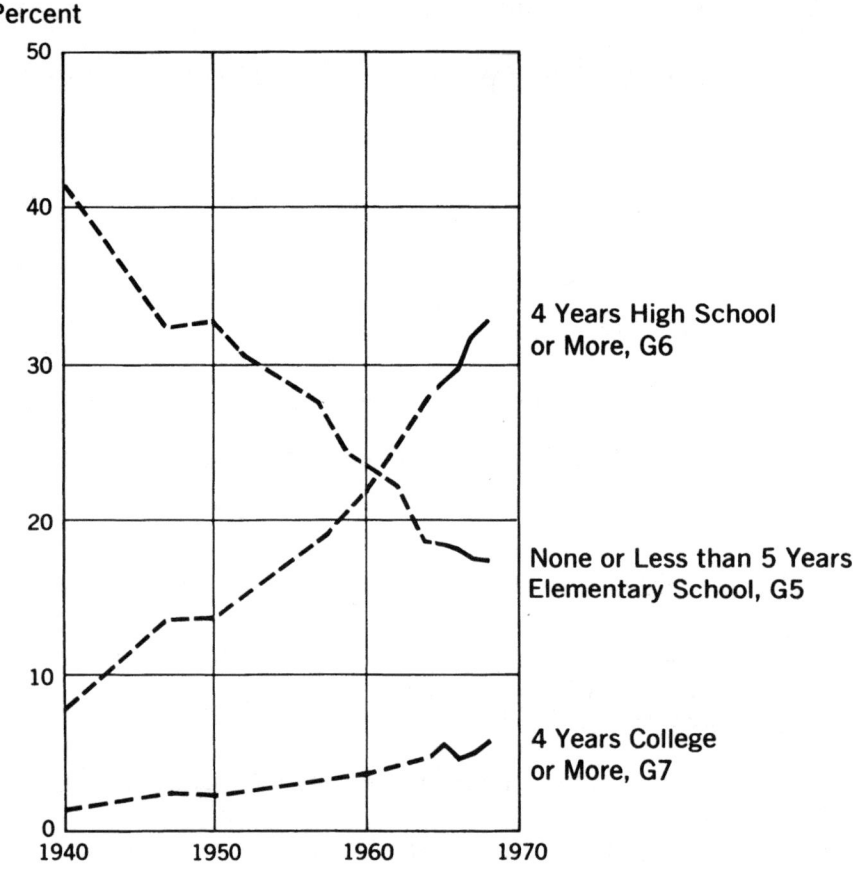

Figure 7.3. Percent of Nonwhite Population 25 Years Old and Over Completing None or Less than 5 Years of Schooling, Series G5, 4 Years of High School or More, Series G6, 4 Years of College or More, Series G7, 1940–1968.

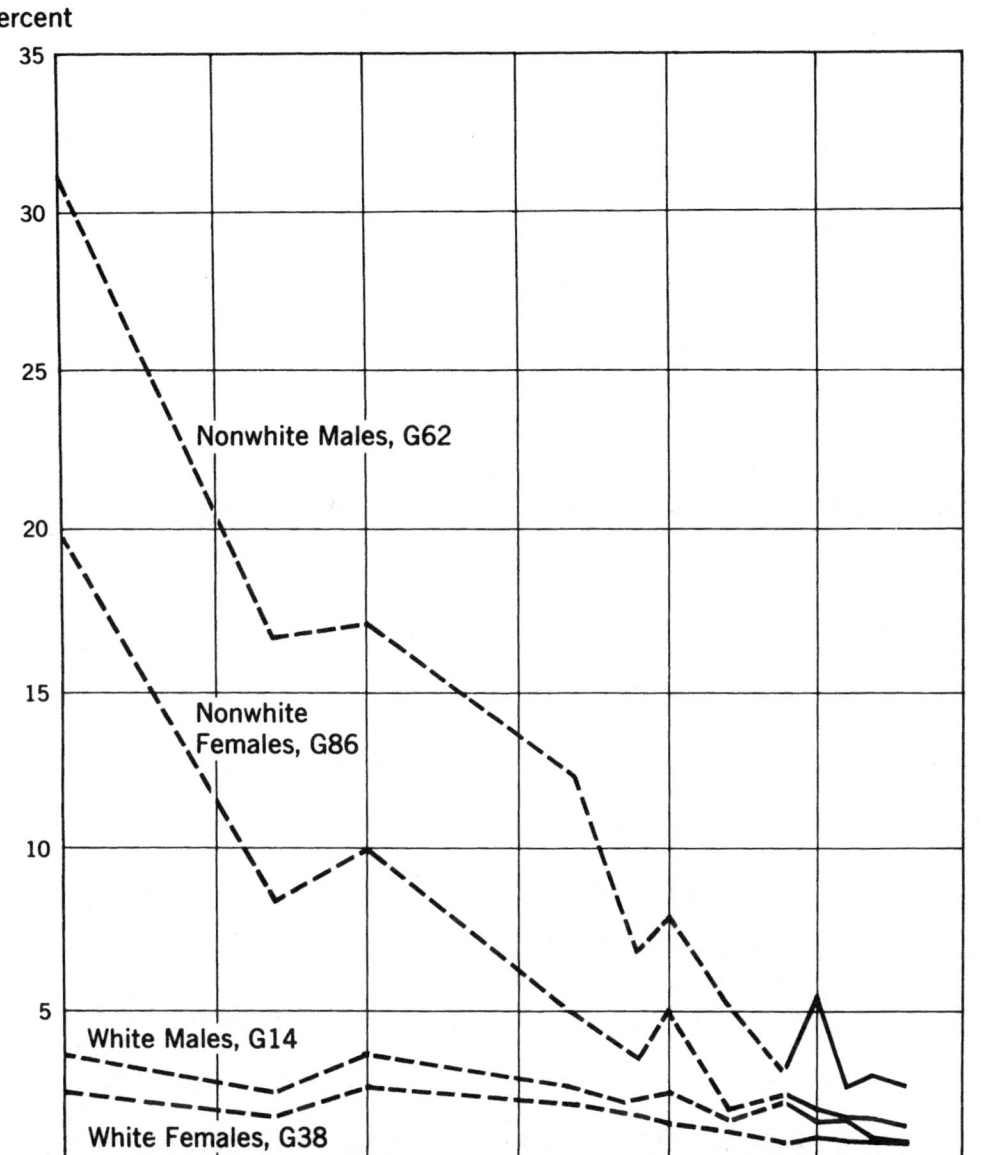

Figure 7.4. Percent of 20–24-Year-Old Population Completing None or Less than 5 Years of School, by Color and Sex, 1940–1968, Series G14, G38, G62, G86.

declined from 31.2 percent to 2.7 percent and nonwhite females have declined from 19.6 to 1.4 percent. These two groups will undoubtedly decline to below 1 percent in the near future.

Figure 7.4 illustrates the use of this indicator in comparing educational trends among sex and color groups of the same age. The same comparison, using four years of high school or more, is next illustrated.

Twelve or More Years Schooling, by Age and Sex, for the Population 20-24 Years of Age

According to this measure (12 years or more schooling) the white population is receiving much more education than the nonwhite, there being a spread of approximately 18 to 24 percentage points between them (Figure 7.5).

White males attained approximately the same educational level as white females in the late 1950s and the two have stepped along together since then. Nonwhite females, on the other hand, have always attained more superior educational levels than have nonwhite males.[3/] Nonwhite males, however, have been gaining more rapidly on nonwhite females since 1960.

A general impression of the present trends in these series may be obtained from the angle of the trend lines on the graph, as follows:

White, male and female, since 1960	32°
Nonwhite female, since 1960, disregarding 1965	40°
Nonwhite male, 1960-1964	60°
Nonwhite male, 1965-67	18°

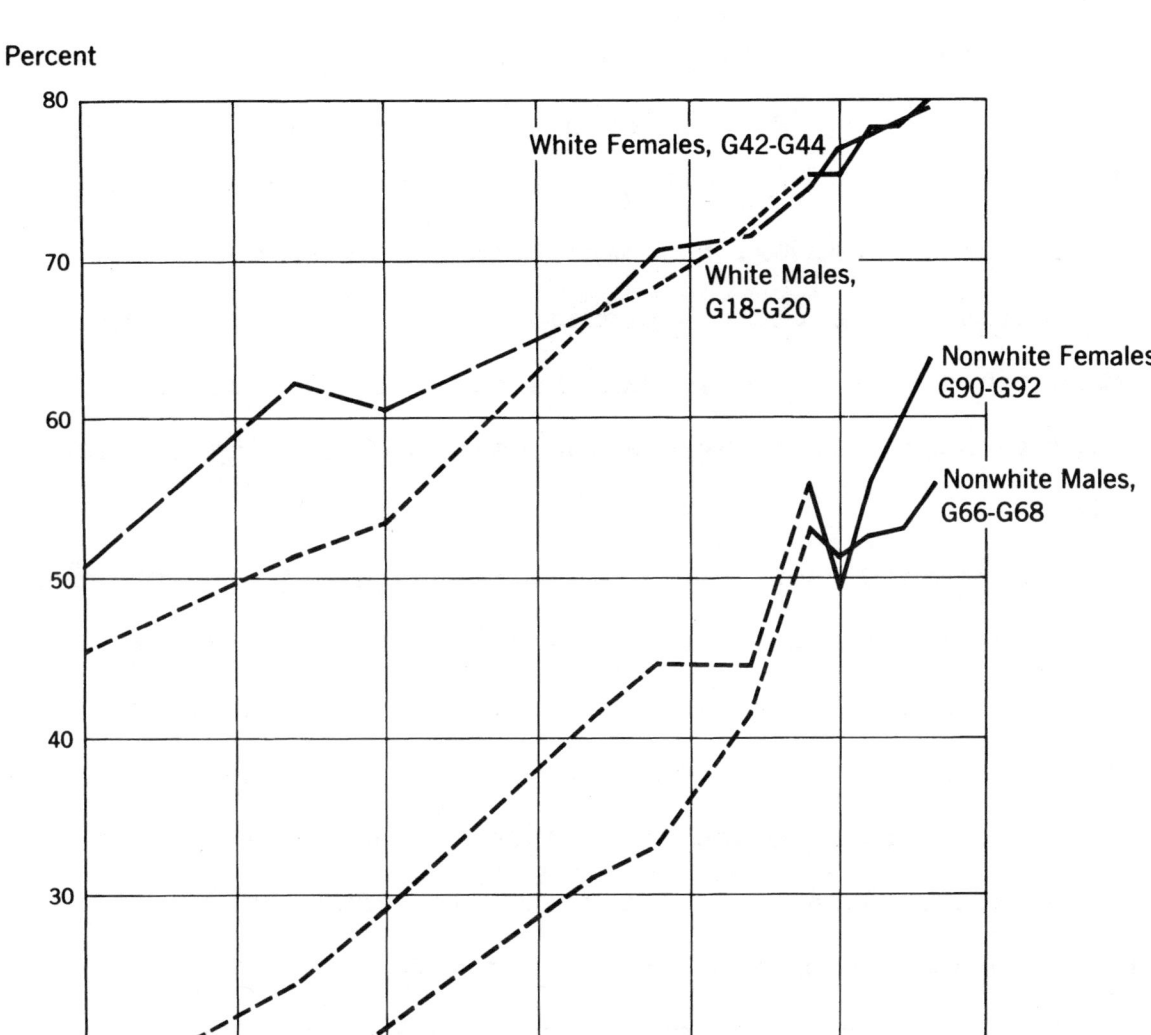

Figure 7.5. Percent of the 20–24-Year-Old Population Completing 4 Years of High School or More by Color and Sex, 1940–1968, Series G18–G20, G42–G44, G66–G68, G90–G92.

The trend for nonwhite females since 1960 may be assumed to be linear if our (footnoted) explanation of the anomalous 1965 sample is correct. The abrupt change in the trend among nonwhite males, however, has persisted for three years. With three consistent results (approximately 52 percent) the notion is reenforced that the observations are not the consequence of a large sampling error, as was the case for nonwhite females in 1965.

It appeared, then, that according to this indicator, the educational attainment of nonwhite males, 20-24 years of age, is increasing at a much slower rate than was the case before 1964. This observation seems inconsistent with the intensification of efforts to improve the lot of nonwhites. What could be the explanation? Let us examine educational attainment and school enrollment in greater detail.

While the percentage of 18-19-year-old nonwhite males enrolled in school, as a series, seems to be somewhat unstable, it has increased since 1962 (Table 7.1). School enrollment of 20-24-year-old nonwhite males, however, also unstable, appears to be relatively constant. This suggests that more nonwhite males may be completing high school and, perhaps, one year of college, but larger numbers are not remaining in college.

The percentage of the 20-24-year-old nonwhite males who have completed four years of high school or more, is fairly constant, 1964-1967. The proportion completing 4 years of high school only is constant. The proportion completing 1 to

Table 7.1. School Enrollment and Educational Attainment of Nonwhite Males, 1962 to Present

	School Enrollment		Educational Attainment 20-24 Years			
	18-19 Years	20-24 Years	20-24 yrs. H.S. or More	4 yrs. H.S.	1-3 yrs. College	4 yrs. College or More
1962 (Oct.)	40.3	12.2 (April)	41.3	29.0	10.9	1.4
1963	46.3	13.6				
1964	40.6	10.0	52.8	36.4	13.0	3.4
1965	47.5	11.7	51.3	36.1	12.3	2.9
1966	49.1	12.3	52.6	35.9	15.0	1.7
1967	50.6	18.9	53.0	36.3	14.2	2.5

Source: Data for school enrollment from Census, 1963b, 1964b, 1966b, 1967a, 1967b, and unpublished data from the U. S. Bureau of the Census. Data for educational attainment from Series G66-G69.

3 years of college only may have increased one or two percentage points over this period while the proportion of those completing 4 years of college, or more appears to be constant.

The evidence on attainment, then, appears to be consistent with the trends in school enrollment for nonwhite males. Nonwhite males in the Armed Forces are not included in the population base. Hence, educational attainment of the combined military and civilian nonwhite male population 20-24 years of age may be slightly higher than that of the civilian noninstitutional population alone.

One Year or More of College for White Females in Three Age Groups

Figure 7.6 (Series G43-G44, G51-G52, G59-G70) presents trends since 1940 in the percent of white females completing one year or more of college. The educational attainment of three age groups is shown for comparison. This measure of attainment over successive points in time shows the improving educational status of women.

The two ten-year age groups display a repetition of the same population with a time lag: the women 25-34 years of age in 1955 appear on the graph ten years later, 1965, as those 35-44 (slightly modified, of course, by some additional educational experience, some loss through mortality, and some change from migration). Slight gains in attainment may be observed by

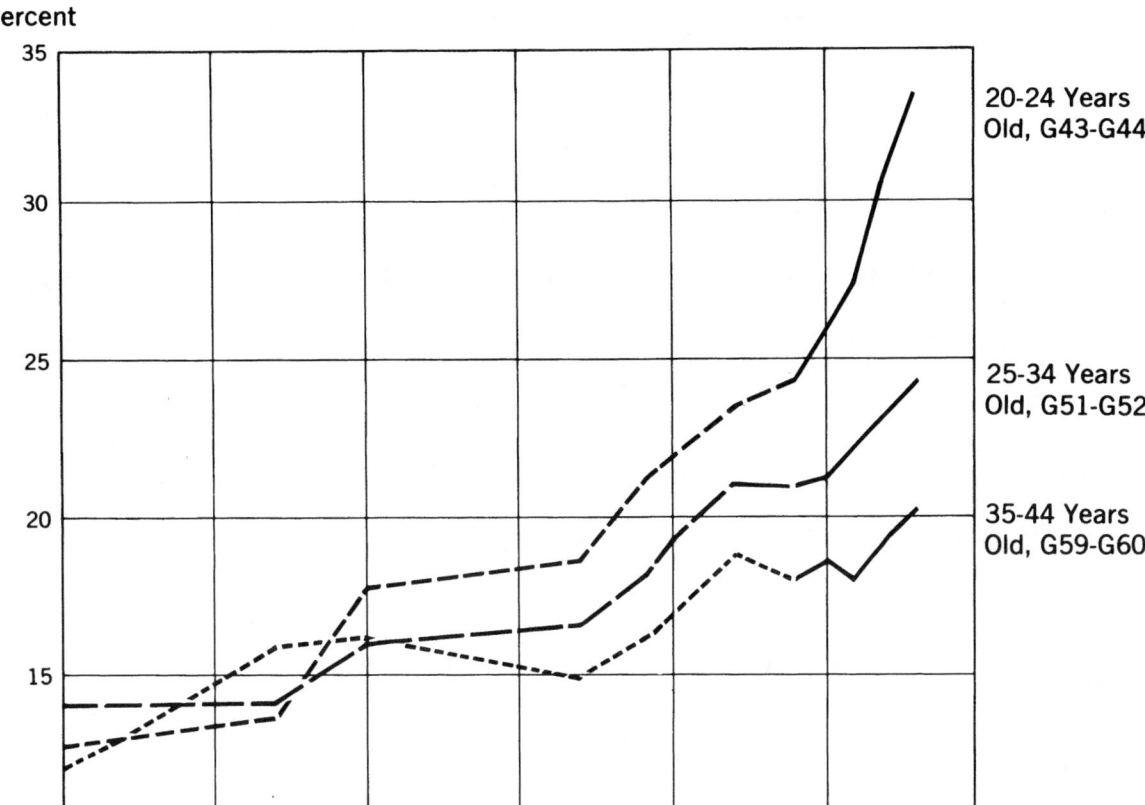

Figure 7.6. Percent of White Females with One Year of College or More, for Three Age Groups, 1940–1968, Series G43–44, G51–52, G59–60.

making this comparison, as is illustrated by the following percentages of white females completing one or more years of college.

    1957, 25-34 years of age (Series G51 plus G52)   16.6%

    1967, 35-44 years of age (Series G59 plus G60)   19.2%

The superior educational attainment of on-coming cohorts, as illustrated by the 20-24 year age group in Figure 7.5, will contribute to the increase in the educational attainment of the older cohorts. The younger group thus forecasts an improvement in attainment of the older age groups.

Cumulative Distributions of Educational Attainment, 20-24 Year-Old Nonwhite Males

Figure 7.7 (selected years, Series G62-G69) illustrates yet another approach to detecting changes in educational attainment of the population. Figure 7.7 shows the educational status of 20-24-year-old nonwhite males at four points in time: 1940, 1947, 1957, and 1967. For a given number of years of school completed, the percentage of the age-sex-color group may be observed changing over time. Thus, those completing eleven or more years of school increased, as follows: (1940) 28.6 percent, (1947) 41.9 percent, (1957) 67.3 percent, and (1967) 84.4 percent, among 20-24 year old nonwhite males.[4]

Another simple indicator that can be derived from the figure is the area under the curve, expressed as a percentage of the total possible area. In Figure 7.7, the area under the curve 1947, is approximately 32 percent of the area from the

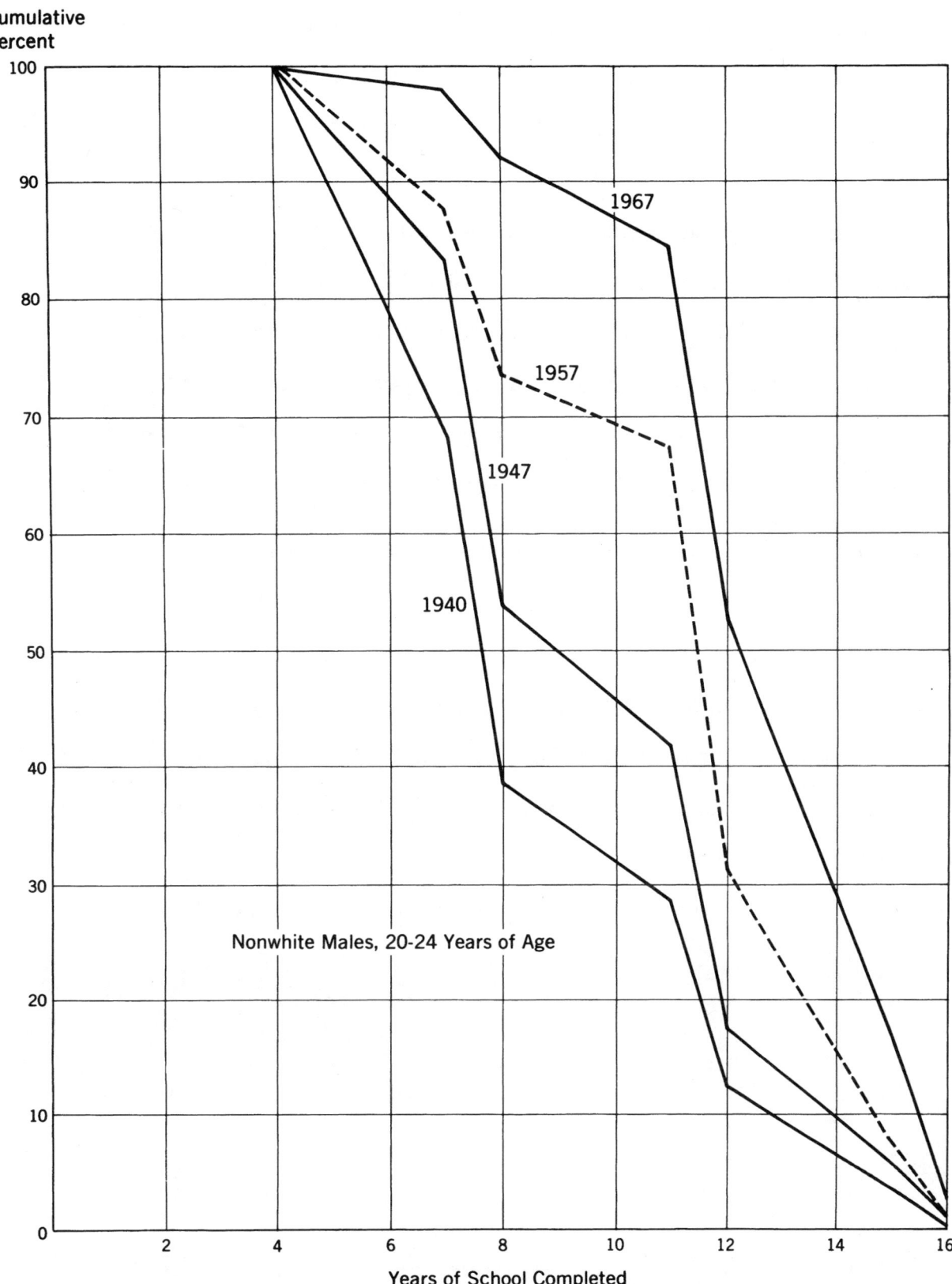

Figure 7.7. Cumulative Percentage Curves of Educational Attainment of Nonwhite Males, 20–24 Years of Age, 1940, 1947, 1957, and 1967, Series G62–G69.

4th year of schooling. The area under the curve for 1967, however, was approximately 68 percent, showing considerable improvement by nonwhite males. By contrast, this indicator for 1967 for white males 20-24 years of age was 81 percent. The difference, 13 percentage points, is a measure of disparity between the two groups in education (Table 7.2).

The median years of education attained typically is used to summarize the distribution of educational attainment. Medians for two population groups are presented in Table 7.2 for comparison with the proportion of the area under the curve. As evidenced by the ratios of nonwhite to white, the two statistics roughly display the same result, as one would expect. Both statistics have upper limits, 100 percent and 16 years, respectively, and both may be fairly easily interpreted. The area statistic, however, makes use of more information on the distribution and could be expected to be more sensitive to changes in educational attainment.

Table 7.2. Comparison of Two Indices of Educational Attainment of White and Nonwhite Males, 20-24 Years of Age, 1947 and 1967

	Area Under Cumulative Curve a/	Median Years of School Completed
1947		
White Males, 20-24	70%	11.4 years
Nonwhite Males, 20-24	32%	6.8 years
1967		
White Males, 20-24	81%	12.8 years
Nonwhite Males, 20-24	68%	12.1 years
Change 1947 to 1967		
White Males, 20-24	+11%	+1.4 years
Nonwhite Males, 20-24	+36%	+5.3 years
Ratio, Nonwhite to White		
1947	.46	.60
1967	.84	.94

a/ "Cumulative curve" refers to the percent of the group attaining each level of education or more. The percentage attaining each level is accumulated from the highest educational level to the lowest.

Source: Series G62-G69 and G14-G21, and Census, 1948b and 1968d.

Footnotes

1/ That years of school completed is a socially significant characteristic is attested by the many studies that have shown it associated with income, socioeconomic status, occupation, recreation behavior, etc.

2/ The data for 1960 are from the decennial census; hence the differences in coverage, sampling, etc., make this observation slightly inconsistent with the series. See series notes.

3/ The "dip" in the curve for nonwhite females in 1965 must be considered in the light of the sampling error. The frequencies upon which percentages are based are much smaller for the nonwhite population than for the white. As a consequence, the estimates for nonwhites are less reliable because of a larger sampling error. The 1965 observation for nonwhite females, 20-24 years of age, illustrates this. Based upon a population base of 818,000, the estimate of approximately 50 percent has a sampling error of approximately 3.2 percentage points, with probability of .68. With probability of .95, the sampling error is approximately 6.4 percentage points. Judging by the trend, the sample of nonwhite females, 20-24 years of age in 1965 was an extreme one. The observed value of 49.4 plus 6.4 is 55.8, a value fairly close to the trend line.

4/ This graphic technique may also be used to illustrate the comparative gains at two points in time of two population categories. See Folger and Nam (1967: 147) where white is compared with nonwhite for 1940 and 1960, using single years of schooling.

8

Attaining Society's Goals for Education

From the perspective of the year 1960, the President's Commission on National Goals (1960) presented proposals and objectives for education for the next ten or 15 years. The goals covered the entire range of educational interests and indicated the direction for governmental and private programs. In a chapter by John W. Gardner, "National Goals in Education," twenty-five goals and a number of subordinate objectives were specified (Gardner, 1960). Some goals were specific and subject to measurable evaluation, such as, "...we must recruit at least 200,000 new teachers every year for the next ten years." (Gardner, 1960: 82) Other goals were less subject to numerical assessment, for example, "...It is essential that the tradition of the comprehensive high school be preserved and strengthened." (Gardner, 1960: 85)

Nearly ten years have passed since these goals were set forth. While they were not endorsed as the official objectives of any governmental or other action agency, the goals, nevertheless, present a number of marks against which the many activities and decisions, public and private, affecting education, may be evaluated. We may now (1969) retrospectively assess whether some of the goals are being attained.[1/]

An attempt will be made to assess thirteen of the goals, some of which were major goals as set forth by the Commission and some subordinate objectives. This effort to bring to bear upon the Commission's specific goals such numerical evidence as may be available is more than an academic exercise. It provides an assessment of progress toward what appeared to be reasonable and necessary goals for the nation ten years ago. It also gives us a notion of how adequate are statistics on education for indicating significant and critical trends in the system. The attempt should benefit current efforts to establish educational goals and to identify statistical series needed to evaluate them. What it will <u>not</u> do, however, is contribute appreciably to our knowledge of the functioning of the social system, of interactions among educational variables, of cause-effect relationships, of sequences in social change, etc. Knowledge of this kind is a necessary prerequisite to altering the educational system in order to move it toward the goals of more effective learning.

Goals Concerning Teachers

1. "To meet both growth and replacement needs, we must recruit at least 200,000 new teachers every year for the next ten years."<u>2/</u> (Gardner, 1960: 82)

As estimated in studies more recent than <u>Goals for Americans</u>, this goal appears to be a realistic specification of the need. The Commission on Human Resources (Folger, 1967: 156) shows an average demand during the 1960s of 197,000 new teachers needed and available annually (Table 8.1). In addition, a recent U. S. Office of Education study (Simon and Fullam, 1966: 45-47), encompassing both public and private school teachers, estimates the total demand for the average year, 1961-1970, to be 210,000. Vincent (1968: 15) has estimated that the colleges and universities, during the 1960s, are supplying an average of 141,000 beginning teachers annually. These from the colleges plus former teachers who have decided to reenter teaching should be sufficient to provide an adequate supply during the decade.

As does Vincent, the Commission on Human Resources estimates an increasing number of new college graduates available to assume teaching positions. Into the 1970s an ever-more adequate supply will be available. On the other hand, new teachers, particularly women teachers, tend to drop out of teaching between 25 and 35 years of age. As their children grow older, they return to their profession, the peak returning ages being 40 to 49. These returnees were 27 and 34 percent, respectively, of new teachers hired in 1958 and 1960, according to two studies (Mason and Bain, 1959; Lindenfeld, 1963: 15). Thus, returning teachers and beginning teachers from colleges, together, will adequately meet the demand for new elementary and secondary teachers into the mid-1970s. While this takes into account the effect of the Elementary and Secondary Education Act of 1965, it makes no allowance for the expansion of educational programs

Table 8.1. Projected Demand for New Elementary and Secondary Teachers, 1959-74

(All Figures in 1000's)

Year	Demand Filled by New College Graduates	Demand Filled by Experienced Returnees	Total Demand	For Enrollment Growth and New Programs	For Replacement of Teachers Leaving and Substandard Teacher
1959	116	38	154	49	105
1960	121	40	161	53	108
1961	124	42	166	53	113
1962	124	41	165	46	119
1963	142	48	190	69	121
1964	136	46	182	56	126
1965	154	52	206	71	135
Projected					
1966	185	63	247	107	140
1967	173	58	231	86	145
1968	160	53	213	64	149
1969	160	53	213	60	153
1970	155	52	207	50	157
1971	154	51	205	45	160
1972	148	50	198	35	163
1973	150	50	200	35	165
1974	152	50	202	35	167

Source: Projections of replacement needs from U. S. Office of Education, Projections of Educational Statistics to 1974-75. Enrollment growth projection from Commission on Human Resources and include estimates of the effects of the Elementary and Secondary Education Acts of 1965. Experienced returnees are projected at 25 percent of total demand.

The above table is reproduced from Folger, 1967: Table 5, p. 156.

to serve larger proportions of kindergarten and pre-school youth, nor for new programs of other types. Neither do these estimates make provision for improving the quality of teachers, except to account for the need to replace teachers with substandard certificates (see Series B7-B8). Considering the nearly 24,500 operating public school districts (1965-66) dispersed throughout the land, local shortages or surplusses are inevitable. In the 1970s, reduction of the student-teacher ratio and improvement of teacher quality appears possible, considering merely the the aggregates.

In summary, the pool of teachers available annually appears to have been and to now be adequate to meet the expected demand for 200,000 new elementary and secondary teachers annually.

2. "Teachers' salaries must be raised until they are competitive with salaries in other fields for jobs involving comparable ability and length of training." (Gardner, 1960: 82)

To properly assess this goal, teachers' salaries should be compared with similar occupations, persons of the same sex, having the same years of education.

Table 8.2 compares the 1959 median salaries of male teachers, both elementary and secondary, with salaries of male professional and technical workers with comparable years of education, and with salaries of selected other professional occupations. Male elementary school teachers received the lowest salaries of any of the teacher categories, but male secondary school teachers were paid very little more. While salaries of other professional

Table 8.2. Median 1959 Income of Males 25-64 Years Old in the Experienced Civilian Labor Force, by Years of School Completed, Selected Occupations

Year of School Completed	Total Civilian Labor Force	Total Professional, Technical, & Kindred Workers	Teachers			College Professors and Instructors	Accountants and Auditors	Chemists
			Total	Elementary	Secondary			
			Median income					
Total	5,083	6,978	5,750	5,379	5,989	7,571	6,821	7,495
High school, 4 yrs.	5,541	6,481	5,500	4,377	5,319	--	6,530	6,163
College 1-3 yrs.	6,119	6,677	4,744	4,310	4,961	5,878	6,600	6,569
4 yrs.	7,428	7,387	4,930	4,749	5,039	5,719	7,149	7,552
5 or more yrs.	7,968	7,968	6,355	5,989	6,532	7,773	7,730	8,580
			Ratio to total professional, etc.					
Total	0.73	1.00	0.82	0.77	0.86	1.08	0.98	1.07
High school, 4 yrs.	0.85	1.00	0.85	0.68	0.82	--	1.01	0.95
College 1-3 yrs.	0.92	1.00	0.71	0.64	0.74	0.88	0.99	0.98
4 yrs.	1.01	1.00	0.67	0.64	0.68	0.77	0.97	1.02
5 or more yrs.	1.00	1.00	0.80	0.75	0.82	0.98	0.97	1.08

Source: Census, 1963g: 2, 4, 6, 14, 44, 62, 64, 66.

and technical occupations might also be compared with teachers' salaires, this evidence of the basic disparity between teachers' 1959 salaries and the other occupations in Table 8.2 with the same length of training, sufficies to document the problem of interest here.

It also may be shown that teachers' salaries differ by sex, school level, and control (public and private). These differences are illustrated in Table 8.3 and compared with other selected professions, each having the same educational attainment, four years of college. Salaries of female teachers in public elementary schools exceed those of males, but males receive higher salaries in other categories. Clergymen receive incomes lower than teachers, but otherwise teachers receive less than the other occupations shown.

Accepting these disparities, we now turn to trends in the ratio of classroom teachers' salaries to salaries in other fields, disregarding educational level (for such detail is not available). From 1960 to 1966 classroom teachers' earnings improved slightly when compared with attorneys, accountants and auditors. Teachers' salaries declined slightly with respect to chemists and held their own when compared with engineers.

None of these changes are great and the general competitive position of classroom teachers' salaries has changed but little in the short run, 1960 to 1966.

Table 8.3. 1959 Income Comparison, by Sex, for 1960 Census Professional Workers, 14 Years of Age and Over, with 4 Years of College Completed

	Males	Females
Accountants & Auditors	7,156	4,959
Clergymen	4,328	2,399
Dentists	10,179	5,480
Editors & Reports	7,243	4,377
Engineers, Technical	8,913	6,472
Pharmacists	7,573	4,483
Teachers, Elementary School	4,760	4,200
Public	4,795	4,340
Private	4,420	2,699
Teachers, Secondary School	5,011	4,097
Public	4,973	4,167
Private	4,825	3,517
Teachers (n.e.c.)	4,987	3,655

Workers with no income excluded from computation of median.

Source: Census, 1964a: 57-58.

Table 8.4. Ratio, Average Earnings of Public School Classroom Teachers to Earnings of Other Professional Occupations, 1960 to 1966

	Accountants & Auditors	Attorneys	Chemists	Engineers	Instructional Staff
1960	.65	.42	.60	.53	.92
1961	.65	.42	.55	.52	.92
1962	.67	.41	.55	.53	.93
1963	.67	.42	.55	.52	.93
1964	.70	.44	.57	.54	.96
1965	.71	.45	.57	.54	.96
1966	.72	.45	.57	.55	.96

Source: National Education Association, 1967a: 27. Teachers' salaries are from NEA studies and other salaries from U. S. Bureau of Labor Statistics surveys.

The right-hand column of Table 8.4 is the ratio of classroom teachers' average salary to salaries of the entire public school instructional staff, a category that includes principals, supervisors, librarians, guidance personnel, etc., as well as classroom teachers.

If Table 8.4 accurately reflects the relative stability of teachers' salaries with respect to other professional and technical occupations, the disparity that existed in 1960 (Tables 8.2 and 8.3) continues to exist. From Table 8.2, for 1959, it is clear that increases in teachers' salaries from 16 percent to 56 percent, depending upon education and level of school, would be required to make the average teacher's salary competitive with those in other professional and technical occupations of equal educational attainment.

In summary, the goal of reducing the disparity between teachers' salaries and salaries of comparable professions had come slightly closer by 1966, but salaries still are far from competitive, and the goal is a long way from being attained.

3. "College faculty members should receive salaries that are competitive with salaries in other fields for jobs involving comparable ability and length of training." (Gardner, 1960: 83)

Academic salaries vary along a number of dimensions: field of specialization, level of the highest earned degree, age, academic rank and years of professional experience, type of employer, major activity (whether research, administration, teaching, etc.), and the sex of the individual (Seltzer, 1965: 99-113). Among educational institutions, salaries vary by whether the institution is publicly or privately controlled, whether it is a university, college, or other type, by size of the institution, and by region (Dunham, Wright, and Chandler, 1966: 39-44).

To assess this goal, salaries of indivuduals comparable in ability and length of training must be compared. Comparability on other factors would be desirable, such as age, sex, specialization, years of professional experience, etc. Comparable data of this kind exist only for selected fields. Perhaps the most satisfactory basis for such a comparison is the National Register of Scientific and Technical Personnel, which provides controls on type of employer, field of specialization and highest degree held.

Doctorate-holding scientists in educational institutions may be compared to those in the Federal government, in business and industry, and the self-employed. Since teaching is primarily the function of educational institutions, type of work may not be entirely comparable. Research and administration, however, is not a specialty of one industry. As to ability, one may assume that doctorates with the same specialty will differ little in ability. In fact, for 11 specialties, Harmon found the mean intelligence test score to be quite similar, varying only from 123.3 to 140.3, and he found variation within specialty to be quite low (Harmon, 1961: 680).[3/]

Table 8.5 presents a comparison of the median annual salaries paid to academic scientists and salaries of scientists having other types of employers, by field. All hold the

Table 8.5. Ratio, Median Annual Salaries, Ph.D. Scientists in Educational Institutions to Ph.D. Scientists Employed by Other Employers

Field and other employer	1956-58	1962	1964	1966	All Scientists (not Ph.D.s) 1968
All Science Fields					
Federal Government	.89	.82	.81	.91	1.00
Business & Industry	.65	.64	.70	.80	.92
Self Employed	--	.60	.58	.64	.95
Chemists					
Federal Government	.84	.82	.76	.86	.82
Business & Industry	.67	.69	.71	.80	.76
Self Employed	--	.60	.67	.68	.65
Physics					
Federal Government	.78	.83	.78	.76	.83
Business & Industry	.70	.67	.69	.71	.74
Self Employed	--	.56	--	--	.65
Mathematics					
Federal Government	.70	.77	.64	.75	.78
Business & Industry	.61	.67	.61	.76	.71
Self Employed	--	--	--	--	.57
Biological Sciences					
Federal Government	.90	.82	.87	.97	1.10
Business & Industry	.71	.69	.75	.87	.99
Self Employed	--	.60	.60	.54	.74
Psychology					
Federal Government	.92	.82	.82	.91	.90
Business & Industry	.65	.64	.63	.71	.83
Self Employed	--	.60	.56	.62	.67
Economics					
Federal Government	--	--	.74	.86	.92
Business & Industry	--	--	.58	.70	.87
Self Employed	--	--	--	--	.78

Note: The median salary of doctorates in educational institutions is divided by the median of the other types of employers.

Source: National Science Foundation, 1968c: 4.

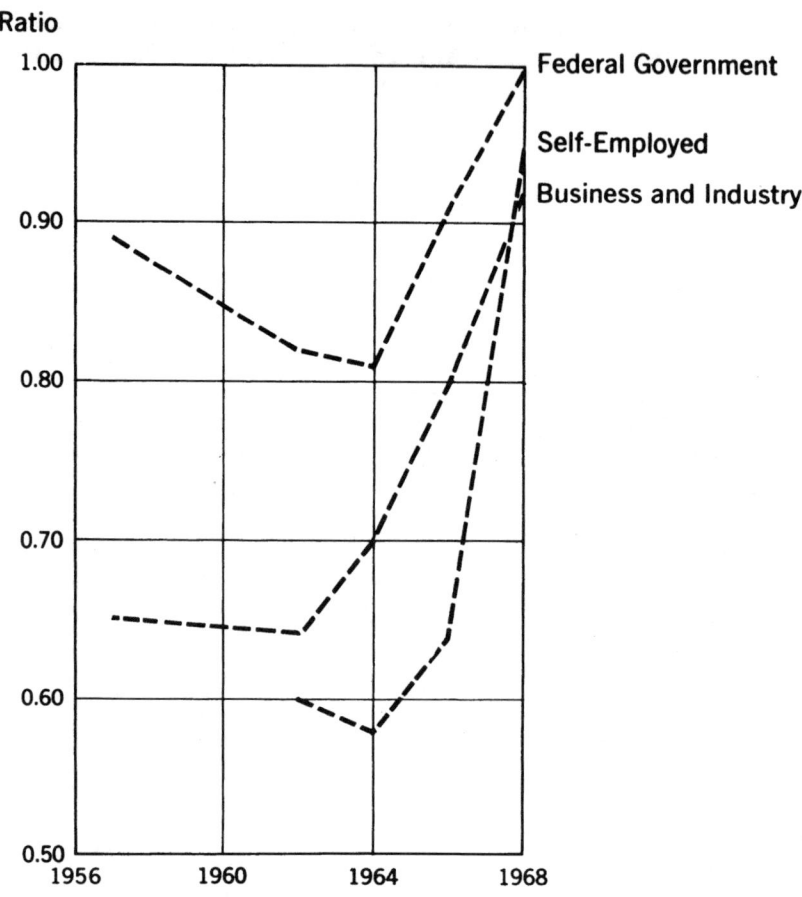

Figure 8.1. Ratio, Median Annual Salaries, Ph.D. Scientists in Educational Institutions, to Ph.D. Scientists, 1957–1966, and All Scientists, 1968, in Federal Government, Business and Industry, and Self-Employed for all Science Fields.

doctorate except in 1968. The evidence is unmistakable that the financial status of doctorate scientists in educational institutions has improved over the past decade. Among the three groups, the self-employed earned the highest salaries, those employed by business and industry had the next highest, while those in the Federal government earned the lowest. The median salary of doctorate scientists working in educational institutions was lower than the median of scientists with other employers, the only exception being the 1968 salaries of biological scientists in the Federal government.

The competitive advantage of salaries of doctorates employed in educational institutions is improving. For most fields, a disparity remains between academic salaries and those in the Federal government, in business and industry, and the self-employed, but the gaps are closing. Allowance must be made for the greater opportunity academic people have for earning outside income, income not represented in Table 8.5. While the goal of competitive salaries for faculty members is yet to be achieved, the trend appears to be toward parity with Federal salaries, if not the other sectors. Physics is an exception.

Goals Concerning Segregation

4. "We should set as our minimum goal that by 1970 there should be no state in which desegregation is prevented by state action, no state that has not moved to comply with the Court on desegregation." (Gardner, 1960: 84)

The trend in desegregation of public schools among Southern and border states is shown in Table 8.6. Before the U. S. Supreme Court ruling of May 17, 1954, the percentage of Negro children in public schools with whites in the Southern and border states was quite minimal. Delaware, Maryland and West Virginia were the only states reporting a few desegregated schools. After 1954, desegregation in the District of Columbia proceeded quite rapidly, and was followed by Delaware, Missouri and West Virginia. Other border states followed at a slower pace. Ten years later, 1964-65, all the border states except Oklahoma and Maryland had at least one-half of the Negro children in integrated schools.

Such was not the case, however, for the remaining 11 Southern states. Ten years after the Supreme Court ruling all Southern states had a "trace" of desegregated schools, but only Texas, Tennessee and Virginia had as many as 5 percent of its Negro pupils in integrated schools. After this date, however, the picture began to change faster.

Title VI of the Civil Rights Act of 1964 required that Federal assistance to a public school district or a public college or university be withheld unless it complied with the provisions of Title VI of the Act. The following year saw marked increases in the percentage of Negroes enrolled in integrated schools in Arkansas, Florida, North Carolina, Tennessee, Texas, and Virginia. The next year general increases in the percentage integrated were observed in all Southern states. By fall 1968, six Southern

Table 8.6. Percent of Negro Pupils Enrolled in Desegregated Schools, Southern and Border States, 1954-55 to Present

Percent

	Southern	Ala.	Ark.	Fla.	Ga.	La.	Miss.	NC	SC	Tenn.	Tex.	Va.	Border	Del.	DC	Ky.	Md.	Mo.	Okla.	W.Va.	Region
1954-55	0.0*	0.0	0.0*	0.0	0.0	0.0	0.0	0.0	0.0	0.0	0.0*	0.0	NA	1.9	NA	0.0	5.1	NA	0.0	4.3	NA
1955-56	0.1	0.0	0.1	0.0	0.0	0.0	0.0	0.0	0.0	0.1	1.1	1.1	NA	11.0	NA	0.8	15.9	NA	NA	NA	NA
1956-57	0.1	0.0	0.0*	0.0	0.0	0.0	0.0	0.0	0.0	0.1	1.4	0.0	NA	28.5	97.0	20.9	19.1	NA	8.7	NA	NA
1957-58	0.2	0.0	0.1	0.0	0.0	0.0	0.0	0.0*	0.0	0.1	1.4	0.0	NA	36.2	88.5	28.4	22.1	0.0	18.2	38.7	NA
1958-59	0.1	0.0	0.1	0.0	0.0	0.0	0.0	0.0*	0.0	0.1	1.2	0.0*	NA	43.7	81.5	27.5	32.4	NA	21.2	39.8	NA
1959-60	0.2	0.0	0.1	0.2	0.0	0.0	0.0	0.0*	0.0	0.1	1.2	0.1	45.4	44.1	81.9	38.9	29.3	42.7	26.0	50.0	6.4
1960-61	0.2	0.0	0.1	0.0*	0.0	0.0*	0.0	0.0*	0.0	0.2	1.2	0.1	49.0	45.0	84.1	47.7	33.6	41.7	24.0	66.6*	7.0
1961-62	0.2	0.0	0.1	0.3	0.0*	0.0*	0.0	0.1	0.0	0.8	1.3	0.2	52.5	53.7	85.6	51.2	41.5	41.4	25.6	62.0	7.6
1962-63	0.4	0.0	0.2	0.7	0.0*	0.0*	0.0	0.3	0.0	1.1	2.3	0.5	51.8	55.9	79.2	54.1	45.1	38.9	23.6	61.4	8.0
1963-64	1.2	0.0*	0.3	1.5	0.1	0.6	0.0	0.5	0.0*	2.7	5.5	1.6	54.8	56.5	83.8	54.4	47.8	42.1	28.0	58.2	9.2
1964-65	2.2	0.0*	0.8	2.7	0.4	1.1	0.0*	1.4	0.1	5.4	7.8	5.2	58.3	62.2	86.0	68.1	50.9	42.3	31.1	63.4	10.9
1965-66	6.1	0.4	6.0	9.8	2.7	0.8*	0.6	5.2	1.6	16.3	17.2	11.0	68.9	83.3	84.8	78.1	55.6	75.1	38.2	79.8	15.9
1966-67	15.9	4.4	15.1	22.3	8.8	3.4	2.5	15.4	5.6	28.6	44.9	25.3	75.7	100.0	86.3	90.1	65.3	77.7	50.8	93.4	25.8
1967-68	13.9a	5.4	16.8	18.0	9.5	6.7	3.9	16.5	6.4	18.4	26.1	20.4									
1968-69	20.3a	7.4	23.3	24.1	14.2	8.8	7.1	27.8	14.9	24.3	38.9	25.7									

* - Less than 0.1.

a - This figure includes desegregated pupils in school districts that signed Form 441 on complete compliance in the year shown.

Source: Data for 1954-55 to 1966-67 from Campbell, Flake and Leeson, 1967: 40-44, for 1967-68 from U. S. Department of Health, Education and Welfare, 1968: Table 1, for 1968-69 from U. S. Department of Health, Education and Welfare, 1969: Table 1.

states had more than one-fifth of the Negro pupils enrolled in integrated schools (Arkansas, Florida, North Carolina, Tennessee, Texas and Virginia), and the remaining states had desegregated seven percent or more of Negro pupils.

It should be noted that the percentage of Negro pupils in desegregated schools are underrepresented in the last three years, particularly the last two.$\underline{4/}$ For the last four years, Table 8.7 shows the number of school districts whose reports on desegregation are included in Table 8.6, and provides an index to the deficiency in the data for the last two years. The table shows 47 percent fewer districts in 1968 than in 1964. The 1968 percentage desegregation for the Southern states shown in Table 8.6 is 20.3 percent. By using estimates from 1967 of the (1968) excluded districts, 1968 is more accurately estimated at approximately 27 percent Negro pupils in desegregated schools.

Despite the inaccuracy of the information, it is quite clear that the minumum goal on desegregation has been achieved and that desegregation of schools in the Southern states is a continuing process.

Obscured in these data is another aspect of the process: the resegregation of schools in large cities. This situation was studied as part of the Equality of Educational Opportunity study (Coleman, et. al., 1966) in ten cities. A summary of the findings says: "Huge metropolitan areas, North and South, are

Table 8.7. Total Number of Southern School Districts Reporting on Desegregation by State, 1964-65 to Fall 1968

	1964-65	1965-66	Fall 1967	Fall 1968
Alabama	118	118	113	89
Arkansas	411	410	144	173
Florida	67	67	66	57
Georgia	196	196	163	144
Louisiana	67	67	46	50
Mississippi	150	149	117	100
North Carolina	170	170	137	143
South Carolina	108	108	93	76
Tennessee	152	152	108	120
Texas	1,379	1,325	381	501
Virginia	130	130	114	115
Total	2,948	2,892	1,482[a]	1,568[b]

a - In the survey for this year, the only school districts not surveyed in the eleven Southern states were the 1,119 districts which have assured the Department (of Health, Education and Welfare) of full compliance with Title VI (HEW Form 441) and which enroll fewer than 3,000 pupils. These districts enroll an estimated 16.5% (1.9 million) of the estimated 11.5 million public school pupils in these eleven states.

b - The Office for Civil Rights estimates that the data on which the 1968 preliminary analysis is based accounts for 85 percent of the estimated 11,677,684 public school students in the eleven Southern states.

Source: Data for 1964-65 and 1965-66 from Campbell, Flake and Leeson, 1967: 43-44; for 1967 from U. S. Department of Health, Education and Welfare, 1968; for 1968 from U. S. Department of Health, Education and Welfare, 1969.

resegregating their schools; the trend is toward more rather than less segregated educational facilities." (Mack, 1966: 5) The prevalence of this phenomenum is not known.

Goals for the Education of Women

5. "Although women win some 30 percent of the B.A. degrees, they take only about 10 percent of the Ph.D's. ...Such waste of talent is a relic of the past. We can afford it no longer. ...Women should be encouraged to enter every field requiring advanced training..." (Gardner, 1960: 84)

The change in the percentage of degrees granted to women since 1959-60 is shown below:

	Bachelor's	Master's	Doctor's
1959-60	35.3	31.6	10.4
1966-67	40.3	34.6	11.9
Change	+5.0	+3.0	+1.5

The percentage of degrees granted to women has increased in each category of degree over the seven-year span, although the increase in Doctor's degrees has been very small. One could not conclude that this goal is being achieved through rapid strides, but the change at least is in the direction of the goal.

The other aspect of this goal, the distribution of women by field, is also somewhat encouraging. In 1959-60 women received Master's degrees in all fields that granted them to men; women also did so in 1966-67. In 1959-60 there were three exclusively masculine fields of the doctorate -- architecture, forestry, and law. In 1966-67, women received the doctorate in all fields in which men received them, except forestry.

Goals for the High School Curriculum

6a. "In High School, every academically talented student should study four years of English, four years of mathematics, four years of one foreign language, at least three years of science, and three years of social studies." (Gardner, 1960: 85)

To assess this goal the number of courses high school graduates have taken in each subject is needed. To couple this information with some measure of academic aptitude will be more difficult. Some of the information to assess this goal has been collected, but it is not accessible in published form (Coleman, et. al., 1966: 652).

Information on graduation requirements of a sample of comprehensive high schools in 31 states has been assembled by Conant (1967). In these 1,874 high schools, the science requirement of 3 years prevails in 64 percent of the schools; the requirement for 4 years of mathematics, in 40 percent of the schools; the requirement for 4 years of a foreign language, in 57 percent of the schools; and the requirement for 3 years of social studies, in 70 percent of the schools. Conant estimates that approximately one-third of all high school students attended medium sized comprehensive schools of this type, 750 to 1,999 students, with 25 percent to 75 percent continuing after graduation to college

(Conant, 1967: 9). This information provides merely a rough approximation to evaluating the adequacy of the high school curriculum and graduation requirements, specified by the goal.

From time to time the U. S. Office of Education collects information on enrollment by subjects in the public secondary schools. Each subject is typically offered in a specific grade, but students in one grade sometimes are allowed to take a subject of another grade. For this reason the data on enrollment by subject and grade present a slightly misleading picture. The gross information provided by the 1961 survey (Wright, 1965), however, may be summarized as follows:

English: Nearly all high school students (above 95 percent each year) take a course in English or an English-related course (such as public speaking, or journalism) each year. The data point to the near universal enrollment in English each year of high school.

Mathematics: All students take a mathematics course in the 9th grade and between 40 and 45 percent of students take courses in the 10th, 11th, and 12th grades.

From the trends shown in Table 8.8, see below, it appears that the percentage of 14-year-olds taking elementary algebra has increased since 1948-49 from 50 percent to 61 percent in 1962-63, and the percentage of 16-year-olds taking intermediate algebra, from 19 percent to 37 percent.

Table 8.8. Estimates of the Enrollment Rates by Age and Subject, Science and Mathematics, Secondary Schools, 1948-49 to 1962-63

	Typical Age	Enrollment Rate					
		1948-49	1954-55	1956-57	1958-59	1960-61	1962-63
Total Science	14-17	.34	.39	.42	.43	.44	.47
General Science	14	.51	.49	.58	.56	.56	.52
Biology	15	.47	.57	.59	.57	.61	.67
Chemistry	16	.19	.22	.23	.26	.26	.31
Physics	17	.13	.14	.14	.16	.13	.14
Other Science	15-17	.03	.04	.04	.05	.07	.05
All Mathematics	14-17	.34	.40	.46	.47	.46	.53
Elementary Algebra	14	.50	.52	.58	.63	.58	.61
Intermediate Algebra	16	.19	.19	.21	.25	.27	.37

Source: Wright, 1965.

Foreign Languages: At any one time only about one-fourth of the high school students are taking a course in a foreign language. This does not mean that the student takes four years of the language, however.

Considered by grade, 52 percent of the 9th grade takes a course in some foreign language. Corresponding percentages for other grades are: 10th, 37 percent; 11th, 9 percent; and 12th, 2 percent (Wright, 1965: 10). This statistic provides a marked contrast to the percentage of schools offering four years of a language (57 percent), according to the Conant study.

Science: Enrollment in science courses, by grade, shows the following: 9th grade, 64 percent enrolled; 10th, 80 percent enrolled; 11th, 37 percent; 12th, 38 percent enrolled.

These data also may be examined in relation to the typical age group in the class where the subject usually is offered. The results are presented in Table 8.8.

Table 8.8 shows that enrollment in general science has changed since 1948-49 but has not changed consistently or permanently. The percentage enrolled was about the same (52 percent) in 1962-63 as in 1948-49. Enrollment of 15-year-olds in biology appears to have increased from 47 percent to 67 percent. Chemistry, the subject typically taught 16-year-olds, increased from 19 percent to 31 percent. Physics and other sciences appear to have maintained a fairly constant proportion of the enrollment.

Social Studies: Subjects in this area are not as uniformly arranged by grade as some of the other subjects. It would appear that nearly all the 11th and 12th graders take some form of social studies, that at least two-thirds in the 10th grade do so, and a minimum of 30 percent in the 9th grade do so.

If one is permitted to generalize from these data concerning the extent of attainment of the stated goal for high school curricula early in the decade, one might conclude the following: English (4 years) and social studies (3 years) are adequately provided in the curriculum and nearly all students enroll in the courses. Mathematics (4 years) is available in approximately two-fifths of the schools and approximately two-fifths of the students are enrolled. Science is available (3 years) in nearly two-thirds of the schools; enrollment is between one-third and two-fifths of the students in the 3rd year. Finally, foreign languages may be available (4 years) in more than one-half of the schools, but only a small percentage of students take as many as 4 years.

Goals for Higher Education

7. "Post-secondary institutions should be prepared to handle up to 50 percent of the college-age population by 1970." (Gardner, 1960: 90)

This goal concerns the capacity of higher educational institutions to provide for the number of youth who might want to apply. A related question is the proportion of the "college age population" actually attending.

Table 8.9 presents the percentage of the population of various ages enrolled in college, as estimated by the Census Bureau from the Census and from the Current Population Survey.

The Census projects an enrollment of 7,424,000 (Census, 1967$_e$) and the Office of Education, 7,832,000, for fall 1970 (Simon and Fullam, 1968). Can institutions provide "spaces" for this many students? The Office reports an enrollment of 7,571,000 in fall 1968. The needed increase of only 261,000 is undoubtedly attainable. "Spaces," then, will be available in institutions for the anticipated enrollment in 1970.

The next question (Is this enrollment 50 percent of the college-age population?) rests upon the ages considered of "college-age." The years 18-21 usually are taken to be the undergraduate years. If this is accepted, there will be 14,377,000 persons in these college ages in 1970.[5/] Fifty percent is 7,188,000. This number, again, is within the evident capacity of higher educational institutions.

However, in 1966, only 33 percent of this age group was enrolled in college, and nearly 10 percent was in the Armed Forces. It does not seem likely that 50 percent of the age group in 1970 will be enrolled in college.

9. "We should be producing 20,000 Ph.D's annually by 1970 (compared with 9,360 in 1958-59) without a drop in quality." (Gardner, 1960: 92)

Quantity and quality are dual aspects of this goal. We must consider each separately.

Table 8.9. Percent of Various Age Groups Enrolled in College, and Percent Total Enrollment of the 18-21 Year Age Group, 1960 to 1968

Year	16-17 Years	18-19 Years	20-21 Years	22-24 Years	25-29 Years	30-34 Years	Ratio, Total College Enrollment to 18-21-Year-Olds
1960 (April)	4.5	31.5	21.7	9.5	5.3	2.5	46.0
1961 (October)	3.9	28.6	20.5	8.0	4.2	2.0	39.3
1962 (October)	4.1	31.4	21.4	9.9	4.7	2.5	43.0
1963 (October)	3.1	34.2	27.1	12.4	5.2	2.5	48.9
1964 (October)	4.1	30.6	24.9	99.6	4.9	2.4	44.4
1965 (October)	3.8	35.0	26.6	12.6	5.6	3.0	50.1
1966 (October)	3.7	36.3	28.7	12.9	6.1	2.4	51.4
1967 (October)	3.4	35.9	31.2	12.7	6.0	3.4	52.6
1968 (October)	3.9	38.0	30.1	13.0	6.4	3.5	53.8

Source: Data for 1960 from Census, 1961; for 1961 from Census, 1962; for 1962 from Census, 1963b; for 1963 from Census, 1964b; for 1964 from Census, 1966b; for 1965 from Census, 1967a; for 1966 from Census, 1967b; and for 1967 and 1968 from unpublished data of the U. S. Bureau of the Census.

Table 8.10 presents trends and projections (U.S.O.E.) of Doctor's degrees by major field. The projections indicate that the goal of 20,000 doctorates is currently (1967-68) being achieved. However, a more important question is whether the degrees are distributed among the fields of greatest need. For example, the National Science Foundation has compared an estimate of doctorates in science fields awarded with the requirements of colleges and universities to 1974-75. During the period 1965-66 to 1969-70, only two-thirds of the requirements for science teaching, research and other activities of colleges and universities can be met. However, the picture brightens during the five-year period ending 1975; during this time, 98 percent of the requirements can be met from doctorate graduating classes. These estimates assume a 2 percent replacement demand arising from death, retirement, and loss to other employers, but the latter is considered quite negligible and is assumed to be largely counteracted by replacements transferring to colleges and universities from other employers (not from graduating classes) (National Science Foundation, 1967c: 5-6, 23-24).

In another recent assessment of the supply-demand balance in higher education, the Office of Program Planning and Evaluation of the U. S. Office of Education has anticipated a deterioration in qualifications of college and university staffs. "The ratio of Ph.D's to total faculty, 50 percent in 1964, is quite likely to be 43.5 percent in 1970 and 46 percent in 1975."

Table 8.10. Earned Doctor's Degrees, Actual to 1966-67 and Projected to 1976-77

Year	Total	Engineering	Physical Sciences & Math.	Biological Sciences	Social Sciences & Psychology	Humanities	Education	Professional and other
Actual								
1956-57	8,756	596	1,923	1,611	1,677	1,067	1,432	450
1957-58	8,942	647	1,902	1,625	1,716	1,073	1,529	450
1958-59	9,361	714	2,094	1,592	1,843	1,189	1,487	442
1959-60	9,829	786	2,141	1,770	1,923	1,250	1,474	485
1960-61	10,575	943	2,335	1,792	2,072	1,345	1,594	494
1961-62	11,622	1,207	2,518	1,959	2,172	1,430	1,737	599
1962-63	12,822	1,378	2,870	2,078	2,401	1,538	1,943	614
1963-64	14,490	1,693	3,051	2,393	2,742	1,753	2,191	667
1964-65	16,467	2,124	3,517	2,675	3,031	1,991	2,372	757
1965-66	17,500	2,350	3,730	2,810	3,190	2,110	2,480	830
1966-67	18,800	2,650	4,000	2,970	3,400	2,270	2,620	890
Projected								
1967-68	21,000	3,110	4,480	3,250	3,750	2,530	2,880	1,000
1968-69	23,600	3,640	5,030	3,630	4,180	2,860	3,170	1,090
1969-70	24,800	3,980	5,280	3,730	4,350	3,030	3,280	1,150
1970-71	24,900	4,140	5,300	3,700	4,350	3,020	3,240	1,150
1971-72	26,800	4,620	5,670	3,920	4,660	3,290	3,420	1,220
1972-73	32,000	5,710	6,770	4,600	5,510	3,930	4,020	1,460
1973-74	35,500	6,630	7,550	5,010	6,020	4,320	4,390	1,580
1974-75	35,800	6,880	7,600	4,990	6,030	4,360	4,350	1,590
1975-76	36,900	7,310	7,820	5,040	6,180	4,500	4,400	1,650
1976-77	38,700	7,660	8,200	5,270	6,490	4,740	4,610	1,730

Source: Simon and Fullam, 1968: 38-39.

(Education, 1968b: 3). This decline in qualifications results from the demand from universities and colleges exceeding the supply of Ph.D's.

The import of the above: while the goal of 20,000 Ph.D's annually by 1970 is being achieved, the goal, in relation to current requirements, is not high enough.

"...without a drop in quality." This aspect of the goal is more difficult to assess. The base-line of quality was not determined in 1958-59, and quality is not currently being evaluated, except for the recent American Council on Education's <u>An Assessment of Quality in Graduate Education</u> (Cartter, 1966), currently (1969) being repeated. If this approach is accepted overall quality might be evaluated by assuming that institutional ratings, as determined in 1964, are constant over a ten-year period (in lieu of the 1969 evidence).

As an example of the application of this approach over a ten-year span, changes in quality of degrees in mathematics and statistics may be estimated. Table 8.11 shows that 36 percent of doctorates were produced by institutions with "Distinguished" faculties in 1954-55 while, in 1964-65, 27 percent were produced by these same institutions. In terms of volume, "Distinguished" institutions had doubled their production (91 to 184), but as a proportion of the total had declined. By weighting the degrees of "Distinguished" institutions with 5, "Strong" with 4, and so forth, we may compute a mean value of quality for the two points in time. This produces a mean of 3.58 for 1954-55 and a mean of 3.10 for 1964-65. By this measure the overall quality of doctorate production in statistics and mathematics has not been improving.

Table 8.11. Doctorates in Mathematics and Statistics, by Quality of Faculty

Quality	Percentage of Doctorates	
	1954-55	1964-65
Distinguished	36	27
Strong	29	26
Good	8	6
Adequate Plus	11	12
Other	16	29
Total	100	100
Number of Doctorates	250	682

A comment upon the procedure for determining quality of graduate faculties and programs may be germane to evaluating the above.

The American Council on Education followed a procedure similar to that of Hayward Keniston in 1957 for evaluating the 15 top graduate institutions in the United States, and another study in 1924 by Raymond Hughes, which had evaluated 38 universities (Cartter, 1966: 5). That there was considerable consistency in the top fifteen institutions in each of these lists, despite differences in time of the study and method of assessment, lends credence to the notion that the evaluation of judges are consistent over time.

In the ACE study, 150 to 200 judges, specialists in that field, chose terms descriptive of the graduate faculty (Distinguished, Strong, etc.). Departments in 106 institutions, altogether, were evaluated. A numerical weight was assigned to the qualitative descriptions, and these weights were averaged to obtain the final numerical score for the department. The critical element of the evaluation is the process by which the judge arrives at his determination.

As the judge recalls his observations and previous experiences relative to a given department he is about to evaluate, he is affected by the number of acquaintances he has among the faculty of the institution and among alumni of the department, as well as his knowledge of the published work of staff and alumni. In such a comparison, institutions with large faculties or large number of graduates are more likely to have come to his attention. The size of staff and alumni of the department, then, is likely to affect the evaluation. As the number of graduates of a department increases over time, the judge is more likely to have formed an opinion through contact with an alumnus of the department.

Despite this and other criticisms of the procedure for determining quality of a graduate department, the use of the assessments show, in the case of mathematics and statistics, that higher quality institutions are increasing their production of doctorates but at the same time the proportion of total degrees from higher quality institutions is declining.

10. "...our medical schools are going to have to turn out more doctors. The Bane Report estimated that we would have to graduate 11,000 annually by 1975 (as against 7,400 in 1959)." (Gardner, 1960: 92)

From 1959 to 1967 the number of graduates in medicine and osteopathy (7,767) increased 6 percent. This small increase, even if continued, will not reach the goal of 11,000 in 1975. However, the projection of degrees by the Commission of Human Resources and Advanced Education[6/] for 1975, when an allotment for osteopathy is made, is 10,400, a figure very close to the goal.

Medical schools are small and maintain relatively constant enrollments. Recommendations have been made to expand the size of medical schools as well as establish new ones. These efforts will undoubtedly be necessary if the goal of 11,000 annually in 1975 is to be reached (National Advisory Commission on Health Manpower, 1967: 19-20).

12. "Experience has demonstrated that voluntary provisions for school district reorganization do not work. States should pass laws making such reorganization mandatory under the direction of the State Department of Education. The approximately 40,000 school districts existing today should be reduced to about 10,000 by 1970." (Gardner, 1960: 95)

Table 8.12 presents the rapid reorganization in school districts that has occurred since 1959. While the number has decreased approximately one-half, the goal of 10,000 remained

Table 8.12. Public School Districts, Fall 1959 to 1967

Fall	School Districts Total	Non-operating
1959	40,520[a]	
1960	NA	NA
1961	35,676[a]	
1962	33,086	4,227
1963	31,705	3,942
1964	29,391	3,400
1965	26,983	2,537
1966	23,464	1,779
1967	21,990	1,602

a - Includes operating and non-operating districts.

Source: Data for 1959 and 1961 from Simon and Grant, 1968: Table 57, p. 46 ; for 1962 from Hobson and Schloss, 1963: Table 1, p. 9 ; and for 1963-1967 from Barr and Foster, 1968: Table 1, p. 6.

approximately 10,000 school districts away in 1967. It seems unlikely that this goal will be attained by 1970.

The purpose of reorganization, of course, is to increase the enrollment size of the school system, 2,000 pupils being the minimum enrollment for an efficient system, according to experts (Gardner, 1960: 95). In 1966-67, as Table 6.1 (page 171) shows, approximately 16 percent of the enrollment in public school systems was smaller than the minimum desirable.

Goals for Financing Higher Education

17a. "By 1970 higher education should be getting approximately 1.9 percent of the Gross National Product (as compared with less than 1 percent in 1957-58)." (Gardner, 1960: 97)

The goal refers to current expenditures, apparently, for, as Table 8.13 shows, they were 0.9 percent of the Gross National Product in 1957-58. The table shows a steady increase in current expenditures as a percent of GNP, the figure being estimated as 1.8 percent in 1968-69. With but a small increase, the 1969-70 expenditures should reach the goal of 1.9 percent.

17b. "Like every other source of funds for higher education, tuition will have to carry its share of the burden of increased costs. If it is to contribute the same proportionate share in financing higher education in 1970 that it does today, tuition in both public and private institutions will have to rise."
(Gardner, 1960: 97)

Table 8.13. Expenditures by Regular Educational Institutions, 1956-57 to 1966-67 and Projected to 1968-69, Compared with Gross National Product

	In Current Dollars (Billions)				Percent	
	Institutions of Higher Education					
	Total	Current Expenditures	Capital Outlay	Total GNP	Total	Current Expenditures
1956-57	$ 4.9	$ 3.8	$ 1.1	430.2	1.1	.9
1957-58	5.3	4.2	1.1	444.2	1.2	.9
1958-59	6.1	4.9	1.2	465.5	1.3	1.0
1959-60	6.7	5.4	1.3	493.7	1.4	1.1
1960-61	7.6	6.0	1.6	511.9	1.5	1.2
1961-62	8.5	6.8	1.7	540.2	1.6	1.2
1962-63	10.3	7.8	2.5	575.4	1.8	1.4
1963-64	11.3	8.8	2.5	611.4	1.8	1.4
1964-65	13.1	9.9	3.2	658.6	2.0	1.5
1965-66	14.9	11.5	3.4	716.2	2.1	1.6
1966-67	16.6	13.2	3.4	768.6	2.2	1.7
1967-68	18.3	14.9	3.4	825.2	2.2	1.8
1968-69	19.8	16.5	3.3	890.7	2.2	1.8

Note: Current expenditures include those for interest from current funds and excludes those from current funds for capital outlay. Estimated capital outlay includes estimated expenditures for replacement and rehabilitation. Expenditures include those for subcollegiate departments of institutions of higher education, estimated at $85 million in 1966-67. Expenditures shown for 1967-68 and 1968-69 are projections. GNP is the average of consecutive years; 1969 is the projection of the Council of Economic Advisers.

Source: Simon and Fullam, 1968: 77-78 and Council of Economic Advisers, 1969b: 55, 227.

Table 8.14 presents the increases in average tuition charges by type of institution and control. Private institutions have increased their student fees approximately 100 percent while public institutions have increased at about half that rate, 55 percent. However, as is shown in Figure 6.9 (page 191), the contribution of student fees to the revenue of institutions of higher education has remained relatively constant, changing only from 20 percent in 1956 to 21 percent in 1966. Tuition income appears to have followed the specification of the President's Commission.

17c. "In the case of private institutions, income from endowment and gifts should be more than doubled. Every college should have an organized program to enable its friends to participate in annual giving. Today about five million alumni are solicited annually by their institutions and give $25 million a year. In 1970 closer to twenty million alumni should be solicited and should give $700 million a year." (Gardner, 1960: 97).

Private gifts and grants to the educational and general income of private institutions of higher education were approximately 298 million in 1959-60 (Lindsay, 1964: 21). By 1965-66 this source of revenue to private institutions had increased to slightly more than 547 million dollars.[7] The average annual increment of 48.5 million dollars, if continued, would bring the total from this source to approximately 740 million dollars in 1969-70, thus slightly exceeding the goal.

Table 8.14. Average Tuition and Required Fees per Full-Time Resident Degree-Credit Student in Higher Educational Institutions by Type and Control, 1958-59 and 1968-69 (Current Dollars)

	1958-59	1968-69	Percentage Increase
All Institutions			
Public	$ 192	$ 298	55
Private	729	1,436	97
4-Year Institutions			
Public	198	339	71
Private	734	1,477	101
2-Year Institutions			
Public	81	121	49
Private	392	992	153

Source: Simon and Grant, 1968: 95.

Footnotes

<u>1/</u> Albert D. Biderman (1966: 133) identified 18 goals for education presented in <u>Goals for Americans</u> on which quantified indicators appear in the report. He also specifies the sources of data for approximately nine of these (1966: 148).

<u>2/</u> The numerical identification of the goals presented here follows that of Gardner's presentation.

<u>3/</u> The test was calibrated around a mean of 100 and a standard deviation of 20. For each field, the standard deviation was below 20, ranging from 14.7 to 17.1, depending upon the field. The coefficient of variability, the standard deviation expressed as a percent of the mean, is low for the specialties, being 11 to 13 percent. Thus, there is some small variation in general ability of doctorates by field of specialization, but, within field the variation is quite low (Harmon, 1961: 680)

<u>4/</u> Through 1966-67, the data were assembled by the Southern Education Reporting Service (Campbell, Flake and Leeson, 1967) from reports by 18 "reporters," one in each state. Their reports include all school districts of the state.

The fall 1967 and 1968 data were assembled by the Office of Civil Rights, Department of Health, Education and Welfare (U. S. Department of Health, Education and Welfare, 1968 and 1969) by survey. The definitions differ from those of the data from the Southern Education Reporting Service. These two years are derived from data from 85 percent of the students. Excluded in fall 1967 were 1,119 districts "which have assured the Department (of Health, Education and Welfare) of full compliance with Title VI (HEW Form 441) <u>and</u> which enroll fewer than 3,000 pupils. These districts enroll an estimated 16.5 percent (1.9 million) of the estimated 11.5 million public school pupils in these eleven states." (U. S. Department of Health, Education and Welfare, 1968: Table 1, footnote 2). Thus, in states where some of the school districts with less than 3,000 pupils are in full compliance with the provisions of Title VI, the percentage shown is less than the actual percentage of Negro students in desegregated schools.

<u>5/</u> The 1970 population is a Census Bureau projection (Census, 1967e: 8). However, the age-grouping provided had to be recombined for the age groups shown. This was done by disaggregating proportional to the number of births of the appropriate cohort. The U. S. Office of Education projection is from Simon and Fullam (1968: 11).

<u>6/</u> Based upon a preliminary report of the Commission. The final report is to be published by the Russell Sage Foundation in 1969.

<u>7/</u> From unpublished data from the National Center for Educational Statistics.

Appendix A

What Contributes Most to an Increase in Degrees: A Change in Rate or Change in Population?

Since the projection of degrees into the immediate future rests upon the experience of the immediate past, the question of the relative value of these two influences upon degree production has relevance to the methodology of projecting degrees. The model for answering the question will be presented and illustrated with data for Master's degrees awarded to females.

Since 1947-48, Master's degrees awarded to women have increased slightly each year except 1953-54. Over this period, however, the size of the cohort (the 24-year-old females) decreased steadily to 1958-59 when it rose, falling again the next year, but afterwards continuing to rise. The rate of awards (degrees to the 24-year-olds) increased slightly each year except two. Among these conflicting influences, what contributed most to the 132 percent increase in annual Master's awards to females over the 17 years?

Let W = the 24-year age cohort of females, in year i

- w = the incremental change in the cohort (plus or minus) to year $i + 1$

- R = the rate of Master's degree awards to females, year i

- r = the incremental change in rate of awards to year $i + 1$, either plus or minus

Then, the awards in year $i + 1$ will be:

$$(W + w)(R + r) = WR + wR + Wr$$

Thus, WR is the production of degrees, year i

Wr is the increment in degrees due to change in rate

wR is the increment in degrees due to change in population

wr is the increment in degrees due to interaction of change in rate and change in population.

While wr has no readily interpretable meaning, it is a relatively unimportant, small value.

Gross totals over the 17 years for these values, show 21,379 degrees due to changes in rates, 1,082 due to a change in population, and 12 due to the interaction of the two. Increase in the rate of degree attainment, then, has contributed the most to the annual increase in Master's degrees awarded to women.

Similarly, the increase in other degrees awarded seems primarily to rest upon increases in rates of attainment. The percentage changes, 1948 to 1965, are, as follows:

	Male			Female		
	B	M	D	B	M	D
Degrees	181	263	420	228	266	360
Age Group	128	101	95	124	99	93
Rate of Attainment	142	258	443	183	275	400

The percentage increase in degrees was greatest for Doctor's degrees, next greatest for Master's degrees and lowest for baccalaureate degrees. On the other hand, during the 1948-1965 period, the proportionate increase in the cohort most typical of the degree recipient, respectively, affected the baccalaureate degree production most, and Doctor's least.

On the other hand, the rate of attainment increased far greater for Doctor's than for Master's and least for baccalaureate degrees. The change in rate, as the above example of change in Master's degrees awarded to females demonstrates, has been by far the most important basis for increases in degrees.

While the increase in the age cohort, brought about by the increases in births during the 1940s, contributed slightly to the increases in degrees, by far the more important factor is the increase in the rate of attainment over this period.

Projections of degrees by the U. S. Office of Education for the next ten years are based upon the experience of the past ten years (Simon and Fullam, 1968: 100-102). Total degrees at each level are projected by applying a rate of attainment to the 18-year-old age cohort, each sex separately considered. For projecting baccalaureate degrees, the 18-year-olds four years earlier are used; for Master's degrees, the 18-year-olds six years earlier are used; and for Doctor's degrees, the 18-year-olds nine years earlier are used. This procedure establishes the expected number of total degrees. Tables 5.4 and 5.5 (pages 143 and 144 in the text) show that the expected increases in rate are greatest for baccalaureate degrees, and smallest for Doctor's degrees, but that positive increments are expected in each level of degree.

Table A1 presents the rate of change in the male and female 18-year-old population, over the previous year. For example, the 1959 population of males was 6.0 percent greater than the 1958 18-year-old male population; this appears in the first column as .060. This change had an effect upon Bachelor's degree production in 1962, upon Master's degree production in 1964, and upon Doctor's degree production in 1967. Because of the variation in age completing high school, age entering college, and age completing the degree, the dates entered in Table A1 only roughly indicate the time when changes in size of the age cohort will effect a change upon degree production.

As one might expect, the rates of increase for males and females are approximately the same. The increment of considerable influence and importance is the change in the size of the cohort attaining 18 years of age in 1965, over the 1964 cohort. Approximately, a 22 percent increase occurred. This population increment affects the 1968 Bachelor's degrees, the 1970 Master's degrees, and the 1973 doctorates, approximately.

The second step in the U. S. Office of Education procedure for projecting earned degrees is to distribute total degrees among the fields of study. This is done by regressing the percentage on time to project the percentage distribution of degrees for each level and sex group. An adjustment sometimes is necessary in the percentages so that the 17 separate equations will equal 100.0 percent of the degrees. The estimating equations, based upon the past ten years experience, provide the annual increment in the percentage for each specialty area. These increments make up the body of Tables 5.4 and 5.5 (pages 143 and 144 in the text).

Table A1. Annual Rate of Change in the 18-Year-Old Population, by Sex, and the Approximate Year the Change Will Affect Degree Production

Year 18 Years of Age	Rate of Change Over Previous Year		Year the Change Will Affect Degrees -		
	Males	Females	B	M	D
1959	.060	.057	1962	1964	1967
1960	.087	.086	1963	1965	1968
1961	.076	.078	1964	1966	1969
1962	-.041	-.042	1965	1967	1970
1963	.004	.001	1966	1968	1971
1964	.083	.083	1967	1969	1972
1965	.226	.220	1968	1970	1973
1966	-.042	-.043	1969	1971	1974
1967	-.002	-.001	1970	1972	1975
1968	.003	.002	1971	1973	1976
1969	.028	.029	1972	1974	1977
1970	.030	.029	1973	1975	1978

Source of population: Simon and Fullam, 1968: 110.

Appendix B

The Development of an Academic Production Index

The degrees awarded annually provide measures of the production of higher education. Some summation or combination of degrees would give us a general index of academic production. Such an index would provide a gross index of trends, a basis for computing ratios and other indices in relation to students, teachers, finances, etc., and a general measure of production subject to disaggregation into its components. Several approaches might be made to developing a differential weighting scheme to enable the summation of degrees into an index:

a) Weights might be assigned proportional to the estimated life-time earnings added by the degree.

b) Weights might be assigned proportional to the cost of obtaining the degree.[1]

c) Weights might be assigned proportional to time required to obtain the degree.

d) Weights might be assigned through use of component analysis, a statistical technique that would take into account the intercorrelation (across time) of the numbers of degrees awarded by type of degree.[2]

These procedures were considered in relation to the adequacy of available data necessary for each, the relative stability of the weights across time, and other factors. In balance, time (c, above) was chosen as a suitable and adequate basis for developing weights. Time is proportional to the student's effort and to institutional costs of providing education. The years typically required to obtain the degree were the basis for developing weights, as follows:

Degree	B4	B5	M	M.D.	Ph.D.
Cumulative Years	2	3	3.25	4	6.25
Divide by 2	1	1.5	1.62	2	3.12
Round to:	1	1.5	1.6	2	3.2

An estimate of the years of required work in the specialty is the basis for the cumulative years on the first row. The number of years college work minus two are shown. The Gross Academic Production Index, then, is computed by summing the products of the weights and the degrees of each kind.

It should be noted that measures based upon these weights are indices of the cumulative educational experiences completed in a given year. For example, the weight for the doctorate includes values for previous educational experiences, such as the baccalaureate, which were acquired during a previous year. Because of this property, the index is not additive across years, nor can it be considered that it measures the "education added" in a given year.[3/]

The weighting procedure assigns the smallest value to baccalaureate degrees and the greatest value to Doctor's degrees. However, the magnitude of baccalaureate degrees, in a typical year, is approximately thirty times greater than

Doctor's degrees. Consequently, the 4-year baccalaureate degrees dominate the index in any year. The trend in the Gross API, presented in Figure 5.18, illustrates this. The peak in 1949-50 and the trough in 1954-55 of the Gross API coincides with the peak and trough in the number of baccalaureates granted.

The U. S. Office of Education has not always reported degrees in the detail presented above. In some years 4-, 5-, and 6-year baccalaureate and first-professional degrees have been combined, and must be separated through an estimating procedure. A procedure for estimating them was developed upon the basis of detail presented in <u>Earned Degrees Conferred</u>, 1964-65 (Mason and Rice, 1967). In this report, first-professional degrees requiring five or more years to complete are enumerated separately from the 4-year Bachelor's degrees. The percentage of 5-year degrees reported as first degrees were developed for all fields having an appreciable number of such degrees.[4/] These adjustments were assumed to apply to all years prior to 1960-61, the time during which the Office of Education requested a report on only one category of baccalaureate degree. While not highly refined, these procedures were judged adequate, considering that the ratios were applied by specialty field.

1/ A weighting system for science and technology degrees has been developed by William V. Consolazio (1967: 99-101). Degree weights are based upon estimated costs to the institution for providing the degree. His Science and Technology Degree Productivity Unit is weighted as follows: Bachelor's degree, 1; Doctor of Veterinary Medicine, 2.2; Master's Degree in Science and Technology, 2.5; Doctor of Medicine and of Dentistry, 4.0; Doctorate in Science and Technology, 4.5.

2/ Component analysis has been employed to develop weights for three levels of degrees in order to assign a degree productivity value to institutions of higher education (Bachelor's Degree Units). The "cases" in this analysis were all degree producing institutions. The weights were: Bachelor's degree, 1; Master's degree, 2.8; and Doctor's degree, 6.8 (Ferriss, 1964).

3/ The annual output of schooling has been analyzed by Beverly Duncan (1968: 601-672), upon the basis of a year's enrollment.

4/ The percentage of first level degrees assigned to the levels indicated, are as follows: to B5: Architecture (75), Business and Commerce, Total (2), Accounting (8), Engineering (5), Forestry (4), Nursing (2), Pharmacy (89), Library Sciences (78), Public Administration (40); to Master's: Social Work (68); to M.D.: Medicine, M.D., Optometry, Osteopathy, and Veterinary

Medicine All (100), Public Health (37), Religion, Total (59), Religious Education and Bible (20), Theology (94). A few other fields gave small numbers of 5-year first-level degrees, but the frequencies were not large and the correction they would entail was judged to be trivial.

Appendix C

Age Cohorts of the Population

A stationary population of students would present no problem for educational planning. Since 1930, the number in each annual newly-born cohort, however, has fluctuated considerably. The sources of this variation are not difficult to find: the birth rate. It had been declining for a long time and continued to fall until about 1936. World War II initially brought on an increase in the birth rate, then a brief decline during the last two years of the war. When the war was over, however, the crude birth rate leaped up during 1946 and 1947. It then subsided and, after 1950, rose again to a peak in 1957. Since that time, however, the rate has declined steadily and, by the end of 1967, stood at approximately 18 live births per 1,000 population. With a declining rate of infant mortality and a continuously rising population, however, the annual absolute number of births reached a peak in 1957, and from this point had declined about 17 percent by 1967.

These shifts in magnitude of successive age cohorts to be served by the educational system create continuous problems of adjustment within the system as a whole. Population changes in specific localities may have even greater consequences, for not only do changes in the birth rate alter the school-age populations, but mobility of the population, also, creates shifts in the numbers to be served at particular locations. The suburbs of metropolitan and urban centers have experienced large population increases for several decades. For this reason, the gross magnitudes of the statistics presented as Series I1 - I35, give us only an unrefined index of the problem. Underneath, the real stress upon the educational system is measured by the population pyramids of fast-growing urban and suburban places. Localized data, then, ultimately are needed to trace the impact of the joint consequence of fertility-mobility upon the educational system. Disaggregation to state, county, and local levels, eventually, is required if age cohort data are to serve their maximal usefulness as indices of demand for education. In fact, analyses of population change within states for educational planning have been carried out in a number of states, such as California, Washington, and North Carolina. See for example, Schmid, et. al. (1967) and Schmid and Miller (1967).

Series I1-I35 illustrate the shifting magnitude of successive population cohorts by sex. The 5-year, 14-year and 18-year cohorts generally represent those entering, respectively, kindergarten, high school, and college, while the "graduating" classes are usually taken as the 13-year, 17-year, and 22-year-old groups. These ages only roughly approximate the entering and leaving students, as a glance at a decennial Census table for year in school by age will reveal. Series I4 presents the population generally attending elementary school and Series I25, the population of undergraduate students in college. Series I35 presents the high school ages. The sources provide additional detail, as one may require, by color as well as sex. Disaggregation to state and local areas requires use of the decennial or special censuses, and state birth records.

These series may be used to analyze educational trends nationally on a per capita basis. This use may be enhanced by projections into the future, for example, see Census (1967c). The future "demand" from students for education, consequently, may be projected with considerable certainty in the short run, and with somewhat less precision in the long run.

Changes in the 5-year cohorts best illustrate the demographic dynamics that affect the educational system.

A small incremental increase may be observed for some cohorts in Series I7 through Series I24, the ages 13 through 18, as each cohort matures. This phenomenum results from immigration into the United States, and is more evident during some periods of time than others.

A Note on the Quality of the Estimates

Like the population as a whole, the size of an age group or of a single year of age, once born, is affected by immigration, emigration and death. Deaths are fairly accurately recorded and some characteristics of immigrants are known, but those departing, citizens or non-citizens, are not known with precision. Other trials besetting the social bookkeeper are erroneous reports of age in the census, the undercount of the census, and the small underregistration of births and deaths. Although many of these errors are thought to be quite small, even small errors when added together, may grow in size as easily as they may counteract one another. These difficulties, plus one other, affect the estimates of the population by single years of age. The one other difficulty is that some estimates fluctuate in magnitude at the end of the decade. The apparent reason for this is that the Census Bureau fitted the year to year estimates to the decennial census enumeration. Fluctuations were created when the "fitting" was not smooth.

One of the most difficult of the above problems is created by the undercount of the U. S. Census (Marks and Waksberg, 1966; Siegel and Zelnick, 1966). With birth and death registration increasingly accurate and with considerable information available on immigration, the annual increments of population by age, sex and color may be posted to the national population account, and successively aged each year. However, the results of this procedure do not balance at the end of the decade with the decennial census. The enumeration is inconsistent with this carefully posted account, sometimes deviating as much as 20 percent for certain age, sex, color groups, e.g., nonwhite males aged 20-24 years. Correcting for such errors is particularly trying when the errors arise from varying rates of net undercount by cohort from census to census. Until the time when this problem is resolved and we are provided with annual single-year-of-age data for the population corrected for net census undercount, the imperfect age/sex estimates presented herein must suffice.

As a consequence of the above, one cannot place unlimited confidence in estimates by single year of age. Indeed, in its introduction to the estimates, the Census authors include the following caveat:

> "<u>Accuracy</u> -- Estimates in single years of age are subject to considerable error. They represent very approximately the size of the population in a given age and reflect very roughly variations from age to age and year to year. They are presented not primarily for use by themselves, but to make possible the particular combinations of ages which may be needed in a given study, for purposes of computing rates, per capita figures, etc. Small differences between figures should be disregarded." (Census, 1965b)

To illustrate some of the properties of the resulting data, a few cohorts were studies, with the following general results:

a) The largest percentage change from one year to the next is the step from one year old to two years. For the period 1945-1950, cohorts increased from one year old to two years by 4.7 percent to 6.8 percent.

b) Cohorts increase in age to the early or middle twenties, immigration exceeding deaths in these young ages. They may hold fairly constant after that, although some increase or decrease may be detected in response to immigration, mass deaths caused by war, etc.

c) Small increases or decreases occur from one year to another, often offsetting one another. Such adjustments, ranging up to 50,000 or 60,000 for a cohort (at least, during the 1940s to 1960s), are more likely to occur around the turn of the decade, such as 1949-1951 or 1958-1960, undoubtedly a consequence of adjustments made to gain consistency with the decennial census.

d) In magnitude of change, over the first twenty years, one cohort among those studied was observed to increase a maximum of 12.2 percent, while others increased by 5 percent, by 8.7 percent, etc. Over the first twenty years the net increase might be as low as 1.5 percent. The absolute value of the rate of change becomes smaller and smaller as the cohort ages.

The 1945 cohort, presented in the table below, illustrates the above.

Changes in Size of the 1945 Cohort, as Estimated in Census
Single Year of Age Data

Year	Age of Cohort	Total Cohort	Change from Previous Year	Rate of Change from Previous Year
1945	1	2,581		
1946	2	2,748	167	.064
1947	3	2,801	53	.019
1948	4	2,795	-6	-.002
1949	5	2,728	-67	-.024
1950	6	2,756	28	.010
1951	7	2,778	22	.008
1952	8	2,764	-14	-.005
1953	9	2,769	5	.002
1954	10	2,811	42	.015
1955	11	2,814	3	.001
1956	12	2,821	7	.002
1957	13	2,799	-22	-.008
1958	14	2,836	37	.013
1959	15	2,804	-32	-.011
1960	16	2,761	-43	-.015
1961	17	2,766	5	.002
1962	18	2,773	7	.002
1963	19	2,781	8	.003
1964	20	2,789	8	.003
1965	21	2,797	8	.003

Source: Census, 1965b.

Appendix D
Notes to the Series

A1. Elementary and Secondary School Enrollment, Public and Non-public Day Schools (in Thousands), 1889-1968, School Year Ending on Date.

Source: Data for 1889-1956 from Census (1960a: Series H223, p. 207); for 1958-1962 from Census (1965a: Series H223, p. 31); for 1964 from Simon and Grant (1968: Table 3, p. 3). Estimates for 1966 and 1967 are from U. S. Department of Health, Education and Welfare (1967); data for 1968 from Simon and Grant (1968: Table 1, p. 2). The following sources are cited in Census (1960a): 1870-1916, <u>Report of the Commissioner of Education</u>, various issues; 1918-1956, <u>Biennial Survey of Education</u>, chapter 2, various issues. Reference is also made to <u>Digest of Educational Statistics</u>, various issues.

The definitions used for this series are as follows:

"A public school is defined as one operated by publicly elected or appointed school officials in which the program and activities are under the control of these officials and which is supported by public funds.... A non-public school is defined as one established by an agency other than the state or its subdivisions, primarily supported by other than public funds, and, the operation of whose program rests with other than publicly elected or appointed officials. Non-public schools include both denominational and non-sectarian schools, but not private schools for exceptional children or private vocational or trade schools." (Census, 1960a: 202-203)

Excluded from this series, therefore, are pupils enrolled in sub-collegiate departments of institutions of higher education,

Federal schools for Indians on Federal installations, residential schools for exceptional children, night and summer schools. In 1960, these excluded pupils were 0.6 percent of the total shown. Elementary schools include kindergarten.

The assumption that these definitions apply equally for all years should not be made. Uniformity in reporting has gradually improved over the years and definitions thus apply more accurately to recent surveys. In addition, it should be noted that non-public enrollments were estimated for those years when surveys of non-public schools were not conducted.

Series A1 may differ from data from the decennial Census of Population or the Current Population Survey for the same year. Nam (1962: 258-269) compared the public school enrollment in the 1960 Census enumeration, the fall 1959 U. S. Office of Education survey and the 1959-60 Biennial Survey. The kindergarten to 12th grade enrollment, as enumerated by the Census, was 100.28 percent of the fall 1959 U.S.O.E. data, and 97.62 percent of the Biennial data. The latter survey is comprehensive, and counts transfer students in more than one school system. In grades K to 8, the Census was 96.51 percent of the U.S.O.E. Biennial Survey; in grades 9 to 12, the Census was 101.2 percent of the Biennial.

Nam identified some of the differences between the Census and Office surveys which might lead to different totals. These are summarized below.

	USOE	Census
Data Collection Methods	Mail questionnaire to state education departments or institutions. (Non-public sometimes collected differently.)	Household interview usually with housewife
Scope	Data collected on teachers, schoolhouses, etc., in addition to students	Data collected on other characteristics of the population, i.e., marital status, labor force status, etc.
	No age limitation	5-34 years
Assembly Methods	States summarize reports from public school districts, using standard definitions	Subject to sampling variability (25% in 1960 decennial census; CPS sample)
Definitions and Time References College	Some terminal-occupational students as well as degree-credit students have been included at various times	Program must lead to a degree
Date of Collection	Fall of the year	Decennial: April, referring (in 1960) to enrollment since February 1st. CPS: Collected in October
Treatment for Non-response, and Missing Data	Supplied by substituting data of prior years	Estimated from survey data

Despite the different methods of assembling the data, when comparisons may be made between similarly defined populations, such as the enrollment data mentioned above, the results from Census and Office are quite similar. However, Nam recommends that those using the two sets of data should not use them interchangeably without qualification.

There are advantages to each set of data. Some purposes are served better by the Census data with the potentiality of associating individual characteristics (age, sex, color, income, occupation, etc.) with the educational variable (years of school completed or enrollment status). Other studies are served best by the institutionally-oriented data assembled by U.S.O.E., with the possibility of relating geographic and institutional characteristics (public-private status, finances, admission policies, etc.) to enrollment, degrees granted, measures of institutional quality, etc. In the analysis of time series, the date the series was initiated and the frequency of "observations" are additional considerations. Both CPS and U.S.O.E. now assemble most series annually, but for time series going back annually prior to 1947, one must rely upon U.S.O.E. data.

A2. Ratio, Elementary and Secondary School Enrollment, per 100 5-17-Year-Old Population, 1889-1968, School Year Ending on Date.

Source: Data for numerator are Series A1. For denominator population estimates for 1889-1899 from Census (1966a: Series B36, p. 196); for 1900-1958 from Census (1965b); for 1960-1964 from Census (1965c); for 1966 and 1967 from Census (1968b); for 1968 from Census (1969a).

The numerator is discussed in detail in Series A1. Population estimates used for the denominator represent the total population of the United States including Armed Forces overseas.

Beginning 1960, Alaska and Hawaii are included. All population estimates are as of July 1 preceding the fall of the school year; they are presented in Series I34.

In summary, this statistic is a ratio of enrollment, as reported chiefly by state departments of education, and population, as estimated by the U. S. Bureau of the Census. Both reporting and estimating errors exist in the two series. One defect of this series is that the population subject to being included in the numerator and denominator is not the same. The magnitude of this inconsistency is not great, as the following table from the 1960 Census illustrates.

Total Enrollment and Percent Enrolled and Not Enrolled by
Age and Level of School, 1960

Age	Grades K-12	College	Percent of the Pop. not Enrolled
5-17 Years, Percent	95.7	2.2	11.1
18-34 Years, Percent	4.3	97.8	87.9
Total, Percent	100.0	100.0	46.9
N (000)	40,613	2,925	81,924

Source: Census, 1963a: Table 167, p. I-374.

The table supports the conclusion that Series A2 overestimates the percentage of the 5- to 17-year-old population enrolled in school.

The advantage of Series A2 is that it extends back to 1889 on an annual or biennial basis.

A3, A4, A5. School Enrollment per 100 Population of School Age, Total and by Color, 1850-1968, School Year Ending on Date.

Source: Data for 1850-1900, 1940, 1954 and 1955, and for white and nonwhite enrollment in 1950, from Census (1960a: Series H374-H376, p. 213); for 1910-1930 from Census (1933: 593-595, 1098); for 1945 and 1947 through 1951 (excluding data for white and nonwhite enrollment in 1947 and 1950) from Census (1952); for 1946 from Census (1948a); for white and nonwhite enrollment in 1947 from Census (1948a); for 1952 from Census (1953); for 1953 from Census (1959); for 1956-1962 from Census (1965a: Series H374-H376, p. 32); for 1963 from Census (1964b); for 1964-1966 from Census (1967b); for 1967 and 1968 from unpublished data from the U. S. Bureau of the Census. The following additional sources are cited: 1950-1930, U. S. Bureau of the Census, Fifteenth Census Reports, Population, vol. II, part 1, pp. 1094 and 1095; 1940, U. S. Census of Population: 1950, vol. II, part 1, p. 1-206; 1954-1962, Current Population Reports, Series P-20, Nos. 12, 54, 66, 74, 80, 93, 117, 126, 129, 148, 162. For notes on CPS, see Notes to Series A27-A37.

Series A3 gives school enrollment from U. S. Bureau of the Census sources per 100 total population of school age; Series A4 and A5 provide corresponding figures for white and nonwhite population, respectively. Figures for 1890 and 1940-1966 refer to the population 5-19 years old; enrollment for 1850-1880 refers to all ages and a population base of those 5-19 years old; 1900-1930 figures refer to the population 5-20 years old.

Except for decennial census years, which refer to the total population within the specified age groups, figures after 1954 refer to the civilian noninstitutional population and are estimates based on Current Population Survey samples taken in October of the year shown.

The definition of enrollment and pertinent information to the enrollment surveys follow. For 1940 and subsequent years,

"enrollment was defined as enrollment in 'regular' schools only -- that is, those schools where enrollment may lead to an elementary or high school diploma, or to a college, university, or professional school degree. Such schools are public, private, or parochial schools; colleges, universities, or professional schools, either day or night. Enrollment was either full-time or part-time.

"If a person was receiving regular instruction at home from a tutor and if the instruction was considered comparable to that of a regular school or college, the person was counted as enrolled. Enrollment in a correspondence course was counted only if the course was given by a regular school, such as a university, and the person received credit thereby in the regular school system.

"Children enrolled in kindergarten were not included in the 'regular' school enrollment figures in the 1950 Census of Population; however, they have been included here to make the data comparable with earlier years and with current practice. In censuses prior to 1950, no attempt was made to exclude children in kindergarten so that the statistics for those years include varying proportions attending kindergarten. Also, in censuses prior to 1940, the data were not restricted as to type of school or college the person was attending.

"In addition to differences in definitions of school enrollment and in population coverage, the enrollment data for different years may differ because of variations in the dates when the questions were asked and time periods to which enrollment referred. Data from the current (population) surveys were obtained in October and refer to enrollment in the current school term. In 1940 and 1950 (and 1960), the censuses were taken as of April 1, but enrollment related to any time after March 1 in 1940 and any time after February 1 in 1950. The corresponding question in the censuses from 1850 to 1930 applied to a somewhat longer period: In 1910, 1920, and 1930, to the period between the preceding September 1 and the census date (April 15 in 1910, January 1 in 1920, and April 1, in 1930); and, in 1850 to 1900, to the 12 months preceding the census date." (Census, 1960a: 205)

Based upon the Current Population Survey, the annual rates are subject to sampling error. Actually, the size of sampling error is small. For example, the 1968 rate for whites, being based upon a much larger population, is more accurate than the rate for nonwhites. Specifically, there are 68 chances out of

100 that the true rate in 1968 for whites lies between 90.8 and 91.2, a range of 0.4; similarly, with the same probability, the true rate for nonwhites lies between 89.1 and 89.7, a range of 0.6.

The following notes refer to the statistical tables:

a - The data for 1960 and thereafter include Hawaii and Alaska.

b - Data for 1930 revised to classify Mexicans as white persons.

c - Data for April, rather than October.

A6, A7. Enrollment in Full-time Public Day Schools, by Grade-Group, Kindergarten and Grades 1-8 (A6) and Grades 9-12 and Postgraduate (A7), 1911-1967, School Year Ending on Date.

Source: Data for 1911-1918 from Education (1923: Table 2, p. 47); for 1919-1930 from Education (1932: Table 2, p. 42); for 1931-1938 from Education (1944b: Table 8, p. 8); for 1939-1949 from Education (1953a:Table 14, p. 18); for 1950 from Education (1959b: Table 1, p. 27); for 1952-1955 from Education (1963: Table 3, p. 8); for 1956-1967 from Simon and Grant (1967: Table 26, p. 23). The following sources are cited in the above: <u>Digest of Educational Statistics</u>, various issues; <u>Biennial Survey of Education</u>, various issues; and U. S. Office of Education estimates.

Accuracy of these data are affected by: (1) Some states and/or schools report figures in terms of organizational level rather than grade level; (2) for recent years, enrollment in ungraded and special classes was not shown separately, but was prorated among the grades.

The following refer to the statistical tables:

a - Alaska and Hawaii included for the first time. If these two states had been excluded for the year noted, Series A6 and A7 would not have been changed, however.

d - Data derived from special studies or estimated by the U. S. Office of Education. In most instances the estimating procedure was to average the preceding and succeeding years.

e - Estimated from data for the fall of the school year.

A8, A9. Enrollment in Full-time Non-public Regular Elementary and Secondary Day Schools (in Thousands), 1934-1967, School Year Ending on Date.

Source: Data for 1934-1964 from Education (1967a: Table I, p. 17); for 1965-1966 from Simon and Grant (1966: Table 27, p. 23); for 1967 from Simon and Grant (1967: Table 34, p. 30).

Non-public schools are defined as those under the operational control of private individuals or church-affiliated or nonsectarian organizations. Excluded are the enrollments of subcollegiate departments of institutions of higher education, residential schools for exceptional children, and Federal schools. Since data are not available for all non-public schools, the total figures given in this series are estimates made by the U. S. Office of Education. Statistics presented for the years 1965, 1966 and 1967 are for the fall of the year, because school year data were not available.

The following refer to the statistical tables:

e - Estimated from data for the fall of the school year.

f - Enrollment for some years are estimates by the U. S. Office of Education.

A10. Average Days Attended per Pupil Enrolled in Public Schools, 1870-1966, School Year Ending on Date.

Source: Data for 1870-1956 from Census (1960a: Series 231, p. 207); for 1958-1962 from Census (1965a: Series 231, p. 31); for 1964 from Simon and Grant (1967: Table 29, p. 27); for 1966 from Simon and Grant (1968: Table 27, p. 26), and unpublished data from the U. S. Office of Education.

Data are for the academic year ending on the date shown. The original data are collected by the U. S. Office of Education through the state departments of education. The total number of days attended by all public school pupils enrolled is divided by the total enrollment, public elementary and secondary day schools.

A11. Pupil-Teacher Ratio: Average Number of Pupils in Daily Attendance per Classroom Teacher (Including Other Nonsupervisory Staff), 1870-1966, School Year Ending on Date.

Source: Data for 1870-1956 from Census (1960a: Series H229, p. 207), divided by Census (1960a: Series H236, p. 208); for 1958-1962 from Census (1965a: Series H229, p. 31) divided by Census (1965a: Series H236, p. 31); for 1964 from Education (1967a: Table 1, p. 21); for 1966 from Hutchins and Barr (1968: Table 1, p. 19). The sources cited in the above are: 1890-1916, Report of the Commissioner of Education, various issues; 1918-1956, Biennial Survey of Education, chapter 2, various issues; Digest of Educational Statistics, various issues.

This series was computed from data on average daily attendance of pupils and the number of pupils and teachers in public elementary and secondary day schools. The definition of public schools given in A1 applies similarly to this series. The category "teachers" includes classroom teachers and other school personnel such as librarians, guidance consultants and psychologists who contribute to the learning experience, when not reported separately. If separately reported such non-teaching instructional staff is excluded.

A12, A13, A14. Pupil-Teacher Ratio in Public Day Schools, Elementary Schools Only (A13), Secondary Schools Only (A14), and Total Elementary and Secondary Schools (A12), 1910-1967, School Year Ending on Date.

Source: Enrollment data are Series A6 and A7; teacher data are Series B5, B6.

Pupil-teacher ratios were computed from data on the number of pupils enrolled and the number of teachers employed in public elementary and secondary day schools. It should be noted that enrollment data are given by grade group while teacher data are based on organizational level of the school. Secondary schools in some systems include teachers in junior high schools. The effect of this variation in definitions is to inflate the pupil-teacher ratio in elementary schools and reduce the ratio in secondary schools.

The following refers to the statistical tables:

a - Figure includes Alaska and Hawaii for the first time.

A15, A16. Pupil-Teacher Ratio in Non-public Elementary (A15) and Secondary (A16) Day Schools, 1890-1966, School Year Ending on Date.

Source for Series A15: Data for 1931 are from Education (1933: 9); for 1933, 1941 and 1966 are from Education (1968a: 10). Data used to calculate the ratios for 1936 through 1940 and 1942 through 1964 are from Education (1967a: Table I, p. 17).

Source for Series A16: Data for 1890 through 1933, 1941 and 1948 are from Education (1951: 8). Data used to calculate the ratios for 1936 through 1940, 1942 through 1946, 1950 through 1960, and for 1962 and 1964 are from Education (1967a: Table I, p. 17). Data for 1961 and 1966 are from Education (1968a: 10).

This ratio was calculated by dividing the number of pupils enrolled by the number of teachers for each year, respectively.

The pupil-teacher ratio of non-public elementary and secondary schools is based upon data that are less reliable than the comparable statistic for public schools, Series A13 and A14. Data for the years 1890, 1900, 1910, 1920, 1930, 1931, 1933, 1941, 1948 (for secondary schools only), 1961, and 1966, are based upon actual surveys of non-public schools conducted by the U. S. Office of Education and hence the ratio for these years may be more reliable than for other years. The ratio for the remaining years is based upon data collected by the U. S. Office of Education from the state departments of education, assembled as part of the Biennial Surveys of Education. Reporting by the schools to the states was sometimes incomplete. To compensate for this, the U.S.O.E. compared the reports from the state departments of education with data on enrollment and number of teachers assembled by a national office of the Roman Catholic Church, data considered to be quite inclusive and data which typically encompass 90 percent of non-public enrollment.

As a result of this comparison, state by state adjustments were made by the U.S.O.E. to attain a better estimate.

In some years (e.g., secondary survey for 1960-61) teaching positions rather than teachers were obtained, in order that the principal who also taught part-time might be counted as a teacher. The 1965-66 ratios are based upon full-time equivalent number of teachers (Education, 1968a: 10, 29, 30). The enrollment component refers only to pupils enrolled in full-time regular non-public day schools.

The following refer to the statistical tables:

a - Figure includes Alaska and Hawaii for the first time.

b - In the enrollment figure for this year only 69 percent of the pupils in Catholic schools is accounted for. "If this average holds true for all schools, it is probable that approximately 60,000 teachers were teaching in private elementary schools in 1930-31." (Education, 1933: 9).

c - This statistic is reported as 35.6 in Education (1936: 9). This occurs due to a slight difference in the figures for enrollment and teachers which were probably refined at a later date.

d - Ratio is based on figures which include the last four years of secondary school, special students, and postgraduates.

e - Ratio is based on total enrollment.

A17. Number of Graduates of Public and Non-public Secondary Schools (in Thousands), 1870-1968, School Year Ending on Date.

Source: Data for 1870-1956 from Census (1960a: Series H232, p. 207); for 1958-1960 from Census (1965a: Series H232, p. 31); for 1962-1964 from Census (1966c: Table 182, p. 130); for 1965 from Simon and Grant (1966: Table 62, p. 49); for 1966 from Simon and Grant (1967: Table 65, p. 51); for 1967 from Simon and Grant (1968: Table 63, p. 51); for 1968 from Simon and Fullam (1968: 30). The sources cited are the same as those listed in Series A1.

Figures exclude those graduates receiving equivalency certificates. Numbers of graduates of non-public secondary schools are estimated for years when surveys of non-public secondary schools were not made. (See Notes to Series A15, A16 for years when surveys of non-public schools were made.)

Graduates of subcollegiate departments of institutions of higher education, Federal schools for Indians, schools on Federal installations and residential schools for exceptional children are included in the data whenever figures were available. See, also, the note for Series A1.

The following refer to the statistical tables:

a - Figure includes Alaska and Hawaii for the first time.

d - Figure is taken from Census (1966c: 130) and differs slightly from the figure given in Census (1960a: 207).

f - Partially estimated by the U. S. Office of Education. 1966 and 1967 figures include reported graduates from public and estimated graduates from non-public schools (Simon and Grant, 1968: 51, 52). 1968 graduates are a projection by the U. S. Office of Education (Simon and Fullam, 1968: 30).

A18. High School Graduates as a Percent of the Population 17 Years Old, 1870-1968, School Year Ending on Date.

Source: Data for 1870-1956 from Census (1960a: Series H233, p. 207); for 1958-1960 from Census (1965a: Series H233, p. 31); for 1962-1964 from Census (1966c: Table 182, p. 130); for 1965 from Simon and Grant (1966: Table 63, p. 50); for 1966 from Simon and Grant (1968: Table 64, p. 52); for 1967 from Simon and Grant (1968: Table 63, p. 51). The statistic for 1968 is estimated upon the basis of a Census Bureau estimate of the Oct. 1, 1967, population (Simon and Grant, 1968: 52). For sources of information on the number of high school graduates refer to those listed in A17. Data for the 1900 to 1964 population by age are from Census Bureau estimates of the July 1 population. Refer to Census (1965b), Census (1965c), and Census (1968b).

Graduates of public and non-public secondary schools are included, but graduates of non-public schools are partially estimated as explained in the notes to Series A17. As in A17 figures for "special" schools are included wherever possible. See, also, the note for Series A1.

The following refer to the statistical tables:

a - Figure includes Alaska and Hawaii for the first time.

d - Figure is taken from Census (1966c: 130) and differs slightly from the figure given in Census (1960a: 207).

A19, A20, A21, A22. Estimated Retention Ratios, Public and Non-public Schools, 5th to 6th Grades (A19), 6th to 7th Grades (A20), 7th to 8th Grades (A21), 8th to 9th Grades (A22), Base Years 1924-1962, School Year Beginning on Date.

Source: Data for 1924-1962 are computed from Simon and Grant (1967: Table 8, p. 7), and unpublished data obtained from the Reference, Estimates, and Projections Branch, the National Center for Educational Statistics, the U. S. Office of Education.

The ratio was computed by dividing the "estimated retention rates," presented in Table 8 of the cited publication, by the rate for the preceding class the preceding year. The base data (Table 8, in Simon and Grant) were developed by the U. S. Office of Education from the Biennial Surveys of Education of public school enrollment and occasional surveys of non-public school enrollment. For some years the non-public enrollment data were estimated upon the basis of Catholic school enrollment solely, a procedure that encompassed about 90 percent of students in non-public schools for most of the years.

The data presented are calibrated to the base year (the school year of the denominator), but represent experience achieved the following year. For example, the probability that a 5th grader enrolled in school in fall 1924 would have continued to the 6th grade the following year is .911, shown in the table opposite the year 1924.

A23, A24, A25. Continuation Ratios in Full-time Public Secondary Day Schools, 9th to 10th Grades (A23), 10th to 11th Grades (A24), and 11th to 12th Grades (A25), Base Years 1910-1966, School Year Beginning on Date.

Source: Data for 1910-1950 from the Biennial Survey(s) of Education. Data for 1910-1911 from Education (1925: 34); for 1912-1913 from Education (1927: 354); for 1914-1916 from Education (1928: 576); for 1917-1925 from Education (1930: 454); for 1926-1937 from Education (1941a: 9); for 1938-1950 from Education (1953a: 18). Data for 1951-1962 from Education (1963: 8); and for 1963-1964 from Simon and Grant (1965: 6); and for 1965 and 1966 unpublished sources of the U. S. Office of Education.

Retention ratios were calculated in the following manner: For the base year 1950 (school year 1950-51), for example, the retention ratio for grades 9 to 10 was calculated by dividing the enrollment in grade 10, 1951-52, by enrollment in grade 9, 1950-51. Base year 1950:

$$\text{Retention ratio Grades 9 to 10} = \frac{\text{Enrollment in grade 10, 1951-52}}{\text{Enrollment in grade 9, 1950-51}}$$

Enrollment in public schools has been collected by the U. S. Office of Education from the state departments of education. In general, definitions have been common throughout the period, but there have been two changes, to be described, that have affected the data to an unknown degree.

Enrollment by grade was obtained from tables of historical summaries published by the U. S. Office of Education. These summaries were prepared by U.S.O.E. personnel with detailed knowledge of the surveys, knowledge seldom made available in published form. However, overlapping sections of these tables were checked to ensure continuity of the series. In cases wherein the data were estimated or based upon preliminary results, the most recent available figures were used.

Enrollment, reported by each state, represents the total number of different pupils registered at any time during the school year. Thus, pupils attending schools in two or more states during a school year are counted more than once. National enrollment figures are increased by the amount of interstate transfer. In the 1953-54 school year, for example, interstate transfers were estimated as approximately 2 percent of the total enrollment of 28,836,000. While total enrollments are thus inflated, the effect upon the continuation ratios is thought to be insignificant.

The series before 1945, particularly, are affected by differences among the states in the number of years schooling provided by the state system. Some state systems required students to complete only 11 years, rather than 12, before being graduated. For example, in 1928, 16 percent of high school students were in states following the 11-year plan. By 1945, however, only 4.6 percent of high school students were so enrolled. In combining the data from the two systems, the U.S. Office of Education tabulated the last four years of high school, combining the 8th to 11th, respectively, with the 9th to 12th years. Secondary school postgraduates and pupils in ungraded schools were excluded.

Prior to 1958, data refer to the contiguous United States. In 1958-59 Alaska was added and in 1959-60, Hawaii.

A26. Continuation Ratios, Grade 12 to College, Public and Non-public, 1945-1967, School Year Beginning on Date.

Source: College enrollment data for 1945-1967 are from Series D1, with territorial enrollment excluded. Grade 12 enrollment data for 1945-1967 are from Simon and Grant (1967: Table 26, p. 23; Table 36, p. 31; and Table 32, p. 29).

The series represents the total first-time degree-credit enrollment in colleges and universities for the fall of the year divided by grade 12 enrollment in public and non-public high schools, the United States and the District of Columbia. The ratio has been multiplied by 1,000 to eliminate the decimal point. The ratio is aligned to the fall of the year of the base year, the latter being the fall enrollment of the 12th grade. As such, the statistic may be considered a probability that a member of the fall 12th grade class will enter college as a freshman for degree-credit work the following fall. The degree-credit category, of course, excludes those enrolled in occupational or general studies programs not chiefly creditable to a Bachelor's degree. In producing this series, several estimates were made, as described below.

The procedure for estimating the continuation ratio from 12th grade enrollment to first-time degree-credit college enrollment is as follows: both the 12th grade public school enrollment and the first-time opening fall degree-credit enrollment in college are available, except for college enrollment in fall 1965 and 1966. Non-public secondary school enrollment is available for alternate years, and non-public enrollment by grade is available for fall 1960 and fall 1964. It was necessary to prorate the non-public secondary school enrollment to obtain an estimate of the non-public 12th grade enrollment. The proportion of secondary school enrollment in the 12th grade non-public schools, obtained from the two given years, was applied to the total non-public secondary enrollment, to estimate the non-public 12th grade enrollment. When added to the public, this gave an estimate of the total 12th grade enrollment for alternate years. From such estimates of the total enrollment, continuation ratios were computed for alternate years, beginning with fall 1945.

The continuation ratios for the remaining, even-numbered years, were estimated, as follows. The ratio between two continuation ratios was computed: (a) the ratio just obtained, that is, the continuation ratio of first-time college degree-credit enrollment to the total (public and non-public) 12th grade enrollment; and (b) the continuation ratio of the total first-time opening fall college degree-credit enrollment to the public only 12th grade enrollment. The ratio between these two continuation ratios is quite stable, varying only from .878 to .895 over the 20-year period. This ratio of the two ratios was available for alternate years (beginning 1945). The interstitial years were estimated by averaging the ratio for the alternate years. For example, the average of the 1945 ratio and the 1947 ratio produced the 1946 ratio. This averaged ratio was then used to adjust continuation ratio (b) above, (based upon public only 12th grade enrollment) to obtain the estimated continuation ratio for public and non-public.

The above "ratio of ratio" procedure applied only to the even-numbered years, 1946 through 1958, and to 1962. All other years, except 1960 and 1964, are based only upon the estimate of the non-public enrollment, previously described.

The statistic for 1965 and 1966 could not be computed, because the fall 1966 and fall 1967 first-time opening fall degree-credit enrollment was not assembled by the U. S. Office of Education.

A27-A37. Percent of Various Age Groups Enrolled in School, 1947-1968, Fall of Year.

Source: Data for 1947-1965 from Census (1967a); for 1966 from Census (1967b) and unpublished data supplied by the U. S. Census Bureau; for 1967 and 1968 from unpublished data supplied by the U. S. Bureau of the Census.

Except for decennial Census years (1950 and 1960), the data are from the Current Population Survey, a monthly sample of the civilian noninstitutional population of the United States. Changes in the size of the sample have made the statistics from the Survey increasingly accurate, but they still are subject to a small sampling error (see below).

The procedure for determining enrollment is, as follows. The enumerator asks whether:

"The person had been enrolled at any time during the current term or school year in any type of graded public, parochial, or other private school in the regular school system. Such schools include kindergartens, elementary schools, high schools, colleges, universities, and professional schools. Attendance may be on either a full-time or part-time basis and during the day or night. Thus, regular schooling is that which may advance a person toward an elementary or high school diploma, or a college, university or professional school degree. Beginning with 1954, children enrolled in kindergarten have been included in the enrollment figures for

'regular' schools, and have also been shown separately. Figures...for years prior to 1954 have been revised to include children in kindergarten.

"'Special' schools are those which are not in the regular school system, such as trade schools or business colleges. Persons attending 'special' schools are not included in the enrollment figures.

"Persons enrolled in classes which do not require physical presence in school, such as correspondence courses or other courses of independent study, and in training courses given directly on the job, are also excluded from the count of those enrolled in school, unless such courses are being counted for credit at a 'regular' school." (Census, 1967a: 3)

Changes in the methodology of the Current Population Survey since it was transferred to the U. S. Bureau of the Census in August 1943, have been documented in several publications (Steinberg, 1953; Census, 1963e; Census, 1964c; and Census, 1967d). The last-named reference, particularly, identifies the changes in detail. The primary improvements in the reliability of estimates of school enrollment have resulted from changes in the number of primary sampling units and the number of households interviewed. Major improvements were instituted in October, 1943, February, 1954, May, 1956, and January, 1967. These changes are presented in the table below.

A number of procedural and processing changes have been made from time to time to speed up the processing and make data more accurate. These chiefly were:

a) August 1947: The method of selecting units within the sample area was changed so that each unit selected could be given the same weight in the tabulations.

b) July 1949: Coverage of the sample was extended to special dwelling places, such as hotels, trailer camps, etc.

c) February 1952: A document sensing card was introduced to speed the recording and transfer of data to IBM processing cards.

d) January 1953: 1950 Census data were first used to make ratio estimates from the sample data.

e) July 1953: A 4-8-4 rotation system replaced a system of keeping households in the sample for 6 consecutive months.

Major Revisions in CPS Sample

Date of Revision	Primary Sampling Units	Counties and Independent Cities	Households Interviewed	Remarks
October 1943	68	125	25,000*	sample converted to strictly probability basis
February 1954	230	453	21,000	25,000 households; Sample expanded geographically
May 1956	330	638	35,000	40,000 households in sample. About 20 percent increase in reliability
January 1960	333	-	-	Alaska & Hawaii added
October 1961	357	-	-	about 5 percent gain in reliability
January 1967	449	863	52,500	60,000 households; about 20 percent increase in reliability

* Less households not interviewed because not at home, vacant, etc.

Source: (Census, 1967d: 15-18)

In the new system, a household was in the sample for 4 months, out for 8 months, and back in the sample for 4 additional months before being retired.

 f) September 1953: High speed electronic computers were first used to process the data.

 g) July 1955: The timing of the survey was changed from the week when fell the 8th of the month, to the week containing the 12th day of the month.

 h) April 1962: Updated population information based upon the 1960 Census was first used.

In addition to these, other changes in definition, coverage etc., affecting the data on the labor force were made (Census, 1967d).

In each publication on school enrollment of the Current Population Survey, except for 1954-1958, a table presents the standard error of estimate. From these the table below has been computed, showing the approximate error in the percentages for each year. One standard error is given below. The chances are 68 out of 100 that the true percentage of the percentages shown in Series A27 through A37 falls within plus or minus the value shown in the table below.

Standard Error of Estimated Percentage of Persons Enrolled
in School (68 chances out of 100), 1947-1966

Series	1947	1948	1949	1950	1951	1952	1953	1954-1958	1959	1960	1961	1962	1963	1964	1965	1966
A27	.4	.4	.4	a	a	.4	.4	N/A	.2	.2	.2	.2	.2	.2	.2	.1
A28	2.4	2.2	2.4	2.4	2.2	2.0	2.1	N/A	1.0	1.0	1.0	.9	.9	.9	.9	.9
A29	1.1	1.0	1.1	.7	1.1	1.0	.6	N/A	.4	.4	.3	.3	.3	.3	.3	.3
A30	.4	.4	.4	.4	.4	.4	.4	N/A	.2	.2	.2	.2	.2	.2	.2	.2
A31	.4	.4	.4	.3	.3	.3	.3	N/A	.2	.2	.2	.2	.2	.2	.2	.2
A32	1.2	.8	.8	.8	.9	.9	.9	N/A	.3	.3	.3	.2	.2	.2	.2	.2
A33	1.6	1.7	1.6	1.7	1.7	1.7	1.7	N/A	.6	.6	.6	.5	.5	.5	.5	.5
A34	1.7	1.7	1.7	1.7	1.7	1.8	1.7	N/A	1.0	1.0	.9	.9	.9	.9	.8	.8
A35	.7	.7	.7	.7	.7	.8	.8	N/A	.4	.4	.4	.4	.4	.4	.5	.5
A36	.3	.3	.3	.3	.3	.3	.3	N/A	.2	.2	.3	.3	.3	.3	.3	.3
A37	.3	.3	.3	a	a	.3	.3	N/A	.2	.2	.2	.2	.2	.2	.2	.2

a - Not available.

Source: Data for 1947-1949 were computed from tables of standard error of the estimated percentage: from Census, 1952; for 1950-1953 from Census, 1954; for 1959 from Census, 1960b; for 1960 and 1961 from Census, 1962; for 1962-1966 from Census, 1967b.

B1, B2, B3, B4, B5, B6. Classroom Teachers and Other Nonsupervisory Staff in Public Elementary and Secondary Day Schools, by Sex, School Year Ending on Date, Total, in Thousands (B1), Male, in Thousands (B2), Female, in Thousands (B3), Female as a Percentage of Total Elementary and Secondary (B4), Elementary Total, in Thousands (B5), and Secondary Total, in Thousands (B6).

Source for B1: Data for 1870-1956 from Census (1960a: Series H236, p. 208); for 1958-1962 from Census (1965a: Series H236, p. 31); for 1964 from Simon and Grant (1967: Table 29, p. 27); for 1966 from Hutchins and Barr (1968: Table 1, p. 19).

Source for B2, B3, B4: Data for 1870-1956 from Census (1960: 208), for B2, Series H237, for B3, Series H238, and for B4, Series H238 divided by Series H236; for 1958 from Census (1965a: 31), for B2, Series H237, for B3, Series H238, for B4, Series H238 divided by H236; for 1960-1964 from Simon and Grant (1967: Table 29, p. 27); for 1966 from Hutchins and Barr (1968: Table 1, p. 19).

Source for B5, B6: Data for 1890-1956 from the respective <u>Report(s) of the Commissioner of Education</u> and the <u>Biennial Survey(s) of Education</u> (Education, 1893; 1901; 1911; 1921; 1923; 1925; 1927; 1928; 1930; 1932; 1935a; 1937a; 1939; 1941a; 1943; 1944b; 1947; 1949a; 1950a; 1953a; 1957a; 1957b; 1959a); for 1958-1961 from Schloss and Hobson (1962: Table 9, pp. 16-17); for 1962-1966 from Schloss (1966: Table 9, p. 21); for 1967 from Simon and Grant (1967: Table 47, p. 37); for 1968 and 1969 from Hutchins and Barr (1968: Table 25, p. 24).

The following sources are cited in the above for B1, B2, B3 and B4: 1870-1916, Report of the Commissioner of Education, various issues; 1918-1958, Biennial Survey of Education, various issues.

Teachers and nonsupervisory staff include classroom teachers and others concerned with instruction, except supervisors of instruction and principals. The nonteaching categories include librarians, guidance and psychological specialists, television instructors, etc. Prior to 1919-20 the data are the number of different persons employed but after that date the number of positions are reported, as is the case at present. Data do not include statistics for subcollegiate departments of institutions of higher education, residential schools for exceptional children, or Federal schools.

The classification as elementary or secondary follows local or state organizational custom, but elementary usually includes kindergarten through grade 8, and secondary, grades 9 through 12. The standard definitions are contained in Handbook I, The Common Core of State Education Information (Education, 1953b) providing uniform terminology and definitions.

In Series B4, for the years 1954 through 1958, only the female teachers are represented by classroom teachers only. For these years the percent of female teachers given may be somewhat lower than actually existed.

The following refer to the statistical tables:

a - Prior to 1938, number of different persons employed rather than number of positions.

b - Includes 231 part-time teachers not classified by sex.

c - Classroom teachers only. Excludes other nonsupervisory instructional staff.

d - Figure includes Alaska and Hawaii for the first time. If these states had been excluded for the year noted, the figure for Series B1 would have been 1,380,161; for Series B2, 391,231; and for Series B3, 957,406.

e - Includes teachers in junior high schools.

f - Estimated.

B7, B8. Teachers with Less than Standard Certificates in Public Elementary Schools (B7) and Secondary Schools (B8) as a Percentage of Total Teachers in Each System, 1954-1967, School Year Beginning on Date.

Source: Data for 1954-1962 from Hobson and Schloss (1963: Table 13, p. 32-33); for 1963-1966 from Hobson and Schloss (1967: Table 9, p. 21); for 1967 from Barr and Foster (1968: Table 1, p. 6).

Standard teaching certificates for a particular state may be obtained when teachers fulfill the qualifications specified by that state. Because of the shortage of qualified teachers "less than standard certificates" are issued for limited periods of time to teachers not meeting all the qualifications. They may, for example, have completed less than the specified educational requirement, or they may lack semester hours of professional education and supervised teaching experience. Teachers who obtained certificates when requirements were different or lower are considered to have standard certificates since current requirements refer only to the issuing of <u>new</u> certificates. Although most states require at least a Bachelor's degree for elementary and secondary teaching, there is considerable variation in other requirements from state to state.

Teachers in public day schools, generally, are defined as classroom teachers only. Administrative personnel, psychological personnel, and all persons having less than half of their workload devoted to teaching are excluded.

B9, B10. Instructional Staff in Full-time Non-public Elementary (B9) and Secondary (B10) Day Schools (in Thousands), 1934-1964, School Year Ending on Date.

Source: Data for 1934-1964 from Education (1967a: Table I, p. 17); for 1968 from Simon and Grant (1968: Table 46, p. 39).

Data are estimates based on incomplete surveys and special studies. Non-public schools are defined as those under the operational control of private individuals or church-affiliated or nonsectarian organizations.

The following refer to Series B10 in the statistical tables:

d - Figure includes Alaska and Hawaii for the first time.

f - Estimated.

B11, B12, B13, B14. Median Age of Elementary and Secondary Teachers, by Color and Sex, 1930-1960.

Source: Data for 1930-1960 from Folger and Nam (1967: Table III-1, p. 84). The following sources are cited in the above: various subject reports in the Census of Population for the years 1930, 1940, 1950, and 1960.

C1. Total Number of Public Elementary Schools (in Thousands), 1930-1966, School Year Ending on Date.

Source: Data for 1930-1964 from Simon and Grant (1967: Table 59, p. 45); and for 1966 from Hutchins and Barr (1968: Table 7, p. 25). The following sources are cited in the above: <u>Biennial Survey of Education</u>, chapters on "Statistical Summary of Education" and "Statistics of State School Systems."

A "school" is defined as follows:

"...a division of the school system consisting of a group of pupils composed of one or more grade groups, organized as one unit with one or more teachers to give instruction of a defined type, and housed in a school plant of one or more buildings. More than one school may be housed in one school plant, as is the case when the elementary and secondary programs are housed in the same school plant."
(Hutchins and Barr, 1968: 4)

The following refer to the statistical tables:

a - Figure includes Alaska and Hawaii for the first time. If these states had been excluded for the year noted, the figure would have been the same.

C2, C3. Number of One-Teacher Public Schools in Use (in Thousands), 1910-1966, School Year Ending on Date (C2), and One-Teacher Schools as a Percentage of Elementary Schools, 1930-1966, School Year Ending on Date (C3).

Source: Data for 1910 from Education (1949b: Table 12, p. 23); for 1916-1928 from Census (1960a: Series H245, p. 208); for 1930-1964 from Simon and Grant (1967: Table 59, p. 45), and for 1966 from Hutchins and Barr (1968: Table 7, p. 25). The following sources are cited in the above: <u>Biennial Survey of Education</u>, various issues; <u>Digest of Educational Statistics</u>, various issues.

The following definition is given:

"One-teacher public schools are schools in which one teacher is employed to teach all grades authorized in the school, regardless of the number of rooms in the building." (Census, 1960a: 203)

Series C3 is calculated by expressing C2 as a percentage of Series C1.

The following refer to the statistical tables:

a - Figure includes Alaska and Hawaii for the first time. If these states had been excluded for the year noted, the figure would have been the same.

b - Partially estimated.

C4. Total Number of Public Secondary Schools (in Thousands), 1930-1966, School Year Ending on Date.

Source: Same as C1.

Secondary Schools include various grades, depending upon the state and district organizational system. The most frequent system is the traditional four-year school, but there are other combinations, as illustrated by the following distribution (Hutchins and Barr, 1968: 25) of the 1965-66 public secondary schools:

```
           Junior High                  7,920
           Senior High                  4,942
           Junior-Senior and
              Undivided High            5,060
           Regular, 4-year High         8,176
           Incomplete, Regular High       232
           Vocational or Trade High       267

           Total, 1965-66              26,597
```

The following refers to the statistical tables:

a - Figure includes Alaska and Hawaii for the first time.

C5. Average Length of School Term (in Days) in Public Elementary and Secondary Schools, 1870-1966, School Year Ending on Date.

Source: Data for 1870-1956 from Census (1960a: Series H230, p. 207); for 1958-1962 from Census (1965a: Series H230, p. 31); for 1964 from Simon and Grant (1967: Table 29, p. 27); and for 1966 from Hutchins and Barr (1968: Table 1, p. 19).

Only the days that pupils are under the guidance and direction of teachers are counted as part of the school term. To compute the average length of the school term, the aggregate pupil-days attendance for the school year is divided by the average number of pupils attending daily, the ADA.

The following refers to the statistical tables:

a - Figure includes Alaska and Hawaii for the first time. If these states had been excluded for the year noted, the figure would have been exactly the same.

C6. Average Number of Days Attended per Pupil Enrolled in Public Elementary and Secondary Schools, 1870-1966, School Year Ending on Date.

Source: Data for 1870-1956 from Census (1960a: Series H231, p. 207); for 1958-1962 from Census (1965a: Series H231, p. 31); for 1964 from Education (1967a: Table 21, p. 48); and for 1966 from Hutchins and Barr (1968: Table 1, p. 19).

The average number of days attended during the school year per pupil enrolled is computed by dividing the aggregate number of days attended by all pupils during the year, by the total enrollment for the year.

The following refer to the statistical tables:

a - Figure includes Alaska and Hawaii for the first time.
c - Estimated.

C7. Expenditures for Public Elementary and Secondary Day Schools per Pupil in Average Daily Attendance, in Current Unadjusted Dollars, 1889-1967, School Year Ending on Date.

Source: Data for 1889-1956 from Census (1960a: Series H254, p. 209); for 1958-1962 from Census (1965a: Series H254, p. 31); for 1964 and 1967 from Simon and Grant (1967: Table 76, p. 62); and for 1966 and 1968 from Simon and Grant (1968: Table 73, p. 61). The sources cited in the above are the same as those listed in Series A1.

Expenditure data are given here in current (unadjusted) dollars. Except prior to 1918 when expenditures for interest are included, current expenditures exclude capital outlay and interest on school debt.

The purchasing power of the dollar has not remained the same over the years and these data are given in unadjusted dollars. A portion of this series is adjusted to 1966 purchasing power in Simon and Grant (1966: Table 71, p. 57). Adjustments, based on the Consumer Price Index, (Bureau of Labor Statistics, U. S. Department of Labor) show that current expenditures of $87, $88, and $209 for the years 1930, 1940 and 1950, respectively, are equivalent to $162, $201 and $281, respectively, in 1966 purchasing power.

Table 6.5 (page 187) presents expenditures in constant (1958) dollars for various purposes on a unit basis (schools or teachers or students, as appropriate).

The following refer to the statistical tables:

a - Figure includes Alaska and Hawaii for the first time.

c - Estimated.

C8. Expenditure per Pupil Enrolled in Public Schools, 1870-1965, School Year Ending on Date.

Source: Data for 1870-1965 from Census (1966a: Series B43, p. 196-197). The following sources are cited in the above: 1870-1952, Report of the Commissioner of Education and Biennial Survey of Education. Reference may also be made to Simon and Grant (1965: Tables 3, 40, 42, pp. 6-7, 58 and 63, respectively) and Education (1967a: Tables H and 1, pp. 13 and 21, respectively).

Total expenditures include total current operating expenditures, capital outlays, interest, and other auxiliary services such as adult education and summer schools. This figure is divided by the total enrollment. Both elementary and secondary schools are included.

The following refers to the statistical tables:

d - Calculated from data in the original source, Education (1967a). This figure is given as 523 in Census (1966a).

D1, D2, D3. First-time Degree-credit Enrollment, All Colleges and Universities (in Thousands), Total (D1), Males (D2), Females (D3), 1939-1967, School Year Beginning on Date.

D4, D5. Total Degree-credit Enrollment, All Colleges and Universities (in Thousands), Males (D4), Females (D5), 1939-1968, School Year Beginning on Date.

Source: Data for 1939-1960 from Huddleston (1961: Table 6, p. 11 and Table 9, p. 15). Data for 1961-1967 are from successive annual reports of the Opening Fall Enrollment in Higher Education survey of which the most recent release is Chandler (1969). In addition to the annual publications of tables and institutional data, two "analytic reports" have been issued (1959 and 1960), the most recent being Huddleston (1961), referred to above.

A "first-time" student is one who has not previously been enrolled in any institution of higher education. A "degree-credit" student is one enrolled in a program of study which is creditable toward a Bachelor's or higher degree. (Definitions are indicated in the instructions for completing the report form.)

Data are collected early in the fall of each year, and, since 1947, the entire universe of institutions listed in the U.S.O.E. Directory of Higher Educational Institutions has been included. Institutional coverage has been uniform and the response rate quite good. Since 1954 the response has been consistently close to 100 percent. Nonresponding institutions have been estimated. The primary sources of year-to-year variation are changes in categories of enrollment. Extension students were excluded until 1953. Correspondence students, TV students, and students in laboratory or preparatory schools have always been excluded. Undergraduate students in programs not creditable toward a Bachelor's degree, particularly students in occupational curriculums or semi-professional programs, were introduced as a separate category in 1963.

In 1966 several changes were introduced. The concept of degree-credit students was dropped. Resident and extension students were separately counted, but no separate accounting was made of non-degree-credit students. In 1967, the 1966 concepts were continued with the additional specification of undergraduate and "post-baccalaureate" within the resident, but not the extension, category, and the specification of first-time freshmen and all freshmen within the resident category (Chandler and Rice, 1967: 136). The fall 1968 survey discontinued the distinction between resident and extension students and reinstituted the degree-credit concept. It also subdivided the first time students into degree-credit students and all others (Chandler, 1969: 36). These changes in concept, 1965-68, interrupted the series, providing no 1966 and 1967 data for the degree-credit category. The changes may have had adverse effects upon the quality of data, particularly as reported by institutions whose data systems could not readily adapt to the frequent changes in concepts. Estimates, based upon the survey data and using proportions observed in 1965, have been made for first-time degree-credit enrollment (D2, D3) and for total degree-credit enrollment (D4, D5).

Except where noted, Series D2 and D3 are for aggregate United States, and Series D4 and D5 are for continental United States.

The following refer to the statistical tables:

e - Estimated.

f - Enrollment data adjusted to fit the 1956 reclassification of institutions by type.

g - Data are for continental United States only.

D6, D7, D8, D9. First-time Degree-credit Enrollment, Junior College (in Thousands), Males (D6), Females (D7), and as a Percent of Total First-time Degree-credit Enrollment (D8, D9), 1939-1968, School Year Beginning on Date.

Sources and Definitions: See Notes to Series D1-D5.

To obtain Series D8 and D9, Series D6 and D7 are divided, respectively, by Series D2 and D3. This series is the best measure of the junior colleges' increasing share of undergraduate enrollment. In Series D6 and D7 the category, junior college, was used up until 1962, after which the more general category, "two-year institutions," replaced it. The difference in these concepts is illustrated in the 1963 report, where to 577 junior colleges are added data from 21 technical institutes and 39 semi-professional schools. The category, two-year institutions, includes community colleges, technical institutes, junior colleges and semi-professional schools. First-time enrollment in two-year institutions, Series D6, D7, for 1966 and 1967 could not be satisfactorily estimated.

Except where noted D6 and D7 refer to the aggregate United States.

The following refer to the statistical tables:

c - Data are for continental United States only.

e - Estimated.

f - Enrollment data adjusted to fit the 1956 reclassification of institutions by type.

D10, D11, D12. Ratio, First-time Opening Fall Degree-credit Enrollment in Institutions of Higher Education, per 100 18-Year-Old Population, Total (D10) and by Sex (D11, D12), 1939 to 1968, School Year Beginning on Date.

Source: Enrollment data are from Series D1-D3. respectively. Population data are from Series I22-I24. respectively. See the notes to these series.

D13, D14, D15. Ratio, Higher Education Enrollment per 100 18-21-Year-Old Population, Total (D13), 1870-1968, and by Sex (D14, D15), 1939-1968

Source: Data for 1870-1944 from Census (1960a: Series 321, pp. 210-211); for fall 1946-1965 from Simon and Grant (1967: Table 85, p. 69); for 1966 and 1967 enrollment from

Chandler and Rice (1967: 6); for 1968 from Chandler (1969). The data for population are from Series I25-I27. Total enrollment in institutions of higher education, resident degree-credit enrollment (full- and part-time students), regular session only (September to June), exclusive of enrollments in extension, correspondence, adult education, short courses, etc., as a percent of the population 18-21 years old is presented to 1946. Data from fall 1946 to date are based on opening (fall) enrollments. Beginning with fall 1953, enrollment figures include resident and extension degree-credit students while data for all earlier periods exclude extension students. Degree-credit enrollment for 1966 and 1967 are estimated from survey data because the degree-credit students were not separately accounted for by the U.S.O.E. surveys. (Refer to Notes to Series D1-D5.)

Beginning in fall 1960, the enrollment data include the 50 States and the District of Columbia; data for all earlier periods include currently existing States and the District of Columbia. The population estimates exclude the Armed Forces overseas from 1870 through 1900 and include them thereafter. The population data used are estimates of the U. S. Bureau of the Census as of July 1 of each year 1900 to 1967, i.e., July 1 preceding the opening of the academic year. For this series, the percentage-enrolled figures are shown according to the fall of the year.

This series relates the reported institutional population to a constant age group. A change in the ratio could be a function of the shifting age structure of the enrolled population. To explore this possibility, the Census reports of the ages of the college-going population were examined for recent years, with the results shown below:

	Percent of the College Enrollment (through age 34), 18-21 Years of Age	Percent of the 18-21 Year-Old Population Enrolled in College
1960	58.5	21.9
1961	63.3	23.0
1962	62.0	24.2
1963	62.6	24.3
1964	62.5	25.6
1965	62.4	29.2
1966	64.3	30.4

Source: Census, 1961, 1962, 1963b, 1964b, 1966b, 1967a, 1967b, 1967c.

During 1960-1966, college enrollment of the population through age 34 is reported. The percent of this population that is 18-21 years of age increased from 58 percent to 64 percent. During the same period, the percent of the population 18-21 years of age enrolled in college increased from about 22 percent to 30 percent.

Evidence from the decennial Census also shows that the college population is becoming more concentrated in the 18-21 age group. Below is the percent of the college population aged 15-29, who are within the ages 18-21 years, inclusive:

	1950	1960
Male	43.2	55.4
Female	72.2	77.0

(In 1960, there were 148,104 males and 61,542 females, aged 30-34 years, enrolled in college; these are not included in the above because comparable 1950 data are not available.)

We infer, then, that Series D13 for degree-credit college students reflects genuine increases in attendance rates, as does the Census data for a more general population of college enrollees.

The following refers to the statistical tables:

e - Estimated.

D16, D17, D18. Degrees Conferred by Institutions of Higher Education, Bachelor's (D16), Master's (D17) and Doctor's (D18), 1870-1967, School Year Ending on Date.

Source: Data for 1870-1948 from Census (1960a: Series H330, H333, H336, p. 211); for 1949-1965 from Mason and Rice (1967: Table 5, pp. 5-6); for 1966 from Simon and Grant (1968: Table 108, p. 87); for 1967 from Chandler (1968: Table 1, p. 4). The sources cited in the above are the following: for 1870-1946, Report of the Commissioner of Education, Biennial Survey of Education, various issues, and, since 1947-48, a special annual survey entitled Earned Degrees Conferred. Other sources cited in Census (1960a: 204) are Education for Victory, August 21, 1944, and Higher Education, vol. XII, no. 7, March, 1956.

By definition the "Bachelor's or first professional" degree is the first degree granted in a particular field, and must be based on at least four years of college work or its equivalent. Thus the first degree in law (LL.B.) is included even though law graduates may have previously earned a degree in another field. "Master's or second professional" degrees are more advanced, but below the doctoral level. Doctor's or equivalent degrees comprise the highest level of earned degrees; honorary degrees are excluded from the count (Census, 1960a: 204).

D18 is also reproduced in Cartter (1964: 1260) with Doctor's and Master's degrees by sex.

The following refer to the statistical tables:

a - Figures include Alaska and Hawaii for the first time. If these states had been excluded for the year noted, the figure for Series D16 would have been 381,923; for Series D17, 69,364; and for Series D18, 9,356.

d - Data are for academic years ending June 30 of the year shown.

D19. Doctor's Degrees Conferred (NAS-NRC), 1880-1968, School Year Ending on Date.

Source: Data for 1880-1957 from Harmon and Soldz (1963: 1); for 1958-1966 from National Academy of Sciences (1967: 5); for 1967 from National Academy of Sciences (1968: 4); for 1968 from unpublished material of the National Academy of Sciences.

Although the U. S. Office of Education provides the basic source of information on degrees during the period 1880-1897, discrepancies apparently are due to greater discrimination in screening out degrees conferred by institutions which were considered to be poorly qualified to grant doctorates at the time. For the period 1889-1915, the National Academy of Sciences relied upon the work of J. McKeen Cattell, who carefully screened the degrees and published his results in *Science*, in the issues of August 30, 1907, and October 22, 1915. After 1915 the series was collected by the staff of NAS-NRC. The latter data, through 1957, are on a calendar year basis. For 1958-1968, the data are for the 12-month period ending June 30. Part of the discrepancy between D18 and D19 arises from a difference in the reporting period.

A slightly different series may be found in National Science Foundation (1955: 72). Another may be found in Singletary and Newman (1968).

The following refers to the statistical tables:

b - Figure includes Puerto Rico for the first time.

D20. Bachelor's Degrees per 1000 23-Year-Old Population, 1900 to 1967, School Year Ending on Date.

Source: Data on degrees from Series D16; for data on population, Series I31.

The choice of 23-year-olds as a base for this statistic rests upon the median age of the population in the fourth year of college in April, 1960, when the U. S. Census of Population was taken. The median age of 4th year males was 23.2 years, and of female 4th year students, 23 years. In a study of 1958 baccalaureate recipients, Sharp (1963) found the median age of male baccalaureate recipients was 23 years and female, 22.4 years. While the median age may have been increasing over the years, lack of data on the age of baccalaureate recipients over the range of years for this series led to the decision to use a constant age group as a base. A series on baccalaureates per 100 22-year-olds -- customarily considered the typical age at graduation -- produces substantially the same trend line as this series.

D21. Ratio of Bachelor's Degrees per 100 High School Graduates Four Years Earlier, 1884-1967, School Year Ending on Date.

Source: Series D16, the Bachelor's and first-professional degrees conferred by institutions of higher education, was divided by Series A17, the number of graduates of public and non-public secondary schools, and the quotient multiplied by 100. For sources, see the respective Series notes.

The graph (Figure 5.4) is presented both by the year of high school graduation and the year of college graduation since one or the other of these dates may be of interest to the analyst. The first ratio of the series presents the June, 1880, high school graduates divided by the June, 1884, baccalaureate graduating class. Until the 1912 high school graduating class, the data were annual, and they were biennial thereafter. Adjacent years might be averaged to give estimates for every year. However, this was not done because there are a few years with abrupt changes in either the numerator or denominator, and it was thought advisable to refrain from introducing an unknown amount of error.

D22. Master's Degrees per 100 Bachelor's Degrees, Two Years Earlier, 1872-1967, School Year Ending on Date.

Source: Calculations based upon D16 and D17. The selection of the two-year lag period rests upon evidence that doctorate recipients complete their Master's degrees 2.3 years after the Bachelor's degree (National Academy of Sciences, 1967: 69).

D23. Doctor's Degrees per 1,000 Bachelor's degrees x-Years Earlier, 1878-1967, School Year Ending on Date.

Source: Calculations based upon D16 and D19 where given and D18 otherwise, using an 8-year lapse time for all calculations prior to 1920, and, thereafter, the lapse time shown in

D47. Ten-year lapses were used for the most recent years. Bachelor's degrees were estimated by averaging the preceding and following year, in the few instances that Bachelor's degrees were not available.

D24, D25, D26. Ratio, Four-Year Bachelor's Degrees per 100 First-time Enrollment Four Years Earlier, Total (D24), and by Sex (D25, D26), 1950-1967, School Year Ending on Date.

Source: Degree data for 1950-1967 from the series <u>Earned Degrees Conferred</u> published for each year by the U. S. Office of Education of which the most recent comprehensive release is by Chandler and Rice (1968). Also, summary data for 1966-67 has been published (Chandler, 1968). First-time opening fall degree-credit enrollment is presented in D1-D3. Ratios for males and females are based upon degrees awarded four years after first-time opening fall degree-credit enrollment.

Prior to the academic year ending 1961, degrees requiring only four years were not separately reported. Consequently, the four-year degrees were estimated from the Bachelor and first professional degrees (the first-level degrees) by continuing the observed proportion of .875 four-year degrees for males and .97 for females. Degrees for 1959-60 and earlier years were estimated in this fashion from the number of reported first-level degrees. Degrees for 1965-66 and 1966-67 required an adjustment to correct for the (revised) U. S. Office of Education practice of pooling four- and five-year degrees while separately reporting six-year degrees.

D27. Grand Total, Academic Production Index (in Thousands), 1949-1967, School Year Ending on Date.

Source: Data are from the U. S. Office of Education Series, Earned Degrees Conferred, the latest comprehensive release being for 1965-66 (Chandler and Rice, 1968). Summary data for 1966-67 has been published (Chandler, 1968). The academic production index is described in Appendix B, p. 264. Briefly, the several levels of degrees are summed after weighting them with a value proportional to the time required to obtain the degree. The grand total is the sum of all fields.

D28. API, Total (in Thousands), Arts, Humanities and Social Sciences, 1949-1967, School Year Ending on Date.

D29. API, Total (in Thousands), Basic and Applied Sciences, 1949-1967, School Year Ending on Date.

D30. API, Total (in Thousands), All Other Fields, 1949-1967, School Year Ending on Date.

Source: The sources are those cited in Series D27; the same calculation procedure was employed. These three series, D28-D30, provide subdivisions of Series D27, the grand total

D31. Higher Education Enrollment per 100 API, 1949-1967.

Source: Total degree-credit enrollment: sum of Series D4 and D5; API: Series D27.

D32. Higher Education Faculty Members per 100 API, 1950-1967.

Source: Full and part-time faculty: Series E5; API: Series D27.

D33. Current Fund Expenditures for Higher Education, per API, in Hundreds of Constant 1958 Dollars, 1950-1966, School Year Ending on Date.

Source: Data for expenditure from Lindsay (1964), National Center for Educational Statistics (1968), Mertins (1969). Implicit price deflators from Council of Economic Advisers (1969: 230). API: Series D27.

Current expenditures for all but capital improvements are available for academic years ending on even-numbered years. Dollars were adjusted to 1958 = 100 by use of Office of Business Economics implicit price deflators for gross national product. Adjacent years were averaged to approximate the conditions prevailing for the academic year.

D34. Expenditures for Student Aid in Higher Education, per API in Constant 1958 Dollars, 1952-1966, School Year Ending on Date.

Source: for expenditure data and for the implicit price deflator is the same as that cited in Series D33. API: Series D27.

D35. API Grand Total, per 100 Graduates, 1949-1967, Academic Year Ending on Date.

Source: Graduates: sum of Series D16, D17, D18; API: Series D27.

"Graduates" are the total number of degrees awarded, rather than the total number of persons graduating. The number of persons receiving two degrees simultaneously (such as law school graduates) is thought to be a small proportion of the total.

D36. API, Total Engineering, Mathematics, Physical Science, per 100 Graduates, 1949-1967, Academic Year Ending on Date.

Source: Degrees: the same as the sources cited in Series D16-D18 (in Chandler, 1968, refer to Table 9, p. 12-19). The classification of degrees by field follows the U. S. Office of Education system. The weights which are applied to the different levels of degrees are presented in Appendix B. The aggregate Academic Production Index for the fields of Engineering, Mathematics, and Physical Science is divided by the total number of degrees, and multiplied by 100, to produce Series D36.

D37. API, Total Biological Science, per 100 Graduates, 1949-1967, Academic Year Ending on Date.

Source: See Series D36.

D38. API, Health Professions, per 100 Graduates, 1949-1967, Academic Year Ending on Date.

Source: See Series D36.

D39. API, Social Science (Excluding Social Work), per 100 Graduates, 1949-1967, Academic Year Ending on Date.

Source: See Series D36.

D40. API, Education, per 100 Graduates, 1949-1967, Academic Year Ending on Date.

Source: See Series D36.

D41. Current Fund Expenditures of Higher Education, in Billions of Constant 1958 Dollars, 1930-1966, Academic Year Ending on Date.

Source: Same as Series F16. Series F16 has been converted to constant 1958 dollars by dividing by the implicit price deflator for GNP developed by the Office of Business Economics (Council of Economic Advisers, 1969: 230). This series is included in order to make readily available an index to constant dollar amounts of current fund expenditures by higher educational institutions.

D42-D47. Mean Lapse Time, B.A. to Ph.D., 1920-1961, by Field and for Total, 1920-1966, as follows:

    D42. Total Physical Sciences, 1920-1961.
    D43. Total Biological Sciences, 1920-1961
    D44. Total Social Sciences, 1920-1961.
    D45. Arts and Professions, 1920-1961.
    D46. Education, 1920-1961.
    D47. All Fields, 1920-1966.

Source: Data for 1920-1961 from Harmon and Soldz (1963: 43); the total (Series D47) for 1962 through 1966 from unpublished data obtained from NAS-NRC. For recent years, medians of 3-year groups of doctoral recipients have been published in National Academy of Sciences (1967: 66-68).

For the years (1920-1961) the data are assembled for the calendar year. Prior to 1957 the data were assembled from graduation announcements of doctorate degree-granting institutions. With 1957, however, NAS-NRC began collecting personal history information by questionnaire directly from the doctorate recipient. The NAS-NRC 1967 publication on doctorate production presents the median rather than the mean lapse time, and hence the recent data are incompatible with the historical series. (Since the distributions are positively skewed, the median actually is the preferred statistic.) Data are oriented on the year the Doctor's degree was awarded.

D48, D49, D50. Estimated Average Starting Salary (per Month) Offered by Selected Business Concerns to Male Bachelor's Degree Graduates Specializing in Engineering, Accounting and Sales, 1947-1968, School Year Ending on Date.

Source: Data from National Education Association (1968). The source cited in the above is: Frank S. Endicott, <u>Trends in Employment of College and University Graduates in Business and Industry</u>, Annual Report, Northwestern University, Evanston, Illinois.

Since 1947, Frank Endicott, of Northwestern University, has conducted a survey of 150-200 business and industrial concerns at the beginning of the recruiting season (November) to obtain estimates of starting salary offers to male graduates. Only those companies which actively recruit college and university graduates are included. The specific companies responding vary from year to year but generally they are large or medium-sized corporations. Smaller companies to which students make direct application are not included.

Comparison of Endicott's data for recent years with that collected by the College Placement Council in a different survey lends support to Endicott's estimates. From the membership in the College Placement Council, a representative and cooperative group of placement offices was selected to collect data "throughout the most competitive part of the recruiting season, representing the most active group of employers making offers to the most desirable candidates as a result of campus interviews." (College Placement Council, 1967a: 10) Employers are not restricted to business and industrial concerns. Although the two surveys vary in many ways, the data itself -- beginning salary offers -- are quite similar. The results of the College Placement Council survey are given in the following table:

National Average Monthly Salary Offers to Male Bachelor Degree Candidates, by Curriculum, for All Types of Employers (Academic Year Ending on Date)

Year	Curriculum		
	Engineering[a]	Accounting	Marketing & Distribution
1960	$ 518	$ 457	$ 423
1961	539	475	431
1962	564	494	466
1963	590	527	465
1964	612	535	493
1965	634	553	516
1966	670	585	549
1967	718	637	588

Source: College Placement Council, 1967b.

[a] Figures represent the simple average of figures given for 8 different fields of engineering study. In 1961, 1962 and 1963 averages represent the 7 fields for which data were available; the figure for 1960 represents only 4 fields.

The absolute differences between annual figures in each of these series and their counterparts in the Endicott survey were computed and the mean difference calculated. For engineering, the mean difference is approximately 7 dollars per month; for accounting, approximately 8 dollars per month; for marketing and distribution -- sales, approximately 12 dollars per month. These small differences lend support to the accuracy of estimates reported by Endicott. However, the two series, 1960-1967, appear to be drifting apart in engineering and accounting but not in sales. College Placement Council data exceed Endicott's data for engineering and accounting during the first three years, but Endicott's data exceed the College Placement data for the last three years. Sales data, on the other hand, do not show a similar drift.

E1, E2, E3, E4. Median Age of College Teachers, by Color and Sex, by Decade, 1930-1960: Male Total (E1), Male Nonwhite (E2), Female Total (E3), Female Nonwhite (E4).

Source: Data for 1930-1960 from Folger and Nam (1967: Table III-1, p. 84). The following sources are cited: various subject reports in the Census of Population for the years 1930, 1940, 1950, and 1960.

E5. Total Faculty, Institutions of Higher Education, 1880-1967, School Year Ending on Date.

Source: Data for 1880 from Education (1882); for 1890 from Education (1893); for 1900 from Education (1901); for 1910 from Education (1911). Data for 1920-1958 from Biennial Survey of Education: Education (1923: 286, 429, 553; 1932: 338, 339, 614; 1935b: 25, 26, 27; 1937b: 31, 32; 1938: 1, 37; 1941b: 43; 1944a: 33; 1946: 37; 1949c: 41; 1950b: 55; 1953a: 35; 1957b: 50; 1959a: 64; 1962: 6). Data for 1960-1964 from Dunham and Wright (1966: Table 1, p. 3) and Simon and Grant (1967: Table 101, p. 79). Data for 1966-1967 are from a fall 1966 survey (Beazley, 1969). Comparable data were not collected for 1965-66.

Where possible faculty and other staff of elementary and secondary educational units of higher educational institutions are removed, sometimes through estimation procedures. Full- and part-time faculty, administrative, and other professional staff are included; excluded are clerical and nonprofessional staff, retired, staff on leave without pay, and staff in branch campuses or extension centers, and elementary and secondary teachers where possible.

Data are for the entire academic year for 1899-1900 through 1951-1952; data are for first or fall term thereafter.

The following refer to the statistical tables:

a - The data for 1960 and thereafter include Alaska and Hawaii.

b - The data were collected through the following categories: colleges, universities, technical schools, women's colleges (Division A and Division B), professional schools, colleges of agriculture and mechanical arts, institutions for Negroes, normal schools (public and private), business schools. These data have been summarized for each volume corresponding to the specific year.

E6. Male Faculty as a Percentage of Total Faculty, Institutions of Higher Education, 1880-1964, School Year Ending on Date.

Source: Same as for Series E5. The sex distribution of the total professional staff, fall 1966, is not available.

The following refers to the statistical tables:

a - The data for 1960 and thereafter include Alaska and Hawaii.

c - Data not available.

F1, F2, F3, F4, F5, F6, F7. Number of Institutions of Higher Education, by Type, 1950-1968, School Year Beginning on Date: Universities (F1), Liberal Arts Colleges (F2), Teachers Colleges (F3), Technological Schools (F4), Theological Religious (F5), Schools of Art (F6), Other Professional (F7).

Source: <u>Opening Fall Enrollment in Higher Education</u>, a series issued annually by the U. S. Office of Education of which the most recent (1968 data) issue is Chandler (1969).

There are several classes of institutions which are defined, as follows:

"The 'university' category contains those institutions of large and complex organization in which several professional schools and colleges (not exclusively technical) are incorporated within the administrative framework of the institution. In the 'independent technical' group are included those institutions in which the curricular emphasis is <u>predominately</u> directed to technical and physical-science fields. It should be pointed out that the term 'independent' as here used, and in the following two categories of institutions, denotes non-university affiliation. The 'independent theological schools' include those schools, which, independent in administration, offer programs specializing in religion and theology. 'Other independent professional schools' include those institutions which offer programs directed to a single field of specialization (law, music, art, etc.). The 'liberal arts colleges' are, by far, the most difficult group to classify because the programs of some of the larger colleges are similar to those in institutions classified as 'universities.' On the whole, however, it may be said that in the schools classified as 'liberal arts colleges,' the principal stress is placed on a program of general undergraduate education. The 'teachers college' group includes those institutions devoted primarily to the training of teachers. 'Junior colleges' are those institutions which do not offer the bachelor's degree and in general offer the first two years of undergraduate education." (Story, 1951: ix-x)

These series are not satisfactory for several reasons: (1) The categories into which institutions are classified have not remained constant over the span of time of the series: for example, schools of art were separated out of the "other professional" category in 1958; beginning in 1965 only three categories were used: universities, four-year institutions and two-year institutions. (2) The distinction between institutions offering degree-credit courses and those offering only non-degree-credit courses appears to have been more rigorously applied at some times than others, for example in 1956 when 35 non-degree-credit technical institutes were excluded, and 1961. (3) In the interests of consistency of definition over the entire series, adjustments were made in certain years, e.g., 1961. (4) There appears to have been inconsistent application of the

distinction between a junior college and an institution offering two years of work. (The category was changed from "junior college" to "two-year institutions" in the 1963 survey.)
(5) The U. S. Office of Education includes in its surveys institutions accredited by regional or professional accrediting agencies and some institutions which are not so accredited but their credits are accepted by accredited institutions (see: Education 1965a: 7).

(6) Finally, there are two other related problems concerning the classification of institutions.

First, the difficulty of making the distinction between an independent, geographically separate institution fostered by a parent institution and one that is a subordinate branch of a parent institution remains unresolved. In 1967, the U. S. Office of Education published a <u>Directory of U. S. Post-Secondary Academic Institutions</u> (Education: 1967b) which lists the institutions and their branches, and introduced the concept of "system" of institutions as well as the distinction between a "branch" and a "component." Even so, no classification by type of institution was presented in this publication, although one was promised.

Secondly, a special problem arises in the category, "independently organized professional schools." While the concept of being organized independently of another institution may provide a basis for a clear-cut distinction, the more important question of the number of schools of a given type is not answered; for example, there are many more schools of art than those categorized as independently organized.

The problems associated with these series, then, lead to a severe condemnation of the the past and present efforts to classify institutions of higher education, and, certainly, indicate a need for a new classification procedure which will answer questions about the educational system, such as: how many geographically separate educational institutions offer a curriculum of a given quality in a particular area. Upon such a base more rational plans for the educational system might be built, plans that would concern physical facilities, enrollment, faculty and other staff, students, and so forth.

F8, F9, F10. Number of Junior Colleges, Total (F8), Public (F9), Private (F10), 1918-1968, School Year Beginning on Date.

Source: Data for 1918-1963 from Simon and Grant (1966: Table 88, p. 71); for 1964 from Education (1964: 84); for 1965 from Education (1967c: 90); for 1966 from Education (1967d: 109); for 1967 from Chandler and Rice (1967: 4) and unpublished data from the U. S. Office of Education; for 1968 from Chandler (1969: 3).

Two definitional problems affect these series: (1) the distinction between a junior college and a two- or three-year college program which may be partly non-degree-credit; (2) the accreditation or other status of the institution which makes it eligible to be included in the enumeration. In the fall 1963 survey the U. S. Office of Education made a distinction between junior colleges and other two-year institutions. At that time there were 577 junior colleges, 21 technical institutes, and 39 two-year semi-professional schools (Huddleston, 1963: 5). Since then, however, all two-year institutions have been grouped together as one category for the U.S.O.E. enrollment publication. The variety of institutions in the two but less than four-year category is illustrated below, from the Educational Directory, 1964-65 (Education, 1965a: 10).

	Number of Institutions
Total	656
Terminal-occupational below Bachelor's degree	51
Liberal Arts and General	67
Liberal Arts and General, and Terminal-occupational	370
Primarily Teacher Preparatory	30
Both Liberal Arts and General and Teacher Preparatory	33
Liberal Arts and General, Terminal-occupational, and Teacher Preparatory	90
Professional Only, Not Including Teacher Preparatory	5
Professional and Teacher Preparatory	4
Professional and Terminal-occupational	6

See also Notes to Series F1-F7.

F11, F12. Total Number of Four-year Institutions of Higher Education (F11), and Total, All Institutions of Higher Education (F12), 1870-1968.

Source: Data for Series F12 for 1870-1910, 1920, 1930 and 1940 from Education (1958: 6); for 1922 from Education (1925: 308, 459); for 1924 from Education (1927: 583, 741); for 1926 from Education (1928: 810, 979); for 1928 from Education (1930: 702, 893); for 1932 from Education (1935a: 2); for

1934 from Education (1937b: 6); for 1936 from Education (1938: 5); for 1938 from Education (1941b: 4); for 1942 from Education (1944a: 2); for 1944 from Education (1946: 4); for 1946 from Education (1949c: 2); for 1948 from Education (1950b: 2); for fall 1950-1968 from the annual series, <u>Opening Fall Enrollment in Higher Education</u>, issued by the U. S. Office of Education.

Data for Series F11 for 1918-1948 has been calculated by subtracting the number of junior colleges or two-year institutions (Series F8) from the total number of institutions of higher education (Series F12); for fall 1959-1968 from the annual series, <u>Opening Fall Enrollment in Higher Education.</u>

Four-year institutions include all institutions with at least a four-year program, excluding only junior colleges and other programs of less than the baccalaureate degree level.

The following refer to the statistical tables:

c - Figure is for continental U. S.; for aggregate U. S., figure is 1,713.

d - Figure represents number of schools reporting to U. S. Office of Education.

F13. Number of Medical Schools, 1850-1966, School Year Ending on Date.

Source: Data for 1850-1962 from Census (1960a: Series B186, p. 34) and Census (1965a: Series B186, p. 7); for 1963-1966 from successive editions of <u>Earned Degrees Conferred</u>, the 1966 edition being Chandler and Rice (1968). The following sources are cited in the Census publications: 1830-1840, 1956 <u>American Medical Directory</u>; 1850-1919, <u>Journal of the American Medical Association</u>, vol. 105, no. 9, August 1935, p. 686; 1931-1957, Edward L. Turner, et. al., <u>Journal of the American Medical Association</u>, vol. 165, no. 11, November, 1957, p. 1420; 1958-1962, Department of Health, Education, and Welfare, Public Health Service; unpublished data of the American Medical Association and American Osteopathic Association.

Although the first medical school in the United States was established in 1765, the accuracy of data recorded for years prior to 1900 is questionable. Inspection and classification of medical schools was initiated by the American Medical Association Council on Medical Education in 1904 and by 1929 there was only one unapproved school. As far as the data permit, only approved medical and basic science schools are included (Census, 1960a:31). Data for 1963-1966 show only schools granting M.D. degrees, as reported to U.S.O.E.

The following refer to the statistical tables:

a - Alaska and Hawaii included for the first time.

b - Puerto Rico included for the first time.

F14. Number of Dental Schools, 1860-1966, School Year Ending on Date.

Source: Data for 1860-1962 from Census (1960a: Series B189, p. 34) and Census (1965a: Series B189, p. 7); for 1963-1966 from successive editions of <u>Earned Degrees Conferred</u>, the

1966 edition being Chandler and Rice (1968). The following sources are cited in the Census publications: 1840-1945, Harlan Hoyt Horner, Dental Education Today, University of Chicago, 1947, p. 30; 1946-1957, American Dental Association Council on Dental Education, Dental Students' Register, Chicago, annual publications; 1958-1962, Department of Health, Education and Welfare, Public Health Service; unpublished data of the American Dental Association.

Before the founding of the first dental school in 1840, dental work was done by medical doctors or by persons who were self-taught or apprentice-trained. By 1880, most states required dental practitioners to be dental school graduates (Census, 1960a:32). For 1840 and 1926-1931, schools offering courses in dentistry are included; for 1850-1925, schools conferring degress; for other years through 1963, schools in operation. Data for 1963-1966 show only schools granting D.D.S. degrees, as reported to U.S.O.E. (Census, 1960a: 34).

The following refer to the statistical tables:

a - Alaska and Hawaii included for the first time.

b - Puerto Rico included for the first time.

F15. Total Income of Institutions of Higher Education, in Thousands of Current Dollars, 1930-1966, School Year Ending on Date.

Source: Data for 1930-1954 are from Census (1960a: Series H339, p. 212); for 1956-1962 from Census (1965a: Series

H339, p. 31); for 1964 from Simon and Grant (1968: Table 115, p. 95); for 1966 from Mertins (1969: Table 1, p. 10). The sources cited in the above for 1930-1962 are Biennial Survey of Education, various issues; for 1964, Financial Statistics of Institutions of Higher Education.

The data for the years prior to 1964 here presented differ slightly from the series presented in Financial Statistics of Institutions of Higher Education (Lindsay, 1964).

Total current income in institutions of higher education is defined as "...funds accruing to, or received by, higher educational institutions, usable for their recurring day-to-day activities." (Census, 1960a: 204). Current-fund income excludes "plant-fund receipts" and "other fund receipts."

The following refers to the statistical tables:

a - Alaska and Hawaii included for the first time.

F16. Total Expenditures in Institutions of Higher Education, in Thousands of Current Dollars, 1930-1966, School Year Ending on Date.

Source: Data for 1930-1954 are from Census (1960a: Series H351, p. 213); for 1956-1962 from Census (1965a: Series H351, p. 32); for 1964 from Simon and Grant (1968: Table 121, p. 100); for 1966 from Mertins (1969: Table 3, p. 12-13). The sources cited in the above for 1930-1962 are <u>Biennial Survey of Education</u>, various issues; for 1964, <u>Financial Statistics of Institutions of Higher Education</u>.

The data for the years prior to 1964 here presented differ slightly from the series presented in <u>Financial Statistics of Institutions of Higher Education</u> (Lindsay, 1964). Current-fund expenditures exclude additions to the physical plant.

The following refers to the statistical tables:

a - Alaska and Hawaii included for the first time.

F17. Income from Student Fees as a Percentage of Total Income of Institutions of Higher Education (F15), 1930-1966, School Year Ending on Date.

Source: Same as that cited in the Notes to Series F15. (Data for 1930-1962 are from Series H341 in the reference cited.)

The percent is based upon current-fund income.

Tuition and fees include tuition and general and specific fees assessed against students for educational and general purposes. Fees received from governmental bodies paying tuition from public funds are reported as income from the governmental body. Scholarships and fellowships for tuition and fees are counted as income. Tuition for nursery, demonstration, or laboratory schools is excluded, as also are fees for athletics, student union, student hospital, etc. (National Center for Educational Statistics, 1968: 74).

The following refer to the statistical tables:

a - Alaska and Hawaii included for the first time.

c - Includes income of $34,680,000 for fees for room, board, or other charges which are not included in income from auziliary enterprises.

i - Tuition and fees received from Veterans under Public Law 550 are reported under student fees and not under income from the Federal Government.

F18. Endowment Earnings Income as a Percentage of Total Income of Institutions of Higher Education (F15), 1930-1966, School Year Ending on Date.

Source: Same as that cited in the Notes to Series F15. (Data for 1930-1962 are from Series 342 in the reference cited.)

The percent is based on current fund income.

Endowment earnings applicable to current educational and general expenditures, only, are included. Included are earnings from funds held in trust outside the institution, from Federal and State land-grant funds, and transfers from reserves for stabilization of endowment. Excluded are endowment earnings that are added to the principal of the endowment, transferred to plant funds, or restricted to Student Aid (which is separately reported). (National Center for Educational Statistics, 1968: 75)

The following refers to the statistical tables:

a - Alaska and Hawaii included for the first time.

F19, F20, F21. Income from Governmental Sources, Federal (F19), State (F20), and Local (F21) as a Percentage of Total Income of Institutions of Higher Education (F15), 1930-1966, School Year Ending on Date.

Source: Same as that cited in the Notes to Series F15. (Data for 1930-1962 are from Series H343-H345 in the reference cited.)

The percent is based on current-fund income.

Income from the Federal Government includes regular appropriations to land-grant institutions for instruction, facilities, research, and cooperative extension, grants or contractual payments for research, performed on or off the campus, and payments for educational services from the Army, Navy, or Veterans Administration. Federal aid received through state channels is reported as income from the state government.

Income from state governments includes Federal funds channeled through the state government, from state appropriations, and interstate compacts. Local governmental income includes funds from cities, counties, or school districts. Included is all income for educational and general purposes, tuition and fees, etc., received from the governmental unit (National Center for Educational Statistics, 1968: 75).

The following refer to the statistical tables:

a - Alaska and Hawaii included for the first time.

d - Includes local government

e - Included with state government.

f - Includes Federal and local governments.

j - Includes Federal aid received through state channels and regional compacts.

F22. Income from Private Gifts and Grants as a Percentage of Total Income of Institutions of Higher Education (F15), 1930-1966, School Year Ending on Date.

Source: Same as that cited in the Notes to Series F15. (Data for 1930-1962 are from Series H346 in the reference cited.)

The percent is based on current-fund income.

Only private gifts and grants that may be applied to current educational and general expenditures are included. Research grants or contracts from nongovernmental sources are included. Excluded are additions to plant funds, endowment funds, and loan funds (National Center for Educational Statistics, 1968: 75).

The following refers to the statistical tables:

a - Alaska and Hawaii included for the first time.

F23. Income from Organized Activities Related to Instructional Departments as a Percentage of Total Income of Institutions of Higher Education (F15), 1932-1966, School Year Ending on Date.

Source: Same as that cited in the Notes to Series F15. (Data for 1932-1962 are from Series H347 in the reference cited.)

The percent is based on current-fund income.

Gross income from enterprises operated in connection with educational departments and conducted to provide training; this includes educational activities such as medical school hospitals, home-economics cafeterias, agricultural college creameries, tuition from laboratory schools, etc. (National Center for Educational Statistics, 1968: 76).

The following refer to the statistical tables:

a - Alaska and Hawaii included for the first time.

b - Includes income from sales and services of educational departments ($65,063,000). This is separately reported for this year and includes incidental income of educational departments from sales and services of agricultural departments, sale of occasional publications, etc. (National Center for Educational Statistics, 1968: 76).

g - Data not collected.

F24. Residual Income as a Percentage of Total Income of Institutions of Higher Education (F15), 1930-1966, School Year Ending on Date.

Source: Same as that cited in the Notes to Series F15. (Data for 1930-1962 are from Series H348 in the reference cited.)

The percent is based on current-fund income.

This includes all other income for current educational funds. Included are interest on investments of current funds, rental of buildings, library fines, but excludes rental of student or faculty housing operated as an auxiliary enterprise, rental property held as part of the endowment, and loans (National Center for Educational Statistics, 1968: 76).

The following refers to the statistical tables:

a - Alaska and Hawaii included for the first time.

F25. Income from Auxiliary Enterprises and Student Aid as a Percentage of Total Income of Institutions of Higher Education (F15), 1930-1966, School Year Ending on Date.

Source: Same as that cited in the Notes to Series F15. (Data for 1930-1962 are from Series H349-H350 in the reference cited. "Student aid income" is termed "other current income" in Census, 1960a.)

The percent is based on current-fund income.

The following is included in income from auxiliary enterprises and activities: income of dormitories, dining halls, cafeterias, union buildings, college bookstores, university presses, student hospitals, faculty housing, intercollegiate athletic programs, concerts, industrial plants operated on a student self-help basis, and other enterprises conducted primarily for students and staff and intended to be self-supporting without competing with the industries of the community in which the institution is located (Census, 1960a: 204-205).

Student aid income includes funds from scholarships, fellowships, prizes, etc., from restricted endowment funds, private and public sources, transfers from other income-accounts, such as remission of tuition and fees (Census, 1960a: 205; National Center for Educational Statistics, 1968: 77).

The following refer to the statistical tables:

a - Alaska and Hawaii included for the first time.

h - Figure represents income from "auxiliary enterprises and activities" only since data in the category "student aid income" were not collected for this year.

k - Student aid income includes specifically designated or earmarked funds.

F26, F27. Total Educational and General Expenditures in Institutions of Higher Education, per Student (F26), and per Faculty Member (F27), in Constant 1958 Dollars, 1930-1966, School Year Ending on Date.

Source: Data for current expenditures for 1930-1954 are cited in the Notes to Series F16. (Data for 1930-1962 are from Series H352 in the reference cited.)

Data for enrollment for 1930-1954 are from Census (1960a: Series H321, p. 210); for 1956-1962 from Census (1965a: Series H321, p. 31); for 1964-1966 are estimates using data in Simon and Fullam (1968: Tables 4 and 30, pp. 11 and 57, respectively). The sources cited in the above for enrollment for 1930-1962 are Report of the Commissioner of Education and Biennial Survey of Education, various issues.

Data for number of faculty for 1930-1954 are from Census (1960a: Series H317, p. 210); for 1956-1962 from Census (1965a: Series H317, p. 31); for 1964-1966 are estimates using data in

Simon and Fullam (1968: Tables 4 and 30, pp. 11 and 57, respectively). The sources cited in the above for the number of faculty for 1930-1962 are Report of the Commissioner of Education and Biennial Survey of Education, various issues.

Total educational and general expenditures include general administrative and executive expense, expenditures for instruction and departmental research, organized research, operation of libraries, operation and maintenance of the physical plant, organized activities relating to educational departments, including expenditures related to sales and services of educational departments, and extension activities and public services (National Center for Educational Statistics, 1968: 77-79).

Expenditures in current dollars for 1930-1966 were converted to constant 1958 dollars by applying the implicit price deflator to the various expenditures per student, per faculty member, or, per institution (Series F26 through Series F36). For 1930-1964 the Office of Business Economics implicit price deflator for the Gross National Product was calculated for the academic year by averaging the price deflator for adjacent years in Census (1966a: Series B63, pp. 200-201); the price deflator used for 1966 is from Council of Economic Advis rs (1969: 230).

The following refers to the statistical tables:

a - Alaska and Hawaii included for the first time.

F28. Administrative and General Expenditures in Institutions of Higher Education per Institution, in Thousands of Constant 1958 Dollars, 1930-1966, School Year Ending on Date.

Source: Data for current expenditures for 1930-1966 are the same as cited in the Notes to Series F26, F27. (Data for 1930-1962 are from Series H353 in the reference cited.)

Data for the number of institutions for 1930-1954 are from Census (1960a: Series H316, p. 210); for 1956-1958 from Census (1965a: Series H316, p. 31); for 1960-1966 from Series F12.

The sources and method for adjusting current expenditures to 1958 dollars are given in the Notes to Series F26, F27.

Administrative and general expenditures include expenses of the executive and administrative offices in the conduct of their services for the institution as a whole -- not specifically for any particular division of the institution. Student personnel services expenses, encompassing admissions, counseling and guidance programs, administrative cost of financial assistance, health services, etc. are included. Excluded are expenditures for libraries and operation and maintenance of the physical plant as well as administrative expenditures for auxiliary enterprises and organized activities relating to instructional departments which are separately accounted for (see Series F32, F33, F34, and F36 for these category definitions).(National Center for Educational Statistics, 1968: 77)

The following refers to the statistical tables:

a - Alaska and Hawaii included for the first time.

F29, F30. Expenditures for Resident Instruction and Departmental Research in Institutions of Higher Education, per Student (F29), and per Faculty Member (F30), in Constant 1958 Dollars, 1930-1966, School Year Ending on Date.

Source: Data for current expenditures, enrollment, and number of faculty for 1930-1966 are the same as cited in the Notes to Series F26, F27. (Data for 1930-1962 for expenditures are from Series H354 in the reference cited).

The sources and method for adjusting current expenditures to constant 1958 dollars are given in the Notes to Series F26, F27.

Expenditures for resident instruction and departmental research includes current outlay of the institutions' instructional departments, colleges, and schools, for research which is not separately budgeted or financed, for office and laboratory operations and equipment, and for salaries for department heads, professors, other instructional staff (student assistants), technicians, secretaries, etc. (National Center for Educational Statistics, 1968: 78).

The following refers to the statistical tables:

a - Alaska and Hawaii included for the first time.

F31. Expenditures for Organized Research in Institutions of Higher Education per Faculty Member, in Constant 1958 Dollars, 1930-1966, School Year Ending on Date.

Source: Data for current expenditures and number of faculty for 1930-1966 are the same as cited in the Notes to Series F26, F27. (Data for 1930-1962 for expenditures are from Series H355 in the reference cited.)

The sources and method for adjusting current expenditures to 1958 dollars are given in the Notes to Series F26, F27.

This item represents total direct organized research expenditures. It includes separately budgeted or financed research expenses, whose sources may be outside contracts or grants or the institutions' regular funds, for research and development on campus, at agricultural experiment stations, in hospitals, or at Federal contract and other off-campus research centers.

The following refers to the statistical tables:

a - Alaska and Hawaii included for the first time.

F32. Library Expenditures in Institutions of Higher Education per Institution, in Thousands of Constant 1958 Dollars, 1930-1966, School Year Ending on Date.

Source: Data for current expenditures for 1930-1966 are the same as cited in the Notes to Series F26, F27. (Data for 1930-1962 are from Series H356 in the reference cited.)

Data for the number of institutions are cited in the Notes to Series F28.

The sources and method for adjusting current expenditures to 1958 dollars are given in the Notes to Series F26, F27.

This item includes all expenditures relating to library services, such as salaries, operating expenses, books, periodicals, binding, etc., for both general and departmental libraries (National Center for Educational Statistics, 1968: 78).

The following refers to the statistical tables:

a - Alaska and Hawaii included for the first time.

F33. Expenditures for Plant Operation and Maintenance in Institutions of Higher Education per Institution, in Thousands of Constant 1958 Dollars, 1930-1966, School Year Ending on Date.

Source: Data for current expenditures for 1930-1966 are the same as cited in the Notes to Series F26, F27. (Data for 1930-1962 are from Series H357 in the reference cited.)

Data for the number of institutions are cited in the Notes to Series F28.

The sources and method for adjusting current expenditures to 1958 dollars are given in the Notes to Series F26, F27.

Only expenditures for salaries, supplies, equipment, etc. relating to the operation and maintenance of the institutional plant are included. Excluded are expenditures attributable to the educational departments or auxiliary enterprises (see Series F34 and Series F36 for these category definitions) (National Center for Educational Statistics, 1968: 78).

The following refers to the statistical tables:

a - Alaska and Hawaii included for the first time.

F34. Expenditures for Organized Activities Related to Instructional Departments in Institutions of Higher Education per Institution, in Thousands of Constant 1958 Dollars, 1932-1966, School Year Ending on Date.

Source: Data for current expenditures for 1930-1966 are the same as cited in the Notes to Series F26, F27. (Data for 1930-1962 are from Series H358 in the reference cited.)

Data for the number of institutions are cited in the Notes to Series F28.

The sources and method for adjusting current expenditures to 1958 dollars are given in the Notes to Series F26, F27.

This item includes expenditures for administration, operation, and maintenance of the physical plant attributable to the various educational departments, agricultural, medical, etc., as a consequence of the work of the departments (National Center for Educational Statistics, 1968: 79; Mertins, 1969: 66).

The following refer to the statistical tables:

a - Alaska and Hawaii included for the first time.

g - Includes expenditures for sales and services of educational departments ($13,832,000). This is separately reported for this year and applies only to land-grant colleges and universities; it includes expenses directly related to sales and services of educational departments, e.g., agricultural departments, services, sale of occasional publications, etc. (National Center for Educational Statistics, 1968: 76, 79).

h - Includes expenditures classified as "other sponsored activities," amounting to $159,145,000, and "other, unspecified," amounting to $153,574,000, these categories not having been included in surveys for previous years. These include expenditures for training institutes and other sponsored activities not specifically financed by outside sources such as the Federal Government (Mertins, 1969: Table 3, pp. 12-13; 66).

i - Amount for expenditures was not tabulated separately and is probably included with "student aid expenditures."

F35. Expenditures for Extension and Public Services in Institutions of Higher Education per Institution, in Thousands of Constant 1958 Dollars, 1930-1966, School Year Ending on Date.

Source: Data for current expenditures for 1930-1966 are the same as cited in the Notes to Series F26, F27. (Data for 1930-1962 are from Series H359 in the reference cited.)

Data for the number of institutions are cited in the Notes to Series F28.

The sources and method for adjusting current expenditures to 1958 dollars are given in the Notes to Series F26, F27.

Included are expenses for all non-degree-credit courses, cooperative extension (in land-grant institutions), public lectures, institutes, ratio and TV programs for the general public; excluded are expenses for instruction and services abroad. (National Center for Educational Statistics, 1968: 78).

The following refers to the statistical tables:

a - Alaska and Hawaii included for the first time.

F36. Expenditures for Auxiliary Enterprises and Student Aid in Institutions of Higher Education per Institution, in Thousands of Constant 1958 Dollars, 1930-1966, School Year Ending on Date.

Source: Data for current expenditures for 1930-1966 are cited in the Notes to Series F26, F27. (Data for 1930-1962 are from Series H360-H361 in the reference cited. "Student aid expenditure" is termed "other current expenditure" in Census, 1960a.)

Data for the number of institutions are cited in the Notes to Series F28.

The sources and method for adjusting current expenditures to 1958 dollars are given in the Notes to Series F26, F27.

Included in auxiliary enterprises expenditures are gross expenditures for administration, operation, and maintenance of the physical plant attributable to the institutions' auxiliary enterprises, i.e., cafeterias and dining halls, student residence halls, college bookstores, student unions and hospitals, faculty housing, concerts, industrial plants operated on a student self-help basis (not part of endowment), etc.

Student aid expenditures includes payments for scholarships, fellowships, and prizes and for remission of fees. Excluded are payments to students for the rendering of services. (National Center for Educational Statistics, 1968: 77, 79).

The following refer to the statistical tables:

a - Alaska and Hawaii included for the first time.

b - Student aid expenditures include unitemized educational and general expenditures of $5,238,649.

c - Student aid expenditures include unitemized educational and general expenditures of $7,502,347.

d - Student aid expenditures include unitemized educational and general expenditures of $2,579,553.

e - Student aid expenditures include unitemized educational and general expenditures of $2,020,311.

f - Student aid expenditures include $97,043,886 expended for Federal contract courses.

F37. New Public Construction Expenditure Estimates, Non-residential, Educational, in Millions of Dollars, 1920-1965.

Source: Data for 1920-1956 from Census (1960a: Series N21, pp. 379-380); for 1958-1962 from Census (1965a: Series N21, p. 55); for 1963-1965 from Census (1966c, Table 1092, p. 735). The following sources are cited in the above: for 1920-1956, Department of Labor and Department of Commerce, "Construction Volume and Costs, 1915-1956," <u>Statistical Supplement to Construction Review</u>, and various monthly issues of <u>Construction Review</u>, 1957 and 1958; for 1958-1962, Department of Commerce, U. S. Bureau of the Census, <u>Construction Reports</u>, C30-61, Supplement: "Value of New Construction Put in Place, 1946-1963 Revised;" for 1963-1965, Department of Commerce, U. S. Bureau of the Census, <u>Construction Reports</u>, Series C30.

The following information on construction is given:

"For Federal construction and State and local projects under Federal-aid programs, the estimates are based on reports of Federal agencies since 1941. For prior years, and for public construction other than Federal or Federal-aid projects, they are derived from the compilations of contract awards by the F. W. Dodge Corporation." (Census: 1960a: 374)

The following refers to the statistical tables:

a - Alaska and Hawaii included for the first time. If they had been excluded, the figure in Series H1 would have been 2,646.

G1. Median School Years Completed for Population 25 Years Old and Over, 1910-1968.

Source: Data for 1910-1940, 1950, 1960 from Census (1966a: Series B40, p. 197); for 1947, 1952-1959, 1962-1967 from Census (1960c; 1963c; 1965d; 1966d; 1968d);for 1968 from unpublished material of the U. S. Bureau of the Census. (Data for 1962-1965 are also in Census, 1966a, cited above.) The following additional sources are cited: John K. Folger and Charles B. Nam, "Educational Trends from Census Data," Demography, 1964, vol. 1, no. 1; the Census of Population, 1940, 1950, and 1960; and Current Population Reports: Population Characteristics, Series P-20, various issues. Estimates by age and sex of the adult population 1910 to 1960 have been made by Bearrentine (1966). The data for the beginning of each decade (e.g., 1940) are from the decennial census; all other are from the Current Population Surveys.

The educational attainment statistics published in Current Population Reports are estimates based on the Current Population Surveys of the U. S. Bureau of the Census. The figures may differ from those of the decennial census for the following reasons:

> "(1) Members of the Armed Forces in the United States living off post or with their families on post are included in the survey, but all other members of the Armed Forces are excluded from it. All members of the Armed Forces in the United States are included in the census data. (2) Statistics from both the census and the CPS are subject to

sampling and response errors. There are differences in coverage, enumeration techniques (self-enumeration versus direct enumeration), and the methods of allocating non-responses." (Census, 1966d: 4)

Except where otherwise noted, figures relate to the population of the 50 states and the District of Columbia. In the surveys, inmates of institutions and members of the Armed Forces living off post or with their families on post are included. All other members of the Armed Forces are excluded from the survey. Age categories refer to the age of a person on his last birthday.

Only progress in "regular" schools is counted in determining years of school completed. The category "regular" schools includes:

"...graded public, private and parochial elementary and high schools (both junior and senior high), colleges, universities, and professional schools or night schools. Thus, regular schooling is that which may advance a person toward an elementary school certificate or high school diploma, or a college, university, or professional school degree. Schooling in other than regular schools was counted only if the credits obtained were regarded as transferable to a school in the regular school system." (Census, 1966d: 4)

For 1950 and later years, information on educational attainment was obtained from the answers to two questions: (a) "What is the highest grade or school he has ever attended?" and (b) "Did he finish this grade?" Before 1950, only one question regarding the last grade completed had been asked, and hence the responses may have been less precise.

There are other reasons, too, why data for the different years are not strictly comparable, for example, slightly different sample variances, different adjustment procedures to obtain estimates, the inclusion of Alaska and Hawaii in 1962 and subsequent surveys, the assignment of educational attainment values to persons not reporting on years of school completed in 1962 and subsequent years. It should also be noted that figures presented are for different months: April in 1940, 1947, 1950 and 1960; October in 1952, and March in 1957, 1959, 1962, 1964, 1965, 1966 and 1967.

Despite differences between the CPS and the Census in coverage and data-gathering procedures, Series G1 follows a consistent trend except for 1960. The median years schooling of the population 25 years old and over is, as follows:

Year	Source	Median	.95 Confidence Interval
1959	CPS	11.0	$\pm$ 0.1
1960	Census	10.5	
1962	CPS	11.4	$\pm$ 0.1

From this, one may infer that differences in coverage between CPS and Census, discussed above, are primarily responsible for the variation, rather than the sampling variability of CPS.

For additional information on CPS, see Notes to Series A27-A37.

The following refer to the statistical tables:

a - Alaska and Hawaii included for the first time. Statistics for 1962 and subsequent years are not strictly comparable with earlier data.

b - In Census (1948b) this figure, although also based on the 1940 Census, was reported as 8.4.

c - Estimated by relating to age cohorts of the 1940 Census data on educational attainment.

d - Based on total (including non-civilian) population, from the decennial census.

G2 - G13. Percent of the Population 25 Years Old and Over, and the Population 25 to 29 Years Old Who Have Completed (a) Less than 5 Years of Elementary School (G2, G5, G8, G11), (b) 4 Years of High School or More (G3, G6, G9, G12), (c) 4 Years of College or More (G4, G7, G10, G13), for Total and Nonwhite Population, 1910-1967.

Source: Data for 1910-1930 are estimated. (See note c below);data for 1940-1967 from Census (1948b; 1953; 1957b; 1960c; 1963a; 1965d; 1966d; 1968d). Estimates by age and sex of the adult population 1910 to 1960 have been made by Bearrentine (1966).

The term, color, denotes two categories, white and nonwhite, the latter consisting of Negroes, Indians, Chinese, Japanese and other nonwhite races. The limitations to comparability described in G1 apply equally to these series.

Variations in Series G2-G4, occurring 1959, 1960, 1962, arise because the 1960 data are taken from the 1960 Census of Population. As noted in discussing Series G1, the total population differs in some characteristics from the CPS civilian noninstitutional population.

Similar variations appear to intrude in the 1950 data for several of the statistics in Series G5-G13, affecting the nonwhite series more than the series for the total population.

For additional comment on the Current Population Survey, see Notes to Series A27-A37.

The following refer to the statistical tables:

a - Alaska and Hawaii included for the first time. Statistics for 1962 and subsequent years are not strictly comparable with earlier data.

c - Estimated by relating to age cohorts of the 1940 Census data on educational attainment.

d - Based on total (including noncivilian) population, from the decennial census.

G14 - G109. Percent of the Population Completing Various Levels of Educational Attainment, by Color and Sex for the Following Age Groups (a) 20-24 Years, (b) 25-34 Years, (c) 35-44 Years, 1940-1967.

Source: Data for 1940 and 1947 from Census (1948b); for 1950 and 1957 from Census (1957b); for 1959 from Census (1960c);

for 1960 from Census (1963d) and Census (1963a); for 1962 from Census (1963c); for 1964 from Census (1965d); for 1965 and 1966 from Census (1966d); for 1967 from Census (1968d).

For ready reference, the following is an index to these series:

Color	Sex	Age	Series
White	Males	20-24 years	Series G14 - G21
White	Males	25-34 years	Series G22 - G29
White	Males	35-44 years	Series G30 - G37
White	Females	20-24 years	Series G38 - G45
White	Females	25-34 years	Series G46 - G53
White	Females	35-44 years	Series G54 - G61
Nonwhite	Males	20-24 years	Series G62 - G69
Nonwhite	Males	25-34 years	Series G70 - G77
Nonwhite	Males	35-44 years	Series G78 - G85
Nonwhite	Females	20-24 years	Series G86 - G93
Nonwhite	Females	25-34 years	Series G94 - G101
Nonwhite	females	35-44 years	Series G102 - G109

Definitions and limitations described with reference to Series G1-G13 apply equally to these series.

Educational Attainment, 1947: Because the numbers attaining 7 and 8 years of schooling were combined in the publication for 1947 (Census, 1948b), the number attaining 7 years of schooling was estimated and the percentages calculated. For the 12 age-sex-color groups the number with 7 years schooling was separated from the combined 7-and-8 year category by estimating the percentage with 7 years. The percentages in 1940 and 1950 were obtained from the respective censuses and the percentage for 1947 was assumed to lie on a linear trend between the two. The percentage achieving 7 years of schooling, based upon the total in the age-sex-color group, was then used to adjust the 1947 CPS educational attainment data.

Educational Attainment, 1960, 20-24-year-old male age groups: The attainment of males in the Armed Forces, being available, was subtracted from the total males for each level of schooling, to provide a population more closely resembling that of the Current Population Survey. Data are from Census (1963d).

For additional notes on CPS, see Notes to Series A27-A37.

The following refer to the statistical tables:

a - Alaska and Hawaii included for the first time. Statistics for 1962 and subsequent years are not strictly comparable with earlier data.

b - Based on total (including noncivilian) population from the decennial census.

c - Data not available.

d - Based on decennial data but the noncivilian population is excluded. See notes above.

G110 - G125. Labor Force Participation Rates of the Civilian Noninstitutional Population, 14-17 Years of Age and 18-24 Years of Age, by School Enrollment Status, Color and Sex, 1959-1967.

Source: Data for 1959 from Katz (1960: Table D, p. A-7); for 1960 from Rosenfeld (1961: Table D, p. A-8); for 1961 from Rosenfeld (1962: Table D, p. A-8); for 1962 from Rosenfeld (1963: Table D, p. A-8); for 1963 from Hamel (1964: Table D, p. A-8); for 1964 from Swanstrom (1965: Table D, p. A-8); for 1965 from Bogan (1966: Table D, p. A-8); for 1966 from Perrella (1967: Table D, p. A-8); for 1967 from Bogan (1969: Table C, p. A-7).

The labor force participation rate is the percent of the civilian noninstitutional population in the civilian labor force, including both employed and unemployed persons, full- or part-time employment.

Persons are classified as being in the labor force if they, (a) were employed and working for pay, or were working without pay for 15 hours or more on a family farm or business, or were employed but not working at the time of the survey due to vacation, illness, etc.; (b) were unemployed but looking for work, or were temporarily laid off, or waiting to start a new job within 30 days from the time of the survey, or would have been looking for a job except for illness, or belief that no job was currently available in their line of work, etc.

School enrollment includes enrollment during the current term "in day or night school or any type of public, parochial, or other private school in the regular school system." Trade schools or business, not in the regular school system, correspondence schools, and training courses given directly on the job are not included. School attendance may be either full- or part-time (Perrella, 1967: A-2-A3).

The data are collected for the Bureau of Labor Statistics through the U. S. Bureau of the Census' Current Population Survey of the labor force in October of each year. This sample survey includes estimates for the civilian noninstitutional population 14 to 34 years of age. Beginning with 1962 data, the estimation procedures for the monthly survey are based on information from the 1960 decennial Census of Population while before that date estimates were based on the 1950 Census of Population. In 1960 Alaska and Hawaii were included in the coverage. These changes in the estimation procedures and the coverage, however, have minor effects on the data when making yearly comparisons.

Since the data are based on a sample survey, they are subject to errors of response and reporting. However, the estimated percentages shown in this series are relatively more reliable than the absolute estimates of the labor force for the two age groups shown in Series G126-G127. Tables of standard errors of the estimates may be found in the sources.

Since the data for nonwhites are based upon samples roughly one-tenth as large as the data for whites the sampling errors are greater. For example, the chances are 19 out of 20 that the 1965 statistic in Series G116 for nonwhite, not enrolled males, 81.2 percent, lies between 71.4 percent and 91.0 percent.

For additional notes to the Current Population Surveys, see notes to Series A27-A37.

The following refer to the statistical tables:

a - Percent not shown where base is less than 100,000.

b - Based on total (including noncivilian) population, from the decennial census.

G126 - G157. Labor Force Status of the Civilian Noninstitutional Population 14-17 years of Age (G126-G141), and 18-24 Years of Age (G142-G157) by Fall School Enrollment, Color and Sex, 1959-1967.

Source: Same as for Series G110-G125.

See Series G110-G125 for definition of labor force, school enrollment, and description of data with respect to population coverage and reliability.

G158. Percent Illiterate Among Persons 10 Years Old and Over, 1870-1959.

Source: Data for 1870-1959 from Folger and Nam (1967: Table IV-1, p. 114). The following sources are cited in the above: U. S. Bureau of the Census, Current Population Reports, Population Characteristics, Series P-20, No. 99, Table A, and Census records.

To be classified as literate, a person must be able to read and write a simple message. "Trends and Patterns of Illiteracy" is discussed in detail by Folger and Nam (1967: 111-130).

The following refers to the statistical tables:

c - Percents apply to the population 14 years old and over and are undoubtedly slightly higher than for the population 10 years old and over. Data on illiteracy were not collected for persons 10 to 13 years old for these dates. Other factors affecting comparability are discussed in the source.

H1, H2, H3. Median Income of Males, Age 25 Years and Over, Who Have Completed: 8 Years of Elementary School (1), 4 Years of High School (H2), and 4 or More Years of College (H3), 1939-1966.

Source: Data for 1939-1964 from Census (1966a: Series B44, B45 and B46, p 196-197); for 1965 from Census (1967f: 34); for 1967 from Census (1967g: 39). The following sources are cited in the above: for 1939, <u>Sixteenth Census of the United States Population: Education</u>; <u>Educational Attainment by Economic Characteristics and Marital Status</u>; for 1949, <u>1950 United States Census of Population: Education</u>, Special Report, PE No. 5B; for 1959, <u>1960 United States Census of Population: Occupation by Earnings and Education</u>, Subject Reports, PC (2) 7B; for 1958, 1961, 1963 and 1964, <u>Current Population Reports: Consumer Income</u>, Series P-60, Nos. 33, 39, 43, 47 and 51. All reports are published by the U. S. Bureau of the Census.

The population coverage of these series is the same as in other series from the Current Population Surveys; see Notes to Series A27-A37. While the Census reports on <u>Consumer Income</u> present information on income of families and unrelated individuals, the tables from which these series are derived present the income of persons. Income is for the calendar year. Data were collected in March of the following year. The person was 25 years of age in March of the year following the date given for the median income. Income is in current dollars and includes that received prior to deductions for taxes; definitions of the various types of income included is defined in Census (1967g: 10-12). Definitions of years of school completed are the same as those presented in the Notes to Series G1; the year of school completed is the highest attained by the person.

The following refer to the statistical tables:

a - Figure excludes males over 64 years old.

b - Includes persons with 7 or 8 years of education since estimates were not separately available for those with 8 years of elementary education.

I1-I35. Population, by Sex, for Selected Ages and Age Groups, 1880-1968.

Source: Data for 1880 and 1890 are from Census (1883); for 1890 from Census (1897); for 1900-1959 from Census (1965b); for 1960-1964 from Census (1965c); for 1965-1967 from Census (1968b); for 1968 from Census (1969a).

A key to the data presented is, as follows:

Age	Total	Male	Female
5	I1	I2	I3
5-13	I4	I5	I6
13	I7	I8	I9
14	I10	I11	I12
15	I13	I14	I15
16	I16	I17	I18
17	I19	I20	I21
18	I22	I23	I24
18-21	I25	I26	I27
22	I28	I29	I30
23	I31	I32	I33
5-17	I34		
14-17	I35		

For comment on the accuracy of the data, see Appendix C, Age Cohorts of the Population.

Appendix E

Notes on Tables

Some educational statistics are logically oriented to the beginning of the school year, such as enrollment, and others, such as graduates, are more logically calibrated to the end of the school year. For this reason, no attempt was made to cast all statistical series in relation to the beginning (fall) of the year or to the end (spring) of the school year. Consequently, the following symbols are found in the statistical tables:

SYEOD: School Year Ending on Date, meaning that the statistic refers to the school year that ends on the date appearing in the row.

SYB: School Year Beginning, meaning that the statistic refers to the school year beginning on the date appearing in the row. This symbol was shortened, that is, OD (on date) was eliminated, in order to more easily distinguish it from SYEOD.

"Base year" refers to the year of the data used as the denominator of the statistic. Continuation ratios, for example, utilize data from two successive years, and are presented on the base year, that is, the year of the denominator of the statistic.

Depending upon his purpose, the analyst may wish to re-orient a statistical series to another year to which the data are relevant.

The sources of data are presented as notes to tables, page 276. Here, also, will be found precautionary notes and information on the data collection methods, etc., where such is appropriate to the series. Some of these notes are keyed to specific statistics of the series.

	Elementary & secondary enrollment		Percent of population of school age enrolled in school			Enrollment in full-time public day schools		Enrollment in full-time nonpublic regular		Average days attended per pupil, public schools	Pupil-teacher ratio (public schools)
	Total (000) SYEOD*	Ratio to pop. 5-17 years SYEOD*	Total SYEOD*	White SYEOD*	Nonwhite SYEOD*	K and 1 - 8 SYEOD*	9 - 12 and post-grad. SYEOD*	Elementary SYEOD*	Secondary SYEOD*	SYEOD*	SYEOD*
	A-1	A-2	A-3	A-4	A-5	A-6	A-7	A-8	A-9	A-10	A-11
1850			47.2	56.2	1.8						
1860			50.6	59.6	1.9						
1870			48.4	54.4	9.9					78.4	20.3
1871										79.4	20.6
1872										79.5	20.3
1873										76.5	20.0
1874										77.0	20.3
1875										77.9	20.4
1876										79.4	20.4
1877										80.0	20.3
1878										80.9	20.9
1879										80.5	21.0
1880			57.8	62.0	33.8					81.1	21.4
1881										80.0	20.9
1882										81.3	21.2
1883										81.1	21.9
1884										82.9	22.5
1885										83.6	22.4
1886										84.1	22.7
1887										84.9	22.6
1888										85.9	22.8
1889	13,661	75.2								86.4	22.5
1890	14,479	78.1	54.3	57.9	32.9					86.3	22.4
1891	14,541	77.3								86.6	22.6
1892	14,556	76.3								88.4	22.9
1893	14,826	76.6								89.6	23.1
1894	15,314	78.0								91.6	23.6
1895	15,455	77.6								93.5	24.0
1896	15,834	78.4								94.8	24.4
1897	16,140	78.8								96.3	24.8
1898	16,459	79.2								98.0	25.2
1899	16,474	78.2								97.9	25.1
1900	16,855	78.3	50.5	53.6	31.1					99.0	25.1
1901	17,072	78.3								98.0	24.8
1902	17,126	77.6								100.6	25.0
1903	17,205	77.1								101.7	24.6
1904	17,560	77.8								102.1	24.9
1905	17,806	77.9								105.2	24.9
1906	18,056	78.0								106.0	25.1
1907	18,200	77.8								107.3	24.8
1908	18,609	78.6								109.8	24.5
1909	18,995	79.1								112.6	25.0
1910	19,372	79.4	62.6	64.9	47.2					113.0	24.5
1911	19,636	79.5				16,551d	1,157d			111.8	24.1
1912	19,830	79.2				16,634d	1,201d			115.6	24.3
1913	20,348	79.8				16,906d	1,333d			115.6	24.1
1914	20,935	80.6				17,330d	1,432d			117.8	24.5

* - SYEOD, see Notes to Tables, preceding page.

Year	(1)	(2)	(3)	(4)	(5)	(6)	(7)	(8)	(9)	(10)	(11)
1915	21,474					17,734d	1,562d			121.2	24.8
1916	22,172	81.5				18,207d	1,711d			120.9	24.7
1917	22,516	83.0				18,283d	1,822d			119.8	23.9
1918		81.8				18,354d	1,934d				
1919						19,149	2,067d				
1920	23,278	83.2	67.5	68.9	56.2	19,378	2,200			121.2	23.8
1921	24,820	85.8				19,872d	2,537d			130.6	25.5
1922	26,016	87.3				20,366	2,873d			132.5	25.1
1923	27,180	88.8				20,633d	3,131d			135.9	25.8
1924	27,810	89.1				20,899	3,390			140.4	24.8
1925						20,999	3,651				
1926						20,984	3,757d				
1927						21,126d	3,834d				
1928						21,268	3,911d				
1929						21,274d	4,155d				
1930	28,329	89.5	73.4	75.0b	62.3b	21,278d	4,399d			143.0	24.9
1931	29,061	91.8				21,207d	4,770d			144.9	25.5
1932		92.6				21,135	5,140d			145.8	26.5
1933	29,163					20,950d	5,404d			146.3	25.6
1934	29,006	92.9				20,765	5,669d			149.3	25.4
1935		93.7				20,579d	5,822d				
1936	28,662					20,392	5,974d				
1937						20,070d	6,101d	2,331	360		
1938						19,748d	6,229d	2,251	387		
1939						19,290d	6,414d	2,241	447		
1940	28,044	94.2	74.8	75.6	68.4	18,832	6,601d	2,153	458	151.7	25.2
1941	27,179	93.5				18,582d	6,714d	2,133	483	149.6	24.5
1942		89.7				18,175	6,388	2,079	421	147.9	23.7
1943	25,758					18,033d	6,122d				
1944						17,713	5,554d				
1945		91.2	79.2			17,666d	5,560d	2,259	565	150.6	23.9
1946	26,124		79.2			17,678d	5,622d				
1947			78.1	75.6c	69.7c	17,821d	5,838d				
1948		91.1	78.3			18,291	5,653d	2,451	602	155.1	24.3
1949	26,998		79.4			18,818d	5,658d				
1950	28,492	92.3	80.8	79.3	74.8	19,387	5,725	2,708	672	157.9	24.4
1951		91.5	81.1			20,681d	5,882d	3,154	656	156.0	24.2
1952	30,372		80.9			21,625d	5,882d				
1953			85.7			22,546	6,290	3,592	747	158.9	24.6
1954	33,175	92.5	86.2	87.0	80.8	23,471d	6,574d	3,886	823	158.5	24.1
1955			86.5	87.0	82.9	24,290	6,873d				
1956	35,872	93.1	87.2	87.8	83.6	25,016d	7,318d	4,297	931	157.4	23.6
1957			87.8	88.2	85.3	25,669	7,860d				
1958	38,756	93.5	88.4	88.9	85.1	26,581a	8,258a	4,460	1,035		
1959			88.5	88.8	85.9	27,602d	8,485d				
1960	42,012	95.0	88.6a	89.0a	86.1a	28,439d	8,821d	4,894	1,120	160.2	23.4
1961		94.9	88.5	88.9	86.3	28,686	9,566	5,200e	1,300e	162.3	23.1
1962	44,316		89.6	89.6	86.3	29,374d	10,372d				
1963		94.8	89.6	89.8	88.0	29,915e	11,110e	5,300e	1,300e	163.2	23.0
1964	46,957		89.6	89.8	88.4	30,652e	11,628e				
1965		95.9	89.6	89.8	88.5	31,162e	11,860e	5,400e	1,300e		
1966	48,780		89.7	89.9	88.5	31,808e	12,147e				
1967	49,599	96.1	90.4	90.8	88.6			5,200e	1,400e	163.5	21.9
1968	50,100	95.8	90.8	91.0	89.4						

377

	Total public schools SYEOD	Pupil-teacher ratio					High school graduates		Estimated retention ratios, public and nonpublic schools, on base year			
		Public day schools		Nonpublic day schools				5th to 6th grade SYB*	6th to 7th grade SYB*	7th to 8th grade SYB*	8th to 9th grade SYB*
		Elementary SYEOD	Secondary SYEOD	Elementary SYEOD	Secondary SYEOD	Total pub. & nonpub. SYEOD (000)	Percent 17 yr. olds SYEOD				
	A-12	A-13	A-14	A-15	A-16	A-17	A-18	A-19	A-20	A-21	A-22
1850											
1860											
1870						16	2.0				
1871						17					
1872						17					
1873						18					
1874						19					
1875						20					
1876						20					
1877						21					
1878						22					
1879						23					
1880						24	2.5				
1881						25					
1882						27					
1883						28					
1884						31					
1885						32					
1886						33					
1887						32					
1888						33					
1889						38					
1890					13.2	44	3.5				
1891						43					
1892						53					
1893						59					
1894						65					
1895						72					
1896						76					
1897						80					
1898						84					
1899						90					
1900					10.9	95	6.4				
1901						97	6.4				
1902						99	6.4				
1903						105	6.6				
1904						112	6.9				
1905						119	7.2				
1906						126	7.4				
1907						127	7.4				
1908						129	7.4				
1909						142	7.9				
1910	33.8	34.4	27.8		10.5	156	8.8				
1911						168	9.2				
1912						181	9.8				
1913						200	10.8				
1914						219	11.7				

* - SYB: School Year Beginning; see the note preceding the statistical tables.

1915						240	12.8				
1916						259	13.8				
1917											
1918	31.4	32.6	23.0			285	15.1				
1919											
1920	31.8	33.6	21.6		12.3	311	16.8				
1921											
1922	32.1	34.3	22.2			357	17.8				
1923											
1924	31.9	33.9	23.5			494	23.4	.911			
1925									.876		
1926	30.4	32.6	22.2			561	25.5	.919		.928	
1927									.897		.826
1928	30.2	33.1	20.7			597	26.2	.939		.915	
1929									.902		.898
1930	30.0	33.2	20.6		14.0	667	29.0	.943		.950	
1931				38.7[b]					.925		.914
1932	30.1	33.0	22.2			827	35.5	.935		.945	
1933				35.8[c]	14.1				.951		.934
1934	31.2	33.5	24.9			915	39.2	.953		.935	
1935									.936		.946
1936	30.3	33.8	22.3	34.0	15.3	1,015	42.7	.954		.944	
1937									.938		.954
1938	29.6	33.2	22.0	33.4	16.0	1,120	45.6	.955		.949	
1939									.951		.988
1940	29.0	32.7	22.0	33.2	15.2	1,221	50.8	.968		.939	
1941				33.2	15.2				.940		.933
1942	28.6	32.5	21.3	32.6	15.3	1,242	51.2	.954		.919	
1943									.953		.934
1944	28.1	32.9	19.2			1,019	42.3	.952		.932	
1945									.976		.953
1946	28.0	32.6	19.4	35.0	15.5	1,080	47.9	.954		.924	
1947									.991		.988
1948	27.8	33.0	18.5	36.4	14.4[d]	1,190	54.0	.984		.972	
1949									.972		.949
1950	27.5	32.9	17.7	35.6	15.9	1,200	59.0	.981		.970	
1951									.987		.929
1952	27.6	33.4	17.1	38.3	15.7	1,196	58.6	.974		.951	
1953									.991		.962
1954	27.9	34.3	16.8	42.3	15.2	1,276	60.0	.980		.970	
1955	26.3	32.0	16.1						.999		.966
1956	27.5	33.6	16.8	41.5	16.2	1,415	62.3	.985		.968	
1957	25.7	31.8	15.4						.999		.965
1958	25.7	31.5	16.0	38.6	17.9	1,506	64.8	.985		.963	
1959	25.7[a]	32.0[a]	15.8[a]					.990	.993		.981
1960	25.6	32.2	15.4	38.8[a]	18.4[a]	1,864[a]	65.1[a]		.993	.982	
1961	25.5	32.7	14.9		18.8[e]					.993	.979
1962	25.4	32.4	15.4	36.9	17.7	1,925[d]	69.5[d]				.990
1963	25.2	32.3	15.5			1,950	70.5				
1964	24.9	31.8	15.7	35.9	17.6	2,290	61.3				
1965	24.6	31.7	15.5			2,638	74.9				
1966	24.1	31.0	15.2	33.5	18.1[e]	2,672[f]	75.8				
1967	23.8	31.0	14.9			2,673[f]	76.3				
1968						2,742[f]	77.8				

	Continuation ratio			Percent of various age groups enrolled in school, fall of year										
	Full-time public secondary day schools, on base year		Pub. & nonpub. 12th to college SYB	Total 5-34 years SYB	5 years SYB	6 years SYB	7-9 years SYB	10-13 years SYB	14&15 years SYB	16&17 years SYB	18&19 years SYB	20-24 years SYB	25-29 years SYB	30-34 years SYB
	9th to 10th grade SYB	10th to 11th grade SYB	11th to 12th grade SYB											
	A-23	A-24	A-25	A-26	A-27	A-28	A-29	A-30	A-31	A-32	A-33	A-34	A-35	A-36	A-37
1850															
1860															
1870															
1871															
1872															
1873															
1874															
1875															
1876															
1877															
1878															
1879															
1880															
1881															
1882															
1883															
1884															
1885															
1886															
1887															
1888															
1889															
1890															
1891															
1892															
1893															
1894															
1895															
1896															
1897															
1898															
1899															
1900															
1901															
1902															
1903															
1904															
1905															
1906															
1907															
1908															
1909															
1910	657	707	750												
1911	716	762	824												
1912	702	743	797												
1913	714	749	821												
1914	721	759	840												

Year															
1915	689	704	794												
1916	682	717	830												
1917	663	728	850												
1918	665	732	845												
1919	740	791	850												
1920	734	760	795												
1921	701	746	827												
1922	724	766	840												
1923	731	778	830												
1924	705	759	826												
1925	719	749	824												
1926	721	749	827												
1927	758	788	862												
1928	768	786	851												
1929	793	816	894												
1930	815	827	896												
1931	823	820	880												
1932	848	826	883												
1933	852	798	856												
1934	847	791	866												
1935	835	811	886												
1936	845	838	875												
1937	868	858	882												
1938	886	865	895												
1939	891	859	890												
1940	838	809	839												
1941	858	806	807												
1942	801	744	735												
1943	862	814	826												
1944	892	821	835												
1945	916	841	892												
1946	853	803	864												
1947	896	843	885	604	42.3	53.4	96.2	98.4	98.6	91.6	67.6	24.3	10.2	3.0	1.0
1948	885	850	886	474	43.1	55.0	96.2	98.3	98.0	92.7	71.2	26.9	9.7	2.6	.9
1949	881	869	885	449	43.9	55.1	96.2	98.5	98.7	93.5	69.5	25.3	9.2	3.8	1.1
1950	888	864	846	439	44.2	51.8	97.0	98.9	98.6	94.7	71.3	29.4	9.0	3.0	.9
1951	868	826	828	403	45.4	53.8	96.0	99.0	99.2	94.8	75.1	26.3	8.3	2.5	.7
1952	923	894	910	367	46.8	57.8	96.8	98.7	98.9	96.2	73.4	28.7	9.5	2.6	1.2
1953	908	885	882	424	48.8	58.4	97.7	99.4	99.4	96.5	74.7	31.2	11.1	2.9	1.7
1954	912	873	874	451	50.0	57.7	96.8	99.2	99.2	95.8	78.0	32.4	11.2	4.1	1.5
1955	921	879	886	462	50.8	58.1	97.0	99.2	99.2	95.9	77.4	31.5	11.1	4.2	1.6
1956	927	891	886	472	52.3	58.9	97.4	99.4	99.2	96.9	78.4	35.4	12.8	5.1	1.9
1957	935	890	894	475	53.6	60.2	97.3	99.5	99.5	97.1	80.5	34.9	14.0	5.5	1.8
1958	936	884	882	470	54.8	63.8	96.9	99.5	99.5	96.9	80.6	37.6	13.4	5.7	2.2
1959	934	884	882	473	55.5	62.9	97.5	99.4	99.4	97.5	82.9	36.8	12.7	5.1	2.2
1960	944	896	897	462	56.4	63.7	98.0	99.6	99.5	97.8	82.6	38.4	13.1	4.9	2.4
1961	945	905	922	468	56.8	66.3	97.4	99.4	99.3	97.6	83.6	38.0	13.7	4.4	2.0
1962	948	922	920	495	57.8	66.8	97.9	99.2	99.3	98.0	84.3	41.8	15.6	5.0	2.6
1963	967	924	933	507	58.5	67.8	97.4	99.4	99.3	98.4	87.1	40.9	17.3	4.9	2.5
1964	970	919	929	496	58.7	68.5	98.2	99.3	99.4	98.6	87.7	41.6	16.8	5.2	2.6
1965	923	923	920	504	59.7	70.1	98.7	99.3	99.1	98.6	87.4	46.3	19.0	6.1	3.2
1966	968	968	919	—	60.0	72.8	97.6	99.3	99.3	98.2	88.5	47.2	19.9	6.5	2.7
1967	978	978	—	—	60.2	76.1	98.4	99.4	99.1	98.0	88.8	47.6	22.0	6.6	4.0
1968	—	—	—	540	60.1	76.8	98.3	99.1	99.1	98.0	90.2	50.4	21.4	7.0	3.9

	Public teachers & other nonsupervisory staff[a]						Public school teachers with less than standard cert.		Instructional staff in full-time, non-public schools		Median age, elementary and secondary teachers, public and nonpublic			
	Elementary & secondary				Elementary SYEOD (000)	Secondary SYEOD (000)	Elementary percent SYB	Secondary percent SYB	Elementary SYEOD (000)	Secondary SYEOD (000)	Total Male SYEOD	Non-white Male SYEOD	Total Female SYEOD	Non-white Female SYEOD
	Total SYEOD (000)	Male SYEOD (000)	Female SYEOD (000)	Percent Female SYEOD										
	B-1	B-2	B-3	B-4	B-5	B-6	B-7	B-8	B-9	B-10	B-11	B-12	B-13	B-14
1850														
1860														
1870	201	78	123	61.3										
1871	220	90	130	59.0										
1872	230	95	135	58.7										
1873	238	98	140	58.8										
1874	248	103	145	58.4										
1875	258	109	149	57.8										
1876	260	110	150	57.7										
1877	267	114	153	57.2										
1878	277	119	158	56.9										
1879	280	121	159	56.7										
1880	286	123	164	57.2										
1881	294	122	171	58.3										
1882	299	119	180	60.2										
1883	304	116	188	61.8										
1884	314	119	195	62.1										
1885	326	122	204	62.6										
1886	331	124	208	62.6										
1887	339	127	212	62.6										
1888	347	126	221	63.6										
1889	356	124	232	65.1										
1890	364	126	238	65.5	355	9								
1891	368	123	245	66.5										
1892	374	122	253	67.5										
1893	383	122	261	68.1										
1894	389	125	264	67.8										
1895	398	130	268	67.4										
1896	400	130	270	67.6										
1897	405	131	274	67.6										
1898	411	132	278	67.8										
1899	414	131	283	68.3										
1900	423	126	296	70.1	403	20								
1901	432	126	306	70.9										
1902	442	121	321	72.6										
1903	**449**	117	332	74.0										
1904	**455**	114	341	**75.0**										
1905	460	111	350	76.0										
1906	466	109	357	76.6										
1907	481	104	377	78.3										
1908	495	104	391	78.9										
1909	506	108	398	78.6	482	42								
1910	523	110	413	78.9										
1911	534	110	423	79.3										
1912	547	114	433	79.1										
1913	565	113	452	80.0										
1914	580	115	465	80.2										

Year													
1915	604	118	486	80.4									
1916	622	123	499	80.2									
1917	651	105	546	83.8									
1918													
1919					562	84							
1920	680[b]	96	584	85.9	576	102							
1921	723	118	605	83.7	593	130							
1922	761	129	632	83.1	617	144							
1923	814	139	675	83.0	645	170							
1924	832	138	694	83.4	643	189[e]							
1925													
1926	854	142	712	83.4	641	213[e]							
1927	872	154	718	82.3	640	231							
1928	847	162	685	80.9	619	228							
1929	871	179	692	79.4	603	268							
1930	877	185	692	78.9	595	282[e]							
1931													
1932	875	195	681	77.8	575	300[e]	8.8	3.8	51		32.1		
1933	859	183	676	78.7	559	300[e]	8.2	4.5	66	21		37.7	28.8
1934					539	289	8.9	5.2	67	25			
1935	828	127	701	84.7	542	289	9.0	4.6	65	28	33.7	34.2	32.0
1936	831	138	693	83.4	555	306	8.4	5.0	66	30			
1937	861	162	699	81.2	590	324	8.2	5.6	64	32			
1938	914	195	719	78.7	620	343							
1939	963	235	728	75.6	658	375	7.9	4.5	67	36	37.9	36.9	36.2
1940	1,042	254[c]	779[c]	74.7	723	410	7.6	4.4	76	42		41.2	
1941	1,149	294[c]	839[c]	73.0	786[c]	473[c]	6.3	4.3	82	42			
1942	1,261	332[c]	906[c]	71.9	815[c]	491[c]	6.1	4.2	85	49			
1943	1,387[d]	402[fd]	985[fd]	71.0[fd]	832[c]	524[c]	5.7	4.1	94	51	35.3	35.8	37.8
1944	1,504	451[f]	1,053[f]	70.0[f]	858[c]	550[c]	5.5	4.2	111	52		44.5	
1945	1,625	506[f]	1,119[f]	68.9[f]	869[c]	592[c]	5.6	4.3	120[d]	56[d]			
1946	1,786	568[f]	1,218[f]	68.2[f]	886[c]	621[c]	5.4	4.2	133	63			
1947					908[c]	669[c]			145	74			
1948					940[c]	708[c]							
1949					968[c]	749[c]			155[f]	87[f]			
1950					1,005[c]	783[c]							
1951					1,040[f]	814[c]							
1952					1,058	852[f]							

	Total public elem'y. schools SYEOD (000)	One-teacher public schools		Total public secondary schools SYEOD (000)	Average days public school term SYEOD	Average days attended per pupil, public SYEOD	Public expenditures per pupil in ADA, SYEOD dollars	Public expenditures per pupil enrolled, SYEOD dollars	Degree-credit enrollment, all institutions SYB (000)				
		Total SYEOD (000)	Percent of elementary schools SYEOD						First-time			Total	
									Total	Male	Female	Male	Female
	C-1	C-2	C-3	C-4	C-5	C-6	C-7	C-8	D-1	D-2	D-3	D-4	D-5
1850													
1860													
1870						132.2	78.4		9				
1871						132.1	79.4		9				
1872						133.4	79.5		9				
1873						129.1	76.5		10				
1874						128.8	77.0		9				
1875						130.4	77.9		10				
1876						133.1	79.4		9				
1877						132.1	80.0		9				
1878						132.0	80.9		8				
1879						130.2	80.5		8				
1880						130.3	81.1		8				
1881						130.1	80.0		8				
1882						131.2	81.3		9				
1883						129.8	81.1		9				
1884						129.1	82.9		9				
1885						130.7	83.6		10				
1886						130.4	84.1		10				
1887						131.3	84.9		10				
1888						132.3	85.9		10				
1889						133.7	86.4	13.6	11				
1890						134.7	86.3	14.0	11				
1891						135.7	86.6	14.5	11				
1892						136.9	88.4	14.8	12				
1893						136.3	89.6	15.1	12				
1894						139.5	91.6	15.5	12				
1895						139.5	93.5	15.3	12				
1896						140.5	94.8	15.4	13				
1897						142.0	96.3	15.4	13				
1898						143.0	98.0	15.7	13				
1899						143.0	97.9	16.3	13				
1900						144.3	99.0	16.7	14				
1901						143.7	98.0	17.5	14				
1902						144.7	100.6	17.9	15				
1903						147.2	101.7	18.6	16				
1904						146.7	102.1	19.8	17				
1905						150.9	105.2	20.5	18				
1906						150.6	106.0	21.1	18				
1907						151.8	107.3	22.8	20				
1908						154.1	109.8	24.5	22				
1909						155.3	112.6	25.2	23				
1910		212.4			157.5	113.0	27.8	24					
1911					156.8	111.8	28.8	25					
1912					158.0	115.6	30.4	27					
1913					158.1	115.6	32.2	28					
1914					158.7	117.8	32.6	29					

Year											
1915											
1916					159.4	121.2	33.6	31			
1917					160.3	120.9	35.0	31			
1918					160.7	119.8	40.5	37			
1919											
1920		200.1[b]			161.9	121.2	53.5	48			
1921		196.0			164.0	130.6	67.0	68			
1922		190.7			168.3	132.5	71.5	75			
1923		180.8			169.3	135.9	77.4	82			
1924		169.7			171.5	140.4	82.8	87			
1925		162.8									
1926		156.1			172.7	143.4	86.7	90			
1927					171.2	144.9	81.4	83			
1928					171.6	145.8	67.5	65			
1929					173.0	146.3	74.3	75			
1930	238.3	149.2	62.6	23.9	173.9	149.3	83.9	86			
1931	232.8	143.4	61.6	26.4							
1932	236.2	139.2	58.9	24.7	175.0	151.7	88.1	92			
1933	232.2	131.1	56.5	25.6	174.7	149.6	98.3	95			
1934	221.7	121.2	54.7	25.5	175.5	147.9	117.0	105			
1935					176.8	150.6	136.4	125			
1936					177.6	155.1	179.4	180			
1937									381	228[eg]	153[eg]	
1938												549[e]
1939												
1940	183.1	113.6	58.8	25.1	177.9	157.9	208.8	232	696	500[eg]	197[eg]	661[e]
1941		107.7	56.7	29.0	178.2	156.0	244.2	276	593	409[g]	193[g]	679
1942	170.0	96.3			178.6	158.9	264.8	315	569	370	199	694
1943	160.2	86.6	54.0	24.3	178.0	158.5	294.2	352	558	357	201	723
1944	146.8	75.1	51.2	25.5	177.6	157.4	341.1	405				
1945									517	320	197	721
1946	128.2	59.6	46.5	24.5	178.0[a]	160.2[a]	375.4[a]	433	472	280	192	711
1947	123.8	50.7	41.0	23.7	179.1	162.3	418.5	480	537	324	213	754
1948	110.9	42.9	38.7	25.6	179.0	163.2[c]	460	519[d]	572	345	227	808
1949	104.4	35.0	33.5	26.0	178.9	163.5	538	547	631	386[f]	244[f]	883[f]
1950	95.5	25.3	26.5	25.5			569[c]		675	418[f]	257[f]	920[f]
1951							623[c]		723	446	277	1,007
1952	91.8[a]	20.2[a]	22.0[a]	25.8[a]					730	445	284	1,052
1953	81.9	13.3	16.3	25.4					781	469	312	1,134
1954	77.6	9.9	12.8	26.4					827	491	336	1,211
1955	73.2	6.5	8.9	26.6								
1956									930	543	387	1,321
1957									1,026	596	430	1,467
1958									1,039	602	437	1,604
1959									1,055	608	446	1,739
1960									1,235	706	528	1,936
1961									1,453	834	618	2,174
1962									1,509[e]	857[e]	652[e]	2,404[e]
1963									1,592[e]	895[e]	696[e]	2,639[e]
1964									1,643	931	713	2,838

Note: Columns to the right (originally positioned higher on the page) continue:

Year			
1937		816[e]	
1940		1,418[e]	
1941		1,659	
1942		1,709	
1943		1,722	
1945		1,560	
1946		1,391	
1947		1,380	
1948		1,422	
1949		1,563[f]	
1950		1,733[f]	
1951		1,911	
1952		1,985	
1953		2,092	
1954		2,154	
1956		2,249	
1957		2,424	
1958		2,603	
1959		2,790	
1960		3,052	
1961		3,396	
1962		3,609[e]	
1963		3,867[e]	
1964		4,146	

	First-time degree-credit enrollment, jr. colleges, SYB				First-time degree-credit enrollment per 100 population 18 years old, SYB			Higher education degree-credit enrollment per 100 population 18-21 years old			Degrees conferred by higher education institutions			
	Male (000)	Female (000)	Percent of Total		Total	Male	Female	Total	Male	Female	Bachelor's (USOE) SYEOD	Master's (USOE) SYEOD	Doctor's (USOE) d/ SYEOD	Doctor's degrees conferred NRC, SYEOD
			Male	Female										
	D-6	D-7	D-8	D-9	D-10	D-11	D-12	D-13	D-14	D-15	D-16	D-17	D-18	D-19
1850														
1860														
1870								1.7			9,371		1	
1871											12,357		13	
1872											7,852		14	
1873											10,807	794	26	
1874											11,493	890	13	
1875											11,932	860	23	
1876											12,005	661	31	
1877											10,145	835	39	
1878											11,533	731	32	
1879											12,081	816	36	
1880								2.7			12,896	919	54	45
1881											14,871	879	37	40
1882											14,998	922	46	43
1883											15,116	884	50	
1884											12,765	863	66	46
1885											14,734	901	77	59
1886											13,097	1,071	84	33
1887											13,402	859	77	
1888											15,256	923	140	79
1889											15,020	987	124	121
1890								3.0			15,539	1,161	149	135
1891											16,840	1,015	187	139
1892											16,802	776	190	166
1893											18,667	730	218	195
1894											21,850	1,104	279	242
1895											24,106	1,223	272	245
1896											24,593	1,334	271	244
1897											25,231	1,478	319	298
1898											25,052	1,413	324	236
1899											25,980	1,440	345	224
												1,542		
1900								4.0			27,410	1,583	382	239
1901											28,681	1,744	365	255
1902											28,966	1,858	293	224
1903											29,907	1,718	337	270
1904											30,501	1,679	334	289
1905											31,519	1,925	369	325
1906											32,019	1,787	383	326
1907											32,234	1,619	349	327
1908											33,800	1,971	391	379
1909								4.9			37,892	2,188	451	391
1910								4.8			37,199	2,113	443	362
1911								4.8			37,481	2,456	497	445
1912								4.9			39,408	3,035	500	484
1913								5.1			42,396	3,025	538	471
1914								5.4			44,268	3,270	559	502

Year	Col1	Col2	Col3	Col4	Col5	Col6	Col7	Col8	Col9	Col10	Col11	Col12	Col13
1915													556
1916													611
1917												611	664
1918												667	558
1919													371
1920							5.8			43,912	3,577	556	560
1921										45,250	3,906		660
1922							5.9					615	780
1923							8.4			38,585	2,900		1,062
1924												836	1,124
1925							9.2			48,622	4,279		1,203
1926												1,098	1,438
1927							10.7			61,668	5,984		1,538
1928							11.4			82,783	8,216	1,409	1,617
1929							12.3			97,263	9,735		1,907
1930							12.4			111,161	12,387	1,447	2,058
1931							12.7			122,484	14,969	2,299	2,329
1932							11.5			138,063	19,367	2,654	2,397
1933							13.1			136,156	18,293	2,830	2,452
1934							14.5			143,125	18,302	2,770	2,692
1935							15.7	17.1	11.4	164,943	21,628	2,932	2,582
1936													2,749
1937							14.4	15.6	10.2	186,500	26,731	3,290	2,749
1938							11.9	5.6	9.6	185,346	24,648	3,497	2,731
1939	46e	36e	20.0	23.3	15.6	18.7				125,863	13,414	2,305	2,847
1940							22.4	7.6	12.0	136,174	19,209	1,966	3,245
1941							25.5	30.3	14.0				3,566
1942							26.4	35.9	14.6				3,386
1943							25.5	37.5	15.1				2,564
1944	78ec	41ec	15.6	20.7	30.4	44.2	25.5	38.4	16.1	271,186	42,432	3,989	1,934
1945	70c	38c	17.4	20.0	26.0	35.2				366,698	50,763	5,050	1,629
1946	65	39	17.6	19.6	25.2	32.7							1,988
1947	72	42	20.2	20.9	24.8	31.4							2,949
1948													3,893
1949													5,396
1950	65	41	20.4	20.9	23.9	29.3	25.5	34.7	18.4	433,734	58,219	6,420	6,517
1951	54	41	19.4	21.4	22.6	26.7	24.1	31.3	18.5	384,352	65,132	7,338	7,332
1952	64	46	19.5	21.3	26.1	31.2	25.1	32.0	20.9	331,924	63,587	7,683	7,710
1953	74	51f	21.6	22.7	26.4	31.7	26.5	33.3	21.2	304,587	61,023	8,309	8,369
1954	77f	53f	20.5	21.8	29.6	36.0	29.2	36.5	23.1	292,680	56,823	8,996	8,716
1955	86f	54f	22.0	21.0	31.5	39.0	31.4	40.1	24.0	287,401	58,204	8,840	8,899
1956	102	61	22.8	22.2	32.2	39.4	33.8	43.1	24.9	311,298	59,294	8,903	8,473
1957	104	64	23.4	22.4	32.1	33.8	34.7	43.9	25.3	340,347	61,955	8,756	8,600
1958	108	67	23.0	21.6	33.8	40.3	36.2	45.6	27.3	365,748	65,614	8,942	8,770
1959	112	71	22.8	21.1	34.0	40.0	36.6	45.7	28.0	385,151a	69,584a	9,360a	9,212
1960	129	86	24.6	22.2	35.7	41.2	37.5	47.2	28.2	394,889	74,497	9,829	9,734
1961	147	99	24.7	23.4	34.9	40.1	37.7	46.9	23.9	401,783	78,269	10,575	10,411
1962	157	105	26.1	24.0	37.4	42.9	38.8	47.9	30.1	420,485	84,889	11,622	11,507
1963	164	109	26.9	24.5	37.8	43.1	36.7	49.5	31.5	450,592	91,418	12,822	12,720
1964	194	129	27.4	24.5	44.5	50.4	43.7	53.4	34.5	502,104	101,122	14,490	14,324
1965	242	160	29.0	26.0	41.4	43.9	45.6	55.4e	36.3	538,930	112,195	16,467	16,302
1966					42.7	47.7	46.5e	56.4e	36.7e	555,613	140,772	18,239	17,865
1967					45.1	49.9	47.5e	56.7e	37.8e				20,295
1968	334	222	35.9	31.1	46.8	52.1	48.6	56.8	40.1	594,862	157,892	20,621	22,834

Year	Bachelor's degrees per 1000 23 yr. olds SYEOD D-20	Bachelor's per 100 H.S. graduates 4 years earlier SYEOD D-21	Master's degrees per 100 bachelor's degrees 2 years earlier SYEOD D-22	Doctor's degrees per 1000 bachelor's degrees x-years earlier SYEOD D-23	4 yr. bachelor's degrees per 100 1st time enrollment 4 yrs. earlier Total SYEOD D-24	Male SYEOD D-25	Female SYEOD D-26	API grand total SYEOD (000) D-27	API total arts, humanities, social science SYEOD (000) D-28	API total basic & applied sciences SYEOD (000) D-29	API all other fields SYEOD (000) D-30	H.E. enrollment per API D-31	H.E. faculty per 100 API D-32
1850													
1860													
1870													
1871													
1872			8										
1873			7										
1874			11										
1875			6										
1876			7										
1877			6										
1878			7	3.4									
1879			9	2.9									
1880			8	5.7									
1881			8	3.7									
1882			7	3.7									
1883			6	4.2									
1884		53	6	3.8									
1885		59	7	5.8									
1886		48	7	2.9									
1887		48	6	6.4									
1888		49	8	6.1									
1889		47	9	8.1									
1890		47	7	9.0									
1891		53	5	9.2									
1892		51	5	13.0									
1893		49	7	13.2									
1894		50	7	18.5									
1895		56	7	18.3									
1896		46	7	16.0									
1897		43	6	19.8									
1898		37	6	15.2									
1899		36	6	13.3									
1900	19	36	6	14.2									
1901	19	36	7	13.7									
1902	19	34	7	10.2									
1903	19	33	6	11.2									
1904	19	32	6	11.8									
1905	19	32	6	12.9									
1906	19	32	6	13.0									
1907	19	31	5	12.6									
1908	19	30	6	13.8									
1909	21	32	7	13.6									
1910	20	30	6	12.5									
1911	20	30	6	14.9									
1912	21	30	8	15.9									
1913	23	30	8	14.9									
1914	24	28	8	15.7									

1915	23	26	8	17.2									
1916	24	25	9	18.1									
1917				17.5									
1918	22	18	7	15.0									
1919				9.9									
1920	26	19	9	14.2									
1921				15.6									
1922	33	22	16	17.6									
1922				24.2									
1924	43	27	17	24.8									
1925													
1926	49	27	16	37.3									
1927													
1928	55	22	15	33.2									
1929													
1930	57	22	15	33.4									
1931													
1932	63	23	17	29.0									
1933													
1934	61	20	15	27.7									
1935													
1936	63	17	13	24.7									
1937													
1938	72	18	16	22.3									
1939													
1940	81	18	19	23.5									
1941													
1942	78	16	15	24.9									
1843													
1944	52	10	7	13.8									
1945													
1946	56	11	10	14.2									
1947													
1948	113	27	37	25.3									
1949	154		37					495	120	155	220	4.8	
1950	182	40	22	34.9	55.9	57.6	51.4	581	146	186	249	4.2	43
1951	161		18		58.4	61.0	53.0	546	136	166	244	4.2	
1952	143	28	15	41.6	52.8	53.5	51.3	492	122	142	228	4.3	50
1953	132		16		49.6	49.1	50.5	461	113	130	218	4.6	
1954	129	24	17	69.2	51.5	51.2	52.0	444	109	127	207	5.0	60
1955	151		19		55.4	57.2	52.7	445	111	126	202	5.5	
1956	147	26	20	62.2	52.7	53.8	51.0	465	124	132	210	5.7	65
1957	163		22		54.0	56.4	50.5	499	132	143	224	5.8	
1958	167	29	21	32.3	64.4	54.9	48.8	531	142	156	234	5.7	66
1959	178		20	25.1	51.7	53.2	49.4	561	149	167	245	5.8	
1960	182	28	20	22.4	49.6	50.0	48.9	580	158	173	250	5.8	66
1961	178		20	27.1	50.1	50.2	49.9	596	165	176	254	6.0	
1962	184	28	22	34.7	49.0	48.7	49.4	624	181	184	260	6.2	68
1963	195		23	41.8	49.6	48.7	50.9	675	204	193	277	6.2	
1964	206	27	24	48.9	50.5	50.1	51.0	749	236	209	304	6.0	66
1965	203		25	56.7	48.4	47.0	49.6	813	259	227	326	6.1	
1966	186	29	28	57.4	49.4	48.6	50.6	874	289	234	351	6.9	
1967	211	30	29	55.5	52.3	51.6	53.2	950	324	248	378	7.9	68

	Current expenditures per API in hundreds of 1958 dollars SYEOD	Student aid expenditures per API, 1958 dollars SYEOD	Total API SYEOD	API per 100 graduates					Current fund expenditures, billions 1958 dollars	Lapse time, years, bachelor's-to-doctor's				
				Engineering, math., physical science SYEOD	Biological science SYEOD	Health professions SYEOD	Social science (excl. social work) SYEOD	Education SYEOD		Physical science	Biological science	Social science	Arts & professions
	D-33	D-34	D-35	D-36	D-37	D-38	D-39	D-40	D-41	D-42	D-43	D-44	D-45
1920										6.6	7.4	7.8	8.6
1921										6.9	8.1	8.2	8.3
1922										6.4	7.3	8.7	8.7
1923										6.7	7.9	8.0	9.0
1924										7.0	8.2	9.2	9.5
1925										6.8	7.9	8.9	9.5
1926										6.9	8.4	8.7	9.6
1927										7.1	8.3	8.9	9.6
1928										6.7	7.9	8.5	10.1
1929										6.8	8.5	9.1	10.0
1930									1.02	6.8	7.7	9.0	9.9
1931										7.1	8.2	9.6	9.9
1932									1.26	7.0	8.0	9.4	10.0
1933										6.8	7.5	9.0	9.8
1934									1.15	6.5	7.6	9.0	9.5
1935										6.7	7.7	9.5	9.7
1936									1.27	6.8	7.9	9.4	10.3
1937										6.9	8.2	9.9	10.3
1938									1.39	7.1	8.0	10.2	10.6
1939										6.7	7.9	9.9	10.9
1940									1.55	6.7	8.1	10.3	10.9
1941										6.3	7.6	9.5	10.7
1942									1.47	6.0	7.4	9.7	10.2
1943										6.3	7.5	10.4	11.0
1944									1.69	6.1	8.3	10.8	10.9
1945										7.2	9.3	11.5	12.3
1946									1.90	7.5	9.6	11.5	12.8
1947										7.8	9.8	11.5	12.5
1948									2.44	8.1	9.5	11.5	12.8
1949			117.2	114.4	111.5	154.8	110.4	119.1		7.8	9.2	10.7	12.0
1950	48.53		116.7	113.5	112.0	153.6	110.2	119.5	2.82	7.6	9.1	10.5	12.1
1951			119.5	117.1	115.8	152.4	113.1	121.3		7.4	8.5	10.0	11.8
1952	58.02	93	121.9	120.1	118.0	151.7	114.5	123.2	2.86	7.3	8.0	9.6	12.3
1953			121.3	122.1	120.2	152.2	115.4	124.3		7.1	8.0	9.6	11.5
1954	72.98	189	123.6	123.8	121.5	149.5	116.3	126.4	3.24	7.0	7.7	9.4	11.8
1955			125.5	124.2	121.4	149.7	116.4	127.4		7.2	8.0	9.5	12.0
1956	81.40	224	122.6	122.2	121.8	147.8	115.0	126.1	3.78	7.5	8.2	10.1	12.5
1957			121.3	120.2	121.1	146.2	113.9	125.0		7.3	8.1	10.5	12.1
1958	86.00	250	120.7	119.4	120.4	145.8	113.5	124.2	4.57	7.4	8.5	10.4	12.5
1959			120.8	119.6	119.4	145.1	113.8	123.3		7.6	8.7	10.4	12.1
1960	94.26	293	121.0	119.7	120.7	144.8	114.0	123.7	5.47	7.8	8.8	10.4	12.0
1961			121.4	121.9	120.8	144.4	114.4	123.4		7.8	8.9	10.4	11.9
1962	108.98	352	120.8	123.4	122.1	144.9	114.2	119.9	6.80				
1963			121.7	125.2	121.2	144.8	114.0	123.6					
1964	113.98	375	121.2	125.7	120.7	143.0	113.4	123.6	8.54				
1965			121.7	127.7	121.5	142.4	113.4	124.1					
1966	128.00	437	122.4	127.6	121.9	142.8	113.2	125.4	11.19				
1967			122.8	128.8	122.3	142.2	113.7	127.1					

	Lapse time, years, bachelor's-to-doctor's		Average (current dollars) starting salary per month offered by businesses to male bachelor's graduates in fields of:			Median age college teachers				Faculty		Institutions	
						Male		Female					
	Education	Total all fields	Engineering SYEOD	Accounting SYEOD	Sales SYEOD	Total	Non-white	Total	Non-white	Total (000) SYEOD	Percent male SYEOD	Univer-sities SYB	Liberal arts col-leges, SYB
	D-46	D-47	D-48	D-49	D-50	E-1	E-2	E-3	E-4	E-5	E-6	F-1	F-2
1850													
1860													
1870													
1871													
1872													
1873													
1874													
1875													
1876													
1877													
1878													
1879													
1880										11.5	63.6		
1881													
1882													
1883													
1884													
1885													
1886													
1887													
1888													
1889													
1890										15.8[b]	80.4		
1891													
1892													
1893													
1894													
1895													
1896													
1897													
1898													
1899													
1900										23.9[b]	80.2		
1901													
1902													
1903													
1904													
1905													
1906													
1907													
1908													
1909													
1910										36.5[b]	79.9		
1911													
1912													
1913													
1914													

Year	(1)	(2)	(3)	(4)	(5)	(6)	(7)	(8)	(9)	(10)	(11)	(12)	(13)
1915													
1916													
1917													
1918													
1919													
1920	10.2	7.7											
1921	9.8	7.9											
1922	11.1	7.8											
1923	9.5	7.8											
1924	9.9	8.4											
1925	11.7	8.5											
1926	11.8	8.6											
1927	11.3	8.7											
1928	11.7	8.4											
1929	11.9	8.8											
1930	12.8	8.7											
1931	12.3	9.0											
1932	13.6	9.1											
1933	13.2	8.6											
1934	13.5	8.5											
1935	13.8	8.7				38.7	34.5	35.9	29.0	48.6	73.7		
1936	14.1	9.2											
1937	14.6	9.2											
1938	14.9	9.5											
1939	14.4	9.3											
1940	14.4	9.4				39.8	36.7	41.1	30.5	82.7	72.8		
1941	14.2	8.9								100.8	71.1		
1942	14.0	8.8								99.9	71.6		
1943	15.4	9.4								110.2	71.0		
1944	15.3	9.4								123.7	71.1		
1945	16.6	10.9								147.8	72.4		
1946	15.9	11.0	244	231	225					134.1	71.8		
1947	16.3	10.9	250	235	226					151.0	70.4		
1948	15.3	10.8	261	240	240					136.0	69.0		
1949	15.3	10.2	260	238	240					223.7	73.6		
1950	15.0	10.2	270	246	247	38.6	37.7	40.5	33.9	248.7	75.4		
1951	14.5	9.8	305	275	275					246.3	76.5		
1952	14.7	9.8	325	297	301					268.0	76.9	131	
1953	14.9	9.7	355	325	328					301.6	77.0	131	
1954	15.4	9.7	371	339	339					348.5	77.5	131	
1955	15.2	9.9	415	372	370					382.7[a]	77.9[a]	131	693
1956	15.4	10.3	454	402	398					427.8	78.0	141	705
1957	15.7	10.2	472	417	412					498.4	77.8	141	705
1958	15.3	10.3	489	433	422					641.0	[c]	141	713
1959	15.3	10.3	510	446	440							141	723
1960	15.6	10.4	529	462	453	39.1	38.3	43.3	39.8			141	718
1961	14.8	10.3	554	488	468							141	732
1962		10.2	595	524	490							141	738
1963		10.2	613	537	506							141	756
1964		10.0	632	561	523							142	764
1965		10.0	676	594	562							143	759
1966		10.0	731	648	587							142	778
1967			764	681	626							146	788
1968												155	797

	Independently organized professional schools						Junior colleges		Total		Medical schools SYEOD	Dental schools SYEOD	Higher education institutions	
	Teachers colleges SYB	Techno- logical schools SYB	Theo- logical, relig- ious,SYB	Schools of art SYB	Other profes- sional SYB	Junior col- leges SYB	Public SYB	Private SYB	4-Yr.	Total			Income (000) SYEOD	Expendi- ture (000) SYEOD
	F-3	F-4	F-5	F-6	F-7	F-8	F-9	F-10	F-11	F-12	F-13	F-14	F-15	F-16
1850											52			
1860											65	3		
1870										563	75	10		
1871														
1872														
1873														
1874														
1875														
1876														
1877														
1878														
1879														
1880										811	100	14		
1881														
1882														
1883														
1884														
1885														
1886												23		
1887														
1888														
1889														
1890										998	133	31		
1891														
1892														
1893												37		
1894														
1895														
1896												48		
1897														
1898												54		
1899														
1900										977	160	57		
1901											160	57		
1902											160	56		
1903											160	55		
1904											160	56		
1905											158	55		
1906											162	55		
1907											159	55		
1908											151	55		
1909										951	140	56		
1910											131	54		
1911											122	54		
1912											118	52		
1913											107	51		
1914											102	48		

Year														
1915														
1916														
1917														
1918														
1919														
1920						46	14				96	49		
1921						52	10	32	934		95	49		
1922						80	17	42	989	980	96	46		
1923								63	1,082	1,041	96	46		
1924						132	39	93	1,163	1,162	90	46		
1925						153	47	106	1,224	1,295	85	46		
1926										1,377	85	46		
1927						248	114	134	1,162	1,410	83	45		
1928											81	45		
1929											80	45		
1930						277	129	148	1,132	1,409	79	43		
1931						324	159	183	1,136	1,460	80	43		
1932											79	44		
1933						322	152	170	1,096	1,418d	80	40		
1934						415	187	228	1,213	1,628d	80	40		
1935						453	209	244	1,237	1,690d	76	40	554,511	507,142
1936													566,264	536,523
1937													486,362	469,329
1938													597,585	541,391
1939													652,631	614,385
1940						456	217	239	1,252	1,708c	76	38	715,211	674,688
1941						461	231	230	1,308	1,769	76	38	783,720	738,168
1942						413	210	203	1,237	1,650	77	38	1,047,298	974,118
1943						464	242	222	1,304	1,768	77	39	1,169,394	1,088,422
1944						472	242	230	1,316	1,788	77	39	2,027,051	1,883,269
1945											77	39		
1946											77	39		
1947											77	39		
1948											77	40		
1949											78	41		
1950	205	51	121		144	506	279	227	1,345	1,859	79	41	2,374,645	2,245,661
1951	206	53	130		155	506	291	215	1,380	1,907	79	42	2,562,451	2,471,008
1952	206	53	130		155				1,350	1,871	79	42		
1953	200	53	115		138	518	293	225	1,344	1,857	79	42	2,945,550	2,882,864
1954	193	48	114		125				1,353	1,858	80b	43		
1955	192	44	124		120	469	276	193	1,368	1,852	81	43	3,603,370	3,499,463
1956	198	45	141	48	125				1,397	1,890	82	43b		
1957	199	45	148	46	132	490	283	207	1,404	1,903	85	45	4,641,387	4,509,666
1958	197	46	155		79					1,952	85	47		
1959	198	51	173		75				1,440	1,952	85	47		
1960	198	50	176	45	75	509	310	199	1,451	1,975	91a	47a	5,785,537a	5,601,376a
1961	194	51	180	45	75	524	329	195	1,447	1,973	92	47	7,429,379	7,154,526
1962	198	56	186	46	73	573	357	216	1,479	2,043	84	47		
1963	186	57	201	46	79	657	408	249	1,503	2,080	83	47	9,591,330	9,224,988
1964	187	54	206	46	81	682	422	260	1,526	2,183	82	47		
1965						755	479	276	1,556	2,238	82	47		
1966						789	521	268	1,582	2,337	85	49	12,796,207	12,569,943
1967						866	595	271	1,593	2,382				
1968									1,625	2,491				

	Educational and general income, percent of total income of higher education institutions									Educational & general expenditures in constant 1958 dollars		
	Student fees SYEOD	Endowment earnings SYEOD	Government			Private gifts & grants SYEOD	Organized activities related to instructional departments	Other sources SYEOD	Auxiliary enterprises and Student aid income SYEOD	Total educational and general expenditures		Administrative and general expenditure per institution (000) SYEOD
			Federal SYEOD	State SYEOD	Local SYEOD					Per student SYEOD	Per teacher SYEOD	
	F-17	F-18	F-19	F-20	F-21	F-22	F-23	F-24	F-25	F-26	F-27	F-28
1920												
1921												
1922												
1923												
1924												
1925												
1926												
1927												
1928												
1929												
1930	26.0	12.4	3.7	27.2^d	e	4.7	g	13.1	12.9	687	9,183	61.1
1931	26.6	10.8	e	30.8f	e	5.3	3.7	2.6	20.2	847	9,697	76.2
1932	28.4	11.4	4.1	24.2^d	e	5.6	3.6	2.5	20.1	842	8,162	74.6
1933	26.4	10.0	7.2	20.0	3.5	6.2	4.2	4.5	17.8^h	809	8,086	69.2
1934	27.4	10.8	4.5	21.6	3.4	5.6	4.3	2.3	20.0^h	792	7,869	75.6
1935												
1936												
1937												
1938												
1939												
1940	28.1	10.0	5.4	21.1	3.4	5.6	4.6	1.6	20.1^h	801	8,155	84.5
1941	25.7	9.4	7.4	21.2	3.4	5.8	5.1	1.6	20.1^h	814	7,565	77.6
1942	14.8	7.2	29.4	16.7	2.5	4.8	5.1	1.9	17.5^h	991	7,573	73.5
1943	18.3	7.7	16.9	19.2	2.6	6.6	5.7	1.9	20.9^h	774	7,850	93.8
1944	15.0	4.3	26.0	17.4	2.3	4.5	4.6	1.8	24.1	690	8,070	124.6
1945												
1946												
1947												
1948												
1949												
1950	16.6	4.0	22.1	20.7	2.6	5.0	4.7	1.4	22.8	806	8,680	144.4
1951	17.4	4.4	17.6	23.8	2.8	5.8	5.3	1.6	21.1	963	9,076	147.4
1952	18.7	4.3	14.2	25.1	3.0	6.5	5.6	2.0	20.6	1,160	9,601	173.9
1953	20.0	4.0	13.6	24.4	3.0	6.8	5.3	2.2	20.6	1,135	10,014	207.7
1954	20.1	3.9	15.2	24.5	2.8	7.0	5.3	1.5	19.6	1,259	10,597	248.8
1955												
1956												
1957												
1958												
1959												
1960	20.0^a	3.6^a	17.9^a	23.8^a	2.6^a	6.6^a	5.0^a	1.5^a	19.0^a	1,369^a	11,576^a	291.6^a
1961	20.2	3.1	20.7	22.7	2.6	6.0	4.8	1.4	18.7	1,472	12,906	351.9
1962	19.8^i	2.8	22.6	22.2^j	2.5	5.8	4.5^b	1.4	18.4^k	1,590	14,237	429.1
1963												
1964												
1965												
1966	21.0^c	2.2	20.3	22.8	2.4	4.8	4.9	2.3	19.2	1,656	15,150	501.1

Educational and general expenditures in constant 1958 dollars

	Resident instruction and departmental research		Organized research per teacher SYEOD	Libraries per institution (000) SYEOD	Plant operation & maintenance per institution (000) SYEOD	Organized activities related to instructional departments per institution SYEOD (000)	Extension and public service per institution (000) SYEOD	Auxiliary enterprises and student aid expenditures per institution (000) SYEOD	New public construction expenditure estimates, non-residential educational (millions of dollars)
	Per student SYEOD	Per teacher SYEOD							
	F-29	F-30	F-31	F-32	F-33	F-34	F-35	F-36	F-37
1920									190
1921									274
1922									342
1923									346
1924									353
1925									400
1926									399
1927									367
1928									378
1929									389
1930	402	5,377	44	13.6	86.7	i	35.4	183.6	364
1931									285
1932	475	5,431	52	18.4	91.5	34.4	38.8	195.3[b]	130
1933									52
1934	473	4,582	39	23.1	88.3	24.5	34.6	185.5[c]	148
1935									153
1936	436	4,362	42	22.3	81.8	29.1	42.4	178.7[d]	366
1937									253
1938	423	4,207	41	23.5	83.9	32.1	45.7	189.1[e]	311
1939									468
1940	432	4,378	44	26.2	93.7	36.5	47.5	205.3	156
1941									158
1942	425	3,944	46	23.0	84.2	43.9	49.3	192.2	128
1943									63
1944	503	3,853	68	21.6	85.6	51.0	46.8	334.8[f]	41
1945									59
1946	354	3,590	84	23.7	99.3	54.3	49.7	239.8	101
1947									287
1948	327	3,816	92	32.0	146.6	61.9	51.6	356.7	618
1949									934
1950	369	3,972	114	38.0	152.6	80.7	58.7	365.6	1,133
1951									1,513
1952	413	3,889	150	38.2	151.5	93.2	61.4	346.6	1,619
1953									1,714
1954	491	4,060	157	44.1	167.7	112.7	67.7	369.0	2,134
1955									2,442
1956	467	4,129	182	50.0	189.6	129.8	80.6	428.8	2,556
1957									2,825
1958	512	4,309	214	57.5	213.2	129.0	92.0	475.1	2,875
1959									2,656[a]
1960	545[a]	4,599[a]	263[a]	67.7[a]	234.9[a]	151.7[a]	102.8[a]	544.2[a]	2,818
1961									3,052
1962	562	4,928	330	85.4	271.9	180.7	117.7	667.9	2,984
1963									3,477
1964	601	5,378	378	105.9	306.7	210.6[g]	132.7	782.5	3,790
1965									4,261
1966	626	5,743	372	138.2	337.2	346.9[h]	176.1	922.8	

Year	Median school years completed, population 25 yrs. old and over	Years of school completed by persons 25 yrs. old and over						Years of school completed by persons 25-29 years old				
		Percent of total completing		Percent of nonwhite completing				Percent of total completing		Percent of nonwhite completing		
		None or <5 years elem.	4 yrs. high school or more	4 yrs. college or more	None or <5 years elem.	4 yrs. high school or more	4 yrs. college or more	None or <5 years elem.	4 yrs. high school or more	4 yrs. college or more	None or <5 years elem.	4 yrs. high school or more	4 yrs. college or more
	G-1	G-2	G-3	G-4	G-5	G-6	G-7	G-8	G-9	G-10	G-11	G-12	G-13
1850													
1860													
1870													
1871													
1872													
1873													
1874													
1875													
1876													
1877													
1878													
1879													
1880													
1881													
1882													
1883													
1884													
1885													
1886													
1887													
1888													
1889													
1890													
1891													
1892													
1893													
1894													
1895													
1896													
1897													
1898													
1899													
1900													
1901													
1902													
1903													
1904													
1905													
1906													
1907													
1908													
1909													
1910	8.1[c]	23.8[c]	13.5[c]	2.7[c]									
1911													
1912													
1913													
1914													

Year												
1915												
1916												
1917												
1918												
1919												
1920	8.2c	22.0c	16.4c	3.3c								
1921												
1922												
1923												
1924												
1925												
1926												
1927												
1928												
1929												
1930	8.4c	17.5c	19.1c	3.9c								
1931												
1932												
1933												
1934												
1935												
1936												
1937												
1938												
1939												
1940	8.6bd	13.7d	24.4d	4.6d	41.8d	7.7d	1.3d	5.9d	38.1d	5.8d	27.0d	12.2d	1.6d
1941												
1942												
1943												
1944												
1945												
1946	9.0	10.6	33.0	5.4	32.2	13.5	2.5	9.0	51.4	5.5	19.2	22.2	2.7
1947												
1948												
1949												
1950	9.3d	11.1d	34.3d	6.2d	32.7d	13.7d	2.3d	4.6d	43.6d	7.7d	16.0d	23.6d	2.9d
1951	10.1	9.2	38.8	7.0	30.8	14.9	2.4	10.2	57.0	10.1	15.4	28.1	4.6
1952												
1953												
1954												
1955												
1956	10.6	9.1	41.5	7.6	27.7	18.4	2.9	2.7	60.2	10.4	8.7	31.6	4.1
1957	11.0	8.2	43.7	8.1	24.2	20.7	3.4	3.0	63.9	11.0	7.8	39.3	4.6
1958												
1959												
1960	10.5d	8.3d	41.1d	7.7d	23.5d	21.7d	3.5d	2.8d	60.7d	11.1d	7.2d	38.6d	5.4d
1961	11.4a	7.8a	46.3a	8.9a	22.1a	24.8a	4.0a	2.4a	65.9a	13.1a	6.1a	41.6a	4.2a
1962												
1963												
1964	11.7	7.1	48.0	9.1	18.6	27.5	4.7	2.1	69.2	12.8	5.3	48.0	7.0
1965	11.8	6.8	49.0	9.4	18.4	28.6	5.5	2.0	70.3	12.4	4.8	52.2	8.3
1966	12.0	6.5	49.9	9.8	18.0	29.5	4.7	1.6	71.0	14.0	3.3	50.4	8.3
1967	12.0	6.1	51.1	10.1	17.4	31.6	5.0	1.1	72.5	14.6	1.6	55.7	8.3
1968	12.1												

	Years of school completed by white males, 20-24 years of age, total United States							Years of school completed by white males, 25-34 years of age, total United States						
	Percent completing							Percent completing						
	None or <5 years	5-7 yrs.	8 yrs.	1-3 yrs. h.s.	4 yrs. h.s.	1-3 yrs. college	4 yrs. college or more	5 yrs. college or more	None or <5 years	5-7 yrs.	8 yrs.	1-3 yrs. h.s.	4 yrs. h.s.	1-3 yrs. college	4 yrs. college or more	5 yrs. college or more
	G-14	G-15	G-16	G-17	G-18	G-19	G-20	G-21	G-22	G-23	G-24	G-25	G-26	G-27	G-28	G-29
1920																
1921																
1922																
1923																
1924																
1925																
1926																
1927																
1928																
1929																
1930																
1931																
1932																
1933																
1934																
1935																
1936																
1937																
1938																
1939																
1940	3.5[b]	10.4[b]	16.7[b]	24.1[b]	30.9[b]	10.4[b]	3.8[b]	c	4.5[b]	13.4[b]	23.8[b]	22.4[b]	21.2[b]	7.1[b]	7.8[b]	c
1941																
1942																
1943																
1944																
1945																
1946																
1947	2.4	7.4	11.0	27.8	38.6	10.6	2.0	c	2.9	8.8	14.7	23.6	32.9	9.9	7.3	c
1948																
1949																
1950	3.5[b]	8.4[b]	11.2[b]	23.6[b]	31.1[b]	17.5[b]	4.8[b]	c	3.8[b]	9.0[b]	13.5[b]	22.0[b]	30.9[b]	10.7[b]	10.0[b]	c
1951																
1952																
1953																
1954																
1955																
1956																
1957	2.5	5.4	6.9	18.6	38.6	22.7	5.3	c	1.6	6.6	10.0	22.1	33.6	11.2	14.7	c
1958	2.0	4.6	7.5	17.4	38.9	22.1	7.5	1.8	2.9	6.3	8.6	19.7	34.4	11.9	16.1	6.1
1959																
1960	2.3[d]	5.5[d]	7.3[d]	20.8[d]	35.1[d]	22.2[d]	6.6[d]	2.0[d]	2.8[b]	7.1[b]	9.7[b]	21.1[b]	31.3[b]	12.3[b]	15.7[b]	6.8[b]
1961																
1962	1.4[a]	3.4[a]	5.4[a]	17.8[a]	38.7[a]	25.3[a]	8.1[a]	2.3[a]	2.4[a]	5.2[a]	8.0[a]	17.4[a]	35.9[a]	12.6[a]	18.5[a]	7.4[a]
1963																
1964	2.0	2.5	4.3	15.3	40.7	27.3	7.4	2.2	2.2	4.6	7.1	16.8	38.7	12.8	17.9	7.8
1965	1.4	2.8	4.0	15.9	39.9	27.4	8.2	1.6	2.5	4.5	6.2	15.7	40.4	12.7	17.9	7.2
1966	1.4	2.3	4.0	14.2	36.4	29.6	10.1	3.1	1.9	4.2	5.5	16.0	40.1	13.5	19.0	7.6
1967	0.8	3.0	3.8	13.7	37.7	31.3	9.7	2.5	1.2	4.1	6.2	15.6	38.8	14.6	19.4	8.0

402

	Years of school completed by white males, 35-44 years of age, total United States							Years of school completed by white females, 20-24 years of age, total United States						
	Percent completing							Percent completing						
	None or <5 years	5-7 yrs.	8 yrs.	1-3 yrs. h.s.	4 yrs. h.s.	1-3 yrs. college	4 yrs. college or more	5 yrs. college or more	None or <5 years	5-7 yrs.	8 yrs.	1-3 yrs. h.s.	4 yrs. h.s.	1-3 yrs. college	4 yrs. college or more	5 yrs. college or more
	G-30	G-31	G-32	G-33	G-34	G-35	G-36	G-37	G-38	G-39	G-40	G-41	G-42	G-43	G-44	G-45
1920																
1921																
1922																
1923																
1924																
1925																
1926																
1927																
1928																
1929																
1930																
1931																
1932																
1933																
1934																
1935																
1936																
1937																
1938																
1939																
1940	8.3b	17.6b	31.5b	17.4b	12.9b	5.8b	6.5b	c	2.4b	8.3b	15.1b	23.6b	37.9b	9.3b	3.4b	c
1941																
1942																
1943																
1944																
1945																
1946																
1947	4.9	14.2	24.4	19.4	20.2	8.1	8.8	c	1.6	5.8	8.6	22.0	48.5	10.4	3.2	c
1948																
1949																
1950	5.4b	13.9b	20.8b	21.0b	21.6b	8.1b	9.1b	c	2.5b	5.8b	8.6b	22.4b	42.9b	12.9b	4.8b	c
1951																
1952																
1953																
1954																
1955																
1956																
1957	3.7	8.4	15.4	20.8	32.5	8.5	10.6	c	1.8	4.4	6.4	20.4	48.3	13.6	5.0	c
1958	3.6	7.3	12.5	20.8	33.4	10.1	12.3	5.7	1.6	3.6	5.0	19.5	49.4	15.7	5.3	0.7
1959																
1960	3.6b	9.0b	13.1b	21.4b	30.3b	10.3b	12.4b	5.9b	1.3b	3.4b	5.2b	22.2b	46.0b	16.8b	5.0b	0.6b
1961																
1962	3.3a	7.3a	11.3a	20.0a	32.4a	10.7a	15.1a	6.5a	1.1a	2.7a	5.3a	19.5a	48.1a	17.6a	5.8a	0.6
1963																
1964	3.1	6.9	10.6	19.5	33.0	11.0	15.9	7.3	0.7	2.4	4.2	18.1	50.3	17.4	6.9	0.6
1965	2.9	6.6	10.6	19.1	33.9	10.6	16.4	7.2	0.9	1.4	4.0	16.8	51.1	19.1	6.8	0.6
1966	2.9	6.2	10.4	18.6	34.5	9.6	17.8	7.7	0.7	1.8	3.3	16.4	50.5	19.5	7.9	0.9
1967	2.9	6.2	9.2	18.5	34.7	11.0	17.7	7.3	0.7	2.0	3.2	15.4	48.1	23.0	7.7	0.8

	Years of school completed by white females, 25-34 years of age, total United States						Years of school completed by white females, 35-44 years of age, total United States					
	Percent completing						Percent completing					
	None or <5 years	5-7 yrs.	8 yrs.	1-3 yrs. h.s.	4 yrs. h.s.	1-3 yrs. college	4 yrs. college or more	5 yrs. college or more	None or <5 years	5-7 yrs.	8 yrs.	1-3 yrs. h.s.	4 yrs. h.s.	1-3 yrs. college	4 yrs. college or more	5 yrs. college or more
	G-46	G-47	G-48	G-49	G-50	G-51	G-52	G-53	G-54	G-55	G-56	G-57	G-58	G-59	G-60	G-61
1920																
1921																
1922																
1923																
1924																
1925																
1926																
1927																
1928																
1929																
1930																
1931																
1932																
1933																
1934																
1935																
1936																
1937																
1938																
1939																
1940	3.4[b]	11.9[b]	21.3[b]	22.5[b]	26.8[b]	8.6[b]	5.5[b]	c	7.4[b]	16.2[b]	28.6[b]	18.1[b]	17.7[b]	7.4[b]	4.6[b]	c
1941																
1942																
1943																
1944																
1945																
1946																
1947	2.5	8.1	14.1	21.8	39.4	8.4	5.7	c	4.1	12.0	22.6	19.7	25.8	9.2	6.5	c
1948																
1949																
1950	3.0[b]	7.8[b]	11.9[b]	21.9[b]	39.6[b]	9.6[b]	6.3[b]	c	4.3[b]	12.4[b]	18.9[b]	21.3[b]	26.8[b]	9.5[b]	6.7[b]	c
1951																
1952																
1953																
1954																
1955																
1956																
1957	2.0	5.0	8.4	20.2	47.7	9.7	6.9	c	2.8	7.5	13.3	21.2	40.3	7.9	7.0	c
1958	2.1	4.4	7.2	20.1	48.3	10.4	7.6	1.7	2.1	7.2	11.5	19.8	43.3	9.0	7.1	1.7
1959																
1960	2.0[b]	5.3[b]	7.7[b]	22.1[b]	43.6[b]	11.4[b]	7.8[b]	1.8[b]	2.5[b]	7.4[b]	12.0[b]	21.6[b]	39.6[b]	10.3[b]	6.5[b]	1.9[b]
1961	1.9[a]	4.2[a]	6.4[a]	19.1[a]	47.2[a]	11.6[a]	9.4[a]	1.8[a]	2.2[a]	5.4[a]	10.5[a]	19.1[a]	44.0[a]	11.2[a]	7.5[a]	1.8[a]
1962																
1963																
1964	1.6	3.9	5.8	18.3	49.5	11.2	9.7	1.9	2.2	5.5	9.3	20.0	45.0	10.5	7.5	1.8
1965	1.7	3.8	5.7	18.4	49.2	11.6	9.6	1.9	2.0	5.2	8.4	19.4	46.6	10.6	7.9	2.1
1966	1.5	3.4	5.1	18.5	49.4	11.8	10.4	2.3	2.4	5.0	8.1	19.5	46.9	9.9	8.1	2.0
1967	1.3	3.6	5.2	17.8	48.8	12.6	10.7	2.2	2.2	5.0	7.8	19.5	46.3	10.6	8.6	2.2

	Years of school completed by nonwhite males, 20-24 years of age, total United States						Years of school completed by nonwhite males, 25-34 years of age, total United States						
	Percent completing						Percent completing						
	None or <5 years G-62	5-7 yrs. G-63	8 yrs. G-64	1-3 yrs. h.s. G-65	4 yrs. h.s. G-66	1-3 yrs. college G-67	4 yrs. college or more G-68	5 yrs. college or more G-69	None or <5 years G-70	5-7 yrs. G-71	8 yrs. G-72	1-3 yrs. h.s. G-73	4 yrs. h.s. G-74	1-3 yrs. college G-75	4 yrs. college or more G-76	5 yrs. college or more G-77
1920																
1921																
1922																
1923																
1924																
1925																
1926																
1927																
1928																
1929																
1930																
1931																
1932																
1933																
1934																
1935																
1936																
1937																
1938																
1939																
1940	31.2[b]	30.2[b]	9.9[b]	16.0[b]	8.9[b]	3.0[b]	0.7[b]	c	34.7[b]	31.8[b]	12.1[b]	11.7[b]	5.9[b]	2.2[b]	1.6[b]	c
1941																
1942																
1943																
1944																
1945																
1946																
1947	16.8	29.0	12.2	24.5	11.6	4.6	1.2	c	23.8	24.8	11.3	19.5	14.3	3.3	3.0	c
1948																
1949																
1950	17.1[b]	25.2[b]	11.8[b]	24.2[b]	14.2[b]	6.2[b]	1.1[b]	c	21.8[b]	27.0[b]	12.1[b]	19.2[b]	12.6[b]	4.6[b]	2.6[b]	c
1951																
1952																
1953																
1954																
1955																
1956																
1957	12.3	14.1	10.0	32.4	23.4	6.7	1.2	c	13.2	23.2	12.4	24.7	19.4	4.8	2.4	c
1958	6.7	14.9	13.0	32.3	23.5	8.5	1.2	c	11.1	19.2	10.0	24.3	23.8	6.4	5.2	2.2
1959																
1960	7.7[d]	14.3[d]	9.7[d]	31.9[d]	25.3[d]	9.2[d]	1.8[d]	0.6[d]	11.2[b]	17.8[b]	11.4[b]	26.6[b]	20.3[b]	7.2[b]	5.4[b]	2.4[b]
1961																
1962	5.2[a]	9.2[a]	11.4[a]	32.9[a]	29.0[a]	10.9[a]	1.4[a]	0.3[a]	9.0[a]	15.0[a]	10.2[a]	29.0[a]	22.5[a]	8.6[a]	5.6[a]	1.8[a]
1963																
1964	2.8	7.8	6.4	30.4	36.4	13.0	3.4	0.5	7.1	11.0	8.4	30.0	27.0	7.4	10.1	3.5
1965	5.1	7.0	5.7	30.9	36.1	12.3	2.9	0.8	6.9	12.1	6.5	25.9	29.6	8.8	10.2	4.1
1966	2.5	7.9	8.7	28.3	35.9	15.0	1.7	0.3	6.1	9.5	10.1	26.7	31.8	7.8	8.0	3.7
1967	2.7	5.6	7.6	31.0	36.3	14.2	2.5	0.5	4.4	10.5	7.8	24.4	35.3	9.2	8.4	4.3

405

	Years of school completed by nonwhite males, 35-44 years of age, total United States						Years of school completed by nonwhite females, 20-24 years of age, total United States					
	Percent completing						Percent completing					
	None or <5 years	5-7 yrs.	8 yrs.	1-3 yrs. h.s.	4 yrs. h.s.	1-3 yrs. college	4 yrs. college or more	5 yrs. college or more	None or <5 years	5-7 yrs.	8 yrs.	1-3 yrs. h.s.	4 yrs. h.s.	1-3 yrs. college	4 yrs. college or more	5 yrs. college or more
	G-78	G-79	G-80	G-81	G-82	G-83	G-84	G-85	G-86	G-87	G-88	G-89	G-90	G-91	G-92	G-93
1920																
1921																
1922																
1923																
1924																
1925																
1926																
1927																
1928																
1929																
1930																
1931																
1932																
1933																
1934																
1935																
1936																
1937																
1938																
1939																
1940	42.3[b]	30.8[b]	12.9[b]	7.3[b]	3.5[b]	1.6[b]	1.4[b]	c	19.6[b]	32.0[b]	11.5[b]	19.8[b]	12.2[b]	3.7[b]	1.1[b]	c
1941																
1942																
1943																
1944																
1945																
1946																
1947	29.4	31.6	14.6	13.0	7.8	1.7	1.8	c	8.4	26.9	12.6	27.6	17.4	5.6	1.5	c
1948																
1949																
1950	32.0[b]	30.0[b]	12.4[b]	12.9[b]	7.5[b]	2.7[b]	2.4[b]	c	10.1[b]	21.6[b]	11.7[b]	27.5[b]	20.1[b]	6.8[b]	2.4[b]	c
1951																
1952																
1953																
1954																
1955																
1956																
1957	24.4	24.9	12.6	18.4	11.1	3.3	5.2	c	4.8	14.0	7.7	31.9	30.7	8.4	2.4	c
1958	22.9	26.4	13.2	19.1	10.1	4.9	3.4	1.6	3.4	6.4	11.7	34.3	32.1	9.8	2.5	c
1959																
1960	18.8[b]	23.0[b]	13.1[b]	20.8[b]	15.2[b]	4.9[b]	4.1[b]	2.1[b]	4.9[b]	12.9[b]	10.6[b]	30.7[b]	24.3[b]	13.0[b]	3.6[b]	0.6[b]
1961																
1962	19.2[a]	19.1[a]	13.5[a]	19.6[a]	18.9[a]	5.0[a]	4.8[a]	1.6[a]	1.7[a]	8.2[a]	10.3[a]	35.5[a]	28.8[a]	10.8[a]	4.7[a]	0.3[a]
1963																
1964	14.0	18.9	12.9	23.9	18.2	5.4	6.5	2.8	2.2	4.1	5.1	32.8	39.0	14.2	2.6	0.3
1965	12.6	17.4	10.2	25.1	20.3	7.1	7.3	3.3	1.7	4.2	5.3	39.7	33.6	11.0	4.8	0.5
1966	13.5	16.3	13.5	24.3	18.5	8.3	5.6	2.4	1.4	4.5	6.8	31.7	38.2	14.8	2.6	0.4
1967	12.1	15.9	13.9	26.1	19.8	6.5	5.6	2.3	1.4	5.1	5.1	29.0	40.3	16.0	3.0	0.7

	Years of school completed by nonwhite females, 25-34 years of age, total United States						Years of school completed by nonwhite females, 35-44 years of age, total United States					
	Percent completing						Percent completing					
	None or <5 years	5-7 yrs.	8 yrs.	1-3 yrs. h.s.	4 yrs. h.s.	1-3 yrs. college	4 yrs. college or more	5 yrs. college or more	None or <5 years	5-7 yrs.	8 yrs.	1-3 yrs. h.s.	4 yrs. h.s.	1-3 yrs. college	4 yrs. college or more	5 yrs. college or more
	G-94	G-95	G-96	G-97	G-98	G-99	G-100	G-101	G-102	G-103	G-104	G-105	G-106	G-107	G-108	G-109
1920																
1921																
1922																
1923																
1924																
1925																
1926																
1927																
1928																
1929																
1930																
1931																
1932																
1933																
1934																
1935																
1936																
1937																
1938																
1939																
1940	23.3[b]	35.1[b]	13.7[b]	15.3[b]	7.8[b]	3.0[b]	1.7[b]	c	33.5[b]	35.0[b]	13.8[b]	9.7[b]	4.7[b]	2.1[b]	1.3[b]	c
1941																
1942																
1943																
1944																
1945																
1946																
1947	16.6	28.1	15.1	18.2	15.3	3.1	3.5	c	19.8	35.3	16.5	13.6	9.2	2.8	2.8	c
1948																
1949																
1950	14.5[b]	27.1[b]	12.9[b]	22.3[b]	15.6[b]	4.4[b]	3.2[b]	c	22.4[b]	32.6[b]	14.2[b]	16.2[b]	8.6[b]	3.3[b]	2.7[b]	c
1951																
1952																
1953																
1954																
1955																
1956	7.9	19.0	14.1	27.0	23.0	4.8	4.2	c	17.4	24.7	13.6	21.4	16.2	3.7	3.0	c
1957																
1958	9.5	14.7	9.7	32.3	24.8	5.7	3.2	0.5	12.3	26.7	13.7	22.2	17.4	3.4	4.3	1.4
1959																
1960	6.1[b]	15.2[b]	11.0[b]	29.8[b]	26.0[b]	6.8[b]	5.1[b]	1.4[b]	12.0[b]	23.1[b]	14.0[b]	23.8[b]	18.3[b]	4.7[b]	4.0[b]	1.5[b]
1961																
1962	4.9[a]	10.6[a]	11.1[a]	32.7[a]	29.8[a]	6.1[a]	4.8[a]	0.7[a]	11.4[a]	18.3[a]	13.1[a]	25.3[a]	21.5[a]	5.1[a]	5.1[a]	1.2[a]
1963																
1964	3.4	9.6	10.8	29.3	34.3	8.1	4.5	1.4	7.1	19.0	10.0	28.6	26.0	4.6	4.6	1.7
1965	3.9	8.1	10.5	31.0	31.9	7.2	7.5	2.0	7.7	16.5	11.4	30.1	24.5	4.9	4.8	1.1
1966	3.0	7.5	7.4	34.1	32.7	7.4	8.1	2.1	4.8	18.2	10.4	28.2	27.7	6.5	4.0	1.8
1967	1.1	8.2	6.2	29.0	38.2	10.0	7.2	1.8	5.8	15.4	11.4	26.8	27.8	6.9	5.6	2.4

Civilian labor force participation rates for students and nonstudents, by sex, color, and age

	14-17 years old								18-24 years old							
	Enrolled				Not Enrolled				Enrolled				Not Enrolled			
	White		Nonwhite		White		Nonwhite		White		Nonwhite		White		Nonwhite	
	M	F	M	F	M	F	M	F	M	F	M	F	M	F	M	F
	G-110	G-111	G-112	G-113	G-114	G-115	G-116	G-117	G-118	G-119	G-120	G-121	G-122	G-123	G-124	G-125
1920																
1921																
1922																
1923																
1924																
1925																
1926																
1927																
1928																
1929																
1930																
1931																
1932																
1933																
1934																
1935																
1936																
1937																
1938																
1939																
1940																
1941																
1942																
1943																
1944																
1945																
1946																
1947																
1948																
1949																
1950																
1951																
1952																
1953																
1954																
1955																
1956																
1957																
1958																
1959	27.0	18.9	25.5	13.0	74.1	44.4	a	31.1	42.0	35.7	51.6	28.3	96.2	49.3	94.0	50.0
1960	25.8[b]	16.8[b]	30.9[b]	16.9[b]	74.6[b]	48.3[b]	a	53.8[b]	38.4[b]	33.2[b]	49.4[b]	26.9[b]	96.3[b]	49.4[b]	95.2[b]	55.3[b]
1961	23.6	16.9	24.3	13.3	72.2	46.2	a	46.0	40.3	34.7	40.3	32.2	94.5	50.9	95.3	55.5
1962	24.6	17.0	18.2	12.7	70.9	37.9	a	40.6	44.3	30.2	36.4	33.1	95.3	53.0	95.8	51.0
1963	25.0	17.2	24.7	11.4	72.7	40.4	a	40.0	43.7	33.0	44.9	31.0	95.4	52.0	95.5	54.6
1964	24.7	17.6	24.8	11.9	70.8	39.5	57.1	48.5	41.9	31.0	47.2	27.6	95.9	53.0	93.4	60.1
1965	28.2	19.4	25.0	12.2	77.6	42.5	81.2	34.7	42.8	34.0	36.5	25.6	95.1	54.0	94.7	59.8
1966	27.7	19.9	19.8	10.9	72.5	42.6	53.7	37.2	42.7	35.6	32.1	36.4	95.8	56.0	93.3	56.5
1967	29.0	21.7	23.2	12.9	69.5	43.3	60.8	27.6	45.5	35.3	41.3	48.6	94.8	57.3	91.7	57.8

408

Labor force status of the civilian noninstitutional population by fall school enrollment, color, sex, in thousands
14-17 years old

	Enrolled								Not Enrolled							
	White				Nonwhite				White				Nonwhite			
	Male		Female		Male		Female		Male		Female		Male		Female	
	in l.f.	Pop.	in l.f.	Pop.	in l.f.	Pop.	in l.f.	Pop.	in l.f.	Pop.	in l.f.	Pop.	in l.f.	Pop.	in l.f.	Pop.
	G-126	G-127	G-128	G-129	G-130	G-131	G-132	G-133	G-134	G-135	G-136	G-137	G-138	G-139	G-140	G-141
1920																
1921																
1922																
1923																
1924																
1925																
1926																
1927																
1928																
1929																
1930																
1931																
1932																
1933																
1934																
1935																
1936																
1937																
1938																
1939																
1940																
1941																
1942																
1943																
1944																
1945																
1946																
1947																
1948																
1949																
1950																
1951																
1952																
1953																
1954																
1955																
1956																
1957																
1958																
1959	1,211	4,479	800	4,241	143	560	72	555	289	390	218	491	77	89	32	103
1960	1,196	4,632	740	4,396	190	615	101	598	311	417	241	499	72	80	56	104
1961	1,190	5,037	814	4,811	162	668	86	647	288	399	211	457	65	86	52	113
1962	1,311	5,339	856	5,408	126	693	84	660	232	327	183	483	72	82	52	128
1963	1,406	5,632	922	5,367	190	770	139	922	242	333	187	463	51	62	40	100
1964	1,443	5,838	975	5,552	203	820	96	804	233	329	185	468	40	70	48	99
1965	1,627	5,770	1,080	5,557	211	843	105	863	291	375	179	421	65	80	26	75
1966	1,633	5,887	1,123	5,650	175	883	95	873	240	331	173	406	36	67	35	94
1967	1,756	6,065	1,252	5,770	211	908	115	893	219	315	185	427	45	74	29	105

Labor force status of the civilian noninstitutional population by fall school enrollment, color, sex, in thousands

18-24 years old

	Enrolled								Not Enrolled							
	White				Nonwhite				White				Nonwhite			
	Male		Female		Male		Female		Male		Female		Male		Female	
	in l.f. G-142	Pop. G-143	in l.f. G-144	Pop. G-145	in l.f. G-146	Pop. G-147	in l.f. G-148	Pop. G-149	in l.f. G-150	Pop. G-151	in l.f. G-152	Pop. G-153	in l.f. G-154	Pop. G-155	in l.f. G-156	Pop. G-157
1920																
1921																
1922																
1923																
1924																
1925																
1926																
1927																
1928																
1929																
1930																
1931																
1932																
1933																
1934																
1935																
1936																
1937																
1938																
1939																
1940																
1941																
1942																
1943																
1944																
1945																
1946																
1947																
1948																
1949																
1950																
1951																
1952																
1953																
1954																
1955																
1956																
1957																
1958																
1959	692	1,649	334	936	83	161	39	138	3,907	4,061	2,920	5,921	658	700	429	858
1960	703	1,832	339	1,022	82	166	39	145	4,023	4,179	2,995	6,067	718	754	497	898
1961	790	1,958	390	1,123	81	201	38	118	4,166	4,408	3,208	6,300	709	744	531	957
1962	974	2,197	401	1,329	70	192	50	151	4,084	4,287	3,367	6,350	683	713	476	934
1963	1,013	2,320	448	1,356	101	225	54	174	4,188	4,392	3,414	6,571	676	708	515	943
1964	995	2,376	460	1,486	91	193	52	188	4,485	4,677	3,586	6,769	732	784	583	970
1965	1,284	2,999	624	1,835	91	249	53	207	4,414	4,642	3,796	7,029	748	790	612	1,023
1966	1,379	3,231	712	2,001	89	277	78	214	4,385	4,576	4,095	7,317	753	807	616	1,090
1967	1,437	3,159	795	2,249	140	339	136	280	4,461	4,705	4,233	7,388	729	795	633	1,095

Year	Percent illiterate among persons 10 yrs. old and over G-158	Median income of males, age 25 yrs. & over who have completed:			Population by sex for selected ages and age groups, in thousands												
		8 yrs. elementary school H-1	4 yrs. h.s. H-2	4 yrs. or more of college H-3	5 yrs.			5-13 yrs.				13 yrs.			14 yrs.		
					Total I-1	Male I-2	Female I-3	Total I-4	Male I-5	Female I-6	Total I-7	Male I-8	Female I-9	Total I-10	Male I-11	Female I-12
1850																	
1860	20.0																
1870																	
1871																	
1872																	
1873																	
1874																	
1875																	
1976																	
1877																	
1878																	
1879																	
1880					1,358	686	671	12,324	6,238	6,086	1,073	542	531	1,070	545	525
1881																	
1882																	
1883																	
1884																	
1885																	
1886																	
1887																	
1888																	
1889																	
1890	13.3				1,549	783	766	13,188	6,682	6,506	1,328	670	658	1,419	723	696
1891																	
1892																	
1893																	
1894																	
1895																	
1896																	
1897																	
1898																	
1899																	
1900	10.7				1,827	921	906	15,402	7,783	7,619	1,585	800	785	1,564	786	778
1901					1,849	932	917	15,572	7,867	7,705	1,605	810	795	1,586	797	789
1902					1,873	944	929	15,750	7,954	7,796	1,625	820	805	1,610	809	801
1903					1,889	952	937	15,893	8,025	7,868	1,644	829	815	1,631	819	812
1904					1,909	962	947	16,044	8,103	7,941	1,664	840	824	1,653	831	822
1905					1,929	972	957	16,210	8,186	8,024	1,686	851	835	1,678	843	835
1906					1,947	982	965	16,365	8,265	8,100	1,708	862	846	1,702	855	847
1907					1,963	990	973	16,513	8,337	8,176	1,730	873	857	1,726	867	859
1908					1,981	999	982	16,687	8,428	8,259	1,753	885	868	1,753	881	872
1909					2,002	1,010	992	16,888	8,530	8,358	1,781	899	882	1,782	896	886
1910	7.7				2,029	1,023	1,006	17,138	8,656	8,482	1,811	914	897	1,812	911	901
1911					2,055	1,036	1,019	17,379	8,778	8,601	1,837	928	909	1,835	923	912
1912					2,080	1,049	1,031	17,645	8,911	8,734	1,865	942	923	1,858	934	924
1913					2,120	1,069	1,051	18,016	9,098	8,918	1,901	960	941	1,888	949	939
1914					2,160	1,089	1,071	18,397	9,290	9,107	1,940	979	961	1,919	964	955

Year													
1915			2,191	1,105	1,086	18,717	9,452	9,265	1,970	994	976	1,943	976	967
1916			2,223	1,121	1,102	19,043	9,615	9,428	2,000	1,009	991	1,965	987	978
1917			2,257	1,138	1,119	19,380	9,786	9,594	2,030	1,025	1,007	1,989	999	990
1918			2,288	1,154	1,134	19,716	9,953	9,763	2,064	1,041	1,023	2,016	1,015	1,001
1919			2,297	1,159	1,138	19,834	10,014	9,820	2,071	1,044	1,027	2,015	1,012	1,003
1920	6.0		2,347	1,187	1,160	20,122	10,157	9,965	2,084	1,048	1,036	2,036	1,021	1,015
1921			2,366	1,195	1,171	20,426	10,296	10,130	2,138	1,074	1,064	2,089	1,048	1,041
1922			2,382	1,203	1,179	20,656	10,404	10,252	2,178	1,094	1,084	2,132	1,068	1,064
1923			2,401	1,213	1,188	20,913	10,532	10,381	2,218	1,113	1,105	2,176	1,090	1,086
1924			2,419	1,224	1,195	21,136	10,649	10,487	2,257	1,132	1,125	2,222	1,112	1,110
1925			2,449	1,242	1,207	21,424	10,773	10,591	2,279	1,141	1,138	2,250	1,124	1,126
1926			2,486	1,262	1,224	21,633	10,918	10,715	2,292	1,148	1,144	2,273	1,136	1,137
1927			2,512	1,275	1,237	21,853	11,034	10,819	2,311	1,158	1,153	2,299	1,150	1,149
1928			2,515	1,276	1,239	21,995	11,113	10,882	2,334	1,172	1,162	2,325	1,165	1,160
1929			2,526	1,280	1,246	22,131	11,192	10,939	2,342	1,179	1,163	2,339	1,175	1,164
1930	4.3		2,490	1,267	1,223	22,266	11,268	10,998	2,376	1,200	1,176	2,365	1,191	1,174
1931			2,444	1,248	1,196	22,262	11,264	10,998	2,387	1,204	1,183	2,366	1,191	1,175
1932			2,435	1,244	1,191	22,238	11,254	10,984	2,411	1,214	1,197	2,376	1,195	1,181
1933			2,365	1,217	1,148	22,130	11,214	10,916	2,445	1,229	1,215	2,402	1,206	1,196
1934			2,314	1,179	1,136	21,964	11,134	10,830	2,491	1,253	1,238	2,438	1,223	1,215
1935			2,286	1,162	1,124	21,731	11,020	10,711	2,517	1,264	1,253	2,483	1,246	1,236
1936			2,257	1,147	1,109	21,435	10,875	10,560	2,482	1,249	1,233	2,508	1,258	1,249
1937			2,177	1,105	1,072	21,083	10,699	10,384	2,479	1,250	1,230	2,482	1,248	1,234
1938		1,061 ab	1,432 a	2,017 a	2,097	1,064	1,033	20,666	10,312	2,479	1,237	1,212	2,478	1,249	1,230
1939			2,064	1,047	1,017	20,253	11,275	9,978	2,420	1,224	1,195	2,448	1,236	1,213
1940	2.9		2,107	1,069	1,038	19,937	10,113	9,824	2,395	1,213	1,182	2,427	1,227	1,200
1941			2,172	1,106	1,066	19,674	9,986	9,688	2,371	1,201	1,169	2,415	1,221	1,194
1942			2,149	1,087	1,062	19,429	9,863	9,566	2,345	1,193	1,152	2,396	1,213	1,182
1943			2,212	1,121	1,091	19,319	9,812	9,507	2,324	1,186	1,138	2,380	1,214	1,166
1944			2,223	1,130	1,093	19,247	9,765	9,482	2,262	1,147	1,115	2,327	1,178	1,148
1945			2,245	1,140	1,105	19,325	9,821	9,504	2,202	1,124	1,078	2,273	1,153	1,120
1946			2,362	1,200	1,162	19,624	9,982	9,642	2,138	1,091	1,047	2,219	1,135	1,084
1947	2.7 c		2,532	1,288	1,244	20,119	10,234	9,885	2,104	1,070	1,034	2,139	1,089	1,049
1948		2,533	3,285	4,407	2,885	1,469	1,416	20,990	10,678	10,312	2,146	1,092	1,054	2,099	1,066	1,033
1949			2,728	1,388	1,340	21,634	11,007	10,627	2,149	1,095	1,053	2,136	1,083	1,054
1950	2.5 c		2,715	1,382	1,332	22,424	11,416	11,008	2,166	1,098	1,068	2,164	1,102	1,062
1951			2,673	1,360	1,313	22,998	11,712	11,286	2,263	1,152	1,111	2,170	1,099	1,071
1952			3,438	1,884	1,554	24,501	12,480	12,021	2,291	1,166	1,125	2,272	1,155	1,117
1953			3,439	1,752	1,687	25,701	13,091	12,610	2,320	1,179	1,141	2,302	1,171	1,131
1954			3,454	1,757	1,697	26,887	13,695	13,191	2,441	1,241	1,200	2,336	1,186	1,150
1955			3,449	1,756	1,693	27,925	14,223	13,702	2,612	1,329	1,283	2,462	1,250	1,212
1956			3,587	1,823	1,764	28,929	14,729	14,201	2,961	1,507	1,454	2,641	1,342	1,299
1957			3,680	1,873	1,807	29,672	15,102	14,570	2,799	1,423	1,376	2,997	1,524	1,473
1958	2.2 c	3,508	4,992 a	6,866 a	3,776	1,921	1,855	30,651	15,596	15,055	2,755	1,401	1,354	2,836	1,440	1,396
1959		4,474 a	5,541 a	7,664 a	3,878	1,972	1,906	31,767	16,157	15,609	2,704	1,372	1,331	2,797	1,421	1,377
1960		3,868	5,552	7,697	3,957	2,014	1,943	32,985	16,773	16,213	3,716	1,827	1,888	2,750	1,394	1,355
1961			3,984	2,026	1,958	33,297	16,932	16,365	3,496	1,717	1,779	3,718	1,889	1,829
1962			4,094	2,081	2,014	33,943	17,255	16,686	3,498	1,721	1,782	3,502	1,782	1,721
1963		4,076	5,999	7,987	4,114	2,092	2,023	34,606	17,592	17,014	3,478	1,708	1,781	3,505	1,781	1,724
1964		3,983	6,266	8,805	4,131	2,097	2,034	35,298	17,940	17,360	3,581	1,760	1,772	3,484	1,772	1,711
1965		4,210	6,458	9,048	4,132	2,101	2,032	35,888	18,237	17,651	3,588	1,807	1,871	3,586	1,874	1,763
1966		4,518	6,924	9,840	4,272	2,180	2,092	36,544	18,575	17,969	3,685	1,882	1,941	3,685	1,874	1,810
1967			4,184	2,136	2,049	36,966	18,799	18,167	3,823	1,923	1,980	3,829	1,944	1,885
1968			4,115	2,101	2,014	37,238	18,950	18,290	4,007	2,037	1,970	3,909	1,983	1,926

Population by sex for selected ages and age groups, in thousands

	15 yrs.			16 yrs.			17 yrs.			18 yrs.			18-21 yrs.		
	Total I-13	Male I-14	Female I-15	Total I-16	Male I-17	Female I-18	Total I-19	Male I-20	Female I-21	Total I-22	Male I-23	Female I-24	Total I-25	Male I-26	Female I-27
1850															
1860															
1870															
1871															
1872															
1873															
1874															
1875															
1876															
1877															
1878															
1879															
1880	934	469	466	988	484	504	949	472	477	1,131	544	587	4,253	2,106	2,147
1881															
1882															
1883															
1884															
1885															
1886															
1887															
1888															
1889															
1890	1,289	644	644	1,388	680	708	1,259	629	630	1,400	679	721	5,151	2,547	2,604
1891															
1892															
1893															
1894															
1895															
1896															
1897															
1898															
1899															
1900	1,544	772	772	1,519	756	763	1,505	746	759	1,500	742	758	6,000	2,962	3,038
1901	1,567	784	783	1,544	769	775	1,531	759	772	1,527	755	772	6,118	3,023	3,095
1902	1,591	796	795	1,572	783	789	1,560	774	786	1,558	772	786	6,248	3,093	3,155
1903	1,615	808	807	1,598	796	802	1,589	789	800	1,588	787	801	6,373	3,159	3,214
1904	1,640	820	820	1,627	811	816	1,619	805	814	1,620	804	816	6,505	3,231	3,274
1905	1,668	835	833	1,656	825	831	1,652	821	831	1,653	821	832	6,648	3,308	3,340
1906	1,696	849	847	1,687	841	846	1,684	838	846	1,688	839	849	6,787	3,383	3,404
1907	1,721	862	859	1,716	856	860	1,715	854	861	1,720	857	863	6,920	3,456	3,464
1908	1,749	876	873	1,748	872	876	1,749	871	878	1,754	874	880	7,060	3,531	3,529
1909	1,780	891	889	1,779	888	891	1,782	887	895	1,789	892	897	7,202	3,608	3,594
1910	1,812	907	905	1,813	905	908	1,815	904	911	1,823	910	913	7,340	3,679	3,661
1911	1,831	917	914	1,826	911	915	1,827	910	917	1,836	915	921	7,389	3,700	3,689
1912	1,849	926	923	1,841	918	923	1,840	916	924	1,844	919	925	7,428	3,715	3,713
1913	1,875	939	936	1,860	928	932	1,854	923	931	1,859	925	934	7,485	3,735	3,750
1914	1,899	951	948	1,878	936	942	1,867	928	939	1,869	929	940	7,529	3,751	3,778

Year														
1915	1,916	959	957	1,889	942	947	1,871	930	941	1,871	929	942	7,534	3,743	3,791
1916	1,932	967	965	1,896	945	951	1,872	930	942	1,869	927	942	7,528	3,731	3,797
1917	1,947	974	973	1,904	949	955	1,875	931	944	1,863	924	944	7,496	3,691	3,805
1918	1,971	990	981	1,971	966	959	1,882	937	945	1,843	899	944	7,156	3,346	3,810
1919	1,959	981	978	1,903	950	953	1,860	923	937	1,839	904	935	7,312	3,538	3,774
1920	1,989	994	995	1,940	967	973	1,904	946	958	1,880	931	949	7,444	3,666	3,778
1921	2,042	1,022	1,020	1,994	996	998	1,954	973	981	1,925	956	969	7,563	3,737	3,826
1922	2,086	1,043	1,043	2,041	1,018	1,023	2,001	995	1,006	1,966	975	991	7,675	3,787	3,888
1923	2,133	1,066	1,067	2,093	1,044	1,049	2,052	1,021	1,031	2,015	1,001	1,014	7,853	3,891	3,962
1924	2,185	1,091	1,094	2,149	1,071	1,078	2,113	1,052	1,061	2,076	1,032	1,044	8,091	4,021	4,070
1925	2,222	1,107	1,115	2,193	1,090	1,103	2,160	1,072	1,088	2,124	1,054	1,070	8,268	4,104	4,164
1926	2,252	1,123	1,129	2,229	1,109	1,120	2,202	1,094	1,108	2,166	1,075	1,091	8,424	4,183	4,241
1927	2,283	1,139	1,144	2,267	1,129	1,138	2,244	1,116	1,128	2,210	1,098	1,112	8,596	4,270	4,326
1928	2,313	1,156	1,157	2,298	1,146	1,152	2,277	1,133	1,144	2,245	1,115	1,130	8,756	4,342	4,414
1929	2,330	1,167	1,163	2,316	1,157	1,159	2,298	1,145	1,153	2,273	1,129	1,144	8,901	4,405	4,496
1930	2,352	1,180	1,171	2,336	1,167	1,167	2,317	1,156	1,161	2,296	1,141	1,155	9,034	4,466	4,568
1931	2,355	1,182	1,172	2,342	1,172	1,169	2,326	1,161	1,164	2,307	1,149	1,158	9,082	4,502	4,580
1932	2,355	1,182	1,173	2,343	1,173	1,170	2,330	1,164	1,166	2,315	1,154	1,161	9,129	4,533	4,596
1933	2,366	1,186	1,180	2,344	1,173	1,171	2,333	1,165	1,168	2,320	1,156	1,164	9,172	4,557	4,615
1934	2,394	1,199	1,196	2,358	1,178	1,180	2,336	1,165	1,171	2,325	1,157	1,167	9,211	4,575	4,636
1935	2,432	1,217	1,214	2,387	1,192	1,195	2,350	1,171	1,179	2,327	1,157	1,170	9,235	4,583	4,652
1936	2,473	1,239	1,234	2,424	1,211	1,213	2,379	1,184	1,194	2,341	1,162	1,178	9,260	4,588	4,672
1937	2,498	1,252	1,245	2,463	1,232	1,231	2,415	1,204	1,212	2,370	1,177	1,193	9,305	4,605	4,700
1938	2,485	1,249	1,236	2,490	1,247	1,243	2,455	1,226	1,229	2,409	1,198	1,211	9,395	4,647	4,748
1939	2,478	1,248	1,230	2,489	1,250	1,239	2,483	1,243	1,240	2,447	1,220	1,227	9,523	4,715	4,808
1940	2,448	1,235	1,213	2,477	1,247	1,230	2,492	1,252	1,240	2,480	1,237	1,243	9,698	4,843	4,863
1941	2,427	1,224	1,203	2,439	1,224	1,214	2,461	1,234	1,226	2,476	1,234	1,242	9,767	4,886	4,881
1942	2,408	1,208	1,201	2,417	1,214	1,203	2,422	1,213	1,218	2,438	1,220	1,218	9,761	4,894	4,867
1943	2,394	1,204	1,189	2,391	1,193	1,198	2,403	1,203	1,209	2,402	1,202	1,199	9,687	4,859	4,828
1944	2,376	1,206	1,170	2,387	1,204	1,184	2,384	1,192	1,192	2,399	1,199	1,207	9,596	4,815	4,781
1945	2,308	1,197	1,148	2,387	1,195	1,161	2,341	1,168	1,174	2,337	1,182	1,182	9,432	4,701	4,731
1946	2,259	1,160	1,121	2,263	1,127	1,137	2,278	1,161	1,148	2,292	1,155	1,161	9,271	4,590	4,681
1947	2,211	1,127	1,084	2,261	1,148	1,113	2,267	1,130	1,129	2,276	1,131	1,139	9,176	4,547	4,629
1948	2,120	1,073	1,046	2,189	1,110	1,079	2,248	1,139	1,111	2,256	1,137	1,126	9,120	4,536	4,584
1949	2,082	1,053	1,029	2,106	1,065	1,041	2,178	1,102	1,076	2,248	1,130	1,143	9,066	4,532	4,534
1950	2,133	1,076	1,057	2,055	1,036	1,019	2,092	1,054	1,038	2,164	1,090	1,074	8,947	4,484	4,463
1951	2,111	1,064	1,047	2,156	1,088	1,068	2,062	1,041	1,021	2,085	1,049	1,036	8,741	4,386	4,355
1952	2,121	1,064	1,057	2,128	1,072	1,056	2,163	1,092	1,071	2,058	1,037	1,021	8,515	4,272	4,243
1953	2,224	1,121	1,102	2,131	1,069	1,062	2,135	1,076	1,059	2,160	1,089	1,071	8,414	4,215	4,199
1954	2,257	1,139	1,118	2,227	1,123	1,104	2,139	1,073	1,066	2,135	1,075	1,060	8,386	4,201	4,185
1955	2,295	1,158	1,137	2,255	1,138	1,117	2,236	1,127	1,109	2,142	1,068	1,074	8,443	4,228	4,215
1956	2,424	1,224	1,200	2,287	1,153	1,134	2,265	1,143	1,123	2,244	1,132	1,113	8,638	4,329	4,309
1957	2,603	1,317	1,286	2,407	1,215	1,192	2,296	1,157	1,139	2,274	1,148	1,126	8,749	4,388	4,361
1958	2,958	1,499	1,459	2,576	1,303	1,274	2,416	1,218	1,198	2,307	1,164	1,143	8,909	4,470	4,439
1959	2,804	1,421	1,384	2,920	1,479	1,441	2,587	1,307	1,280	2,431	1,228	1,203	9,190	4,621	4,569
1960	2,769	1,405	1,365	2,761	1,397	1,363	2,932	1,483	1,449	2,606	1,319	1,287	9,549	4,807	4,742
1961	2,754	1,396	1,358	2,759	1,406	1,361	2,766	1,399	1,367	2,939	1,485	1,454	10,253	5,169	5,084
1962	2,723	1,391	1,332	2,728	1,398	1,361	2,780	1,408	1,371	2,773	1,402	1,371	10,761	5,431	5,330
1963	3,509	1,785	1,775	3,728	1,893	1,835	2,765	1,400	1,365	2,787	1,411	1,376	11,155	5,632	5,523
1964	3,512	1,784	1,728	3,517	1,788	1,729	3,735	1,895	1,840	2,772	1,402	1,370	11,319	5,714	5,606
1965	3,488	1,774	1,714	3,517	1,786	1,731	3,522	1,790	1,732	3,743	1,899	1,844	12,128	6,133	5,995
1966	3,593	1,827	1,766	3,496	1,778	1,718	3,525	1,790	1,735	3,531	1,795	1,736	12,887	6,529	6,358
1967	3,691	1,877	1,814	3,660	1,830	1,770	3,496	1,782	1,714	3,533	1,794	1,739	13,632	6,912	6,720
1968	3,836	1,948	1,889	3,699	1,881	1,818	3,608	1,834	1,774	3,512	1,786	1,726	14,372	7,296	7,076

415

Population by sex for selected ages and age groups, in thousands

	22 yrs.			23 yrs.			5-17 yrs.	14-17 yrs.
	Total I-28	Male I-29	Female I-30	Total I-31	Male I-32	Female I-33	Total I-34	Total I-35
1850								
1860								
1870								
1871								
1872								
1873								
1874								
1875								
1876								
1877								
1878								
1879								
1880	1,054	524	531				16,265	3,941
1881								
1882								
1883								
1884								
1885								
1886								
1887								
1888								
1889								
1890	1,275	635	640				18,543	5,355
1891								
1892								
1893								
1894								
1895								
1896								
1897								
1898								
1899								
1900	1,491	736	755	1,465	726	739	21,534	6,132
1901	1,524	753	771	1,498	744	754	21,800	6,228
1902	1,557	771	786	1,532	762	770	22,083	6,333
1903	1,591	790	801	1,565	781	784	22,326	6,433
1904	1,625	809	816	1,599	800	799	22,583	6,539
1905	1,664	831	833	1,638	822	816	22,864	6,654
1906	1,699	851	848	1,675	843	832	23,134	6,769
1907	1,734	871	863	1,709	863	846	23,391	6,878
1908	1,770	892	878	1,744	883	861	23,686	6,999
1909	1,806	912	894	1,781	904	877	24,011	7,123
1910	1,841	931	910	1,815	922	893	24,390	7,252
1911	1,854	936	918	1,832	929	903	24,698	7,319
1912	1,864	939	925	1,844	933	911	25,033	7,388
1913	1,880	944	936	1,862	939	923	25,493	7,477
1914	1,893	947	946	1,878	944	934	25,960	7,563

Year									
1915	1,893	943	950	1,881	941	940	26,336	7,619
1916	1,894	939	955	1,884	937	947	26,708	7,665
1917	1,880	922	958	1,872	921	951	27,095	7,715
1918	1,711	749	962	1,709	752	957	27,510	7,794
1919	1,811	857	954	1,810	860	950	27,571	7,737
1920	1,835	897	938	1,845	904	941	27,991	7,869
1921	1,845	906	939	1,858	914	944	28,505	8,079
1922	1,853	909	944	1,861	913	948	28,916	8,260
1923	1,888	932	956	1,885	931	954	29,367	8,454
1924	1,941	964	977	1,923	955	968	29,805	8,669
1925	1,978	984	994	1,947	968	979	30,249	8,825
1926	2,012	1,000	1,012	1,976	982	994	30,598	8,965
1927	2,052	1,019	1,033	2,013	999	1,014	30,946	9,093
1928	2,097	1,038	1,059	2,056	1,017	1,039	31,208	9,213
1929	2,143	1,055	1,088	2,103	1,035	1,068	31,414	9,283
1930	2,190	1,074	1,116	2,152	1,056	1,097	31,636	9,370
1931	2,204	1,084	1,120	2,173	1,067	1,107	31,651	9,389
1932	2,216	1,093	1,123	2,187	1,077	1,111	31,642	9,414
1933	2,232	1,103	1,129	2,202	1,086	1,115	31,575	9,445
1934	2,252	1,114	1,138	2,221	1,097	1,124	31,490	9,526
1935	2,270	1,123	1,147	2,243	1,109	1,135	31,383	9,652
1936	2,280	1,127	1,153	2,261	1,117	1,144	31,219	9,784
1937	2,285	1,127	1,157	2,277	1,120	1,150	30,941	9,858
1938	2,289	1,127	1,162	2,277	1,121	1,156	30,574	9,908
1939	2,293	1,125	1,167	2,282	1,120	1,162	30,151	9,898
1940	2,326	1,149	1,177	2,302	1,135	1,167	29,781	9,844
1941	2,360	1,172	1,188	2,322	1,148	1,174	29,416	9,742
1942	2,397	1,201	1,196	2,362	1,179	1,184	29,072	9,643
1943	2,420	1,221	1,200	2,400	1,207	1,193	28,887	9,568
1944	2,438	1,233	1,205	2,416	1,216	1,201	28,721	9,474
1945	2,422	1,216	1,206	2,446	1,236	1,210	28,576	9,251
1946	2,402	1,200	1,203	2,441	1,222	1,218	28,643	9,019
1947	2,361	1,165	1,195	2,402	1,186	1,216	28,997	8,878
1948	2,357	1,165	1,192	2,393	1,183	1,210	29,646	8,656
1949	2,343	1,157	1,187	2,380	1,173	1,207	30,136	8,502
1950	2,325	1,151	1,173	2,391	1,183	1,208	30,868	8,444
1951	2,258	1,119	1,139	2,384	1,184	1,200	31,497	8,499
1952	2,255	1,123	1,131	2,314	1,149	1,165	33,185	8,684
1953	2,224	1,112	1,112	2,305	1,151	1,154	34,493	8,792
1954	2,140	1,065	1,075	2,274	1,141	1,133	35,846	8,959
1955	2,066	1,027	1,036	2,187	1,093	1,094	37,173	9,248
1956	2,045	1,019	1,026	2,111	1,054	1,057	38,546	9,617
1957	2,151	1,074	1,077	2,087	1,045	1,042	39,975	10,303
1958	2,129	1,061	1,067	2,190	1,098	1,092	41,437	10,786
1959	2,138	1,062	1,076	2,167	1,087	1,080	42,875	11,108
1960	2,238	1,118	1,120	2,175	1,087	1,088	44,197	11,212
1961	2,274	1,135	1,139	2,250	1,122	1,127	45,309	12,012
1962	2,303	1,152	1,151	2,285	1,138	1,147	46,707	12,764
1963	2,427	1,219	1,208	2,312	1,154	1,158	48,113	13,507
1964	2,642	1,329	1,313	2,437	1,222	1,215	49,546	14,248
1965	2,975	1,497	1,478	2,653	1,334	1,319	50,001	14,113
1966	2,810	1,415	1,395	2,985	1,500	1,485	50,843	14,299
1967	2,823	1,424	1,399	2,819	1,418	1,401	51,590	14,624
1968	2,809	1,416	1,392	2,833	1,427	1,405	52,292	15,052

Bibliography

Astin, Alexander W., Robert J. Panos, and John A. Creager.

    1966   A Program of Longitudinal Research on the Higher Educational System. ACE Research Reports, vol. 1, no. 1, Washington: American Council on Education.

    1967a   National Norms for Entering College Freshmen, Fall 1966. ACE Research Reports, vol. 2, no. 1. Washington: American Council on Education.

    1967b   Implications of a Program of Research on Student Development in Higher Education. ACE Research Reports, vol. 2, no. 6. Washington: American Council on Education.

Barr, Richard, and Betty J. Foster.

    1968   Fall 1967 Statistics of Public Elementary and Secondary Day Schools, Pupils, Teachers, Instruction Rooms, and Expenditures. Office of Education, OE-20007-67. Washington: U. S. Government Printing Office.

Barzun, Jacques

    1968   The American University. New York: Harper and Row.

Bearrentine, Susan O.

    1966   An Estimate of the "True" Educational Distribution of the United States Adult Population: 1910 to 1960. Tallahassee, Florida: unpublished Ph.D. dissertation, Florida State University.

Beazley, Richard

    1969   Numbers and Characteristics of Employees in Institutions of Higher Education, Fall 1966. Office of Education, OE-50057-66. Washington: U. S. Government Printing Office.

Berelson, Bernard

    1960   Graduate Education in the United States. New York: McGraw-Hill Book Co.

Biderman, Albert D.

    1966   "Social indicators and goals." Pp. 68-153 in Raymond A. Bauer (ed.), Social Indicators. Cambridge, Massachusetts: M.I.T. Press.

Blough, Telford Benjamin

    1956   A Critical Analysis of Selected Research Literature on the Problem of School Dropouts. Pittsburgh, Pa.: unpublished D.Ed. dissertation, University of Pittsburgh.

Bogan, Forrest A.

    1966   "Employment of school age youth, October 1965." Special Labor Force Report, No. 68. Reprinted from the Monthly Labor Review, July 1966. Reprint No. 2493. Washington: U. S. Government Printing Office.

    1969   "Employment of school age youth." Special Labor Force Report, No. 98. Reprinted from the Monthly Labor Review, October 1968. Reprint No. 2588. Washington: U. S. Government Printing Office.

Bokelman, W. Robert

    1958   Higher Education Planning and Management Data, 1957-58. Office of Education, Cir. 517. Washington: U. S. Government Printing Office.

    1959   Higher Education Planning and Management Data, 1958-59. Office of Education, Cir. 549. Washington: U. S. Government Printing Office.

    1960   Higher Education Planning and Management Data, 1959-60. Office of Education, OE-53004. Washington: U. S. Government Printing Office.

    1961   Higher Education Planning and Management Data, 1960-61. Office of Education, OE-53004-61. Washington: U. S. Government Printing Office.

Bokelman, W. Robert, and Louis A. D'Amico.

    1962   Higher Education Basic Student Charges, 1961-62, Tuition and Fees, Board and Room. Office of Education, OE-52005-62. Washington: U. S. Government Printing Office.

Bowker, Albert H.

    1965   "Quality and quantity in higher education." Journal of the American Statistical Association 60 (March): 1-15.

Campbell, Robert F., Tom Flake, and Jim Leeson.

    1967   A Statistical Summary, State by State, of School Segregation-Desegregation in the Southern and Border Area from 1954 to the Present. Nashville, Tennessee: Southern Education Reporting Service.

Cartter, Allan M. (ed.)

   1964   American Universities and Colleges. Washington: American Council on Education.

Cartter, Allan M.

   1966   An Assessment of Quality in Graduate Education. Washington: American Council on Education.

Census, U. S. Bureau of the

   1883   Statistics of the Population of the United States. Tenth Census: 1880, vol. 1. Washington: U. S. Government Printing Office.

   1897   Report on Population of the United States. Eleventh Census, 1890, part 2. Washington: U. S. Government Printing Office.

   1933   Fifteenth Census of the United States: 1930. Population, vol. 2. Washington: U. S. Government Printing Office.

   1948a   "School enrollment of the civilian population: April 1947." Current Population Reports, Population Characteristics, Series P-20, No. 12 (February). Washington: U. S. Bureau of the Census.

   1948b   "Educational attainment of the civilian population: April 1947." Current Population Reports, Population Characteristics, Series P-20, No. 15 (May). Washington: U. S. Bureau of the Census.

1949 "School enrollment of the civilian population: October 1948." Current Population Reports, Population Characteristics, Series P-20, No. 24 (April). Washington: U. S. Bureau of the Census.

1950 "School enrollment of the civilian population: October 1949." Current Population Reports, Population Characteristics, Series P-20, No. 30 (April). Washington: U. S. Bureau of the Census.

1951 "School enrollment of the civilian population: October 1950." Current Population Reports, Population Characteristics, Series P-20, No. 34 (July). Washington: U. S. Bureau of the Census.

1952 "School enrollment: October 1951." Current Population Reports, Population Characteristics, Series P-20, No. 40 (July). Washington: U. S. Bureau of the Census.

1953 "School enrollment, educational attainment, and illiteracy, October 1952." Current Population Reports, Population Characteristics, Series P-20, No. 45 (October). Washington: U. S. Bureau of the Census.

1954 "School enrollment: October 1953." Current Population Reports, Population Characteristics, Series P-20, No. 52 (January). Washington: U. S. Bureau of the Census.

1955 "School enrollment: October 1954." Current Population Reports, Population Characteristics, Series P-20, No. 54 (January). Washington: U. S. Bureau of the Census.

1956   "School enrollment: October 1955." Current Population Reports, Population Characteristics, Series P-20, No. 66 (April). Washington: U. S. Bureau of the Census.

1957a   "School enrollment: October 1956." Current Population Reports, Population Characteristics, Series P-20, No. 74 (April). Washington: U. S. Bureau of the Census.

1957b   "Educational attainment: March 1957." Current Population Reports, Population Characteristics, Series P-20, No. 77 (December). Washington: U. S. Bureau of the Census.

1958   "School enrollment: October 1957." Current Population Reports, Population Characteristics, Series P-20, No. 80 (February). Washington: U. S. Bureau of the Census.

1959   "School enrollment: October 1958." Current Population Reports, Population Characteristics, Series P-20, No. 93 (March). Washington: U. S. Bureau of the Census.

1960a   Historical Statistics of the United States, Colonial Times to 1957. Washington: U. S. Government Printing Office.

1960b   "School enrollment: October 1959." Current Population Reports, Population Characteristics, Series P-20, No. 101 (May). Washington: U. S. Bureau of the Census.

1960c   "Literacy and educational attainment: March 1959." Current Population Reports, Population Characteristics, Series P-20, No. 99 (February). Washington: U. S. Bureau of the Census.

1961 "School enrollment and education of young adults and their fathers: October 1960." Current Population Reports, Population Characteristics, Series P-20, No. 110 (July). Washington: U. S. Bureau of the Census.

1962 "School enrollment: October 1961." Current Population Reports, Population Characteristics, Series P-20, No. 117 (July). Washington: U. S. Bureau of the Census.

1963a United States Census of Population: 1960. Detailed Characteristics. United States Summary. Final Report, PC(1)-1D. Washington: U. S. Government Printing Office.

1963b "School enrollment: October 1962." Current Population Reports, Population Characteristics, Series P-20, No. 126 (September). Washington: U. S. Bureau of the Census.

1963c "Educational attainment: March 1962." Current Population Reports, Population Characteristics, Series P-20, No. 121 (February). Washington: U. S. Bureau of the Census.

1963d United States Census of Population: 1960. Educational Attainment, PC(2)-5B. Washington: U. S. Government Printing Office.

1963e The Current Population Survey, A Report on Methodology. Technical Paper No. 7. Washington: U. S. Government Printing Office.

1963f Census of Governments: 1962. Governmental Organization, vol. 1. Washington: U. S. Government Printing Office.

1963g United States Census of Population: 1960. Occupation by Earnings and Education, PC(2)-7B. Washington: U. S. Government Printing Office.

1964a U. S. Census of Population: 1960. Subject Reports, Characteristics of Professional Workers. Final Report, PC(2)-7E. Washington: U. S. Government Printing Office.

1964b "School enrollment: October 1963." Current Population Reports, Population Characteristics, Series P-20, No. 129 (July). Washington: U. S. Bureau of the Census.

1964c "Concepts and methods used in manpower statistics from the Current Population Survey, June 1964." Bureau of Labor Statistics Report No. 279, Current Population Reports, Series P-23, No. 13. Washington: U. S. Government Printing Office.

1965a Historical Statistics of the United States, Continuation to 1962 and Revisions. Washington: U. S. Government Printing Office.

1965b "Estimates of the population of the United States by single years of age, color, and sex, 1900-1959." Current Population Reports, Population Estimates, Series P-25, No. 311 (July). Washington: U. S. Bureau of the Census.

1965c "Estimates of the population of the United States, by single years of age, color, and sex, 1960-1964." Current Population Reports, Population Estimates, Series P-25, No. 314 (August). Washington: U. S. Bureau of the Census.

1965d "Educational attainment: March 1964." Current Population Reports, Population Characteristics, Series P-20, No. 138(May). Washington: U. S. Bureau of the Census.

1966a Long Term Economic Growth 1860-1965, A Statistical Compendium. ES-4, No. 1. Washington: U. S. Government Printing Office.

1966b "School enrollment: October 1964." Current Population Reports, Population Characteristics, Series P-20, No. 148 (February). Washington: U. S. Bureau of the Census.

1966c Statistical Abstract of the United States, 1966, 87th Annual Edition. Washington: U. S. Government Printing Office.

1966d "Educational attainment: March 1966 and 1965." Current Population Reports, Population Characteristics, Series P-20, No. 158 (December). Washington: U. S. Bureau of the Census.

1967a "School enrollment: October 1965." Current Population Reports, Population Characteristics, Series P-20, No. 162 (March). Washington: U. S. Bureau of the Census.

1967b   "School enrollment: October 1966." Current Population Reports, Population Characteristics, Series P-20, No. 167 (August). Washington: U. S. Bureau of the Census.

1967c   "Projections of the population of the United States by age, sex, and color, to 1990, with extensions of the population by age and sex to 2015." Current Population Reports, Population Estimates, Series P-25, No. 381 (December). Washington: U. S. Bureau of the Census.

1967d   "Concepts and methods used in manpower statistics from the Current Population Survey, June 1967." Bureau of Labor Statistics Report No. 313, Current Population Reports, Series P-23, No. 22, Washington: U.S. Government Printing Office.

1967e   "Revised projections of school and college enrollment in the United States to 1985." Current Population Reports, Population Estimates, Series P-25, No. 365 (May). Washington: U. S. Bureau of the Census.

1967f   "Income in 1965 of families and persons in the United States." Current Population Reports, Consumer Income, Series P-60, No. 51 (January). Washington: U. S. Bureau of the Census.

1967g   "Income in 1966 of families and persons in the United States." Current Population Reports, Consumer Income, Series P-60, No. 53 (December). Washington: U. S. Bureau of the Census.

1968a Statistical Abstract of the United States, 1968, 89th Annual Edition. Washington: U. S. Government Printing Office.

1968b "Estimates of the population of the United States, by age, race, and sex, July 1, 1964 to 1967." Current Population Reports, Population Estimates, Series P-25, No. 385 (February). Washington: U. S. Bureau of the Census.

1968c "Marital status and family status: March 1967." Current Population Reports, Population Characteristics, Series P-20, No. 170 (February). Washington: U. S. Bureau of the Census.

1968d "Education attainment: March 1967." Current Population Reports, Population Characteristics, Series P-20, No. 169 (February). Washington: U. S. Bureau of the Census.

1968e Census of Governments, 1967. Governmental Organization, vol. 1. Washington: U. S. Government Printing Office.

1969a "Estimates of the population of the United States, by age, race, and sex: July 1, 1968." Current Population Reports, Population Estimates, Series P-25, No. 416 (February). Washington: U. S. Bureau of the Census.

1969b "Fall school enrollment approximately 58.8 million (advance data, October 1968 survey)." Current Population Reports, Population Characteristics, Series P-20, No. 179 (March). Washington: U. S. Bureau of the Census.

Chandler, Marjorie O.

1968 Earned Degrees Conferred: 1966-67. Part A - Summary Data. Office of Education, OE-54013-67. Washington: U. S. Government Printing Office.

1969 Opening Fall Enrollment in Higher Education, 1968: Part A - Summary Data. Office of Education, OE-54003-68. Washington: U. S. Government Printing Office.

Chandler, Marjorie O., and Mabel C. Rice.

1967 Opening Fall Enrollment in Higher Education, 1967. Office of Education, OE-54003-67. Washington: U. S. Government Printing Office.

1968 Earned Degrees Conferred, 1965-66. Office of Education, OE-54013-66. Washington: U. S. Government Printing Office.

Cohen, Wilbur J.

1967 "Education and learning." The Annals 373 (September): 79-101.

Coleman, James S. et al.

1966 Equality of Educational Opportunity. Office of Education, OE-38001. Washington: U. S. Government Printing Office.

College Placement Council, Salary Survey Committee.

    1967a   Study of Beginning Salary Offers. Bethlehem, Pennsylvania: College Placement Council.

    1967b   Salary Survey, A Study of 1966-67 Beginning Offers. Bethlehem, Pennsylvania: College Placement Council.

Combs, Janet, and William W. Cooley.

    1968   "Dropouts: in high school and after high school." American Educational Research Journal 5 (May): 343-364.

Conant, James Bryant

    1964   Slums and Suburbs. New York: The New American Library of World Literature, Inc.

    1967   The Comprehensive High School. New York: McGraw-Hill Book Co.

Consolazio, William V.

    1967   The Dynamics of Academic Science, A Degree Profile of Academic Science and Technology and the Contributions of Federal Funds for Academic Science to Universities and Colleges. NSF 67-6. Washington: National Science Foundation.

Council of Economic Advisers.

    1969a   Economic Indicators. February 1969. Prepared for the Subcommittee on Economic Statistics of the Joint Economic Committee. 91st Congress, 1st Session. Washington: U. S. Government Printing Office.

1969b   Economic Report of the President. January 1969. 91st Congress, 1st Session, House Document No. 28. Washington: U. S. Government Printing Office.

Creager, John A.

1968   "General purpose sampling in the domain of higher education." ACE Research Reports, vol. 3, no. 2. Washington: American Council on Education.

D'Amico, Louis A.

1964   Higher Education Basic Student Charges, 1963-64. Tuition and Fees, Board and Room. Office of Education, OE-52005-64. Washington: U. S. Government Printing Office.

D'Amico, Louis A., and W. Robert Bokelman.

1963   Higher Education Basic Student Charges, 1962-63. Tuition and Fees, Board and Room. Office of Education, OE-52005-63. Washington: U. S. Government Printing Office.

Davis, James A.

1964   Great Aspirations, The Graduate School Plans of America's College Seniors. Chicago, Illinois: Aldine Publishing Company.

Duncan, Beverly

1965   "Dropouts and the unemployed." The Journal of Political Economy LXXIII (April): 121-134.

1968   "Trends in output and distribution of schooling." Pp. 601-674 in Eleanor Bernert Sheldon and Wilbert E. Moore (eds.), Indicators of Social Change. New York: The Russell Sage Foundation.

Dunham, Ralph E., and Patricia S. Wright.

    1966   Faculty and Other Professional Staff in Institutions of Higher Education Fall Term, 1963-64. Office of Education, OE-53000-64. Washington: U. S. Government Printing Office.

Dunham, Ralph E., Patricia S. Wright, and Marjorie O. Chandler.

    1966   Teaching Faculty in Universities and Four-Year Colleges, Spring 1963. Office of Education, OE-53022-63. Washington: U. S. Government Printing Office.

Eckland, Bruce K.

    1964   "College dropouts who came back." Harvard Educational Review 34 (Summer): 402-420.

Education, Commissioner of

    1882   Report of the Commissioner of Education for the Year 1880. Washington: U. S. Government Printing Office.

    1893   Report of the Commissioner of Education for the Year 1889-90, vol. 2. Washington: U. S. Government Printing Office.

    1901   Report of the Commissioner of Education for the Year 1899-1900, vol. 2. Washington: U. S. Government Printing Office.

    1911   Report of the Commissioner of Education for the Year 1910, vol. 2. Washington: U. S. Government Printing Office.

Education, Office of *

- 1921 Biennial Survey of Education, 1916-18, vol. 3. Washington: U. S. Government Printing Office.
- 1923 Biennial Survey of Education, 1918-20. Statistics. Washington: U. S. Government Printing Office.
- 1925 Biennial Survey of Education, 1920-22, vol. 2. Washington: U. S. Government Printing Office.
- 1927 Biennial Survey of Education, 1922-24. Washington: U. S. Government Printing Office.
- 1928 Biennial Survey of Education, 1924-26. Washington: U. S. Government Printing Office.
- 1930 Biennial Survey of Education, 1926-28. Washington: U. S. Government Printing Office.
- 1932 Biennial Survey of Education, 1928-30, vol. 2. Washington: U. S. Government Printing Office.
- 1933 Biennial Survey of Education, 1930-32. Chapter 5, "Statistics of Private Elementary Schools for the Year 1930-31." Washington: U. S. Government Printing Office.

* (1) In the earlier years of publication, the U. S. Office of Education was entitled the Bureau of Education, but for simplification, all such references are cited under the "Office of Education." (2) With the 1930-32 publication the various segments of the Biennial Surveys of Education were published separately in different chapters and are so cited, but previous to that date chapters are not cited in the bibliography.

1935a   Biennial Survey of Education, 1930-32. Chapter 1, "Statistical Summary of Education, 1931-32." Washington: U. S. Government Printing Office.

1935b   Biennial Survey of Education, 1930-32. Chapter 3, "Statistics of Higher Education, 1931-32." Washington: U. S. Government Printing Office.

1936   Biennial Survey of Education, 1932-34. Chapter 6, "Statistics of Private Elementary and Secondary Schools, 1932-33." Washington: U. S. Government Printing Office.

1937a   Biennial Survey of Education, 1932-34. Chapter 1, "Statistical Summary of Education, 1933-34." Washington: U. S. Government Printing Office.

1937b   Biennial Survey of Education, 1932-34. Chapter 4, "Statistics of Higher Education, 1933-34." Washington: U. S. Government Printing Office.

1938   Biennial Survey of Education, 1934-36, vol. 2. Chapter 4, "Statistics of Higher Education, 1935-36." Washington: U. S. Government Printing Office.

1939   Biennial Survey of Education, 1934-36, vol. 2. Chapter 1, "Statistical Summary of Education, 1935-36." Washington: U. S. Government Printing Office.

1941a   Biennial Survey of Education, 1936-38. Chapter 1, "Statistical Summary of Education, 1937-38." Washington: U. S. Government Printing Office.

1941b   Biennial Survey of Education, 1936-38. Chapter 4, "Statistics of Higher Education, 1937-38." Washington: U. S. Government Printing Office.

1943   Biennial Survey of Education, 1938-40, vol. 2. Chapter 1, "Statistical Summary of Education, 1939-40." Washington: U. S. Government Printing Office.

1944a   Biennial Survey of Education, 1938-40 and 1940-42, vol. 2. Chapter 4, "Statistics of Higher Education, 1939-40 and 1941-42." Washington: U. S. Government Printing Office.

1944b   Biennial Survey of Education, 1940-42, vol. 2. Chapter 2, "Statistical Summary of Education, 1941-42." Washington: U. S. Government Printing Office.

1946   Biennial Survey of Education, 1942-44. Chapter 4, "Statistics of Higher Education, 1943-44." Washington: U. S. Government Printing Office.

1947   Biennial Survey of Education, 1942-44. Chapter 1, "Statistical Summary of Education, 1943-44." Washington: U. S. Government Printing Office.

1949a   Biennial Survey of Education, 1944-46. Chapter 1, "Statistical Summary of Education, 1945-46." Washington: U. S. Government Printing Office.

1949b   Biennial Survey of Education, 1944-46. Chapter 2, "Statistics of State School Systems, 1945-46." Washington: U. S. Government Printing Office.

1949c   Biennial Survey of Education, 1944-46. Chapter 4, "Statistics of Higher Education, 1945-46." Washington: U. S. Government Printing Office.

1950a   Biennial Survey of Education, 1946-48. Chapter 1, "Statistical Summary of Education, 1947-48." Washington: U. S. Government Printing Office.

1950b   Biennial Survey of Education, 1946-48. Chapter 4, "Statistics of Higher Education, 1947-48." Washington: U. S. Government Printing Office.

1951   Biennial Survey of Education, 1946-48. Chapter 7, "Statistics of Non-public Secondary Schools, 1947-48." Washington: U. S. Government Printing Office.

1953a   Biennial Survey of Education, 1948-50. Chapter 1, "Statistical Summary of Education, 1949-50." Washington: U. S. Government Printing Office.

1953b   Handbook I, The Common Core of State Education Information. Bulletin 1953, No. 8. Washington: U. S. Government Printing Office.

1957a   Biennial Survey of Education, 1950-52. Chapter 1, "Statistical Summary of Education." Washington: U. S. Government Printing Office.

1957b   Biennial Survey of Education, 1952-54. Chapter 1, "Statistical Summary of Education, 1953-54." Washington: U. S. Government Printing Office.

1958   Biennial Survey of Education, 1954-56. Chapter 4, "Statistics of Higher Education, 1955-56." Washington: U. S. Government Printing Office.

1959a   Biennial Survey of Education, 1954-56. Chapter 1, "Statistical Summary of Education, 1955-56." Washington: U. S. Government Printing Office.

1959b   Biennial Survey of Education, 1954-56. Chapter 2, "Statistics of State School Systems, 1955-56." Washington: U. S. Government Printing Office.

1962   Biennial Survey of Education, 1956-58. Chapter 4, Section 1, "Statistics of Higher Education, 1957-58." Washington: U. S. Government Printing Office.

1963   Digest of Educational Statistics, 1963 Edition. OE-10024-63. Washington: U. S. Government Printing Office.

1964   Opening Fall Enrollment in Higher Education, 1964. OE-54003-64. Washington: U. S. Government Printing Office.

1965   Education Directory, 1964-1965. Part 3, Higher Education. OE-50000-65. Washington: U. S. Govenment Printing Office.

1967a   Statistics of State School Systems, 1963-64. OE-20020-64. Washington: U. S. Government Printing Office.

1967b   Directory of U. S. Post-Secondary Academic Institutions. Washington: U. S. Government Printing Office.

1967c   Opening Fall Enrollment in Higher Education, 1965. OE-54003-65. Washington: U. S. Government Printing Office.

1967d   Opening Fall Enrollment in Higher Education, 1966. OE-54003-66. Washington: U. S. Government Printing Office.

1968a   Statistics of Nonpublic Elementary and Secondary Schools, 1965-66. OE-20111. Washington: U. S. Government Printing Office.

1968b   Education in the Seventies. OE-10051. Washington: U. S. Government Printing Office.

1968c   Basic Student Charges, 1966-67. OE-52005-67. Washington: U. S. Government Printing Office.

Educational Testing Service.

1957   Background Factors Relating to College Plans and College Enrollment Among Public High School Students. Princeton, N.J.: Educational Testing Service.

1968   State Testing Programs: A Survey of Functions, Tests, Materials and Services. Princeton, N.J.: Educational Testing Service.

Etzioni, Amitai, and Edward W. Lehman.

1967   "Some dangers in 'valid' social measurement." The Annals 373 (September): 1-15.

Ferriss, Abbott

1964   "A method for combining earned degrees granted into an index of production of scientists by institution." Unpublished paper. Washington: National Science Foundation, mimeo.

Flanagan, John C. et al.
- 1962 Studies of the American High School. Project Talent Monograph Series, Monograph No. 2. Pittsburgh: Project Talent, University of Pittsburgh.

Flanagan, John C.
- 1965 The Project Talent Data Bank. Pittsburgh: Project Talent, University of Pittsburgh.

Folger, John K.
- 1967 "The balance between supply and demand for college graduates." The Journal of Human Resources 2 (Spring): 143-169.

Folger, John K., and Charles B. Nam.
- 1967 Education of the American Population. A 1960 Census Monograph. Washington: U. S. Government Printing Office.

Gardner, John W.
- 1960 "National goals in education." Pp. 81-100 in The President's Commission on National Goals, Goals for Americans. New York: Prentice-Hall, Inc.

Gertler, Diane B.
- 1959 Earned Degrees Conferred by Higher Educational Institutions, 1957-1958. Office of Education, Cir. 570. Washington: U. S. Government Printing Office.

Gertler, Diane B., and Virginia W. Keith.
- 1958 Earned Degrees Conferred by Higher Educational Institutions, 1956-1957. Office of Education, Cir. 527. Washington: U. S. Government Printing Office.

Goslin, D. A.

    1968   "Standardized ability tests and testing." Science 159 (February): 851-855.

Hamel, Harvey R.

    1964   "Employment of school age youth, October 1963." Special Labor Force Report, No. 4. Preprinted from the Monthly Labor Review, July 1964. Preprint No. 2441. Washington: U. S. Government Printing Office.

Harmon, Lindsey R.

    1961   "High school backgrounds of science doctorates." Science 133 (March 10): 679-688.

Harmon, Lindsey R., and Herbert Soldz.

    1963   Doctorate Production in United States Universities, 1920-1962 With Baccalaureate Origins of Doctorates in Science, Arts and Professions. Pub. No. 1142. Washington: National Academy of Sciences-National Research Council.

Hightower, Caroline

    1968   How Much Are Students Learning? (Plans for a National Assessment of Education). Ann Arbor, Michigan: The Committee on Assessing the Progress of Education.

Hobson, Carol Joy, and Samuel Schloss.

    1963   Fall 1962 Statistics on Enrollments, Teachers and Schoolhousing in Full-time Public Elementary and Secondary Day Schools. Office of Education, OE-20007-62. Washington: U. S. Government Printing Office.

1967 Fall 1966 Statistics of Public Elementary and Secondary Day Schools, Pupils, Teachers, Instruction Rooms, and Expenditures. Office of Education, OE-20007-66. Washington: U. S. Government Printing Office.

Huddleston, Edith M.

1961 Opening (Fall) Enrollment in Higher Education, 1960: Analytic Report. Office of Education, OE-54007-60. Washington: U. S. Government Printing Office.

1963 Opening (Fall) Enrollment in Higher Education, 1963. Office of Education, OE-54003-63. Washington: U. S. Government Printing Office.

Hutchins, Clayton D., and Richard H. Barr.

1968 Statistics of State School Systems, 1965-66. Office of Education, OE-20020-66. Washington: U. S. Government Printing Office.

Institute of International Education, The

1966 Open Doors, 1966. New York: The Institute of International Education.

Jaracz, William A.

1955 Fall Enrollment in Higher Educational Institutions, 1954. Office of Education, Cir. 419. Washington: U. S. Government Printing Office.

Judd, Charles H.

1933 "Education." Pp. 325-381 in The President's Research Committee on Social Trends (ed.), Recent Social Trends in the United States, vol. 1. New York: McGraw-Hill Book Co.

Katz, Arnold

    1960   "The employment of students, October 1959." Special Labor Force Report, No. 6. Preprinted from the Monthly Labor Review, July 1960. Preprint No. 2340. Washington: U. S. Government Printing Office.

Keniston, Hayward

    1959   Graduate Study in the Arts and Sciences at the University of Pennsylvania. Philadelphia: University of Pennsylvania Press.

Knoell, Dorothy M., and Leland L. Medsker.

    1964a   Factors Affecting Performance of Transfer Students from Two- to Four-Year Colleges: With Implications for Coordination and Articulation. Berkeley, California: Center for Study of Higher Education, University of California.

    1964b   Articulation Between Two-Year and Four-Year Colleges. Berkeley, California: Center for Study of Higher Education, University of California.

Lannholm, Gerald V.

    1962   "Trends in liberal arts outcomes in seventy-nine colleges during a five-year period." Paper presented to the American Educational Research Association, February 20, 1962, annual meeting, mimeo.

Lindenfeld, Frank

    1963   Teacher Turnover in Public Elementary and Secondary Schools, 1959-60. Office of Education, OE-23002-60. Washington: U. S. Government Printing Office.

Lindsay, Felix H. I.
    1964   Financial Statistics of Institutions of Higher Education, 1959-60, Receipts, Expenditures, and Property. Office of Education, OE-50023-60. Washington: U. S. Government Printing Office.

Mack, Raymond W.
    1966   "School integration and social change." Paper presented to the American Sociological Association, August 31, 1966, annual meeting.

Marks, Eli S., and Joseph Waksberg.
    1966   "Evaluation of coverage in the 1960 Census of Population through case-by-case checking." Pp. 62-70 in Proceedings of the Social Statistics Section of the American Statistical Association, 1966. Washington: American Statistical Association.

Mason, Paul L., and Mabel C. Rice.
    1967   Earned Degrees Conferred, 1964-65. Office of Education, OE-54013-65. Washington: U. S. Government Printing Office.

Mason, Ward, and Robert Bain.
    1959   Teacher Turnover in Public Schools, 1957-58. Office of Education, OE-23002. Washington: U. S. Government Printing Office.

Maul, Ray C.
    1964   Class Size in Secondary Schools, January 1964. Research Report 1964-R16. Washington: National Education Association.

Mertins, Paul F.

    1969   Financial Statistics of Institutions of Higher Education: Current Funds Revenues, and Expenditures, 1965-66. Office of Education, OE-52010-66. Washington: U. S. Government Printing Office.

Moore, Geoffrey H.

    1967a   "What is a recession?" The American Statistician 21 (October): 16-19.

    1967b   "Some needed improvements in economic statistics." The American Statistician 21 (December): 27-32.

Nam, Charles B.

    1962   "Some comparisons of Office of Education and Census Bureau statistics on education." Pp. 258-261 in Proceedings of the Social Statistics Section of the American Statistical Association, 1966. Washington: American Statistical Association.

Nam, Charles B., and John K. Folger.

    1965   "Factors related to school retention." Demography 2 (1965): 456-462.

National Academy of Sciences, Office of Scientific Personnel.

    1967   Doctorate Recipients from United States Universities, 1958-1966. Pub. No. 1489. Washington: National Academy of Sciences.

    1968   Summary Report, 1967, Doctorate Recipients from United States Universities. Washington: National Academy of Sciences.

National Advisory Commission on Health Manpower.

    1967   Report of the National Advisory Commission on Health Manpower, vol. I. Washington: U. S. Government Printing Office.

National Center for Educational Statistics.

    1968   Higher Education Finances, Selected Trend and Summary Data. Office of Education, OE-52009. Washington: U. S.Government Printing Office.

National Education Association.

    1965a   Estimates of School Statistics, 1965-66. Research Report 1965-R17. Washington: National Education Association.

    1965b   Teacher Supply and Demand in Universities, Colleges, and Junior Colleges, 1963-64 and 1964-65. Research Report 1965-R4. Washington: National Education Association.

    1967a   Economic Status of Teachers, 1966-67. Research Report 1967-R8. Washington: National Education Association.

    1967b   Teacher Supply and Demand in Public Schools, 1967. Research Report 1967-R18. Washington: National Education Association.

    1968   Beginning Salaries for College Graduates, June 1968. National Education Association Research Memo 1968-2 (January). Washington: National Education Association.

National Science Foundation.

- 1955 Scientific Personnel Resources. A Summary of Data on Supply, Utilization, and Training of Scientists and Engineers. Washington: National Science Foundation.
- 1961 American Science Manpower, 1956-58. NSF 61-45. Washington: National Science Foundation.
- 1962 American Science Manpower, 1960. NSF 62-43. Washington: National Science Foundation.
- 1964 American Science Manpower, 1962. NSF 64-16. Washington: National Science Foundation.
- 1967a The Junior College and Education in the Sciences. Prepared for the Subcommittee on Science, Research and Development, Committee on Science & Astronautics, U. S. House of Representatives, 90th Congress, 1st Session, Series H. Washington: U. S. Government Printing Office.
- 1967b American Science Manpower, 1964. NSF 66-29. Washington: National Science Foundation.
- 1967c Science and Engineering Staff in Universities and Colleges, 1965-1975. NSF 67-11. Washington: National Science Foundation.
- 1968a American Science Manpower, 1966. NSF 68-7. Washington: National Science Foundation.
- 1968b Employment of Scientists and Engineers in the United States, 1950-66. NSF 68-30. Washington: National Science Foundation.

    1968c   "Salaries and selected characteristics of U. S. scientists, 1968." Reviews of Data on Science Resources. NSF 69-5, No. 16. Washington: National Science Foundation.

National Youth Administration, Division of Reports and Records.

    1944   Final Report of the National Youth Administration, Fiscal Years 1936-1943. Washington: Federal Security Agency, War Manpower Commission.

Panos, Robert J., Alexander W. Astin, and John A. Creager.

    1967   National Norms for Entering College Freshmen - Fall 1967. ACE Research Reports, vol. 2, no. 7. Washington: American Council on Education.

Perrella, Vera C.

    1967   "Employment of school age youth, October 1966." Special Labor Force Report, No. 87. Reprinted from the Monthly Labor Review, August 1967. Reprint No. 2538. Washington: U. S. Government Printing Office.

President's Commission on National Goals, The

    1960   Goals for Americans. New York: Prentice-Hall, Inc.

Rice, Mabel C., and Neva A. Carlson.

    1955   Earned Degrees Conferred by Higher Educational Institutions, 1953-54. Office of Education, Cir. 418. Washington: U. S. Government Printing Office.

    1956   Earned Degrees Conferred by Higher Educational Institutions, 1954-55. Office of Education, Cir. 461. Washington: U. S. Government Printing Office.

Rice, Mabel C., and Hazel Poole.

    1957   Earned Degrees Conferred by Higher Educational Institutions, 1955-1956. Office of Education, Cir. 499. Washington: U. S. Government Printing Office.

Rosenfeld, Carl

    1961   "The employment of students, October 1960." Special Labor Force Report, No. 16. Preprinted from the Monthly Labor Review, July 1961. Preprint No. 2369. Washington: U. S. Government Printing Office.

    1962   "The employment of students, October 1961." Special Labor Force Report, No. 22. Reprinted from the Monthly Labor Review, June 1962. Reprint No. 2394. Washington: U. S. Government Printing Office.

    1963   "Employment of school age youth, October 1962." Special Labor Force Report, No. 34. Preprinted from the Monthly Labor Review, August 1963. Preprint No. 2420. Washington: U. S. Government Printing Office.

Schloss, Samuel

    1966   Fall 1965 Statistics of Public Elementary and Secondary Day Schools. Office of Education, OE-20007-65. Washington: U. S. Government Printing Office.

Schloss, Samuel, and Carol Joy Hobson.

    1962   Fall 1961 Statistics on Enrollment, Teachers, and Schoolhousing in Full-time Public Elementary and Secondary Day Schools. Office of Education, OE-20007-61. Washington: U. S. Government Printing Office.

Schmid, Calvin F. et. al.

    1967   Population Trends, Cities and Towns, State of Washington, 1900 to 1967. Seattle: Washington State Census Board.

Schmid, Calvin F., and Vincent A. Miller.

    1967   Enrollment Forecasts, State of Washington, 1967 to 1975. Seattle: Washington State Census Board.

Seltzer, Norman

    1965   Scientific and Technical Manpower Resources. NSF 64-28. Washington: National Science Foundation.

Sharp, Laure M.

    1963   Two Years After the College Degree. NSF 63-26. Washington: National Science Foundation.

    1965   Five Years After the College Degree, Part I, Graduate and Professional Education. Washington: Bureau of Social Science Research, Inc.

Siegel, Jacob S., and Melvin Zelnik.

    1966   "An evaluation of coverage in the 1960 Census of Population by techniques of demographic analysis and by composite methods." Pp. 71-85 in Proceedings of the Social Statistics Section of the American Statistical Association, 1966. Washington: American Statistical Association.

Simon, Kenneth A., and Marie G. Fullam.

    1966   Projections of Educational Statistics to 1975-76. Office of Education, OE-10030-66. Washington: U. S. Government Printing Office.

1968 Projections of Educational Statistics to 1976-77. Office of Education, OE-10030-67. Washington: U. S. Government Printing Office.

Simon, Kenneth A., and W. Vance Grant.

1965 Digest of Educational Statistics, 1965 Edition. Office of Education, OE-10024-64. Washington: U. S. Government Printing Office.

1966 Digest of Educational Statistics, 1966 Edition. Office of Education, OE-10024-66. Washington: U.S. Government Printing Office.

1967 Digest of Educational Statistics, 1967 Edition. Office of Education, OE-10024-67. Washington: U. S. Government Printing Office.

1968 Digest of Educational Statistics, 1968 Edition. Office of Education, OE-10024-68. Washington: U. S. Government Printing Office.

Singletary, Otis A., and Jane P. Newman (eds.)

1968 American Universities and Colleges. Washington: American Council on Education.

Steinberg, Joseph

1953 "The current population survey." Pp. 559-582 in Morris H. Hansen, William N. Hurwitz, and William G. Madow (eds.), Sample Survey Methods and Theory, Methods and Applications, vol. 1. New York: John Wiley & Sons, Inc.

Story, Robert C.

    1949   Earned Degrees Conferred by Higher Educational Institutions, 1948-49. Office of Education, Cir. 262. Washington: U. S. Government Printing Office.

    1950a   Earned Degrees Conferred by Higher Educational Institutions, 1949-50. Office of Education, Cir. 282. Washington: U. S. Government Printing Office.

    1950b   1950 Fall Enrollment in Higher Educational Institutions. Office of Education, Cir. 281. Washington: U. S. Government Printing Office.

    1951   1951 Fall Enrollment in Higher Educational Institutions. Office of Education, Cir. 328. Washington: U. S. Government Printing Office.

    1952   Earned Degrees Conferred by Higher Educational Institutions, 1950-51. Office of Education, Cir. 333. Washington: U. S. Government Printing Office.

    1953   Earned Degrees Conferred by Higher Educational Institutions, 1951-52. Office of Education, Cir. 360. Washington: U. S. Government Printing Office.

Swanstrom, Thomas E.

    1965   "Employment of school age youth, October 1964." Special Labor Force Report, No. 55. Preprinted from the Monthly Labor Review, July 1965. Preprint No. 2465. Washington: U. S. Government Printing Office.

Tolliver, Wayne E.

    1961   Earned Degrees Conferred, 1958-1959. Office of Education, OE-54013. Washington: U. S. Government Printing Office.

    1962   Earned Degrees Conferred, 1959-1960. Office of Education, OE-54013-60. Washington: U. S. Government Printing Office.

    1963a   Earned Degrees Conferred, 1960-1961. Office of Education, OE-54013-61. Washington: U. S. Government Printing Office.

    1963b   Earned Degrees Conferred, 1961-1962. Office of Education, OE-54013-62. Washington: U. S. Government Printing Office.

Trow, Martin

    1961   "The second transformation of American secondary education." International Journal of Comparative Sociology II (September): 144-166.

U. S. Bureau of the Budget, Office of Statistical Standards.

    1962   A Federal Statistics Program for the 1960s. Prepared for the Subcommittee on Economic Statistics of the Joint Economic Committee. 87th Congress, 2nd Session. Washington: U. S. Government Printing Office.

    1967   1967 Supplement to Economic Indicators. Prepared for the Subcommittee on Economic Statistics of the Joint Economic Committee. 90th Congress, 1st Session. Washington: U. S. Government Printing Office.

U. S. Department of Health, Education and Welfare.

    1966   Health, Education and Welfare Trends, 1965 Edition. Washington: U. S. Government Printing Office.

1967 Press Release of August 24, 1967, No. HEW-R68. Washington: U. S. Department of Health, Education, and Welfare.

U. S. Department of Health, Education and Welfare, Office of Civil Rights.

1968 Untitled Press Release of May 27, 1968. Washington: U. S. Department of Health, Education and Welfare.

1969 Untitled Press Release of January 16, 1969. Washington: U. S. Department of Health, Education and Welfare.

Vincent, Howard L.

1968 "Supply and demand of elementary and secondary school teachers." Pp. 11-16 in Office of Program Planning and Evaluation, Education in the Seventies. Office of Education, OE-10051. Washington: U. S. Government Printing Office.

Wilson, Kenneth M.

1965 Of Time and the Doctorate. SREB Research Monograph No. 9. Atlanta, Ga.: Southern Regional Education Board.

Wolfle, Dael

1954 America's Resources of Specialized Talent. Commission on Human Resources and Advanced Training. New York: Harper and Bros.

Wright, Grace S.

1965 Subject Offerings and Enrollments in Public Secondary Schools. Office of Education, OE-24015-61. Washington: U. S. Government Printing Office.

Wright, Patricia

1965   Earned Degrees Conferred, 1962-63, Bachelor's and Higher Degrees. Office of Education, OE-54013-63, Cir. 777. Washington: U. S. Government Printing Office.

1966   Earned Degrees Conferred, 1963-64, Bachelor's and Higher Degrees. Office of Education, OE-54013-64, Misc. No. 54. Washington: U. S. Government Printing Office.